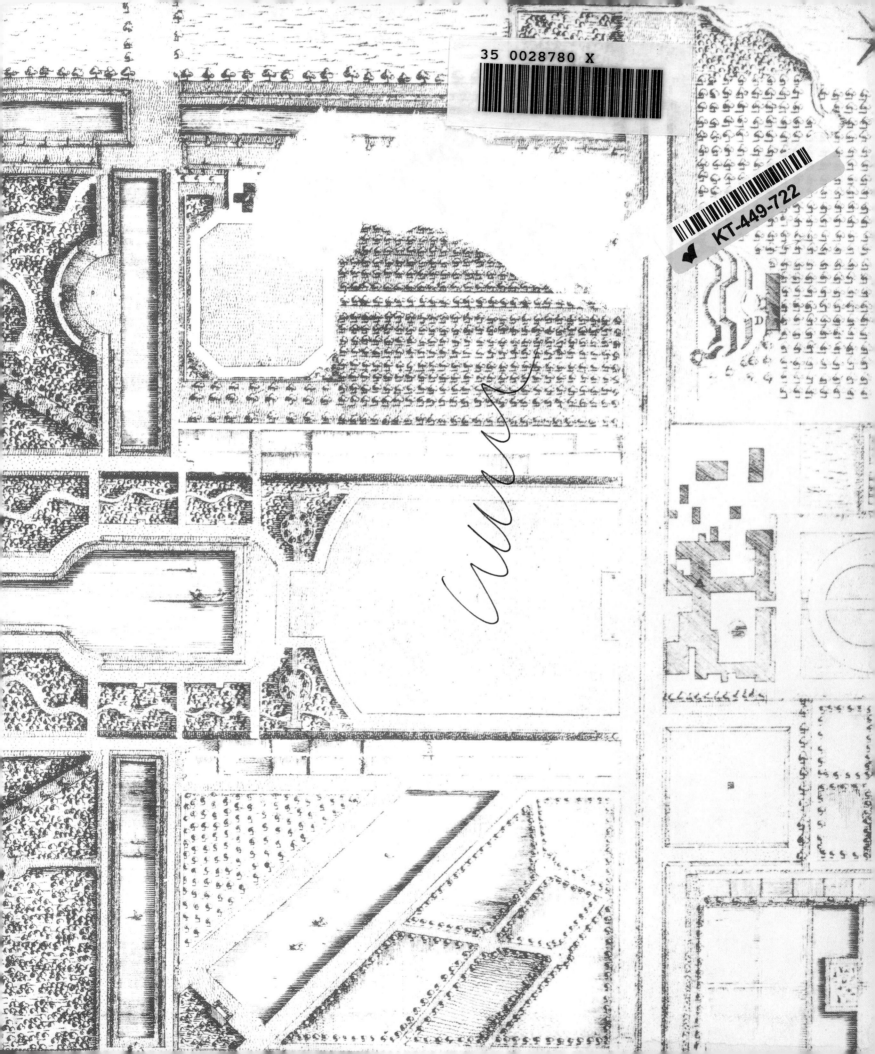
35 0028780 X

KT-449-722

CREATING
PERIOD
GARDENS

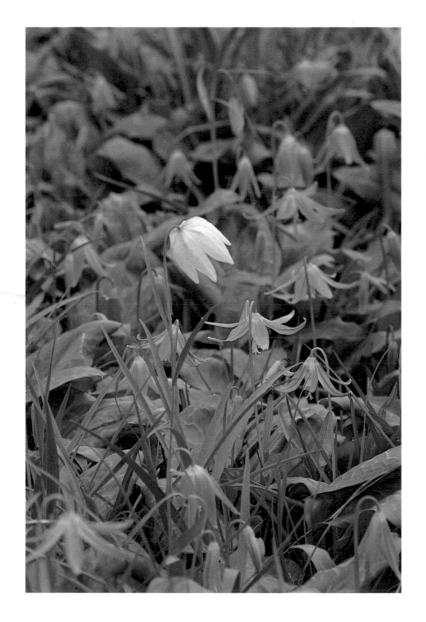

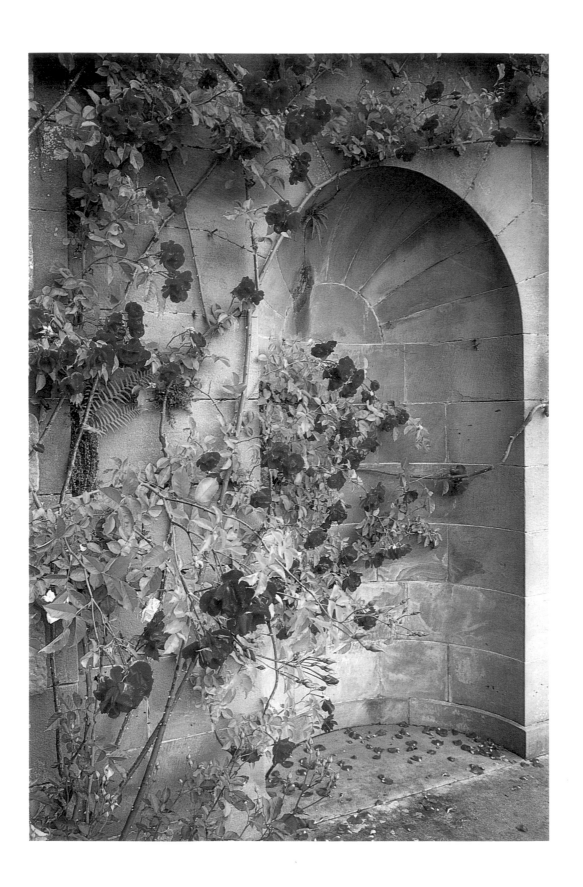

CREATING
PERIOD
GARDENS

Elizabeth Banks

photographs by
Jerry Harpur

UNIVERSITY OF HUMBERSIDE

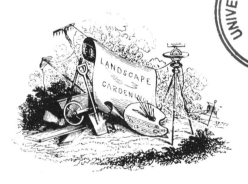

Phaidon · Oxford

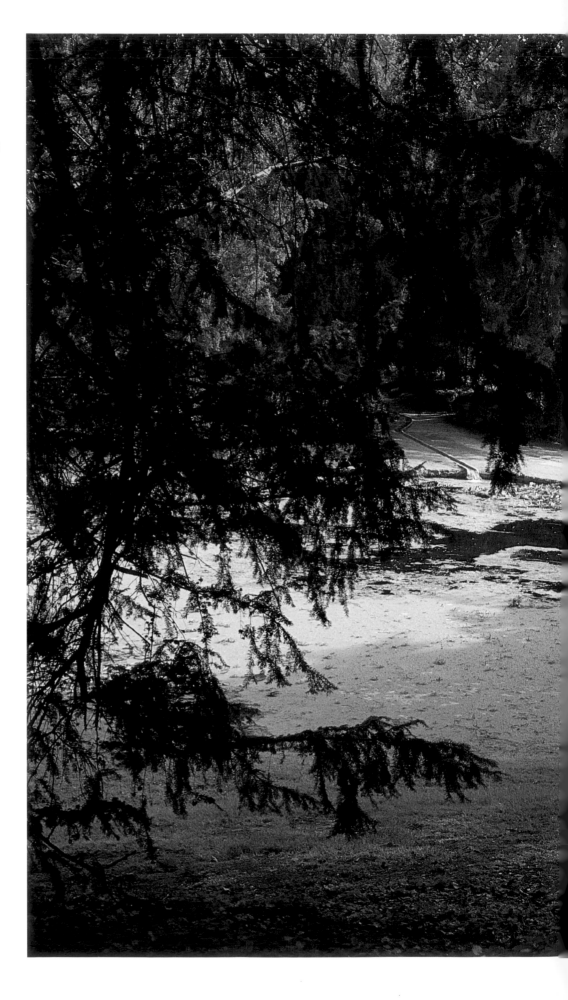

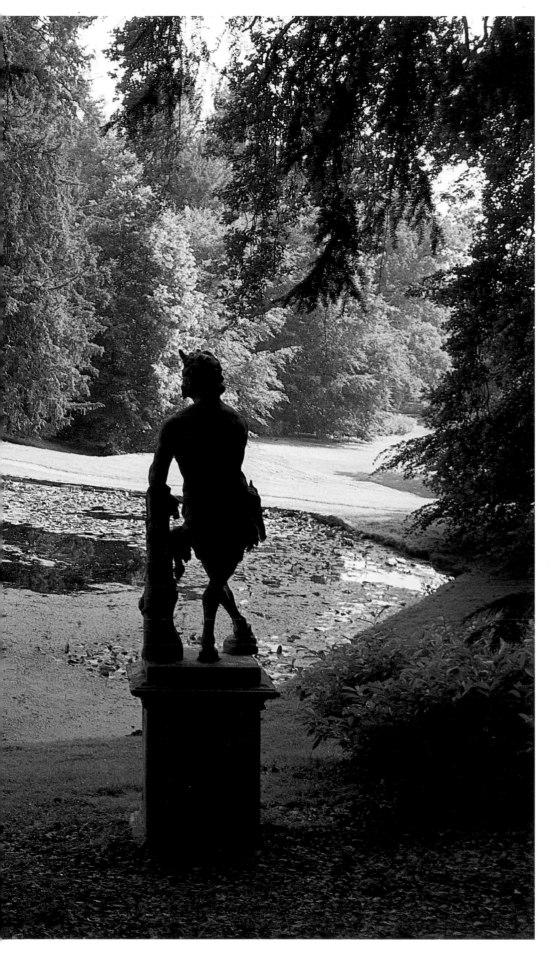

BELOW
*The key to the symbols used in the drawings
of garden styles.*

KEY

 DECIDUOUS TREES

 CONIFEROUS TREES

 SHRUB PLANTING

 HERBACEOUS PLANTING

HEDGES

 GRASS

 WATER

GRAVEL PATHS

WALLS

FENCES

 BUILDINGS

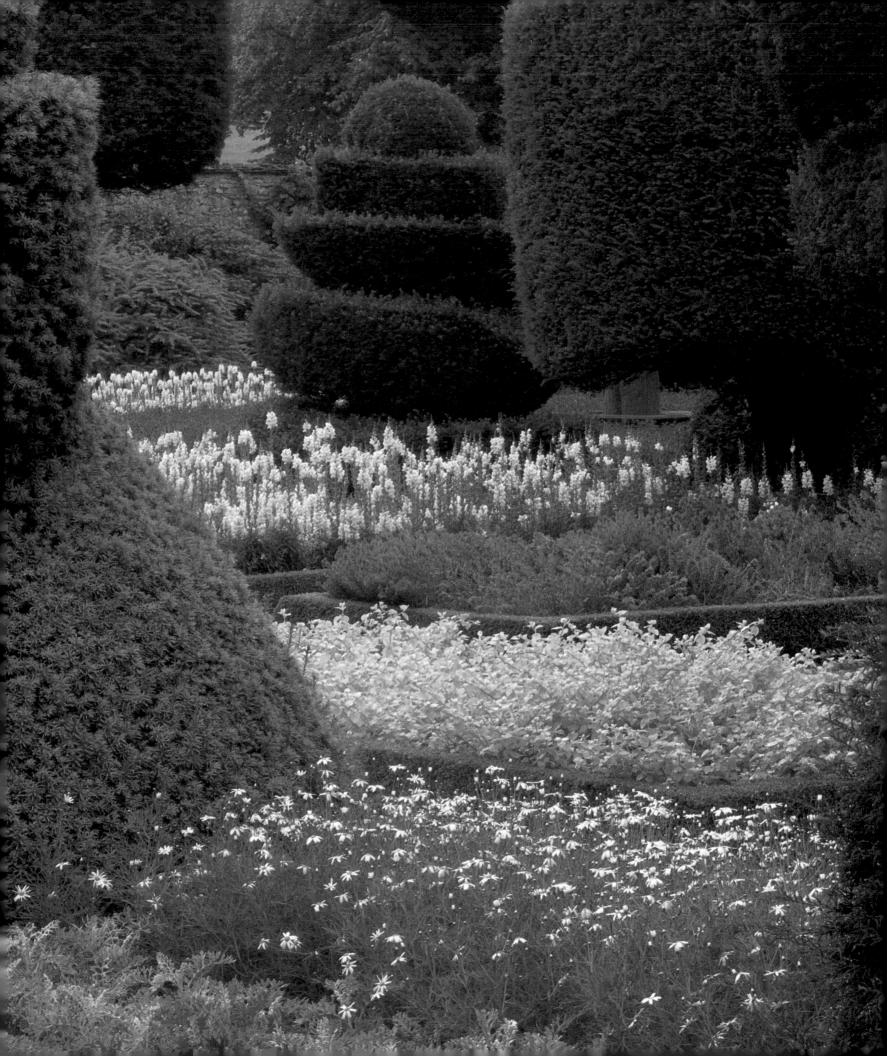

Contents

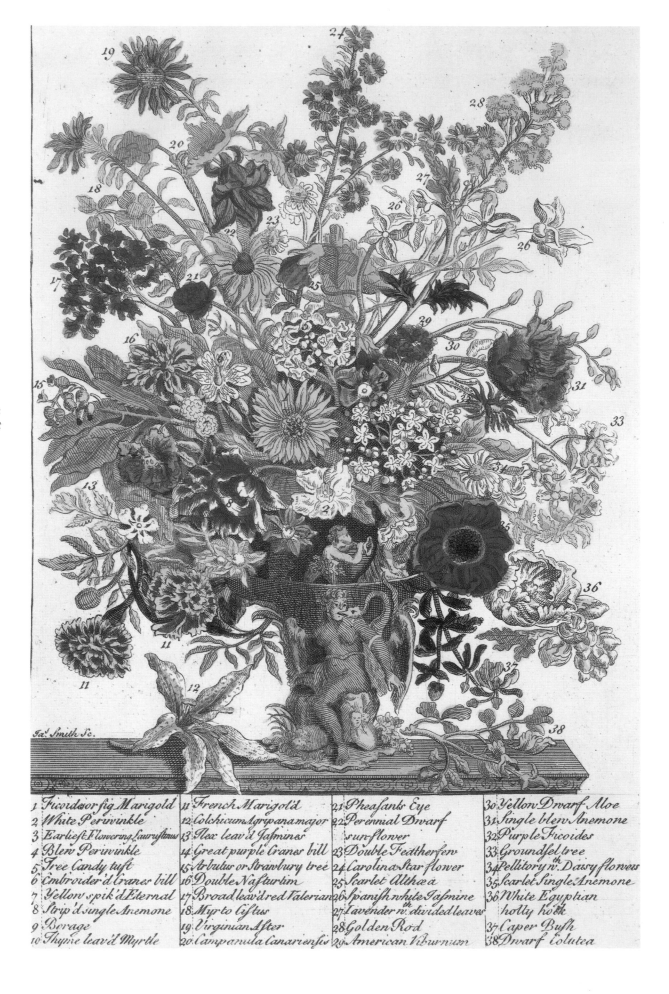

A plate from Robert Furber's Flower Garden Display'd, *a nurseryman's catalogue, published in 1734, showing the flowers available for an English 18th-century garden in November.*

OPPOSITE
An outdoor plant table in the ornamental garden at Shrubland Hall.

Ia: Smith Sc.

1 Ficoidæor fig Marigold	11 French Marigold	21 Pheasants Eye	30 Yellow Dwarf Aloe
2 White Periwinkle	12 Colchicum Agripanamajor	22 Perennial Dwarf	31 Single blew Anemone
3 Earliest Flowering Laurustinus	13 Ilex leav'd Jasmines	sun-flower	32 Purple Ficoides
4 Blew Periwinkle	14 Great purple Cranes bill	23 Double Featherfew	33 Groundsel tree
5 Tree Candy tuft	15 Arbutus or Strawbury tree	24 Carolina Star flower	34 Pellitory wth Daisy flowers
6 Embroider'd Cranes bill	16 Double Nasturtim	25 Scarlet Althæa	35 Scarlet Single Anemone
7 Yellow spik'd Eternal	17 Broad leav'd red Valerian	26 Spanish white Jasmine	36 White Egyptian
8 Strip'd single Anemone	18 Myrto Cistus	27 Lavender wth divided leaves	holly hock
9 Borage	19 Virginian After	28 Golden Rod	37 Caper Bush
10 Thyme leav'd Myrtle	20 Campanula Canariensis	29 American Viburnum	38 Dwarf Colutea

Preface

PERIOD gardens can be an inspiration – a source of ideas. Whether your garden is old and needs restoring or whether it is new and complements a modern house, there is a period style which will flatter and enhance it. Making a period garden for yourself can be a great pleasure and this book explains in detail the stimulating ideas and styles of famous period designers and how they may be re-created today.

The early Gardens of Embroidery were laid out in simple designs for growing fruit, flowers and vegetables together to display and consume. Gradually they developed into the formal landscapes of the great geometric gardens and the early eighteenth century. Such gardens were made from many small compartments, and it is possible to pick out a particular part or 'cabinet' and re-create it in precise and perfect proportions – so satisfying to behold.

The Gardens of Paradise of the eighteenth century imitated nature, with gentle curves and sinuous lines that created pleasing and beautiful shapes carefully thought out. In the nineteenth century the Gardens of Romance were full of rich decoration and interesting plants, which gave a striking and colourful effect.

Much help has been given in guiding the untried team of the artist Lucy Cuddon and myself through the hazards of book production. Without the support of Penelope Marcus and Simon Bell this book would not have been created. Jerry Harpur's photographs provided inspiration. Annette Lace, Camilla Beresford and Krysia Bilikowski contributed to the contents, which are based on detailed research. Many thanks to my family and friends for their encouragement and to the clients and staff of Elizabeth Banks Associates, who have been most supportive, and finally to Ruth Maccormac and Jennifer Speake, who have assisted in editing the text.

Elizabeth Banks
February 1991

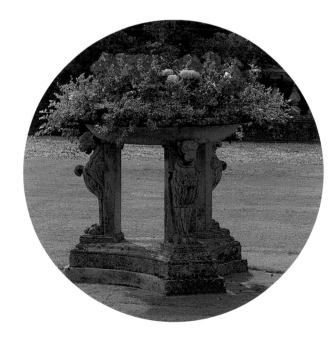

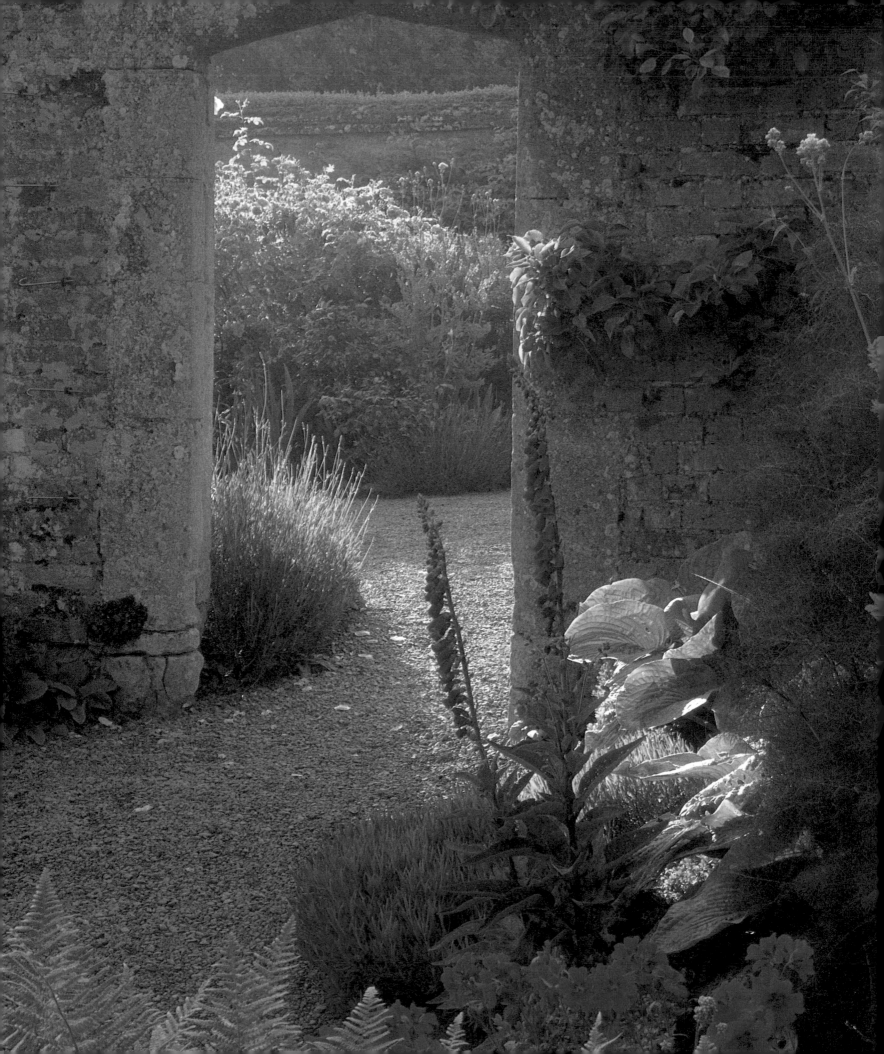

Introduction

IN THE words of Francis Bacon, 'God Almighty first planted a garden' and people have been gardening ever since. Growing flowers in gardens of beauty has fulfilled a human desire for at least the last two thousand years and the search for paradise, for peace and happiness in serene surroundings has inspired many gardens, especially in the benign climate of Britain. In the gentle moist conditions delicate plants grow and thrive so successfully that gardening has become a national pastime. From the monk's garden in medieval times to the small modern courtyard, the desire has been the same – to make a beautiful place out of doors.

The study of period gardens can ease this challenge. Ideas and inspiration can be gleaned from period styles to create a beautiful new garden or to restore an old one. This book sets out to stimulate the gardener to re-create, to restore or just to use some of the ideas shown in a period style. Most styles evolved from gardens laid out by some of the most famous and successful designers of their time, so by reproducing their ideas, the gardener today can benefit from their skill and experience.

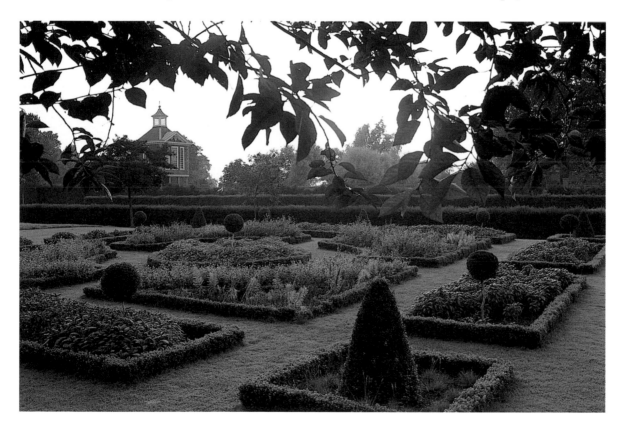

The magnificence of the knot garden at Westbury Court lies in the classical formality and precision of the colourful flower beds set off by the dark green of low box hedges.

OPPOSITE
Through the stone doorway bursts the full glory of an English summer garden, caught in shafts of sunlight.

There have been gardens in Britain since the time of the Romans. Garden design developed distinctive styles as historical events or social changes occurred. Some were closely related to architecture whilst others were more influenced by plants. Many were conceived by great statesmen inspired by famous designers. Much intellectual energy wad concentrated on their creation and this resulted in some remarkable gardens which still stand today as magnificent works of art in their own right.

In *Creating Period Gardens* a selection of fifteen particular styles dating from 1500 to about 1930 is described in detail. They are set out in chronological order beginning with the medieval Pleasaunce Garden and ending with the Exotic Conservatory of the twentieth century.

The book divides into three sections and each style is described in a chapter which can be read on its own or with the others of the same period. In Section I the great sixteenth- and seventeenth-century Gardens of Embroidery are illustrated by four styles: the Pleasaunce Garden, the Fantasy Garden, the Knot Garden and the Geometric Garden. The Pleasaunce Garden portrays the modest, enclosed, flower, vegetable and herb garden which first originated in the medieval monastery. The Fantasy Garden shows the influence of the Italian Renaissance. The Knot Garden explains how to create the intricate patterns of a parterre. The Geometric Garden shows how to lay out the mathematical designs and construct the hedges and avenues of large formal gardens.

The eighteenth-century Gardens of Paradise are represented by five styles: the Theatrical Garden describes the transition from the formal and authoritarian to the informal and liberal approach; the Landscape Garden explains the principles behind the great landscape parks, many designed by Capability Brown; the English Flower Garden shows the design of one of the first flower gardens to imitate nature; the Villa Garden illustrates how all the previous ideas can be combined into one small garden which, for the first time, shows off

The rich planting around the grand staircase in Montacute garden, embellished with its vases, epitomizes the opulence of the ornamental garden.

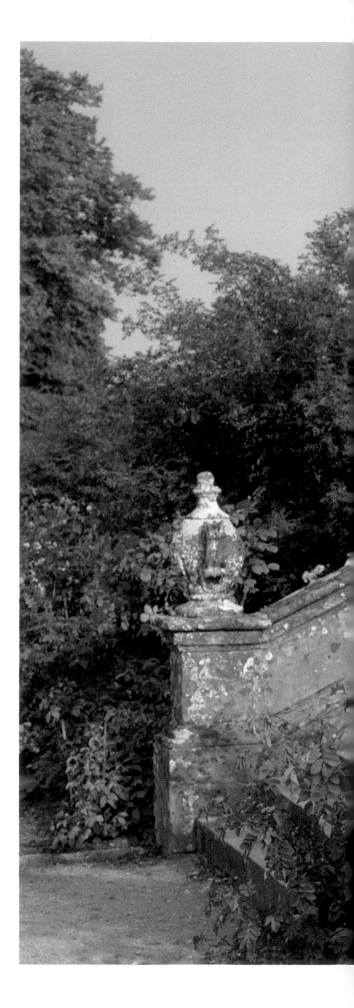

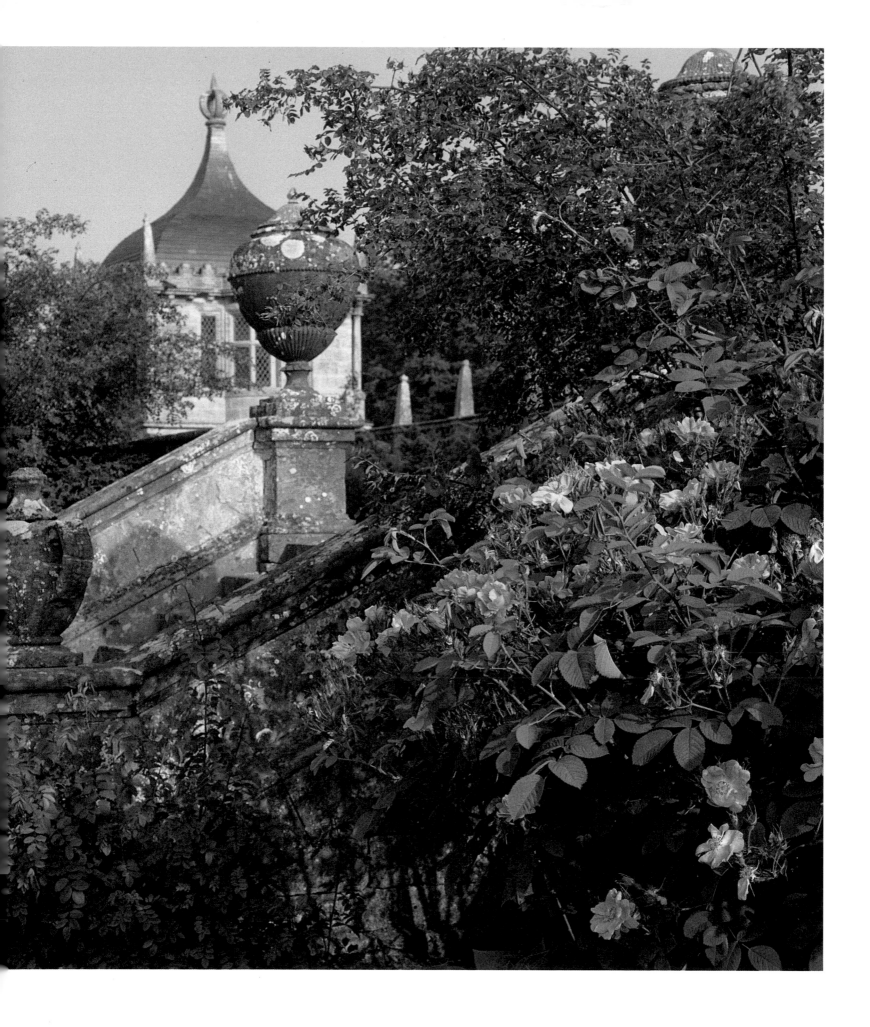

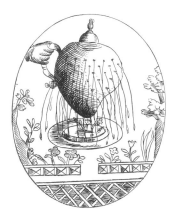

The fine gentle spray of a 15th-century watering can.

A rustic summerhouse, designed by Thomas Wright, was one of the many elements of fantasy found in an 18th-century garden.

plants for their botanical interest; and the Walled Garden displays the designs for an enclosed fruit, vegetable and flower garden.

The Gardens of Romance illustrate six exuberant Victorian styles: the Ornamental Garden, describing the brightly coloured carpet bedding schemes; the Rosarie, showing how to create a rose garden; the Rock and Quarry Garden, explaining how to set out a rockery and the plants which grow in it; the Wild and Woodland Garden, illustrating how to grow exotic plants naturally; the Sheltered Garden, portraying the enclosed gardens planted by Gertrude Jekyll; and finally the Victorian indoor garden – the Exotic Conservatory.

The design and construction details are explained so that they can be adapted to fit into gardens of all sizes, although of course some of the styles are more suitable than others for a particular space. For example, the Pleasaunce Garden is suitable for small courtyards whereas the Landscape Garden is more appropriate for larger areas.

Information is provided so that each style can be created in the same way as it was originally constructed or it can be adjusted to fit different conditions today. Lists of appropriate plants for each style are given and for the earlier periods they have been arranged chronologically by the dates when they became

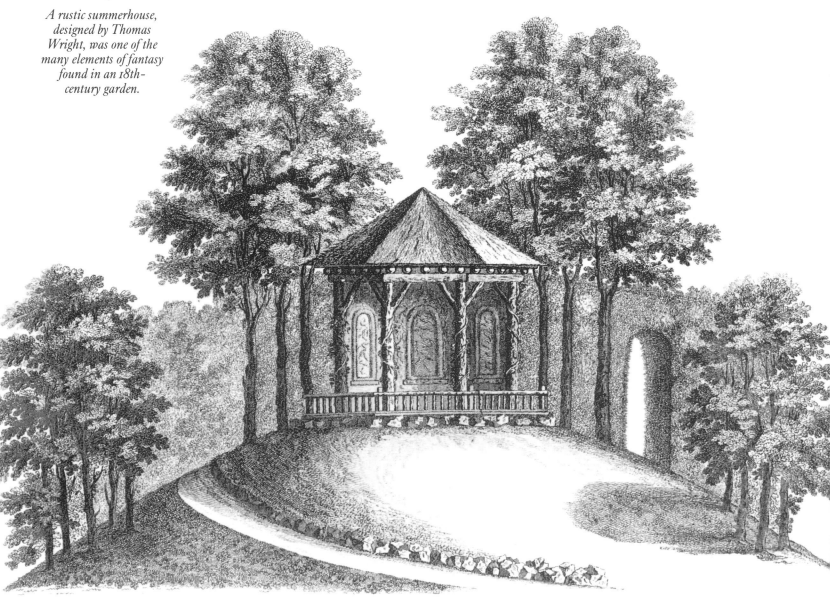

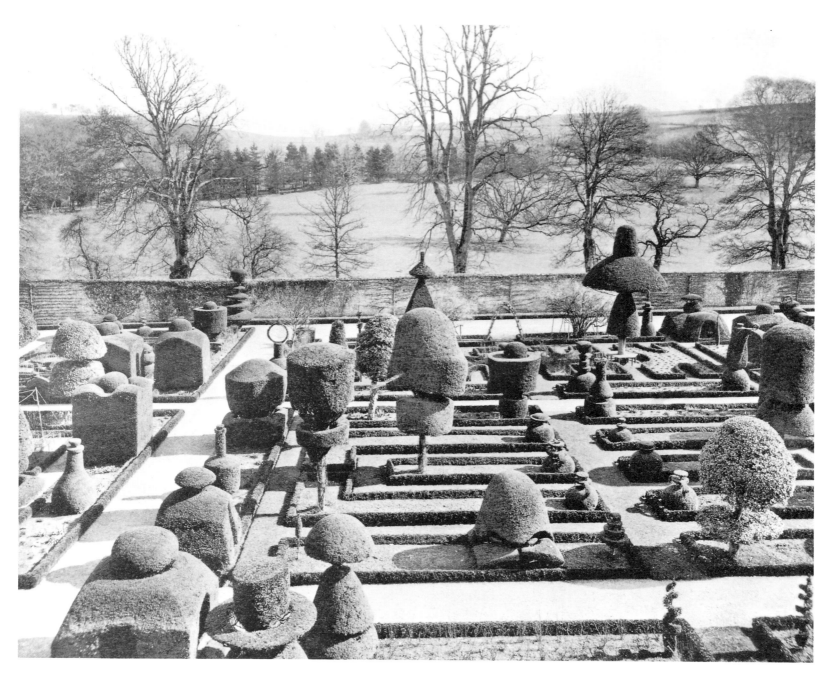

available. Plants have always been brought back from foreign travels, and the enormous influx during the nineteenth century greatly affected garden design. They are listed by their common and Latin names; where the original seventeenth- or eighteenth-century common name is very different from the one in use today, these have been given in a subsidiary list.

The design of each style is clearly illustrated by an aerial sketch and the details are shown by further sketches or sections. More information about the construction or planting is given in the page of features in each chapter and in the section at the back of the book on Planting and Structural Techniques.

The original principles of design are described so that they can be adapted to any site. For example, in the Fantasy Garden the proportions of the width of the paths to the length of the beds are given and in the Geometric Garden the proportions of the rides, avenues and allées are also provided so these can be adjusted to fit into the available space.

As the Victorians discovered, the climate of

The wit, extravagance and unexpected shapes of the Victorian yew topiary at Levens Hall reached its full humour in the Edwardian period – with bottles, top hats, corkscrews and jugs galore.

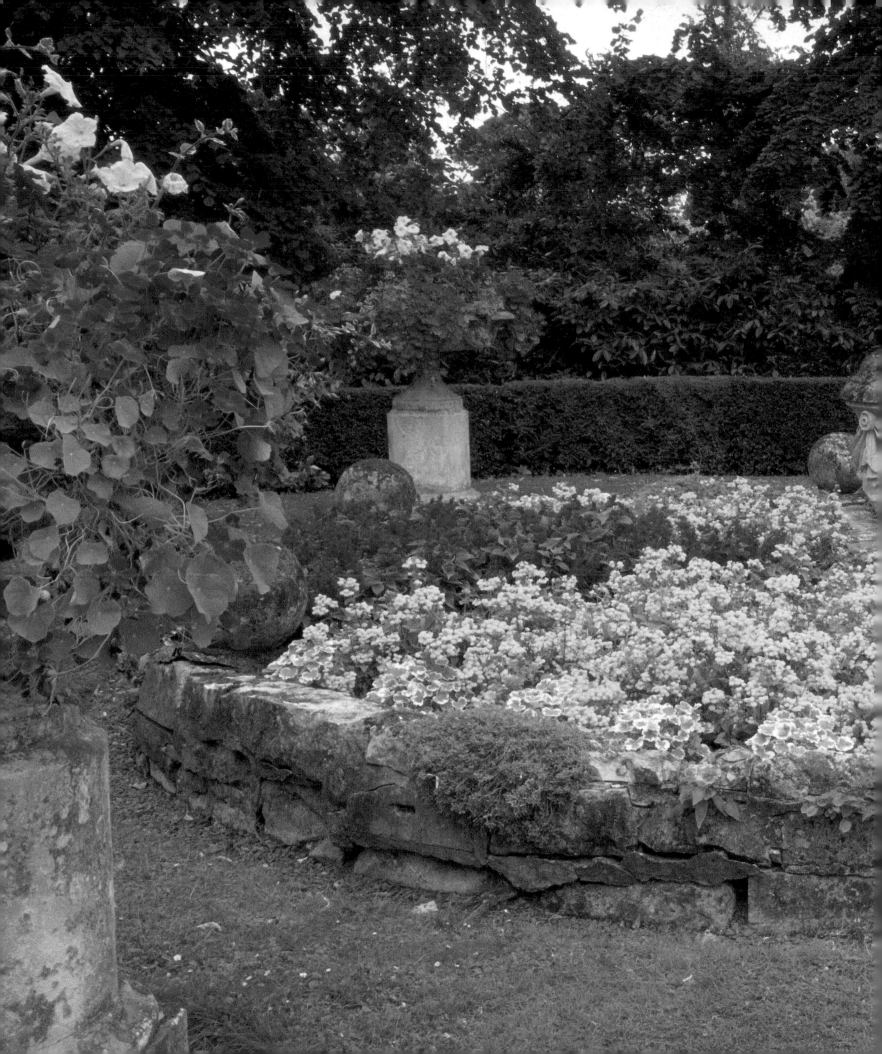

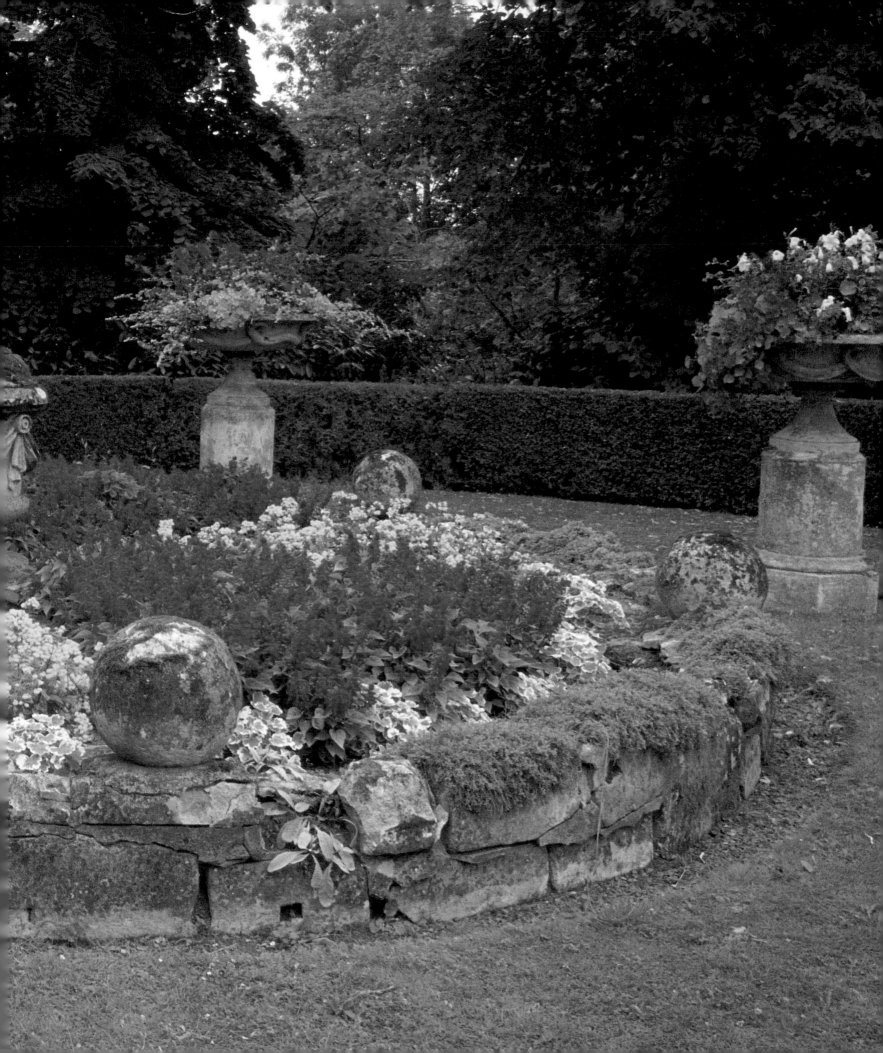

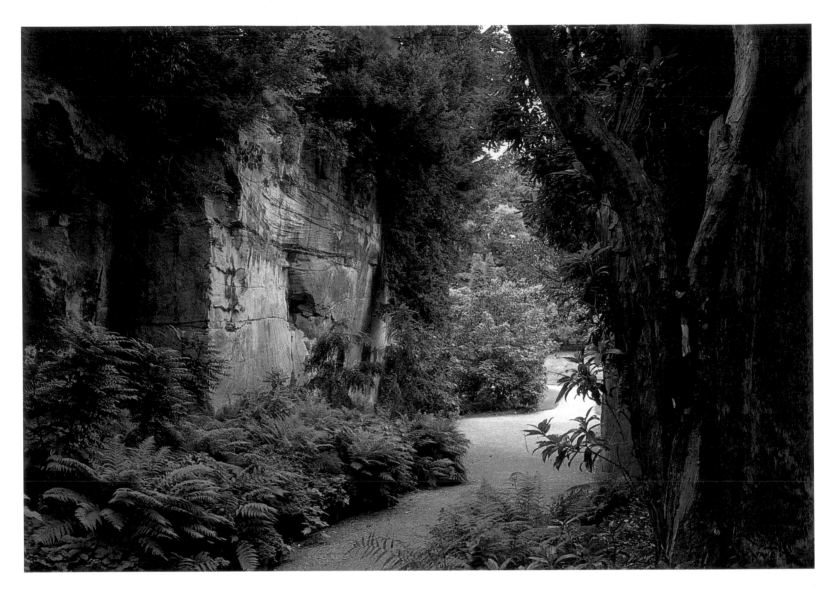

The drama of natural rock shapes and the varied textures of green plants create the mystery of the rock and quarry garden at Belsay.

PREVIOUS PAGES
Victorian gardens are unrestrained displays of exuberant and gaudy colour.

Britain and America is most suitable to grow many of the plants from India and the Far East. For example, along the west of the British Isles and America the damp maritime climate creates perfect conditions to grow rhododendrons from the Himalayas. Good gardening practices have not been included in this book except where they affect the design, nor have the details of how to build the steps and walls and so on, but this information can be obtained from books listed in the bibliography or from a good local builder. Sources of much of the material and plants is given in the Direc-

tory. Also included is a list of gardens that can be visited, and the comprehensive Bibliography refers to other books which may be used if further information on a particular style is required.

This is a book in which to browse, to pick up ideas, to study a style or a period. It may be read from cover to cover or thumbed through and dipped into when needing inspiration or information. Here can be found ideas that will suit a small corner or a secluded part of the garden; or a combination of several different styles can be created in a larger garden.

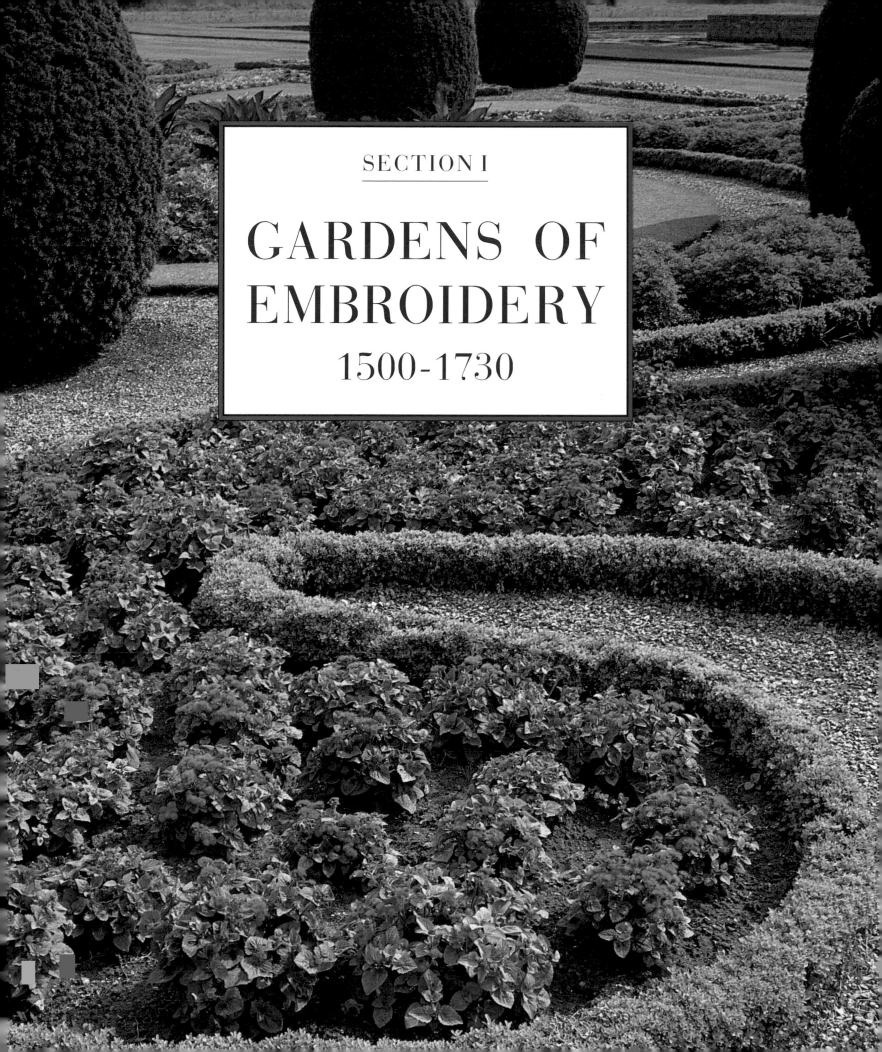

SECTION I

GARDENS OF EMBROIDERY

1500-1730

Introduction

PREVIOUS PAGE
The swirling line of the box hedge establishes the scrollwork outline in the embroidery garden at Oxburgh.

A medieval gardener pruning his vines on simple hazel-rod frames and tying in the tendrils with willow shoots.

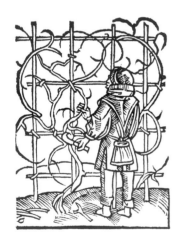

RIGHT
Two 16th-century woodcuts showing a selection of designs for ornamental trellises in a pleasaunce garden.

The Gardens of Embroidery developed during medieval times and lasted into the mid-eighteenth century, when these great formal designs were swept away in favour of the more relaxed style of the landscape park.

The beauty of the earliest embroidery style, the Pleasaunce Garden, lay in the intricate patterns set out in small enclosures surrounded by walls or hedges. In this garden the sun shone, flowers bloomed and life was pleasant. This idea of creating paradise, excluding the bustle and noise of the outside world, is as appealing today as it was to monks and noblemen five hundred years ago. At that time the monk's garden was a sanctuary from the rough-and-tumble of the military skirmishes of the world outside. Its sense of peace as a place for social gatherings to take place without interruption is just as needed today.

These patterns made from just a few plants can easily be set out in any small courtyard or enclosed area. Here, as during the Tudor period, guests and friends can admire and enjoy the atmosphere of calm perhaps broken only by the soothing splashing of a fountain.

Inside the medieval enclosure of the Pleasaunce Garden the order of the daily life of a monk was echoed in the symmetry and detail of the design, which was made from patterns of evergreens. This simple palette of different textures of green plants has been used by many great designers of contemplative gardens – from the Christian monasteries of Europe to the Buddhist temples of Japan. Flowers are present but they are of secondary importance, to be appreciated for their own beauty like special works of art and not used as an integral part of the design.

Many of the plants were brought back to Britain by itinerant monks, who travelled to the Middle East with the Crusades and whose concern for healing the sick encouraged the spread of herbal remedies and herbs. This movement throughout Europe allowed the spread of new gardening techniques and designs. Many of the gardens are beautifully illustrated in illuminated manuscripts painted by the monks and where some of the influences can be seen. Such paintings are one of the few sources showing the details of these gardens, as all of the gardens themselves have now vanished.

During the sixteenth century the extrovert Tudor king Henry VIII and his love of display stimulated gardening on a grand scale. The gardens of this period are not only beautiful but also create illusions, especially of space. The larger the garden appeared to be, the greater the consequence of the owner. Today these

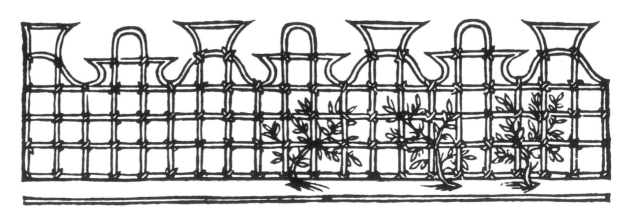

illusions are equally appropriate, particularly when space is at a premium.

Many of the original gardens were attached to great houses built after the upheaval of the dissolution of the monasteries. When the wealth and authority of the Church passed into the hands of noblemen, Thomas Wolsey, a prince of the Church as well as a minister of the Crown, built Hampton Court Palace, with its terraces, maze and large mount with a summer-house on top. Meanwhile, his successor, a layman, William Cecil, 1st Lord Burghley, built another vast house and garden, Theobalds in Surrey. Both of these were 'acquired' by Henry VIII, who himself built the amazing Nonsuch Palace. Not to be outdone at the loss of Theobalds, William Cecil remodelled Hatfield House, where his descendants still live and care for his garden. Contemporary descriptions of these three gardens provide much information on the style of this period.

By the seventeenth century, gardeners had scaled new heights of fancy with the Fantasy Garden. These were gardens in which to show off works of art, statues or other objects. They served as outdoor rooms – living galleries to entertain in. At this time, the main rooms were on the first floor and the gardens were designed so that the intricate pattern of the terrace below could be seen from above at a single glance. However, from the ground itself the complex pattern could not be seen and only became clear once the visitor had walked around the garden. Below the first terrace there was often a second or even a third one unseen at first

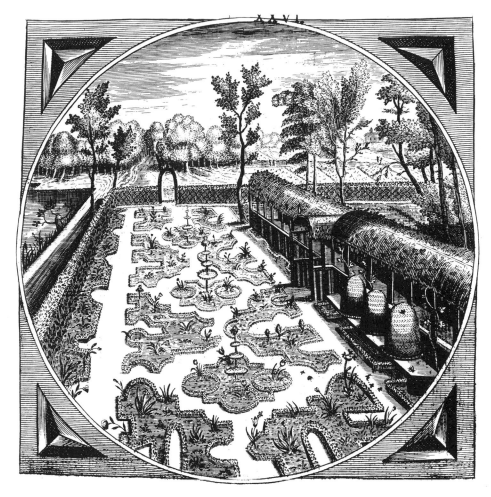

glance from the main room. Each terrace displayed yet another fountain or arbour, summer-house or special plant. Extraordinary plants or those requiring special cultivation were also exhibited like works of art for all to see and admire.

Colour was important too, but as few flowers could display it over a season, brightly painted balustrades, grotesque wooden figures or coloured trellis were used instead.

Enjoyment of the garden went further than one might expect. It was a special entertainment to play tricks on one's guests by terri-

Within the simple shape of a pleasaunce garden elaborate patterns of beds show off individual plants. The beds are separated by gravel and edged by a low hedge, usually box. In the 16th century, hives of bees were important for pollination. Alongside the garden runs a wooden arbour covered by climbers and vines.

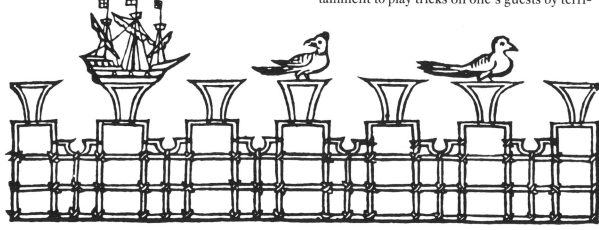

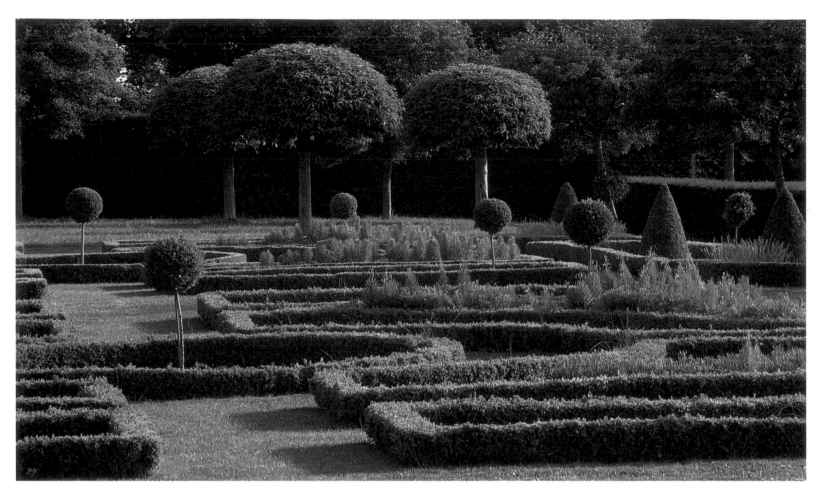

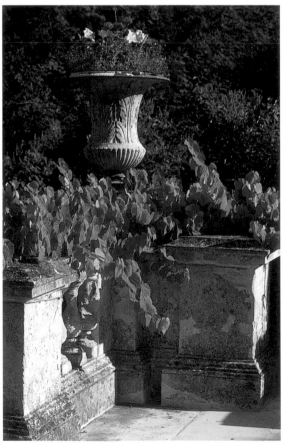

The very fine knot garden at Westbury is a triumph of simplicity – just a combination of low hedges and mown grass, to which annual plants are added in the spring and the summer.

An eye-catching ornament gives height and decoration to the fantasy garden.

fying them with groaning and hissing gods, surprising them with laughing nymphs, or annoying them, especially the ladies, by squirting water up their skirts or into their eyes from, for example, the breasts of statues. These 'fantastic' events transformed the sophisticated garden designs into unexpected adventures.

During the seventeenth century and up until the mid-nineteenth century, garden design was much influenced by the thinking and ideas generated by the Italian Renaissance, which provided an extraordinary intellectual stimulus. From this distance, it is difficult to appreciate the effect of these ideas on all forms of artistic creation and why the study of the Roman and Greek way of life should have had such an impact on creative thinking. In the simplest terms it could be seen as the releasing of ideas from the authoritarian control of medieval Christianity and the return to the more liberal concepts of the classical world.

At this time there was no demarcation be-

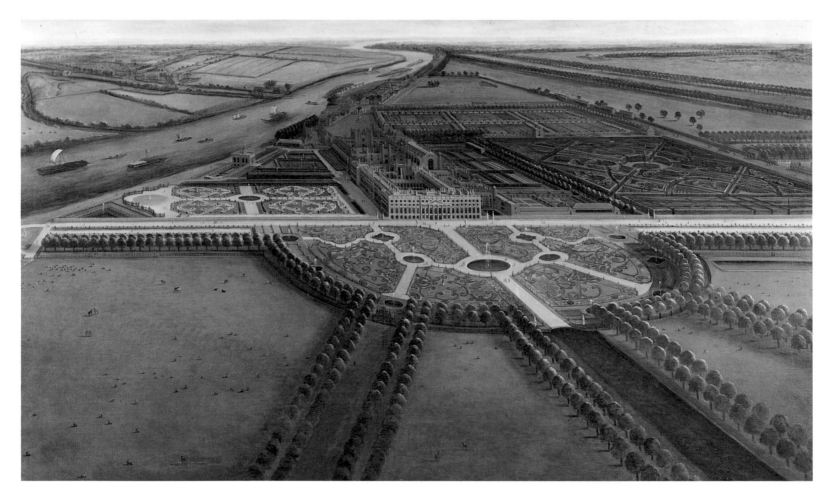

tween the humanities or sciences, no difference between artist and engineer nor between amateur and professional. This produced artists with great engineering skills and engineers with artistic ones, such as Leonardo da Vinci. They played an important role in devising the complex engineering necessary to make the fantasies work. Many of these artists came to Britain from Europe especially France. One of the most influential was Salomon de Caus (1576–1626), who with his son Isaac constructed many fantasies for Prince Henry, eldest son of James I, and for the Earl of Bedford at Woburn and the Earl of Pembroke at Wilton House, amongst others. Most of these ornamental gardens were destroyed during the Civil War, and their designers exiled to Europe.

The return of Charles II in 1660 and the repatriation of many of his followers to their properties decimated by twenty years of neglect caused one of the greatest periods of garden design ever known in England. Many of the

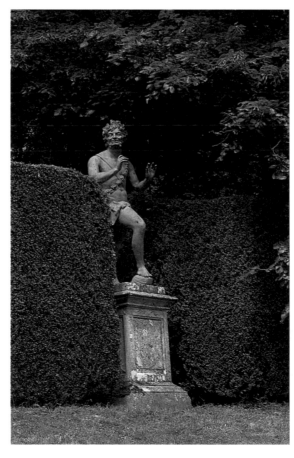

Hampton Court Palace was the most magnificent of English Baroque gardens and among the greatest of European gardens at the beginning of the 18th century. This painting of 1702 by Leonard Knyff shows the ornate parterre created by Dutch and French gardeners of William of Orange. Its form still exists.

Geometric gardens are full of theatrical surprises, such as this statue of a faun leaping out from behind a tall hedge.

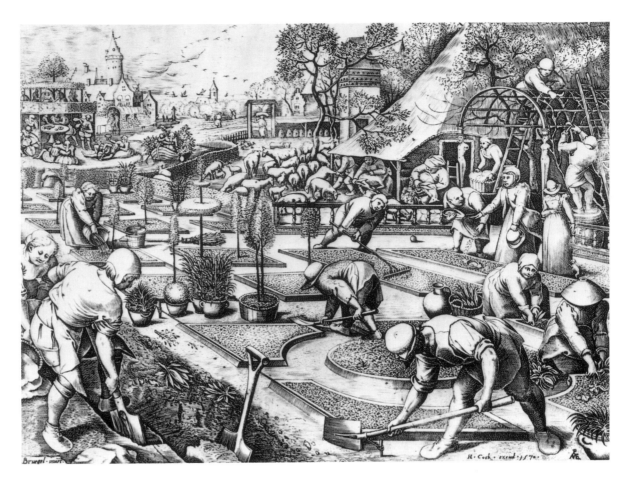

Many of the activities required to look after a pleasaunce garden during the spring are shown in this print – preparing the border of vegetables by deep digging, beating the soil to form the raised sides of the beds, pricking out the seedlings; in the middle distance a woman waters, a man rakes, and another sows the seed, while the family look on. Behind them, gardeners fix vines to an elegant trellis.

gardens which can be seen today were laid out during this period, which lasted until *c.* 1730.

These grand landscapes were highly influenced by the designs of André Le Nôtre (1613–1700) in France especially for Louis XIV at Versailles and Nicolas Fouquet at Vaux-le-Vicomte. Le Nôtre's designs were based on a series of principles which were used to create the last two styles in this section – the Knot Garden and the Geometric Garden. His plan for a country house was simple: to organize the landscape into one mighty scene that would express the dignity and elegance of Man and delight his senses. All nature should conform. Enormous fêtes or extravagant parties with entertainments such as fireworks on the canals were held in these gardens and were thought to be symbolic of the unity of a nation, an idea much appreciated by the politically insecure

Stuarts and their noblemen, who were anxious to demonstrate their newly acquired authority.

In 1712 John James published an English version of Le Nôtre's ideas in his very influential book *The Theory and Practice of Gardening*. It describes in detail various features which compose a formal landscape. Each feature or compartment can be re-created as one unit or linked together to make a larger garden. The size can be reduced or enlarged but in order to ensure the success of the design the proportions should be kept to the formula calculated in the eighteenth century. It is the proportion of the features and their shape and geometry which give these gardens their dramatic effect. Some of the grandest designs are made from the simplest shapes, which can be at once breathtaking in their scale and satisfying in their symmetry.

1

The Pleasaunce Garden

ENCLOSED and private, a pleasaunce garden is an intimate outdoor room directly related to the house. Flowers, herbs, lawns and fruit are grown to satisfy all senses – to see, to smell, to taste, to hear and to enjoy and to contemplate. Its arbours are covered with honeysuckle, its seats with camomile, and raised benches with delicate flowers are enclosed by luscious apples, pears and other fruit growing on lattice-work. The beds are laid out in simple patterns which can also be enjoyed from windows above. The aim is to create a restful garden, a sanctuary away from the bustle of the outside world, where flowers, herbs, fruit and vegetables can all be appreciated in a modest setting.

Most of these gardens are square or rectangular and divide into four, six or eight compartments. The larger ones can be further subdivided into smaller oblong beds. Often a fountain splashes noisily in the centre. Shade is produced by arched tunnels of climbers or a

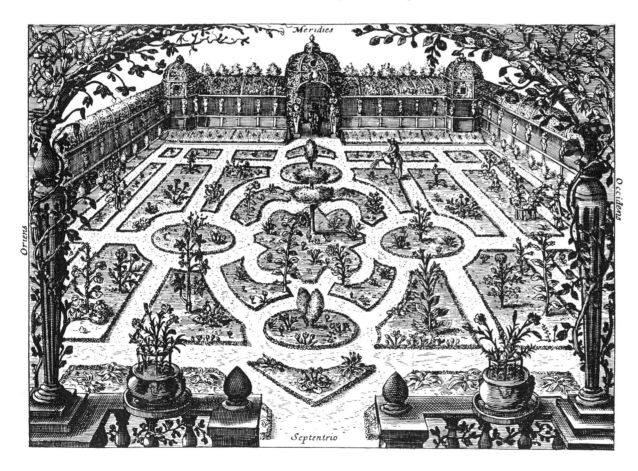

This 17th-century engraving from the Hortus Floridus *by Van der Pass shows the formal layout of a contemporary garden. The simple shaped beds are separated by pale gravel. The deliberate sparse planting was intended to ensure that each plant could be seen individually and separately. The garden is surrounded by an elaborate and complicated lattice-arbour, which resembles a cloister, and over which grow vines and ivy.*

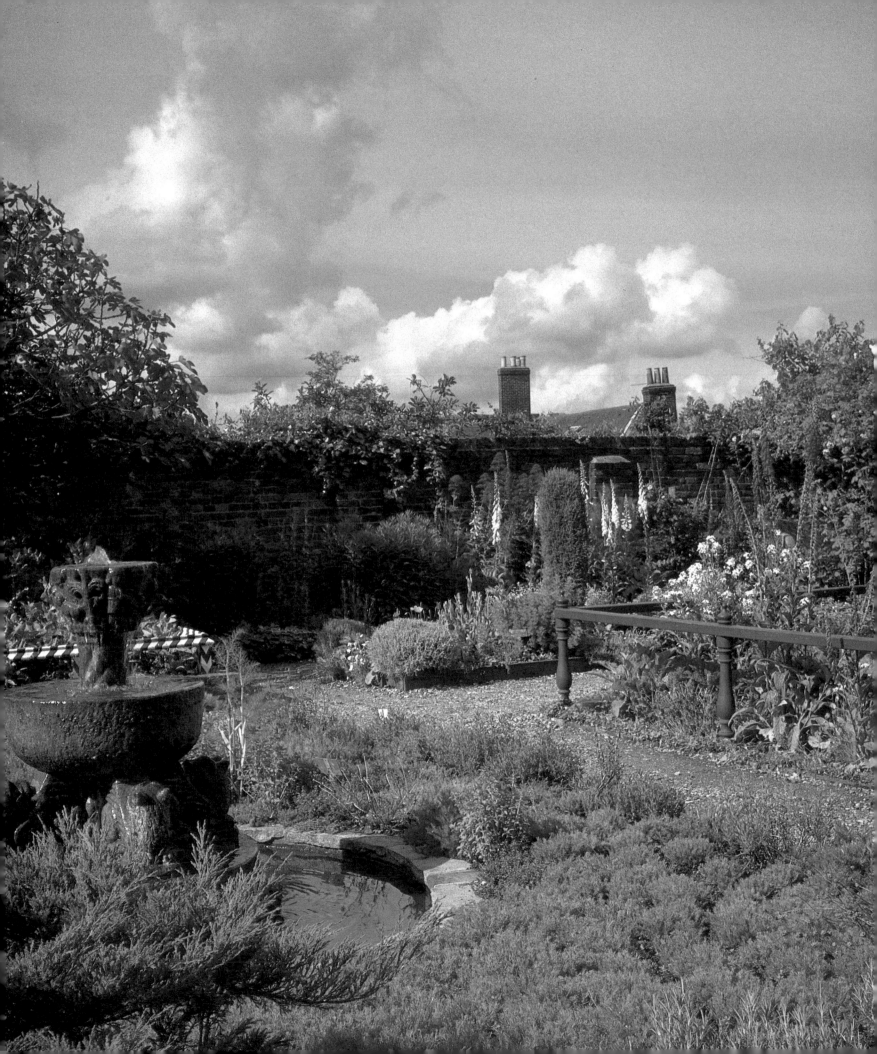

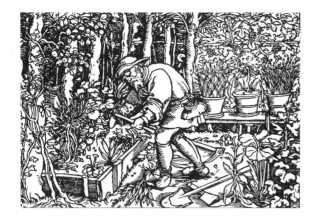

covered gallery. Decoration is provided by elaborately trained flowers growing either in the flower beds or in brightly coloured vases of all shapes and sizes. Created on a flat or gently sloping terrace, the compartments of the pleasaunce garden are divided by paths. Some of the quarters grow fruit and vegetables while others are grassy meads or lawns bordered by turf benches and seats or banks for lying against. Herbs are grown with the vegetables and fruit, and certain varieties are planted in a special quarter in knot patterns. Flowers are grown throughout the garden.

During the medieval period the garden was an essential part of the household. It not only produced most of the food, but medicines as well. Orchards and vineyards provided apples and grapes not just for eating, but for making cider and wine. Monks, particularly the Cistercians, Benedictines and Carthusians, developed herbaria or physic gardens to grow herbs for curing disease or for distilling essential oils to make tinctures, cordials and other ointments or medicines. Pleasaunce gardens evolved in monasteries as places of beauty offering a sanctuary for meditation and relaxation surrounded by scents and colourful flowers.

The Tudors' passion for order is illustrated by the neatness and formality of their gardens, which they felt should form an extension to the house and be enclosed by a strong boundary in the same way that a frame encloses a picture.

Pleasaunce gardens consequently require little space and this style suits enclosed areas such as town gardens or walled courtyards.

In the thirteenth century the Spanish-Moorish tradition of fountains, pools and water channels was introduced into England, probably by Queen Eleanor. The walls of one of her gardens still survive in the courtyard at Rockingham Castle, Northamptonshire. But today medieval enclosing walls remain in only a small number of monasteries or castles, and where they do survive, they are seldom complete, and so their original design can only be seen in medieval manuscripts. In these illustrations the Virgin Mary is often depicted sitting in a pleasaunce garden. By the fifteenth century nobles were painted relaxing in them and during the Tudor period many portraits showed them in the background. Throughout this long period there were changes in detail, as architectural styles evolved and gardening techniques improved, but the concept of an enclosed sanctuary never altered.

The Tudors, influenced by the Flemish style, decorated their gardens with painted wooden figures of grotesque heraldic beasts. Heraldic patterns of these beasts were also set out in the squares of grass. Replicas can be seen in the entrance yard at Hampton Court Palace,

OPPOSITE
Tudor House has a pleasaunce garden, with painted fences, either red or striped, a fountain, and a striped perch for heraldic beasts.

LEFT
A 16th-century gardener plants flowers including daisies in a raised bed, edged by wooden boards. In the background is a vine against a trellis, and flowerpots of carnations, with wattle supports. A vine grows up an apple tree on the left; a hollyhock is on the right.

A late 15th-century garden with a hazel or willow wattle fence, a tiered fountain, a 'live' palisade fence behind the evergreen trees, a pear tree and lilies in front. The gardener is tending carnations.

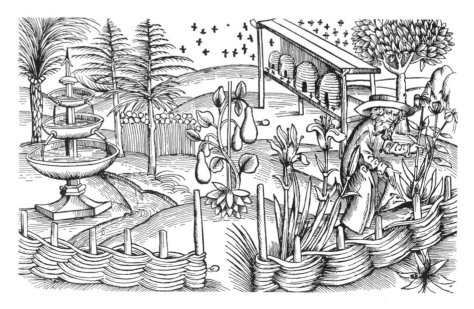

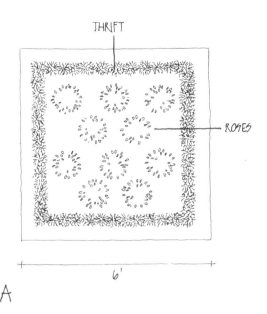

THRIFT

ROSES

A

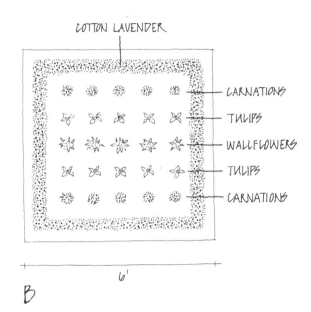

COTTON LAVENDER

CARNATIONS

TULIPS

WALLFLOWERS

TULIPS

CARNATIONS

B

A is a detail of a flower bed growing individual plants, and B is a layout showing the lines of planting in a typical flower bed, which is edged by a low hedge.

Surrey, and a heraldic knot garden has been recently re-created at Pitmedden near Aberdeen. A late Tudor garden recently restored by Dr Sylvia Landsberg at the Tudor House Museum in Southampton is an excellent example of this style and contains many of the features. Dr Landsberg is also creating a simpler yeoman's garden attached to the sixteenth-century farmhouse at the Weald and Downland Museum, Singleton, West Sussex.

Throughout the Middle Ages the range of plants available was limited mostly to those

This is the layout plan of a pleasaunce garden. Features from this garden can be included in other gardens.

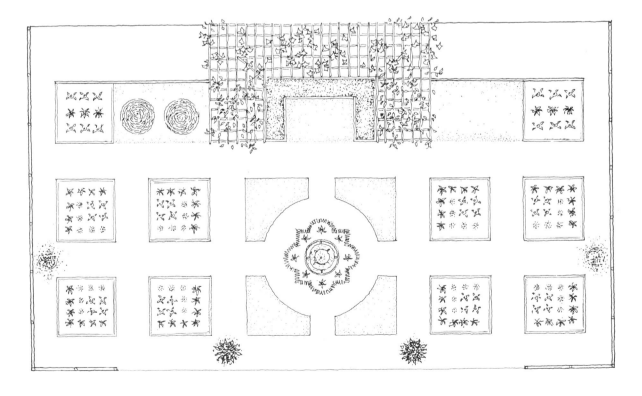

0   1   2   3   4M

native to Europe and a few Middle Eastern plants which had been introduced by itinerant monks during the Crusades. However, during the sixteenth century many more plants arrived from abroad, and primitive methods of hybridizing facilitated the cult for carnations and, later, tulips. Enthusiasm for plants spilled over into the passion for symbolism using flowers as images. This symbolism was widely apparent during the reign of Queen Elizabeth, the Virgin Queen, who was linked to the white eglantine rose and was often shown in portraits as Flora, the goddess of flowers.

Pleasaunce gardens should be laid out on a variation of the quadrangle, divided into quarters by paths. These meet at a central feature, which may be a fountain or well-head as a supply of water. This simple layout is still used as the basic plan in most kitchen gardens today.

'Medieval' herb gardens are laid out in plain square beds, small enough for every inch to be cultivated without having to step on the soil, and divided by paths just big enough to work from. In pleasaunce gardens the square beds are more decorative and are laid out in more ornate geometric patterns but their size is governed by the same principles as the herb garden.

These patterns are usually based on a square formation like graph paper and can be made from a variable number of blocks. Circular beds and those with wavy edges developed towards the end of the sixteenth century. The outline of the curves should be fitted into a rectangular form. Low hedges or fences divide the garden into compartments. One compartment should be primarily for growing plants and another can be made into a 'flowery mede', with grass liberally filled with wild flowers. These areas often have raised benches constructed from brick, timber boards or wicker work, varying in height from about 16 in (0.4 m) to 22 in (0.5 m). If the bench is to be sat on it is filled with turf or if it is used as a back rest and lent against it can be filled with herbs or flowers. These seats look like chunky window boxes. A camomile seat is filled with the herb camomile, so that the smell wafts across the sitter when it is crushed. Other sweet-smelling herbs such as thyme, eau de Cologne mint or pennyroyal may be used. The flower beds are about 3–4 ft (0.9–1.2 m) wide and may be raised about 3 in (7.5 cm) above the level of the path.

Detail of a camomile seat, made from brick, with a trellis frame for climbers behind.

BELOW
A section of the pleasaunce garden relating the height of the raised bed to the trellis behind and the camomile seat. Pinks grow in the pot.

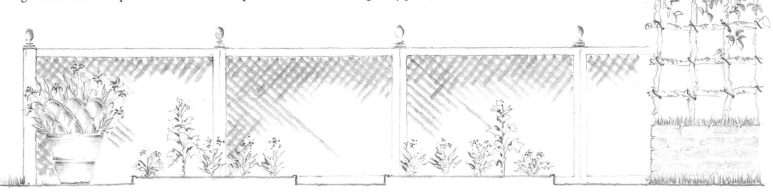

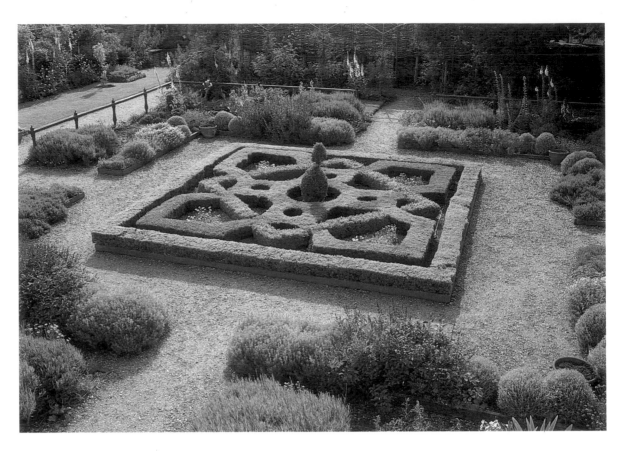

The knot garden at Tudor House. It is made from box and cotton lavender and set in a rectangular garden, and surrounded by the typical red painted and single railed fence. Around the outside is a selection of flower beds set in pale gravel.

Paths can be constructed by compacting the soil, making a smooth, even surface. They should be covered with a layer of sand or fine gravel and be at least 2 ft (0.6 m) wide.

If following the earlier medieval style, arbours should be made from poles of poplar or willow, either arched like a tunnel or square like a pergola. Later arbours became more sophisticated, with plants such as vines, melons and cucumbers 'running and spreading all over them': these could be constructed from wooden trellis made from laths. Other climbers include jasmine, musk and damask roses. The arbours provide shelter from the hot sun and dampening rain, and they can run around the edge of the garden like a cloister or be constructed like a round pavilion with wooden seats, or even as a tunnel with seats.

The pleasaunce garden should always be enclosed and protected from the outside world. The enclosure takes many forms and ranges from the humble wattle fence to ornate brick or high stone walls. Brick walls can be roofed with tiles or reed thatch. The external walls of smaller gardens may well be made from woven fences, but in larger gardens these decorative fences are usually used to divide the ornamental areas into compartments.

Most woven fences are made from the pliable sticks of hazel, aspen or willow and are tied with the flexible shoots of the osier willow or with wire or string. They can be tied into intricate lattice-work screens 'made with small Poles and wand bound with wire about 2 ft (0.6 m) off the ground'. A lighter trellis can also be made from these sticks. These frames can be placed around a quarter and are 'especially good if your ground be little ... as they take not half so much room as borders' or hedges. Sound advice from Thomas Hill in *The Gardener's Labyrinth*. This was the first popular gardening book and was published in 1577.

Illustrations of medieval pleasaunce gardens show attractive diamond-shaped fences made from straight thin sticks contained within panels surrounded by sturdy wooden rails and supported by posts. The posts are sometimes colourfully painted and may be decorated with finials, balls or grotesque figures. Roses and other climbers are shown entwined around them. Sometimes these fences are made out of trellis.

There are many examples of wattle fences where shoots are interwoven around stouter stakes. Such fences can be varied in texture from fine basket work to more rustic and thicker woven sticks. This technique of weaving branches around posts is still used today on live wood when laying hedges. Wattle can also be used to make frames for supporting flowers and for primitive tree guards.

Other forms of wooden fencing such as woven panels and chestnut paling are still in use today. Wooden palings with the tops cut into triangular points may be nailed to two horizontal rails fixed to upright stakes. Vertical cleft sticks may be spaced at different distances according to the use – for example, if the fence divides the more elegant part of the garden they are more widely spaced or, if enclosing a vegetable plot, they are fixed closer together.

Balustrades made from stone or painted wood can be used to separate the more functional compartments from the pleasure garden and to frame the entrance to a terrace in front of the house. Heraldic beasts may be carved on top of the main posts at the corners of the quarters.

'Living fences' are created by climbers trained up light trellis and clipped close to it. Sticks of live hawthorn and willow can be planted close together as if they are stakes and backed by a single horizontal rail supported by posts. Most of the live stakes will strike and grow into a hedge. Quickset hedges can also be made from a mixture of hawthorn, briar rose, gooseberries, brambles and berberis, most of which have vicious thorns!

The borders of the garden may be edged with various materials, including earthenware or stone tiles, cobble stones, thin strips of lead, or even knuckle-bones of animals placed upright. Sometimes the soil around the edge of the border is compacted into a firm battered slope. Boards are frequently used and held in place by long wooden pegs nailed to the timber.

Plants such as thrift, cotton lavender, germander or box can be used and clipped to form compact low hedges around the beds. In the medieval pleasaunce garden individual plants

This sketch shows the typical layout and elements of a pleasaunce garden: the raised beds of the flower garden; the three-tiered fountain; a camomile seat in the centre, surrounded by an arbour made of hazel; in the corner are beehives. The whole garden is surrounded by a wooden balustrade.

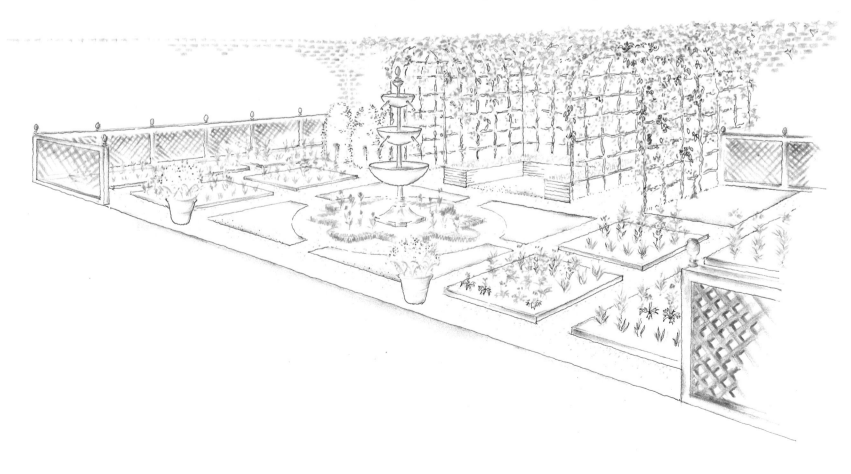

were neatly trimmed and by the Tudor period topiary was starting to become popular. The most commonly used plant for topiary was box, which was cut into fantastic birds, beasts or geometric forms. Such trimmed plants can also be used as features in the centre of beds or to mark the edges of a particular pattern.

Frames supporting plants are made of wood and vary from rustic poles to dressed timber. They come in all shapes and sizes, from the twisted holder for a single carnation to a tiered frame for climbers. Individual plants whose blooms are greatly prized are often carefully supported by wicker twigs tied together to make a stand, which is placed either in a vase or directly in the flower beds.

Woven hazel hoops can be used to support plants grown in containers. They should be bent over so that both the ends are securely fixed in the pot, and each hoop should be evenly spaced around it. Simpler supports may also be used, such as a single horizontal circle supported by upright sticks.

Sometimes small trees are grown on circular mounds which are neatly retained by wicker work and topped by turf. Fruit trees are often attached with twine or osier to a wooden frame or trellis, which may enclose part of the garden or be attached to the surrounding wall. Apples, pears and plums may be grown in an area set aside for an orchard but peaches and Morello cherries, traditionally highly prized, frequently grow in the pleasaunce garden itself. Grapes are often trained on frames or covered arbours. If a vine is not suitable other vigorous climbers can be treated in the same way.

This garden at Drummond Castle, shows the different kind of patterns for a knot garden within a pleasaunce garden.

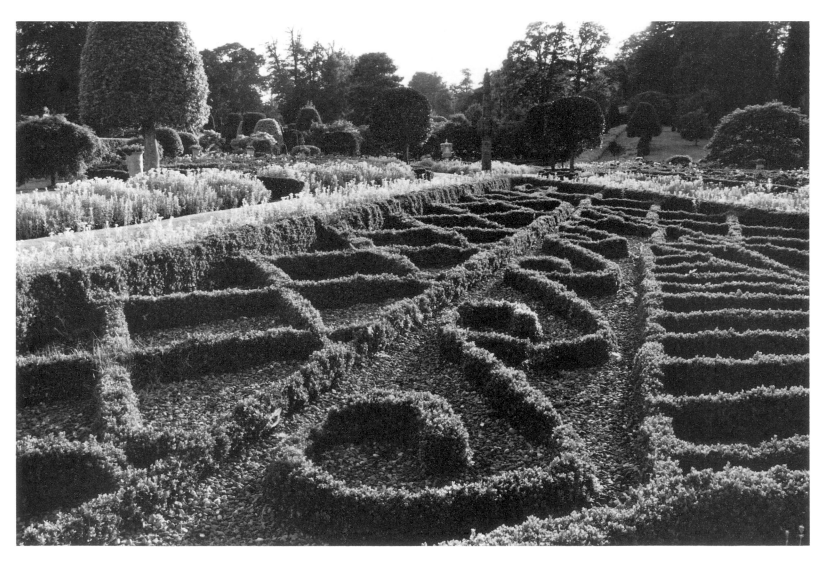

Wooden Fencing and Flower Bed Edging

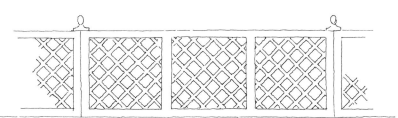

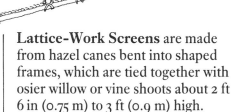

Trellis in Panels is usually highly colourful and decorated. A solid wooden frame supports the timber laths, forming a diamond or square pattern. Tall posts with carved symbols such as heraldic beasts can be fixed between each panel. The height can vary from about 2 ft 6 in (0.75 m) to 5 ft (1.5 m).

Rustic Trellis can be made from straight canes fixed to poles with the bark left on. More sophisticated **Trellis** is made from laths fixed to sawn posts. The diamonds can vary from 2 in (0.05 m) to 8 in (0.2 m) wide and the height can be from about 3 ft (0.9 m) to 6 ft (1.8 m).

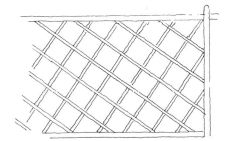

Wattle Fence is woven like a basket using thick canes of hazel twisted

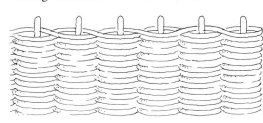

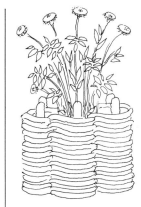

Wickerwork Planters are woven around special plants such as pinks to protect them.

Live Fence is made from long live shoots of willow, hazel or hawthorn stuck into the soil as tall cuttings. Each stem is tied to a supporting rail fixed to posts. The twigs grow rapidly and soon form a thick hedge.

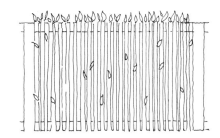

around poles. **Wickerwork Fence** uses thin whips of willow. For fences up to about 2 ft 6 in (0.75 m) high each post can be driven directly into the ground between 4 in (0.1 m) to 6 in (0.15 m) apart. Fences up to 6 ft (1.8 m) can be made from panels of about 3 ft (0.9 m) long and fixed to a stout pole.

Lattice-Work Screens are made from hazel canes bent into shaped frames, which are tied together with osier willow or vine shoots about 2 ft 6 in (0.75 m) to 3 ft (0.9 m) high.

Wooden Balustrades can be plain or brightly painted, with turned finials decorating the posts. The height varies from about 2 ft (0.6 m) for edging borders to about 4 ft (1.2 m) when enclosing a garden.

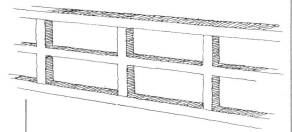

Wooden Edge around Raised Beds can be highly decorated and painted in bright colours, with carved finials at the corners. Alternatively, this edging may be made from more rustic wooden planks strong enough to support the soil in beds about 8 in (0.2 m) to 1 ft (0.3 m) high.

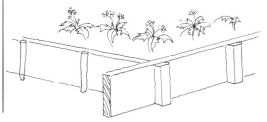

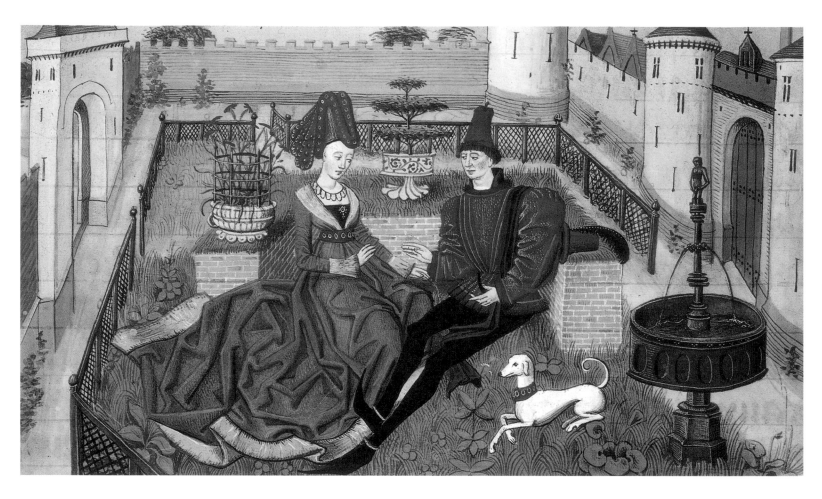

This miniature from Roman de Renaud de Montauban, *c. 1475, shows two figures in a pleasaunce garden. They are seated in a meadow and lean against a camomile seat. They are surrounded by a trellis fence. They listen to the trickle of fountain water. Between them is a formal vase with a clipped evergreen shrub, while to their left is a pot of pinks.*

Plants with interesting flowers should not carpet the beds as it is important to see how the individual specimens actually grow. This is particularly true of the more unusual ones such as lilies, roses and other exotics, which should be planted with plenty of room around them. *The Gardener's Labyrinth* explains how the 'most delectable Flowers and Hearbs in use, for adorning a Summer Garden, or Garden of pleasure and delight' should be planted or sown. It continues by listing the flowers, and the sixteenth-century language vividly invokes the pleasure they can give:

Roses are of several sorts and Colours, as white, Red, Damask, Province, Musk and Sweet-bryer … this is the chief for beauty and sweetness: Rose-trees are commonly planted in a plot by themselves, (if you have roome enough) leaving a pretty space betwixt them for gathering

… Gilly-flowers, Carnations, or July-flowers, these for beauty and sent (scent) are next to the rose; they are of several curious colours and smelleth like cloves … Wall-July-flowers, or Wall-flowers, usually grow on walls; for they delight to grow in lime and Morter. Tulips are very beautiful flower but have no sent [scent], they adorn a garden wel

… Lavender is wondrous sweet both leaf and flower. Flowers of the Sun [Sunflower] groweth very high, and beareth a great yellow Flower as big as the crown of a hat

… Penny-royal is good to set in the edges of your beds, or border, so are Daisies. Camomel [Camomile] is also good for edges of border and it may be set in banks to sit on.

These descriptions conjure up the simplicity and tranquillity of the pleasaunce garden, which can provide a refuge from the tumult of life as well as pander to the senses. Perhaps it is best described by Hill: 'What rarer object can there be on earth … than a beautifull and Ode-riferous Garden plat Artificially composed.'

2

The Fantasy Garden

FANTASY gardens are primarily entertaining rather than intimate and contemplative like the pleasaunce garden. Although the designs appear deceptively simple, just variations on squares of grass, they are highly sophisticated and often contain unexpected and thrilling surprises to excite the imagination of the viewer. Containing indulgent almost childish tricks, the fantasy garden is full of illusions, demonstrating control over nature.

These gardens are to be seen and to be seen in. They are for display – to show off objects, to flaunt plants and to parade in with guests. Made from broad open terraces filled with patterned green lawns picked out by coloured paths, they are like outdoor galleries exhibiting works of art in a living space except that the scale of the objects is larger than life, so that the viewer should feel part of a 'heroic' landscape.

This style first flourished in the seventeenth century and is sometimes called the 'Italian Garden'. Statues, vases, urns or busts are displayed within the grass compartments on a broad flat terrace. Such objects were frequently brought back from Grand Tours to Europe and especially Italy.

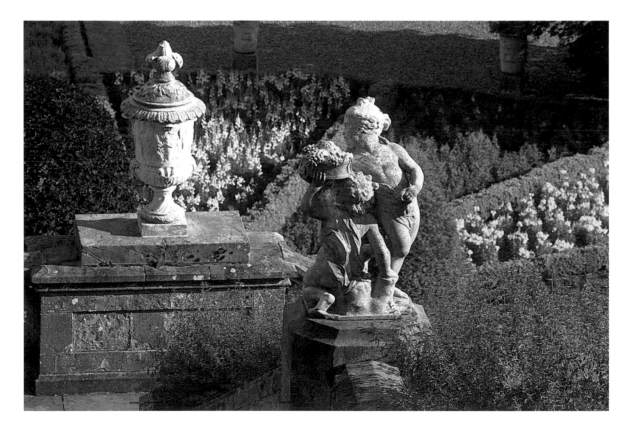

The garden at Drummond Castle shows the element of fantasy that statues add to a garden.

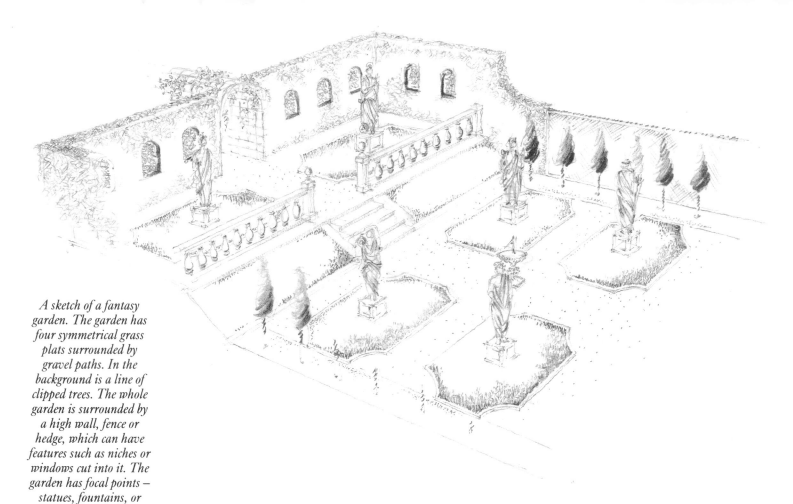

A sketch of a fantasy garden. The garden has four symmetrical grass plats surrounded by gravel paths. In the background is a line of clipped trees. The whole garden is surrounded by a high wall, fence or hedge, which can have features such as niches or windows cut into it. The garden has focal points – statues, fountains, or even small trees in pots.

BELOW
A section drawing of the details and different levels found in a fantasy garden.

PAGES 38–9
Most of the features of a fantasy garden are in this painting of Massey's Court, Llanech, Denbighshire, of 1662. In the top terrace the lawn is edged by plattes bandes *of clipped trees. The second terrace is reached by two flights of steps around a fountain. The lower terrace contains an orange house and another fountain. In the field is the grand amphitheatre with an enormous pool in the middle.*

The size of the terrace creates the grandeur of the garden, and its space is broken only by the statues or other imposing features. In more modest gardens these works of art can be replaced by simple pyramids or cones made from wooden trellis entwined with climbers such as passion flowers, or formed by yew or box clipped into balls or other fancy shapes. It is important that these objects can be viewed both from the house and when walking around the garden. In the Stuart period the main rooms were often on the first floor and these gardens were designed to be seen from above. The full extent of the layout could often be appreciated from the salon or *piano-nobile*, but the detail could only be savoured by walking around it. The garden was approached down a flight of steps from the first floor, and might sometimes be sunk slightly lower than the ground floor so that more of the pattern could be seen when approaching it.

Whilst touring the garden, the visitor was supposed to discover a mythical legend or story. Each object evoked part of a classical scene or told a tale; discovering the details of the allegory titillated and entranced the viewer.

These gardens were designed to be used all the year round and so did not rely on flowers to create their effect. Sheltered by walls and hedges, they looked inward. Views to the countryside could only be seen from particular places such as mounts, banks, terraces, raised platforms or summer-houses, banqueting rooms or pavilions.

The Renaissance and its interpretation of the

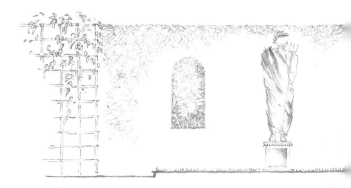

Greek and Roman classical world influenced the designers and patrons, many of whom were both artists and engineers. In Italy the most famous of these was Leonardo da Vinci, who turned his brilliant mind to anything. Stimulated by the emerging sciences of hydraulics and engineering, the artist/engineer happily designed extraordinary mechanical figures which moved, groaned, roared, hissed and even laughed. Such devices were operated without the benefits of modern power, pressurized water or instant electricity. Viewers were entranced by fantasies such as the tinkling laughter of nymphs dancing around a grotto bathed in a rainbow of refracted light. These complex phenomena were made out of only the simplest of materials such as wood, iron, fire, water, rope and stone.

In Britain the passion for these devices lasted throughout the seventeenth century except for the interregnum of the Civil War and the Commonwealth. The most famous designer/engineers were Salomon de Caus and his son Isaac, the architect Inigo Jones, and Claude and André Mollet; all of these designers had royal connections to the courts of Charles I and Charles II. Today few gardens of this period remain except in outline. Examples of the terracing can be seen at Wilton House, Wiltshire; at Powis Castle, Powys, Wales; and in Scotland at Drumlanrig Castle, Dumfries; and Drummond Castle, Crieff. Later gardens have been planted in most of them. The fantastic grotto at Woburn Palace, built by Isaac de Caus before 1627, can still be seen today.

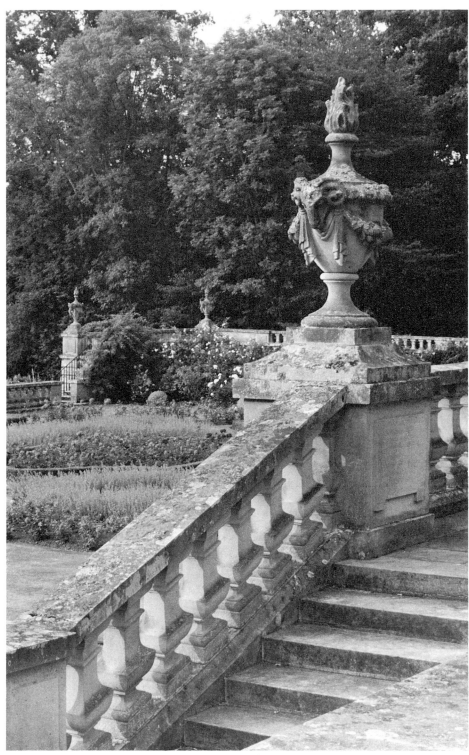

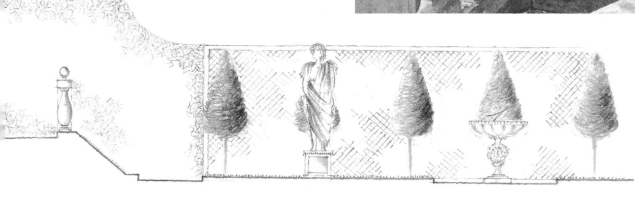

The apt position of a vase on its plinth at Mellerstain gives decoration and drama to the terrace and garden below.

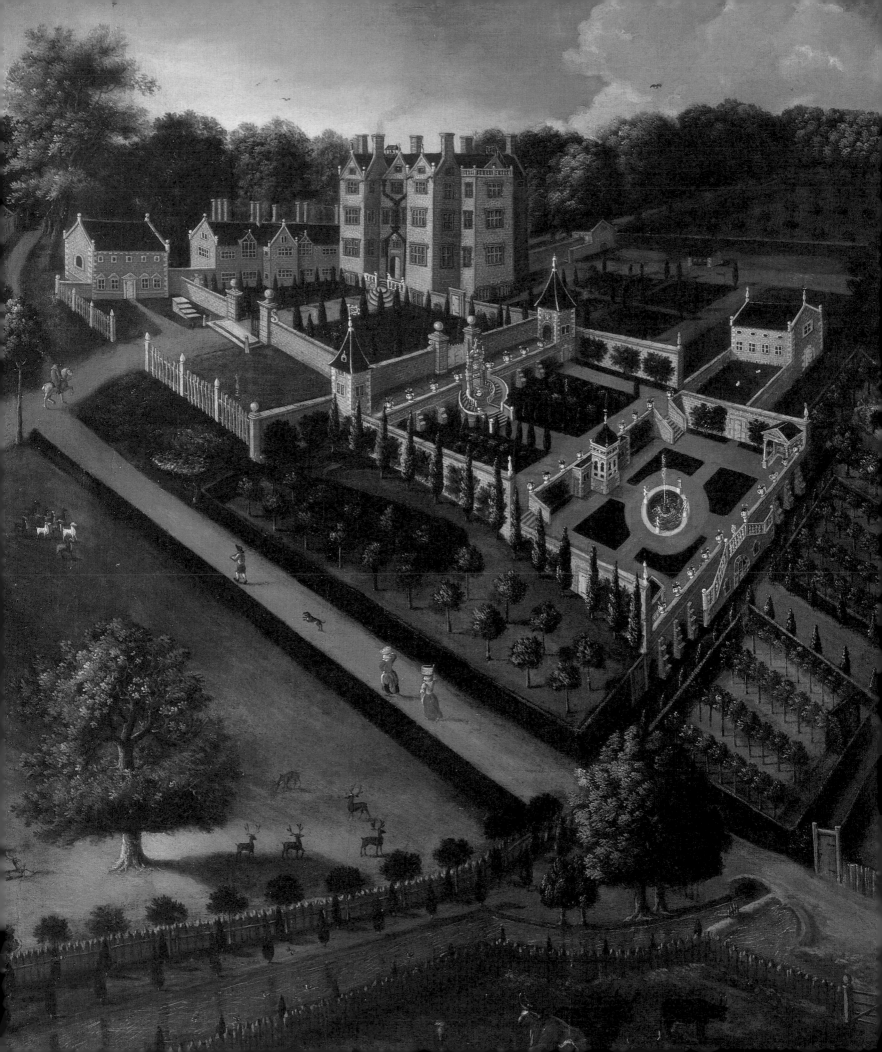

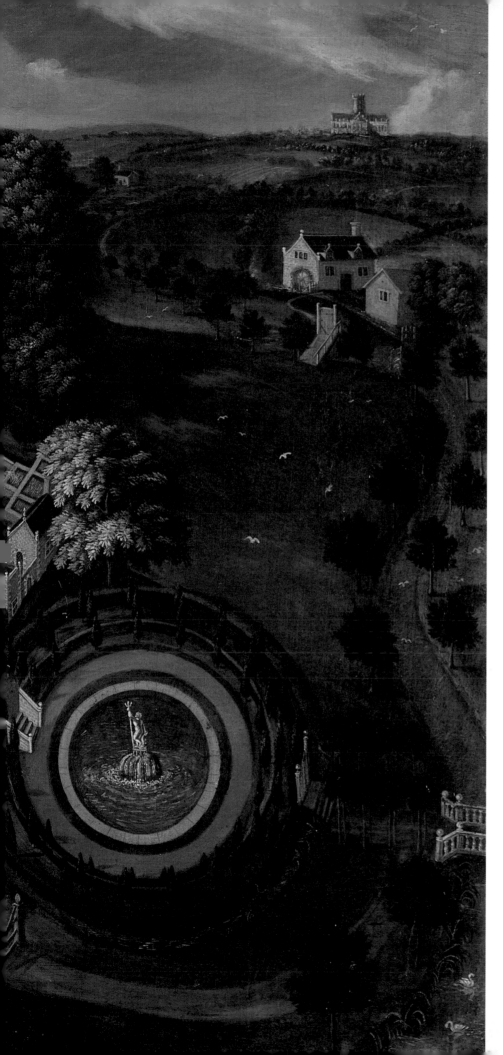

At the time, the style was well illustrated and many of the most important gardens were included as backgrounds to portraits. The grandest of these was the garden at Arundel House, attributed to Inigo Jones, glimpsed at the back of the portrait of Thomas Howard, the 'collector' Earl of Arundel. At the height of its grandeur it is said to have displayed over thirty-two full-sized statues, 128 busts, 250 inscriptions, sarcophagi and many other classical fragments brought back from the Earl's travels in Italy. It must have been magnificent!

Other examples of work by Inigo Jones can be seen in the stage sets for a court masque *The Shepherd's Paradise* of about 1633 and in the little courtyard he is reputed to have designed for Chevening House in Kent.

Fantasy was further elaborated by the workings of mechanical devices, such as jets of water squirting from fountains or the waving arms of gods, who occasionally even roared or hissed. Sometimes these fantasies verged on the vulgar, with water sprayed from the breasts of goddesses. Another childish trick was to squirt water up the voluminous skirts of surprised ladies. This was triggered by the host stepping on a particular stone which activated the device.

Fantasies were sometimes assembled in grottoes or caves hidden under terraces, or on the edge of mounds, where special effects heightened the drama. There was a close relationship between gardens, theatre and open-air masques, so popular in the Elizabethan and Stuart periods.

The fantasy garden terrace is based on a geometrical pattern and is often rectangular, and the aim is to make it look as large as possible. The garden is divided into four quarters, with a large principal feature in the centre, usually circular and often containing a spectacular fountain or statue.

Opposite the main entrance on the central path there can be another architectural feature such as an arbour, arcade, summer-house or grotto designed in the classical style. The central axis can be focused onto such a feature, and

Caption on page 36

Trellis Frames and Bowers

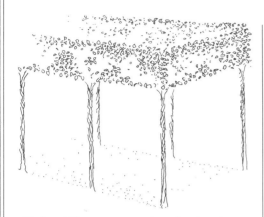

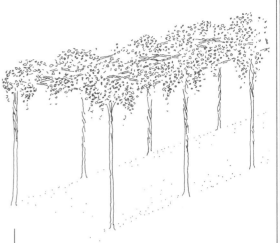

Covered Bowers have a simple wooden frame supported between two stout posts at least 3 ft (0.9 m) apart and 7 ft (2.1 m) high. Like the arbour, they arch over paths. Prolific climbers such as vines, honeysuckle and old man's beard romp over the bower with their flowers dangling down.

Simple Trellis supports many types of plants such as vines, honeysuckles, scarlet bean, passion flower or even bindweed. Straight canes of hazel, chestnut or elm are tied together into squares with young shoots of willow or twisted twine. If it is to be free-standing the frame can be supported by stout poles, or it can be fixed to a wall.

Raised Bowers consist of a simple wooden frame raised and fixed on edge between stout posts. The climbers are clipped so that the sky can be seen between the struts.

Lattice Arbours are delicate outdoor galleries for walking through. The lattice work is assembled from 'fillets' or strips of oak, 1 in (0.025 m) square, fixed into 'checker' squares, 6–7 in (0.15–0.175 m) wide, tied together with wire. These are supported on carved wooden columns, often in the Ionic classical style, and braced by cross-rails holding decorations of circles and arches. In the more elaborate ones mouldings such as cornices and wainscotting are added.

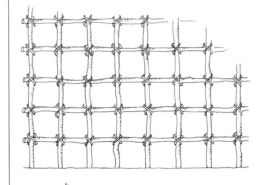

Versailles Boxes were much used as inexpensive objects in French gardens, where climbers such as ivy were treated as architectural features. They are square wooden boxes usually painted green or white, ranging in size from 1 ft 6 in (0.46 m) to 3 ft (0.92 m). Pyramids of wooden lattice fit into the boxes and their height can range from 3 ft 9 in (1.14 m) to 8 ft 3 in (2.5 m).

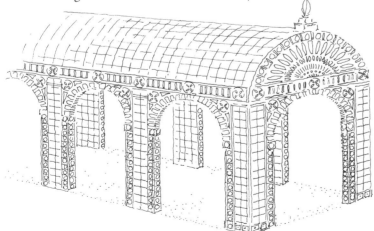

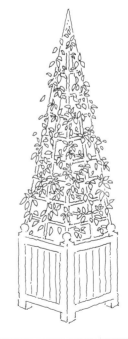

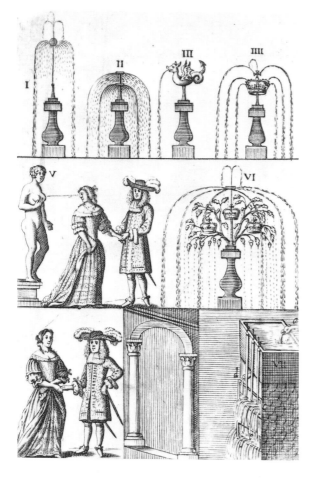

if this is outside the terrace, the path can be used to set up a series of perspectives. This linear arrangement may be emphasized by the siting of statues or other objects which can be placed on a plinth in the middle or at the corners of the grass quarters.

If the ground naturally slopes up or down, another terrace may be added either lower or higher than the principal one, linked by a double flight of steps. Stone or painted wooden balustrades run along the top of the high retaining walls and may run down the steps adjoining the two terraces. Such terraces may include a grotto, fountain, loggia, summer-house or other feature.

Steep and sharply graded banks may be used instead of retaining walls, or on their own as strong geometrical shapes. Some may be formed as steps or like canals upside-down. There is a good example of this at Holme Lacy near Hereford. The angle of the grass bank may be up to 45 degrees (or a 1:3 slope).

The compartments are always made from grass surrounded and divided by gravel paths. The length of the quadrangle is related to its width and by the end of the seventeenth century certain rules defined the size. These rules are connected to the width of the central path. For example, if the path is 12 ft (3.6 m) wide the width of the quarter should be a ratio of it – twice the width at 24 ft (7.3 m); three times at 36 ft (11 m); or even four times at 48 ft (14.6 m); but in no case wider than four times the width of the path. If the beds must be wider, then the path must also be widened in accordance with this formula.

The design is always symmetrical and the shape of one quarter is copied in the other three parts. The measurements appear precise but often on the ground they are not quite right and one side is not exactly the same size as the other. This lack of precision can be confusing when restoring such gardens.

The pattern made by the line of the junction between the path and grass around the outside of the quarters or grass 'plats' can be varied from one garden to the next. This line facilitates the sophistication of design. Patterns can be created of curves, ovals or circles, volutes or serpentines, squares or rectangles. The geometrical shape of the quarters can be emphasized by a narrow strip of planting like a ribbon running around the outside, called a *platte bande*.

A page from John Woolridge's Systema Horticulturae, *1700, with examples of fountains. Note V, where the man with his foot has set off a contraption that makes the statue squirt water at his companion; VI is a vase that spectacularly turns into a fountain; at the bottom is a tank, with water trickling gently from level to level.*

The unexpected positioning of a statue of faun above a box hedge, in William Kent's garden at Rousham, is the witty combination of statues and hedges.

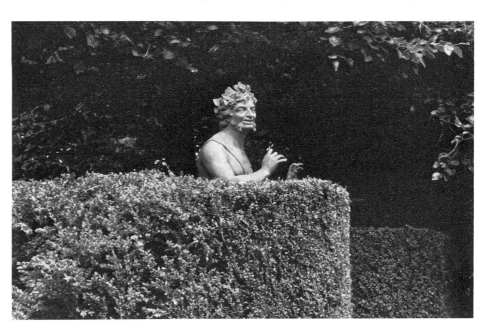

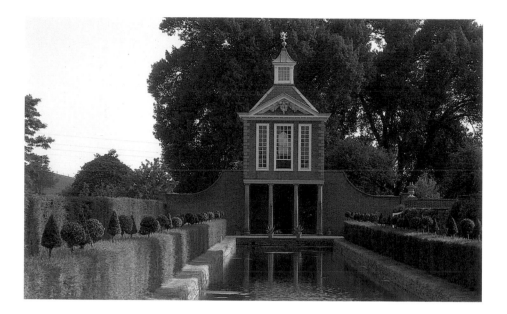

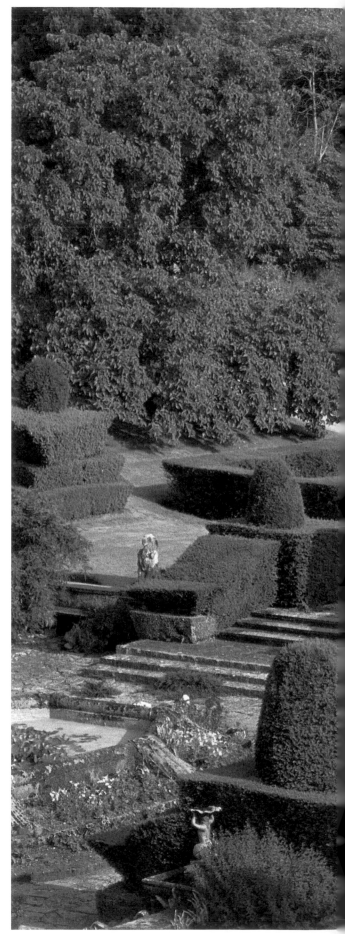

What is remarkable about the fantasy garden at Westbury is the simplicity of the design: a canal edged by a yew hedge leads to a pavilion in the distance. Out of the hedges dramatically emerge shaped finials.

RIGHT
This garden at Mapperton presents the structure of a typical fantasy garden and the importance of architectural features. It has changes of levels and includes many elements such as statues, vases, steps and topiary.

In his book *Systema Horticulturae, or the Art of Gardening* (1700), John Woolridge states that 'statues are commendable in the middle of fountains, and [in] green squares in groves and at the end of obscure walks.' He also advocates the use of sundials as the central feature and using a vane to tell the time. He is aware of the cost of statuary and recommends the more modest use of 'Flower Pots, which painted white and placed on pedestals, either on the ground in a streight line on the edge of your walks, on your walls, or at the corners of your squares are exceeding pleasant.'

Statuary and artefacts play a significant part and the figures usually represent classical gods such as Jupiter, Mars or Apollo, who are often depicted with virtues such as Honour, Truth and Valour. The more important gods are placed nearer the centre in the 'open centres and lawns of a grand design'. They are usually elevated on a pedestal or column and may be surrounded by their attendants, apparently 'ready to execute the Command of their great Masters'. Neptune, god of the sea, may be placed in or near water. Venus, Diana, Daphne and Flora with their attendants appear in the flower garden and orchard. Generally the size of the figures is also significant and they

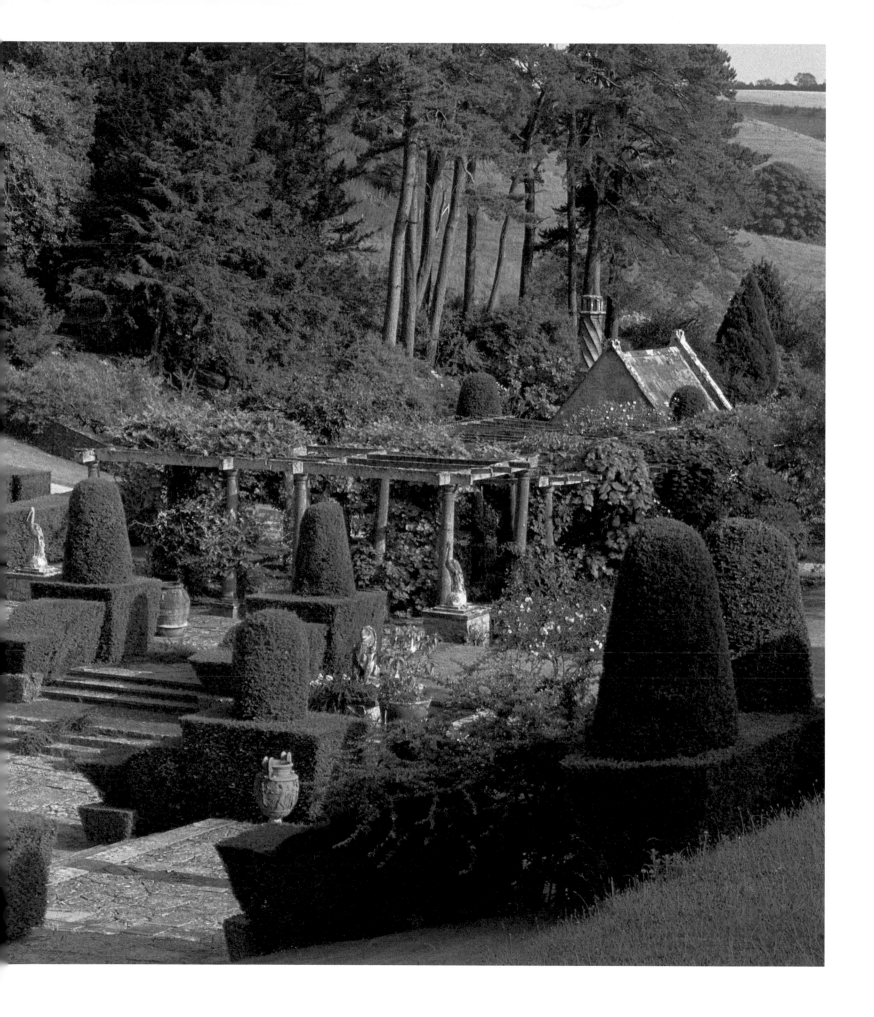

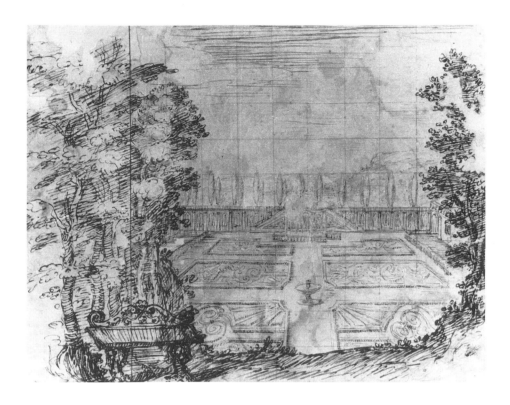

ABOVE
Inigo Jones's stage set for
The Shepherd's
Paradise, *1633, depicts a
fantasy garden. The
fountain splashes among
the grass plats, and an
elaborate grotto is framed
by two flights of steps,
leading to the terrace.*

any time in those places of never dying Pleasure.'

The brick walls enclosing smaller gardens are used as sun traps to ripen fruit. Gravel is considered to absorb more heat than grass so it is used to edge the borders along the wall. If the ground is almost level the paths should be constructed with a slight camber. The edges can be protected in several ways including by thinnish bricks laid on edge, by narrow wooden boards, thin lead strips, or turf cut to a precise line. The paths should be maintained by raking, rolling and spraying with the most basic of weedkillers – salted water. Weeds of any kind should be discouraged.

The quality of the grass in the plats is also important, and seventeenth-century gardeners were recommended to use either turf 'from sheep walks coming off poorer land' or to sow seed from a local hayfield. Daisies, low-growing clover and other smaller wild flowers are to be encouraged but it is essential to keep the grass low and mow the lawn regularly.

Some designs have *plattes bandes* or bands of planting around the outside and this decoration is particularly useful if there are only a few objects to display. In these narrow borders the centre part is kept for yew or box clipped into balls or miniature obelisks. Flowering shrubs such as lilacs, taller roses and honeysuckle may be planted alternately between the evergreen yew or box pyramids and clipped into decorative shapes, such as balls on poles.

Border flowers can be planted in rows between the standard clipped shrubs and box hedges bordering the beds but they should not be more than about 18 in (0.45 m) high. Annuals such as snapdragons or special plants such as lilies may also be planted in these narrow rows. In plainer gardens the beds are filled with ground cover such as ivy, which is clipped to keep it within the bed. A fuller description of these borders is given in the next chapter.

Plants are also used as architectural features, and beautiful or unusual trees can be placed as accents in the centre of a terrace or to empha-

'should not be too small but bigger than Life, especially in large Gardens' so that they can depict the heroic scale of the landscape.

Eventually enthusiastic gardeners set out very many statues; as John Woolridge ironically remarks, 'many have placed in their gardens, Statues, and Figures of several Animals and a great variety of other curious pieces of workmanship, that their walks might be pleasant at

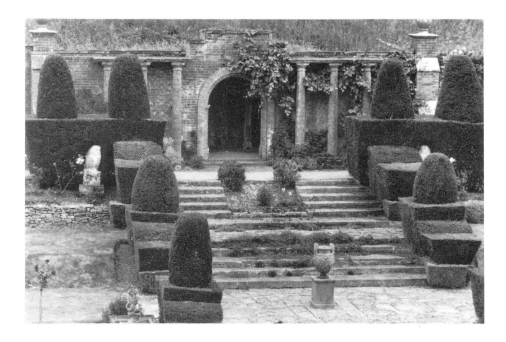

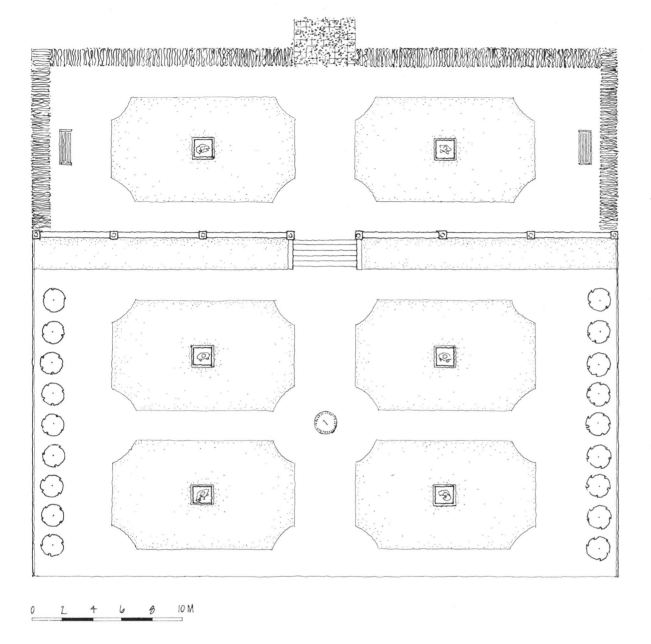

The ground plan of a fantasy garden, which is planned on two levels or terraces. The upper level is enclosed on three sides by a tall yew or beech hedge, which can have windows cut into it. It is separated from the lower garden by a bank surmounted by a balustrade, and steps lead to the lower garden. Four symmetrical quarters or compartments surrounded by gravel paths divide the lower terrace. The design of the garden relies on the whole pattern that is created by the four identical compartments together with the paths that relate in exact proportion to them and to each other. The upper terrace is smaller but retains the same proportions.

0   2   4   6   8   10 M

size the shape of the quarters. Tubs or plant cases can be used in the same way as statues, the tub giving the effect of a pedestal or base and the trunk and foliage acting as the object. In the seventeenth century orange and lemon trees were particular favourites grown in boxes because they could be moved into the greenhouse during the winter. Other delicate shrubs such as myrtles, roses and tender lilies were also planted out in tubs or pots and protected or taken indoors during winter.

More vigorous and colourful climbers can be trained over interesting frames, such as the pyramid-shaped trellis attached to a square box, called a 'Versailles' case.

The devices of the fantasy garden can provide amusement and childish delight. The shape is clear, precise and simple and the garden requires relatively low maintenance. It is designed to appear decorative from the house and its interesting shape will look good all year round.

FAR LEFT
Steps are an attractive element of a garden, and here their breadth serves to make the grotto above a grander feature.

3

The Knot Garden

EMBROIDERY, cutwork, compartments, scrolls, volutes, cartoozes – these names describe the intricate designs of the knot garden or parterre. The patterns are similar to embroidery or needlepoint, embellished to create a grand living tapestry laid out on a broad terrace.

The knot garden is a magnificent array of colour to admire and to entertain in. The designs are contrived and regular. The complex patterning is often to be viewed from above where the whole tableau is displayed. The intricate details may also be appreciated by walking around the garden.

The designs are laid out on level or gently sloping terraces and the effect should be open, with only the occasional feature such as a fountain or statue accentuating the broad space. The patterns are symmetrical, colourful and complicated and are very similar to the beautifully scrolled plasterwork and delicate carving of the Baroque period of Grinling Gibbons, Sir Christopher Wren and others.

By the early eighteenth century five styles of parterre had developed – knot, embroidery, compartments, the English manner and cutwork. These styles were rarely mixed together in the same parterre, but in grand gardens several parterres of different styles made up a large display 'divided at convenient distances by Cross-walks taking care that the Parterre of Embroidery be always next to the building as being the richest and most magnificent'. Smaller gardens tended to concentrate on only one style.

These richly patterned gardens evolved from the more modest and enclosed medieval herb garden. The knot garden style developed first and the more complicated patterns emerged in the early eighteenth century. At the beginning of the seventeenth century the patterns were simpler and similar to the grass terraces described in the previous chapter.

With the Restoration of Charles II in 1660, the returning exiled gentlemen brought with them French ideas for 'Broderie' parterres, which were transposed into English gardens by the Mollet brothers, pupils of the famous French designer, André Le Nôtre (1612–1700). Later in the seventeenth century William and Mary brought with them the Dutch style of parterres, which used more intricate shapes made from clipped topiary, especially box hedges. Examples can be seen in contemporary illustrations of Hampton Court Palace and Kensington Palace Gardens.

Many designs for knot gardens and parterres are shown in the beautiful aerial perspectives engraved in the book *Le Nouveau Théâtre de la Grande Bretagne* by J. Knyff. It illustrates all sorts and sizes of gentlemen's residences and offers a superb record of formal gardens, and in particular the styles of parterres. With the engraver J. Kip, Knyff produced several other books, including *Britannia Illustrata*. In 1711 Colen Campbell published *Vitruvius Britannicus*, which illustrates the facades of many country houses. Volume 3 includes a large number of engravings of grand landscapes.

Victorians copied designs for many of their enormous parterres from eighteenth-century gardening books, especially John James's translation from French of *The Theory and Practice of Gardening*, first published in 1712.

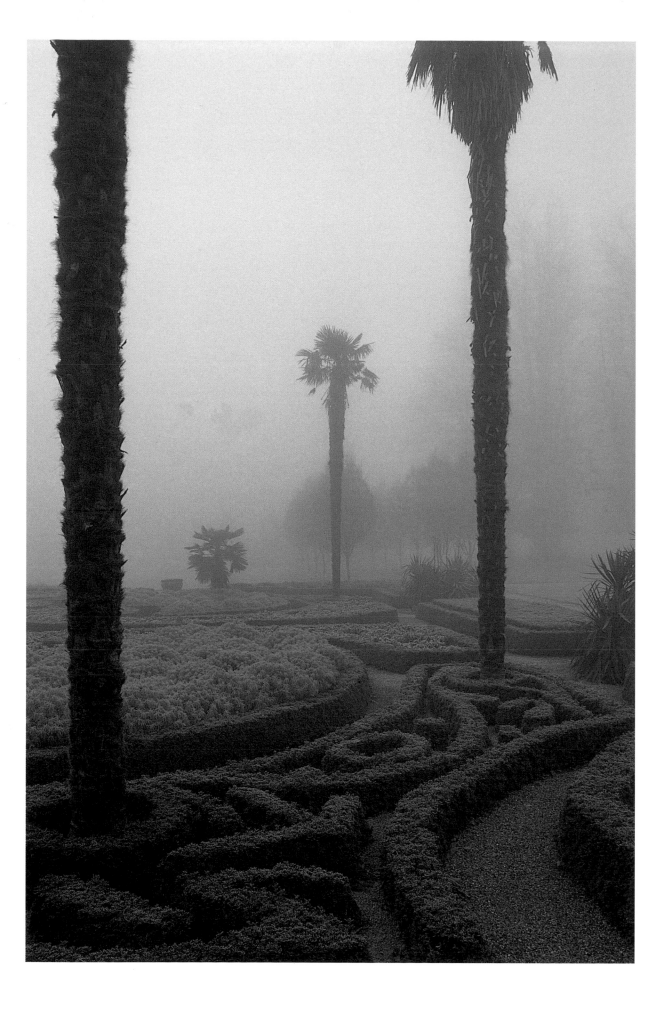

The graceful patterns of a box knot garden at Chevening.

Parterre Patterns

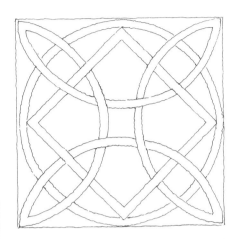

The Knot Parterre can be created in two styles – with the intertwining figures based on symbolic forms such as the one illustrated, or as the representation of a heraldic emblem. The pattern is always symmetrical. Symbolic forms are usually smaller than heraldic ones and the shapes are made entirely from plants clipped to the same height.

In the pattern illustrated here the knot can be enclosed by a brick edging or a border of marjoram. The circle and square might be made out of dwarf box and the interconnecting half-circles planted with hyssop. In the centre there might be a feature such as a ball of rosemary or a statue surrounded with pennyroyal, and the four sections of the square might be planted with wormwood. Yellow-leaved thyme can be set in each of the three parts of the oval created by the half-circles while the eight beds between the circle and the square may be planted with cotton lavender. Finally, sage may be placed in the eight beds around the circle.

Coloured stones or sand are used to

feature the more intricate shapes of the heraldic knot. The motto and date is usually placed in a border around the square. The emblem is set within a swirling circle of, for example, box and the larger sections are emphasized by colourful annuals such as marigolds.

The Cutwork Parterre can be of any size but the shape must be symmetrical. Here flowers are grown in raised beds edged by clipped box. The beds should be separated by hard-surfaced paths: grass ones would wear out quickly, particularly since each flower should be viewed close up and the gardener will use the path frequently in order to maintain the plants.

In the cutwork parterre many different kinds of plants can be grown. The range is shown in the plant lists at the back of the book. Usually each bed is devoted to one type but bulbs can be planted with herbaceous or annuals. Unlike the other parterres colour does not unify the design and it can be mixed.

In the centre of the parterre there is usually a main feature, which can

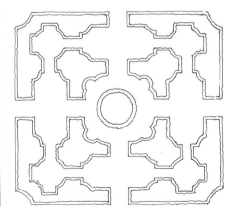

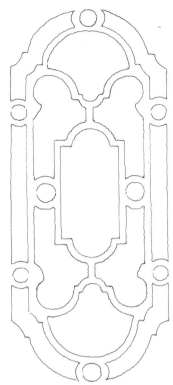

either be a statue or fountain or, when this is not suitable, a round bed can be filled with special plants.

Grasswork in the English Manner is the term used to describe the shapes created by cutting a pattern out of a closely mown lawn or grass platt and filling the grooves with gravel or crushed coloured stone. It was called 'in the English manner' because grass grows so well in the damp British climate, much better than it does in Europe. So more parterres in this style were made in England than anywhere else.

These parterres were often surrounded by *plattes bandes* or narrow borders separated from the grasswork by a path 2–3 ft (0.6–0.9 m) wide 'laid smooth and sanded over to make a greater distinction'.

Today there are still some of these Victorian re-creations surviving, such as the great garden at Drummond Castle, Crieff, Scotland; Shrubland Hall near Ipswich; and Levens Hall, Cumbria. Few of the earlier eighteenth-century parterres actually remain but there are some good twentieth-century re-creations which can be seen, for example, at Ashbourne House, Wiltshire; and Oxburgh Hall, Norfolk.

Plants, grass and gravel are used like paints to create the abstract forms. Elements of the embroidery parterre include 'Branches, flowers, Palms, foliage, Hawk's-bill, Darts, Tendrells, Roots, Clasps, Beads, Stalks, Wreaths, Frets or interlacing, as well as designs of Flowers themselves such as Roses, Pinks, Tulips', blended into delicate designs. Using this rich palette the plants are mixed to create the ornate and decorative patterns. Shape is important, the plants themselves are not.

The length of the knot garden or parterre should generally be about one and a third times the width. This proportion can be extended to one and a half times the width but should not be any longer. If the proportions are altered then the terrace or plat on which the parterre is planted will be too narrow and the garden unbalanced. The rectangular plats should be created on an open and flat surface, which can have a gentle slope inclining towards the house but not away from it.

In the eighteenth century the broad terrace was longer than the width of the facade of the house facing the parterre, but this is not really necessary and these proportions can be adjusted to fit any size. 'Figures somewhat oblong appear better upon the ground than those of a square', states John James. The knot pattern was often based on a square or circle but other motifs were added to form an oblong shape.

Even in the eighteenth century, when designers had a great deal of experience setting out these complicated patterns, they did not always fit precisely onto the ground. The square was sometimes not a perfect square nor the rectangle precisely accurate. If the terrace

is of quite a large size the eye does not see these small discrepancies.

Once the site has been chosen and levelled, the parterre should be carefully laid out. Each line of the delicate tendrils of the branch work in the embroidery should flow smoothly and should be mirrored exactly in each quarter. The easiest method is to set out the pattern on a piece of graph paper and transpose it on site by using grid lines set out on the ground, in the same way as embroidery patterns are transcribed onto canvas.

In order to create the best effect each parterre should be enclosed by walls, hedges or trees. The choice of material depends on the size of the garden and the budget. Hedges and groves can be planted in several different styles described in Chapter 4.

The 'knot garden' is the oldest style of this particular type of garden design, and is composed of intertwining figures delineating knots, bows, ropes, swags and complicated ties. These are made from low-growing and coloured hedging plants of contrasting leaf shapes

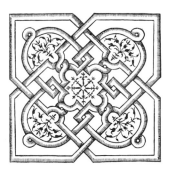

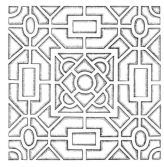

Two examples of knot gardens show the repetition and seemingly elaborate intertwining of several basic forms. In fact the patterns are quite simple.

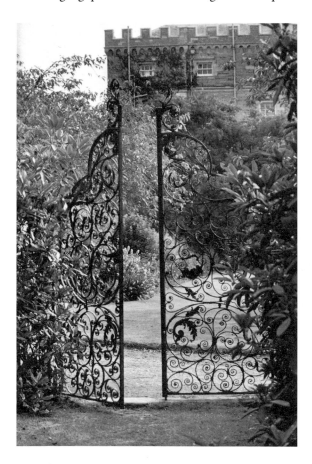

A wrought-iron gate at Mellerstain echoes the complexity of an embroidery patterning in a parterre.

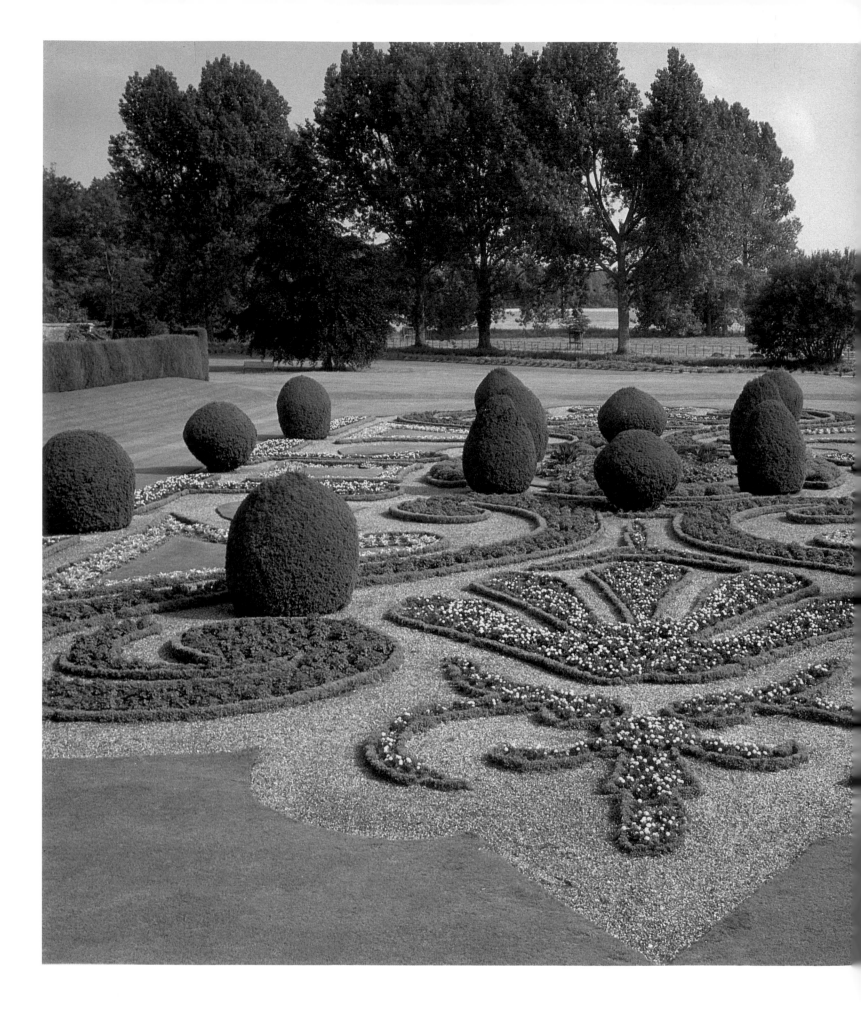

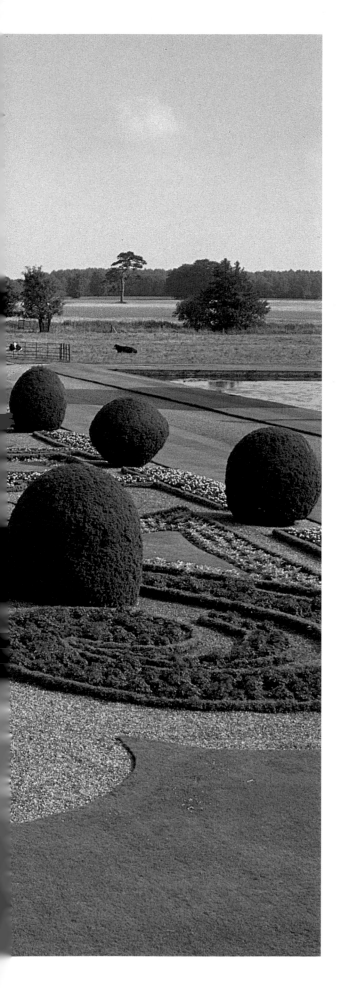

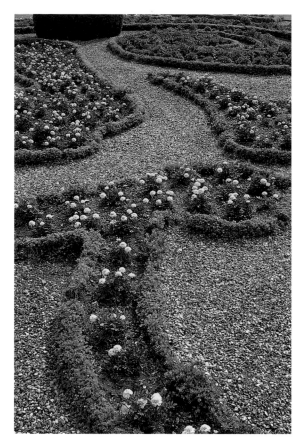

LEFT
Detail of scrolling embroidery pattern created by box hedging. It can be reproduced in one of two styles: by filling it either with colourful low flowering plants, and this is termed cutwork, or with gravel, and this is called embroidery. A modern equivalent of embroidery is to use coloured foliage, such as Santolina, instead of the gravel.

FAR LEFT
The dramatic embroidery parterre at Oxburgh. The scrolls are edged by box and set off by pale gravel. These patterns can be used in any size garden, but it is important to keep the effect of their simplicity and grandeur. It may be better to reproduce a detail than reduce the whole pattern to fit, and thereby spoil the scale and sense of space. The grandeur is also achieved by keeping the plants low.

and colours appearing to swirl through each other. Other patterns may be shaped to look like some heraldic beast, crest or motto. Starting from simple abstract patterns indicating, for example, a lover's knot, over many years the designs evolved into large-scale cartoons often displaying the heraldic symbols of the family concerned. They are mainly made from clipped dwarf box, with contrasting colours produced by the grey leaves of santolina, rue and sage; the yellows of golden thyme and other variegated plants; purples from the purple sage and many others.

The 'embroidery' style was much influenced by seventeenth-century French designs. It is also made from hedging, coloured gravel and grass, but the pattern is much lighter and more delicate. Simplified and abstracted shapes of flowers, leaves, stalks and details such as tendrils are formed into scrolls of swirling and

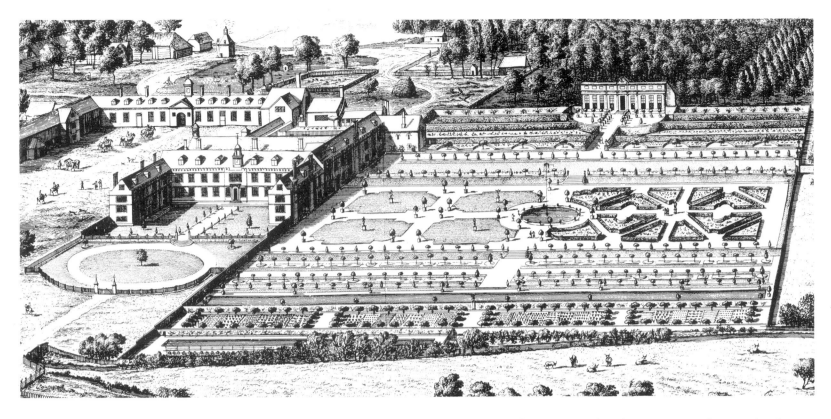

A late 17th-century garden at Southwick, near Southampton. The whole garden is laid out in a series of terraces and enclosed by a wall. At the top of the garden is an orangery, with orange bushes in boxes set out in a pattern and fruit trees trained against the walls. On the upper terrace, high hedges enclose beds of flowers. Below, the principal terrace displays a fantasy garden on the left and a cutwork knot garden on the right. A long parterre and a narrow canal separate these two gardens from the lower one where flowers and vegetables grow together in neat rows.

curving lines very similar to those used in plasterwork, woodwork and tapestry. Dwarf box or 'flourish work' is used to mark the outside lines of the pattern, which should be set in coloured sand or fine gravel but rarely on a close-mown lawn.

If the pattern of the stalk, leaf, palm volute or cartooze – the name given to a complicated design made from combining the other shapes – is wider than the two lines of box marking it out, the centre part between the box should be filled with black earth or 'smith's dust', which was the chippings off a blacksmith's anvil. Red sand or brick dust should be laid in a narrow band outside the box pattern to highlight the delicate shape. Today there is a greater range of coloured gravels and other materials which can be used to emphasize the planting, but the principle of a dark colour within the design to show off the pattern and the contrasting red rim around the outside should be adhered to. If other colours are used they should stand out in the same way.

In smaller embroideries the remainder of the design should be covered with white or yellow sand. In larger ones a fine pea gravel and even a fine form of hoggin can be laid instead of sand.

Grass is used only as a ground cover in the largest parterres, and even in the eighteenth century using grass in small areas was not recommended because of the maintenance needed to keep it in good condition.

The delicate leaf-like scrolling of the embroidery was called 'branch work' and John James also states that its pattern should not be made too large or complicated as 'the Eye at one view may not lose the general intention of the Embroidery'. Designs of larger flowers and leaves should be used in moderation. The pattern should be clear and precise, 'without confusion'. This clarity can be seen in some of James's designs illustrated in his book.

'Cutwork' is another form of parterre where the design is made by clearly shaped flower beds edged in box laid out in a symmetrical pattern. James states that 'flowers must surround every side and rise in different situations for the sake of Symmetry, especially in pieces of cutwork'. The widest range of herbaceous and annual plants and flowering shrubs that was available in the early eighteenth century was planted in these borders. The taller shrubs were usually in the middle and the smaller ones around the outside but it was important that if the design was repeated within the parterre then the shape and height of the planting had to be repeated too.

The soil inside the beds should be slightly raised, and the larger paths between the borders should be laid with sand or fine gravel so that they can be walked on. If there is only a narrow strip separating the beds, it should be filled with powdered tile or brick dust mixed with lime. This mixture forms a hard crust to the surface rather like an elementary cement. According to James, these narrower paths were not meant to be walked on but only used to 'distinguish pieces of compartiments'.

The cutwork style was much copied by the Victorians and there are still some rose gardens laid out in this way. They also used this style to set out ornate displays of seasonal bedding plants.

'Grasswork in the English manner' is the name given to parterres made mainly from grass. These are large close-mown lawns with no patterning in the centre grass, but ornate shapes often in the form of a shell are cut out and filled with gravel at either end. The shape of the grass plat or quarter can be emphasized by a narrow border of flowers, which may be separated from the lawn by a slender path, 2–3 ft (0.6–0.9 m) wide, dressed with sand.

If the border of flowers is separated from the quarter it is called the *platte bande isolée*. In the smaller gardens these borders are about 4 ft (1.2 m) wide and in the larger parterres they can be increased to 5–6 ft (1.5–1.8 m). They are nearly always edged in box, although occasionally daisies, thrift and pansies may be used as an edging. In the centre, standard flowering shrubs can be clipped into round balls or other shapes and planted alternately between pyramids or balls of yew or box.

The flowers in gardens of 'the English manner' should be planted in rows along the length of the border, about 4–5 in (0.1–0.12 m) apart. If the border is 6 ft (1.8 m) wide there should be four rows on either side of the centre shrubs, making a total of eight rows. If it is only 3–4 ft

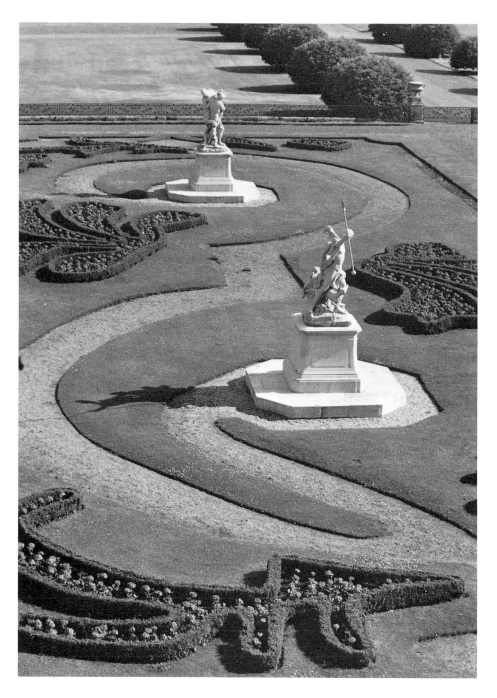

(0.9–1.2 m) wide then there should be only two rows on each side. These borders may be planted with seasonal plants or bulbs such as tulips and hyacinths, or with middle-size herbaceous plants growing to about 12–18 in (0.3–0.45 m) high such as snapdragons, wallflowers, crown imperials and martagon lilies. Although the outside rows should be kept for bulbous roots and non-spreading plants, bulbs generally should be kept separate from herbaceous plants.

At Wrest Park a parterre combines the swirling form of the 'grasswork in the English manner' with details of the embroidery pattern.

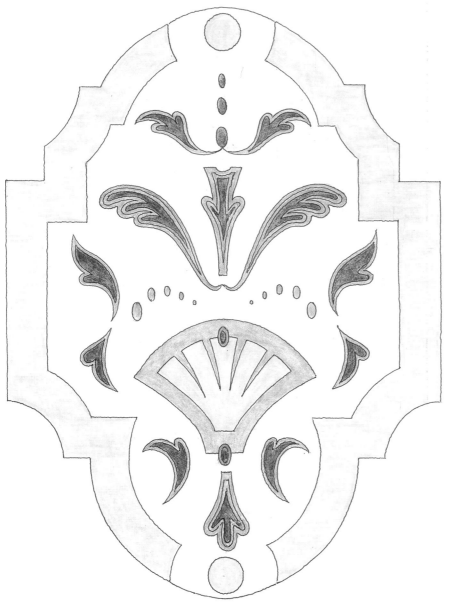

The plan shows the mixing of the two styles of knot gardens – embroidery and 'grasswork in the English manner'. The scrolls of the Embroidery are emphasized by placing red brick dust outside box hedging and further heightening the pattern inside by spreading dark-coloured dust.

Chests, cases or boxes of orange and lemon trees can be ranged at regular intervals around the grass. Sometimes clipped yew can be set between each of the fruit trees. This is to provide some pattern all year round, especially during the winter when the citrus fruit trees have to be protected in the greenhouse.

Sometimes, and especially during the early eighteenth century, the parterre styles were mixed together and these were either called 'composite' or 'compartiments'. Again the patterns should be repeated at the ends and sides of the quarters, like mirror images. Some of the designs shown by James contain scrolls or shell-like patterns of cut grass, knotwork hedging, sculptured borders filled with flowers, and small designs of embroidery. The shape is highlighted using the same techniques as in the individual styles. Coloured sands and dust outline the pattern and darker tones fill in the body. The narrow paths that separate the compartiments are filled with powdered tile or brick and lime. The planting follows the principles set out for each of the styles.

Occasionally there were dwarf borders cut into shapes filled with one variety of low-growing flowers such as primroses, violets, sea-thrift or daisies. These beds were smaller versions of the seasonal bedding borders planted out in many public parks today.

The complicated designs of the parterre, created by swirling lines of box emphasized by coloured gravels, are suitable for any size of rectangular site, from a small patio to a large garden. It is also a suitable style of garden for a courtyard or terrace, particularly if it is to be seen by many people, for example, those working in an office. When laid out, the designs are a most effective way of producing all-year-round patterns close to the house. The emblems of the knot garden can also be adapted for a special occasion such as a wedding, or may incorporate initials to celebrate moving into a property or to commemorate an anniversary. Once established the garden requires relatively little maintenance although it must be kept tidy.

If the terrace is rather small another type of border may be used to adorn the 'English grasswork', and this is a flat and even strip of grass bordered by two narrow paths raked smooth but not rolled. These may be decorated with clipped yews and flowering shrubs such as lilac, syringa and viburnums planted alternately in the same way as the *platte bande isolée*, or with vases and flower pots, boxes or wooden tubs set regularly along the middle of the grass strip.

Boxes or cases were also used in special gardens called 'parterres of orangeries'. These are composed of strips of gravel running around the outside of the shaped lawn, with a box hedge parallel to the outside of the strip.

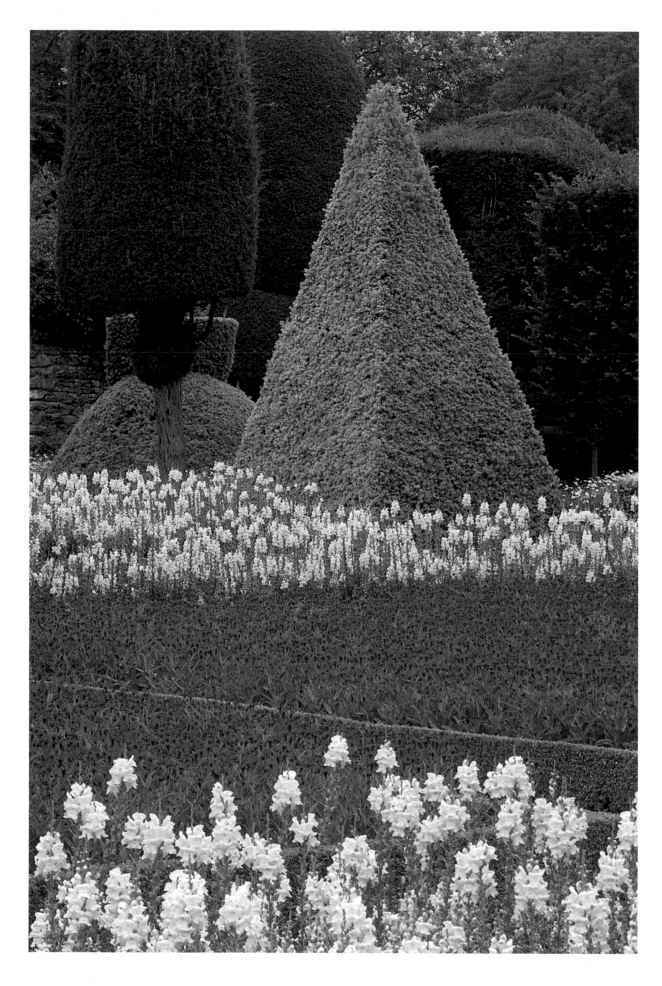

This garden at Levens Hall, is a good example of a cut-work parterre, where the flowers are grown in beds, edged by clipped box. A yew pyramid serves as a feature.

55

4

The Geometric Garden

THE geometric garden is made from clipped hedges, tall trees, long avenues, narrow canals, formal shrubs and grass. Precise, regular and three-dimensional, the layouts are highly sophisticated. Made from a series of straight lines of geometrical patterns, the immediate effect is grand but severe. However, the walks and rides are full of surprises, illusions and mock perspectives. All of the spacious design appears to be visible at the first glance, but more and more unexpected delights are revealed whilst walking through the garden.

The strong and clear patterns produced by the precise proportions create regular and harmonious shapes. For example, the ratio of the height of trees or hedge to the width of a ride or allée, or the size of a path and its relationship to the length of ride are all worked out to a mathematical formula. These calculations were influenced by early scientific and mathematical theories of geometry and optics.

This style produces gardens of great stature and was used on a grand scale to lay out the magnificent formal gardens of the early eight-

The different decorative hedges used in the geometric garden. All, between 7–10ft high, are made from single rows of trees, either with the trunk showing, or grown like a traditional hedge from the base. The finial decorations are made from the main trunk of each tree, which emerge from the hedge below and are clipped into shape. In 'A Hedge cut with Pilasters', the base or plinth of the column can be box, supporting a beech or hornbeam hedge above.

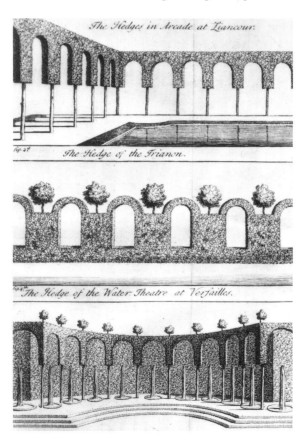

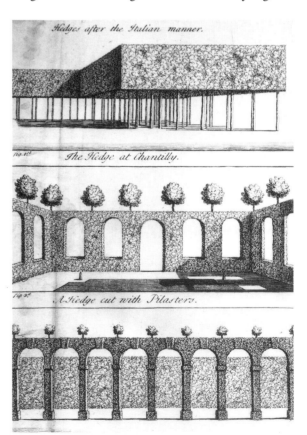

eenth century. In some cases, the landscapes extended into nearby woods and avenues strode across valleys. However, these large landscapes were made up of smaller compartments each designed in a particular way. So, this style is very versatile and can be re-created in almost any size of garden, using one or more compartments linked together.

Grand names described these compartments or 'cabinets', suggesting a greater size than many of them actually were. Some of the more exotic ones were called groves, labyrinths, halls, porticoes, colonnades, arbours, wildernesses, mounts, basons, canals, cascades, grottoes, ruins, serpentine meanders, cold baths, aviaries, cabinets, obelisks, manazeries, bowling greens, dials, precipices and amphitheatres. Most of the grander houses also had kitchen gardens, flower gardens and all the usual requirements for supplying produce to a large establishment.

The first designer who developed these large-scale gardens was the famous gardener of Louis XIV of France, André Le Nôtre, who laid out Versailles and Vaux-le-Vicomte amongst others. His skill was 'to organize the landscape into one mighty scene that would express the dignity and elegance of man and delight his senses. All nature should conform.' Le Nôtre used all the techniques available to him to compose his designs. He used illusions to enlarge features or to make them look further away. His layouts controlled the views by restricting the vision with hedges or trees, while providing unexpected openings or glades contrasting strongly with the previous enclosure. Unity between earth and heaven was produced by reflections of water and sky framed at the end of avenues.

Although Le Nôtre designed very little in Britain, able pupils such as the Mollet brothers came from France after the Restoration of Charles II to advise on landscape design. Towards the end of the seventeenth century home-based designers emerged such as George London and Henry Wise. London

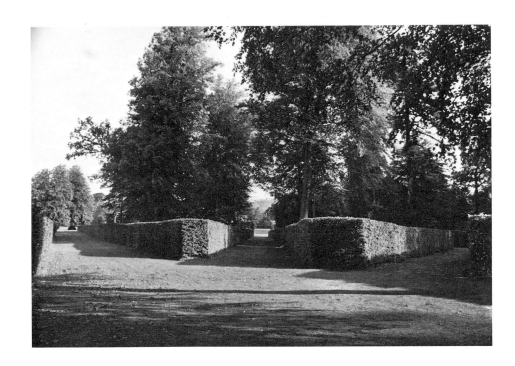

travelled all over the country advising on the laying out of landscape parks.

The influence of the geometric style is considerable and ranges from gardens associated with great houses such as Blenheim Palace, to more modest manor house gardens usually designed by the owner. Layouts attached to country houses of the period can still be seen. Walls around a parterre built then remain, even though the planting may have changed. Gardens which show this style well are Chevening House in Kent; Melbourne Hall, Derbyshire; Bramham Park, West Yorkshire; and Wrest Park, Bedfordshire.

The principal walk or avenue always extends from the centre of the house as far as it can, often ending at an eyecatching feature or other building. In grander gardens there may be a banqueting house or major folly such as the one at Wrest Park. In others a nearby church steeple, a beautifully shaped tree, or a natural feature is used. Nearer the house there is usually a wide and long ride crossing the principal one at right angles known as the 'cross ride'. Again this often frames an eyecatcher. Together the rides form the shape of a cross.

These strong axial lines are often joined together by subsidiary rides creating more geometric forms which can only be seen on plan. They are often based on either an equilateral or

Clipped hornbeam hedges at Chevening at the centre of the patte d'oie, *or 'goosefoot' plan, from which six avenues radiate.*

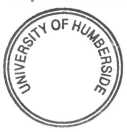
UNIVERSITY OF HUMBERSIDE

right-angled triangle. Sometimes the tail of the right-angled one extends beyond the garden into the adjoining wood.

Woven between these lines are smaller walks linking various compartments such as cabinets, wildernesses, bowling greens, basons and canals. The walks are also formed in geometric shapes such as parallelograms, rectangles, crosses, trapeziums and so on. These minor walks can be clearly seen in the eighteenth-century engraving by J. Kip of the plan of Wrest Park (end papers).

The main walks should be wider than the subsidiary ones, and from the far end the walk should be wide enough to be able to see the facade of the house. All the principal walks should have a focal point. Many have descriptive names: for example, 'parallel walk, strait

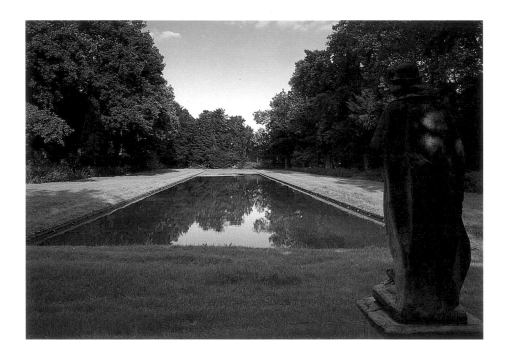

The Lady's Canal at Wrest. The simple and impressive geometric shape of the canal is emphasized by the tall trees and the smooth edge of the grass as it meets the water.

walk, cross walk, winding or circular walk, diagonal or bevel walk'.

In the eighteenth century, avenues were planted in 'single walks' with two rows of trees, or in 'double' or sometimes 'triple' walks, which have four or six rows of trees respectively. The proportion of the length to the width

of these walks or rides is very important and John James in his *Theory and Practice of Gardening* set out the formula for rides and allées:

If the single walk is:

200 feet long the width walk should be
14–15 ft [4.2–4.5 m]
600 feet long the width should be
30–36 ft [9.1–11 m]
1,200 feet long the width should be
42–48 ft [12.8–14.6 m]
1,800 feet long the width should be
54–60 ft [16.5–18.3 m]
2,400 feet long the width should be
60–72 ft [18.3–22 m]

James points out that it is important that the proportions should be right – if they are 'defective' the walk or avenue will look unsatisfactory.

The width for a double walk or four rows of trees is double those given above. The ride in the middle should be larger than the two outside rides or 'counter walks' and about half the total width of the feature. The counter walks should be about a quarter of the total width. Thus if the total width of a double avenue is 48 ft (14.6 m) then the width of the middle walk should be 24 ft (7.3 m) and the counter walk 12 ft (3.6 m) each. If there is not enough room the counter walks may be reduced in width, rather than the central one - from which it is important not to hide the facade of the house or feature being framed. However the counter walks should not be reduced to less than 6 ft (1.8 m) wide.

The apparent size of a walk can be shortened or lengthened by exaggerating the perspective. This is done by gradually narrowing the width of the walk towards the further end, giving the illusion of distance; conversely, to foreshorten the object at the end of the walk, the far end is widened. This only works if the lines of the edge gradually ease inward or outward.

In larger gardens the principal walks should be about 30-36 ft wide (9.1–11 m) and the less important ones about 24 ft wide (7.3 m). The minor paths can be as narrow as 6 ft (1.8 m), but this does depend on the length of the path and the material used. For example, grass paths should be wider than gravel ones.

For longer avenues, elms and limes are favoured. Horse chestnut, sweet chestnut and beech are also used, whilst willow and poplar are recommended for damper ground. Hedges are often used to mark out the minor walks, or to enclose features like canals, labyrinths, and halls displaying statues or fountains. They can also form complex patterns, such as a *patte d'oie* or goosefoot, where three rides join together, with the same angle between each ride. Hedges create much of the beauty and delight of these gardens as well as the surprises, as, for instance, when a tall hedge hides a feature behind it. In labyrinths and mazes nearer the house hedges can be free standing and clipped on both sides, often in fantastic shapes. Mazes still exist at Hampton Court Palace, Hatfield House and Chevening House.

Batty Langley describes three types of hedging called 'hedges in the wood', 'palisade hedging' and 'hedges in walks'. 'Hedges in the wood' are used to edge subsidiary rides or to frame the halls or cabinets within groves. The hedge should stand proud of the line of trees, with a clearing of about 7–8 ft (2.1–2.4 m) behind it to leave enough room for a ladder from which to clip the hedge on both sides to about 10–12 ft (3–3.6 m).

A 'palisade' hedge is made like a wooden stockade around an old castle. The hedging plants and trees are planted in the same row quite close together creating the palisade. The hedge growing up from the base should be

The drama of the beech avenue leading to Drummond Castle comes from the regularity and close planting of the trees, spaced only 15 feet apart.

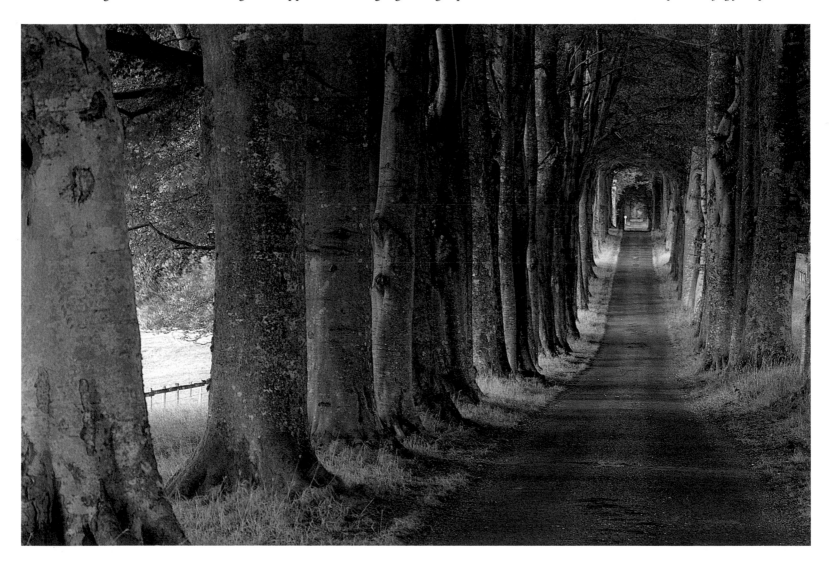

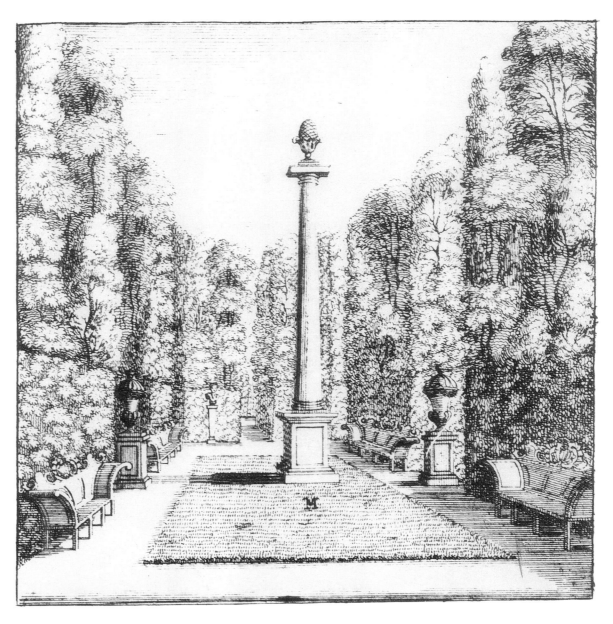

'The Lady Dutches's Square' from A Plan and View of the Buildings and Gardens at Wrest, *1737, by Rocque. It shows the many seats, alcoves, and statues in a garden room at Wrest Park.*

clipped up to about 10–12 ft (3–3.6 m). When the tree canopy grows over the hedge it should be pruned up to a height of about 20–30 ft (6–9.1 m). Once the trees have reached 30 ft they should be pollarded so they do not grow any taller.

A variation of this palisade is to plant the hedge along a line of standard trees and clip it to about 3–4 ft (0.9–1.2 m) high. The canopy of standard trees should be pruned up to about 5–6 ft (1.5–1.8 m) above the ground leaving a line of exposed trunks. Behind this the lower branches of a second row of trees should be clipped but not pruned up to the canopy. This makes a second tier of hedge growing behind the first line of trunks.

'Hedges in walks' are used to frame lines of avenues. The row of trees on each side of the walk should stand detached from the wood behind. A thicket hedge should be planted 3–4 ft (0.9–1.2 m) behind it and clipped upright.

Hornbeam was the most popular hedging

Hedging

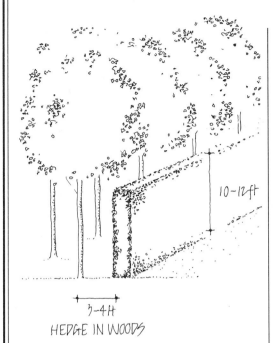

HEDGE IN WOODS

Hedges in the Wood stand proud from the trees behind and are clipped on both sides to a height of about 10–12 ft (3–3.6 m) depending on the length of the ride but they can be reduced to about 5 ft (1.5 m) in short spans. If an evergreen hedge is required, laurel, holly, yew or a mixture may be used, the plants spaced about 10 in (0.25 m) apart. Beech and hornbeam are the best broad-leaved examples.

Palisade Hedges The hedging plants are set very close together, between 2 and 3 in (0.05–0.07 m) apart, like a palisade. In woodlands, elm, lime or horse chestnuts line the back of the hedge, which is often planted with hornbeam, beech and maple.

Palisade **A** shows the hedge clipped on two sides only and the trees behind are cut back in line with the inner side of the top of the hedge. The height can vary from about 5–12 ft (1.5–3.6 m).

The trees behind the hedge should be lopped off at 10–12 ft (3–3.6 m) high. The wood behind should be planted in the style of Groves in Wood.

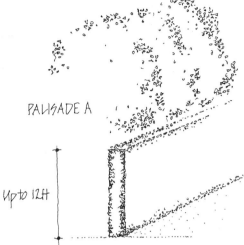

PALISADE A

Palisade **B** shows the closely clipped hedge no more than 3–4 ft (0.9–1.2 m) high, with the clear stems of the avenue of trees rising about 5–6 ft (1.5–1.8 m) above it. The trees are shaped to prevent them from shading the hedge beneath.

PALISADE B

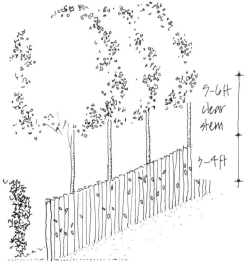

Palisade **C** shows the hedge clipped on both sides 3–4 ft (0.9–1.2 m) high in front of the line of trees. A 6 ft (1.8 m) grass strip is mown on either side of the trees.

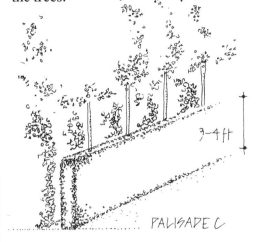

PALISADE C

Hedges in Walks grow in front of an avenue of regularly spaced trees. A grass strip about 3–4 ft (0.9–1.2 m) wide runs between the hedge and the trees. The hedges are clipped like Hedges in the Wood, with a woodland thicket of elm, lime, horse chestnut and sweet chestnut behind. The hedge can be evergreen, using plants such as yew, laurel, juniper or holly.

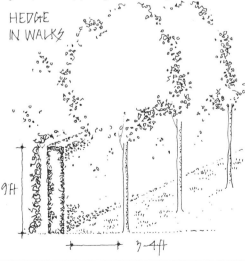

HEDGE IN WALKS

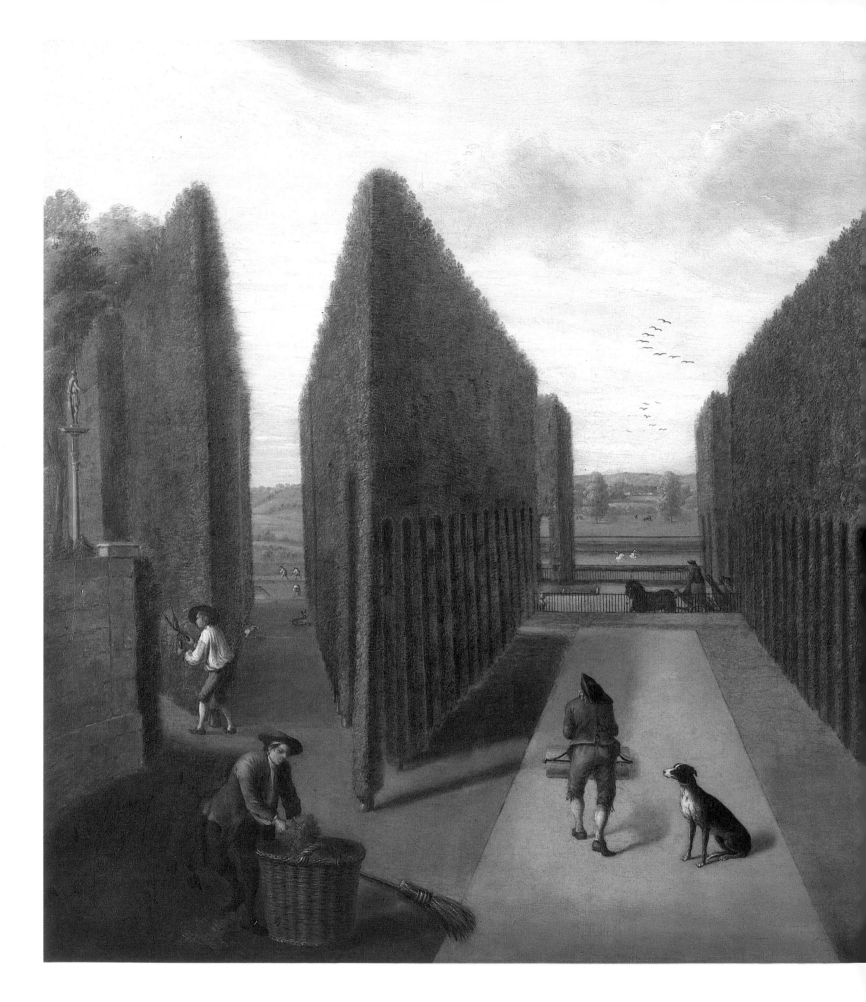

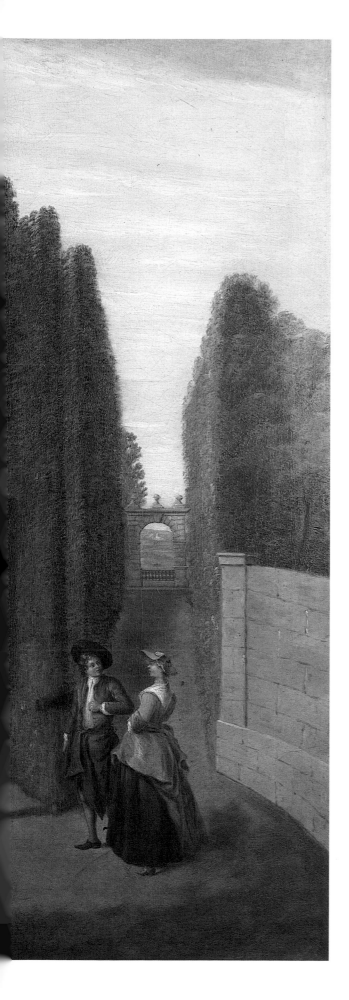

plant in eighteenth-century gardens, but beech was also recommended. Maple was used in shady conditions. Evergreen hedges were mainly planted with yew. Palisade evergreen hedges contained a mixture of box, *Phillyrea*, Italian cypress and holm oak. The hedges in walks should be planted with a mixture of common juniper, savin juniper, laurel, buckthorn and holly.

Walks can be made from gravel or from sand and should be raked. Most of the green walks have two strips of raked gravel about 2 ft (0.6 m) wide between the grass and the hedges to ease maintenance. In order to create the sharp effect it is very important to have clean lines between the hedge and grass.

Hedges can also be trained into different patterns such as colonnades, arcades, arbours, porticoes or balls. In an 'arcade', the hedge can have windows cut in it. If the window opening is clipped at an angle, from the beginning of the ride the hedge will look as if it is intact and the window will only be seen when walking along it. In arched arcades with larger windows the walls can be made from hornbeam and the stanchions from elm or lime supported by a frame. These can be further embellished by clipping the tree into a ball, which gives the appearance of a vase or decoration on the top of a built arcade.

A 'colonnade' is made in almost the same way but the arches are wider. The pillars of the arches are made from the bare trunks of trees, or from clipped hornbeam. Another type is the 'pleached hedge', which is formed by clipping the canopy into a solid block about 6–8 ft (1.8–2.4 m) above the ground, leaving freestanding trunks as support.

A 'green arbour' or 'gallery' is similar to arched vaulting in Gothic cathedrals. The gallery is created by narrow arching lime or elm trees which line up along either side of the walk, with four trees forming a square. The foliage of each tree crosses over the walk to meet the foliage of either the tree opposite or the one in the opposing corner. Various decorations

The Garden of Hartwell House, Buckinghamshire, 1738, by Balthasar Nebot is a scene of early morning activity in one of the great 18th-century gardens. It shows some of the magnificent colonnades that were grown in the garden. Although the painting greatly exaggerates their scale, yet these dynamic narrow hedges were achieved by precise and razor-sharp clipping. The colonnades have windows or openings through to other parts of the garden.

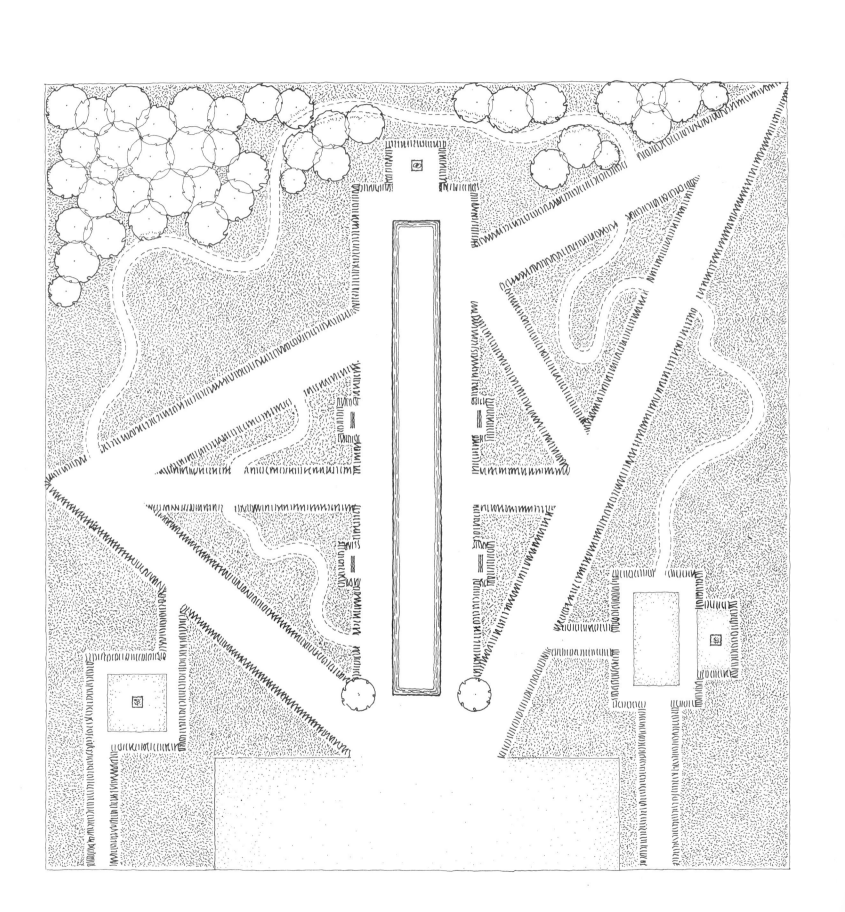

0 2 4 6 8 10 12 14 16 18 20 M

can be added to embellish the corners. A good example of a gallery can be seen at Château Beloil in Belgium.

A 'green portico' is the term used to describe the training of trees into an extravagant shape like a portico or gate made from stone or brick, with pilasters or other types of columns. In the most fancy ones, hornbeam is used for the plinths and lime or elm for the walls. Often they enclose a seat. They make attractive features at the end of a walk.

The geometric garden is often part of a woodland, which can be carved out of an existing wood or created in a new one. Between the rides and features of the woodland flowering shrubs are planted to provide beauty and scent.

In 1714 six kinds of woodland were described, and they are: 'forests, coppice woods,

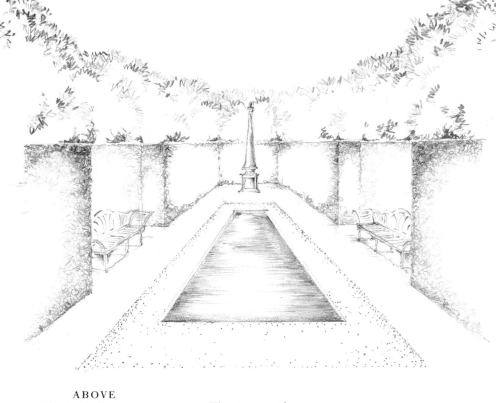

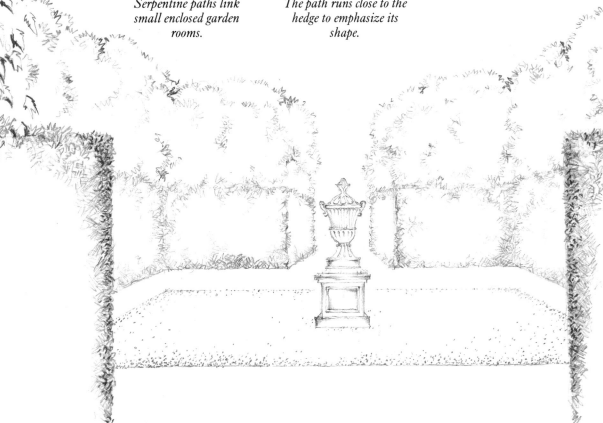

OPPOSITE
The ground plan of a geometric garden. The canal is intersected by a geometric pattern of grass allees, lined by hedges. Serpentine paths link small enclosed garden rooms.

ABOVE
The sketch illustrates a garden 'room' edged with a palisade hedge which may contain alcoves for statues or garden seats. The path runs close to the hedge to emphasize its shape.

This is a secret but simple garden room in a grove. It is enclosed by a hedge, and at its centre is a grass lawn.

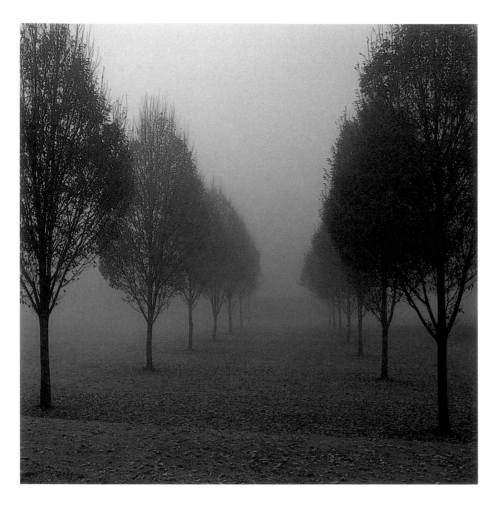

This grand and splendid formal avenue of hornbeam at Chevening was planted only ten years ago.

tain a coppice on a fifteen-year rotation. He also recommended leaving about sixteen oak standards to an acre.

'Groves of middle height with tall hedges' are much used in geometric gardens and according to James are 'truly Groves of Delight and Delicacy'. They form the background to the halls, cabinets, galleries, fountains and any other room in the wood. The trees are only allowed to grow about 30–40 ft (9–12 m) high before being cut back and pollarded. This allows in light to keep the hedges in good condition.

'Groves open in compartments' have no trees in the middle of the glade. The walks bordering them are planted with lime or horse chestnut. A low palisade hedge is trimmed to about 3–5 ft (0.9–1.5 m) high and runs around them. In the squares or grass plats within the compartments there is often a grass gravel path 2 ft (0.6 m) wide bordering the hedge and grass to keep the hedge tidy and the grass edge sharp. The core of the grove or 'bosquet' is planted with yew and flowering shrubs.

'Groves in Quincunx or squares' is the term used to describe the open planting of trees without a hedge or understorey, similar to an orchard. Sometimes the rows are in chequer pattern, or in symmetrical lines at right angles to one another or in parallel rows. The grass between them is always kept mown. In the seventeenth century such a grove was often planted in the shape of a five in playing cards.

'Woods of evergreens' are planted with conifers and evergreen broad-leaved trees such as holm oak and holly.

A geometric garden can be created by using some of the techniques described but there is no need to use them all. Even in the eighteenth century there were only a few gardens in which you could have seen all of these hedge types. It is best to choose the kinds that suit the garden, its size and the effect desired. The hedges must be cut once a year but otherwise the maintenance is fairly moderate. If the proportions are correctly calculated, this style is simple, satisfying and gives an effect all year round.

groves of middle height with tall hedges, groves open in compartments, groves planted in Quincunx or squares, and woods of evergreen'. Most of the forest trees were pruned up to form a clear stem to about 20–30 ft (6–9 m) below any lateral branches. Pruning to a single leader and other care produced trees of between 15–20 ft (4.5–6 m) within seven years of planting.

The 'forest' woodland is similar to a broad-leaved plantation. It can be planted as a star with a great circle in the middle where all the rides meet. This formation can be seen at Haddington Great Wood at Tyninghame, Scotland, which was laid out in about 1714.

'Coppice woods' are usually planted with sweet chestnut and oak. John James recommended cutting down about a ninth of the coppice each year, but it is more usual to main-

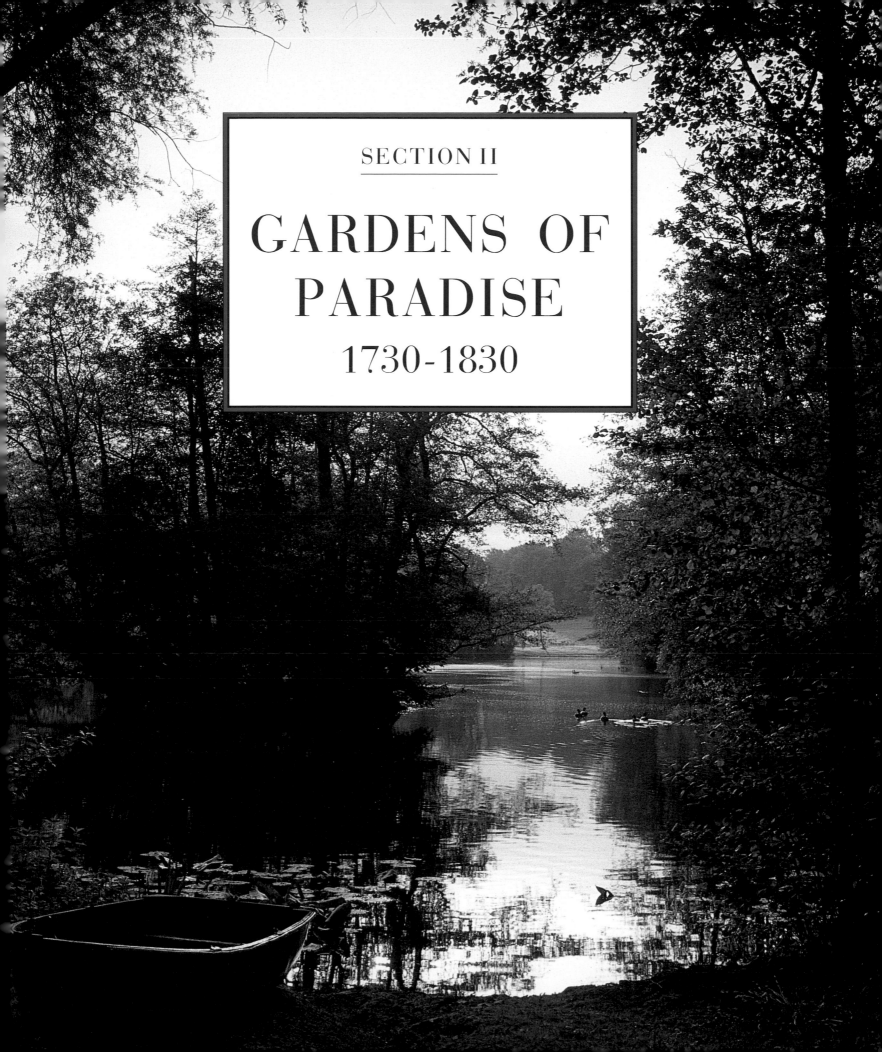

SECTION II

GARDENS OF PARADISE

1730-1830

Introduction

PREVIOUS PAGE
The lure of the Gardens of Paradise is a dream-like fantasy, evocative of nature, that enticed the visitor to gentle exploration.

THIS section describes five styles, four of which are developments of the natural style. The fifth, the Walled Garden, describes a typical early nineteenth-century kitchen garden.

Creating 'the amiable simplicity of unadorned nature, that spreads over the mind a noble sort of tranquillity' – this was one of the main aims of the eighteenth-century Theatrical Garden style. The areas within the garden were laid out to be viewed from a particular route and the design was precisely worked out. As one walked through the different areas one was supposed to experience a series of emotional sensations, rather like viewing the several acts of a play. Many scenes ended at a pleasant folly or special feature. The arrangement of objects or statues could tell an allegorical story which could only be interpreted by informed guests. Today, with our reduced knowledge of classical literature, we cannot always appreciate the references in these gardens but even so this style remains one of the most pleasing and stimulating. It is perhaps ambitious to design but its beauty is most rewarding.

Another new idea was to 'consult the genius of the place', to look at those features which made a particular place special and which could be emphasized. The third principle was to 'correct or to conceal any particular object that is disagreeable'. This is still essential today, although some of the ugly objects in our landscape are much larger and more obtrusive than they were in the eighteenth century.

The Landscape Garden style enhances the best features of a site and masks the unsightly ones. In this garden the visitor experiences more of a flowing narrative than in the Theatrical Garden, where his visit is punctuated by clearly defined episodes.

In the eighteenth century the Landscape Garden portrayed the relaxed pastoral Gardens of Paradise. The idea of imitating nature and using natural features as decoration was the inspiration behind the designs of these great gardens. The aim was to create a haven of beauty where trees, grass and flowers mingled appearing as if they had always grown there. The creative talent which flowed into these designs is considered to be one of Britain's greatest contributions to world art.

Today, we are so familiar with these gardens that it is hard to conceive the radical change in the ideas required to create such 'natural' gardens. The style was such a success that it captured the imagination of many landowners, who created landscape parks around their new or refurbished houses. Many of these parks can still be seen on the outskirts of most villages, where the clusters of artistically placed trees stand out amongst the patchwork of fields. The love of nature and the desire to imitate it is still as seductive now as it was in the eighteenth century. Surprisingly, the inspiration came from landscape painting and not, as one might imagine, from a detailed study of nature itself. That had to wait another century for the more scientific approach of the Victorians. Literature, poetry and the study of art provided the intellectual stimulus, particularly the study of the great landscape paintings of the seventeenth century. The huge canvases of Claude Lorrain, Salvator Rosa and Nicolas Poussin depicting totally mythical scenes of the classical world of Rome and Greece inspired many young and impressionable aristocrats, particularly those participating in the Grand Tour to Italy. The study of the classical world was considered to be the best education for an aspiring young gentleman. Where better to study it than in Rome itself. So, many sons of wealthy landowners were sent to Italy for several years.

One of the most influential of these was Richard Boyle, 3rd Earl of Burlington, who during his long stay in Italy became convinced that the key to perfection lay in the theories and works of Andrea Palladio (1508–80). Palladio himself was deeply influenced by classical Roman architecture. Burlington collected a group of like-minded intellectuals including William Temple, Henry Hoare, Charles Hamilton and William Kent, and when they returned to Britain they created gardens to represent these heroic landscape paintings.

Like so many radical changes, the timing was right for several reasons. One was simply the cost of maintaining vast formal landscapes containing miles of hedges. Another was the changing attitude towards farming – it became more fashionable to look at grazing cows or sheep or browsing deer in large fields or parks. The size of the park and the number of animals indicated the wealth and success of the owner. Finally, the political stability under the Hanoverian kings and their Whig government had generated a new prosperity, which brought with it an enthusiasm for setting the mansion in a fitting landscaped park.

Thus the idea of imitating nature fell on fertile ground. The desire to create heroic landscapes combined with changes in farming practice promoted the use of large areas of land. In fact it even led owners to 'borrow' land outside the boundaries of their own holdings. These were gardens on a large scale, nevertheless the design ideas can be used very successfully in smaller gardens or when designing a modern development on a green field site.

The Father of Psyche Sacrificing to Apollo *by Claude Lorrain represented the kind of landscape that many 18th-century gardeners wished to imitate in the paradise gardens. They wanted to experience moving from the foreground, perhaps from a temple, down towards a bridge, and then up to the spectacular views across the countryside afforded from the rotunda.*

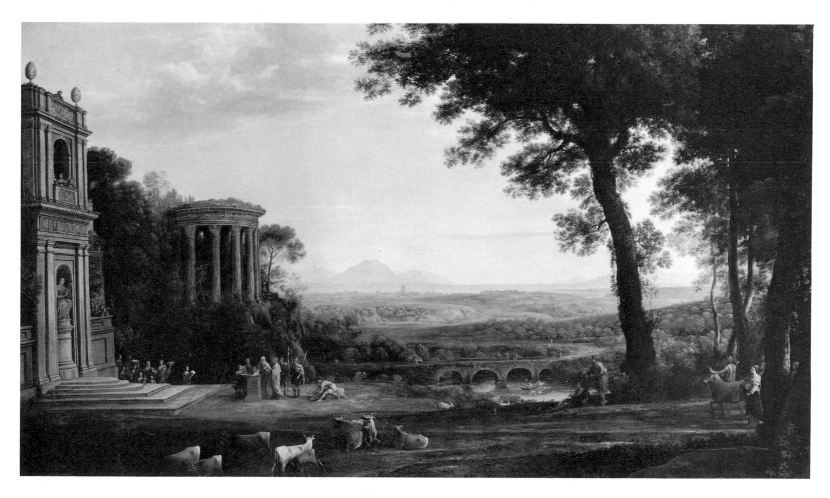

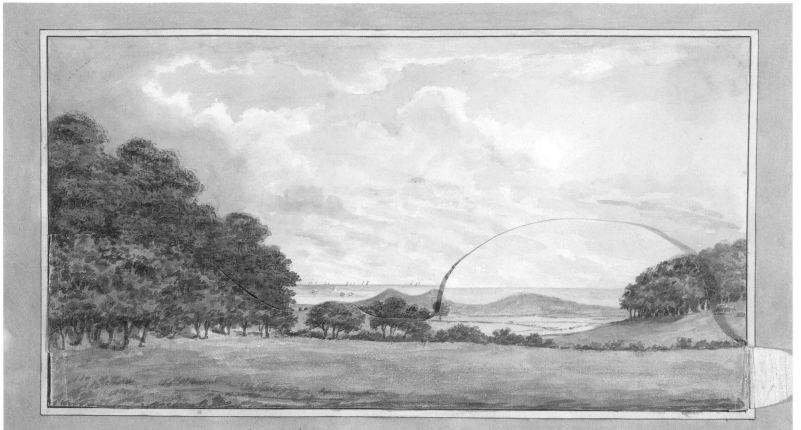

View from the proposed Site looking towards the East.

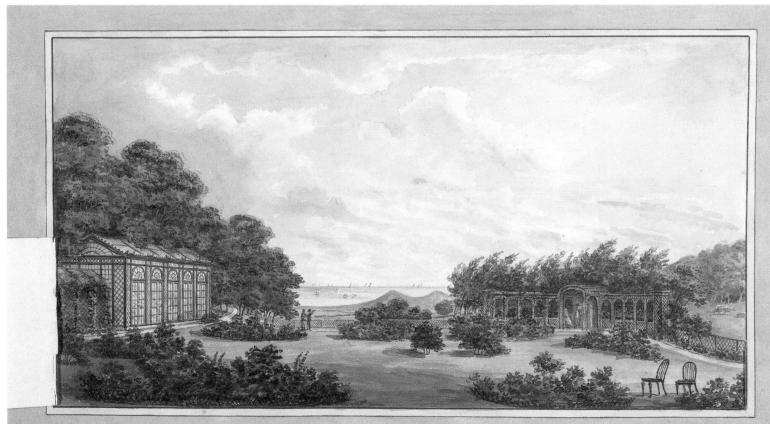

View from the proposed Site looking towards the East.

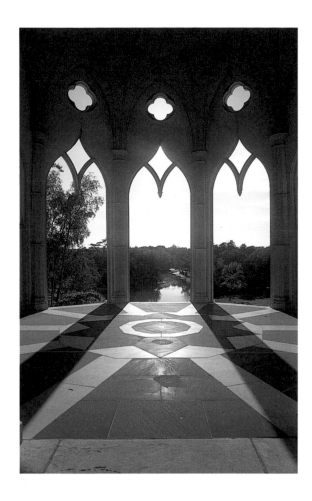

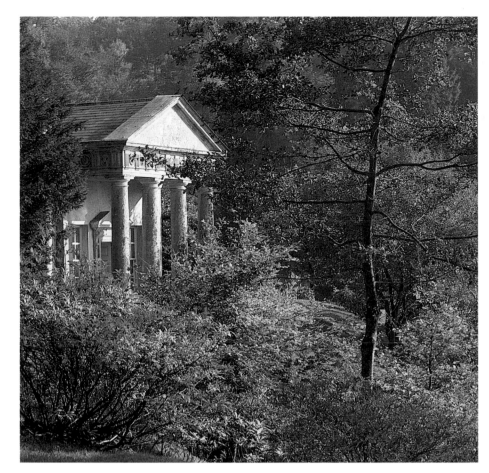

Much of garden design today is based on the idea of making the plants look natural, and often the success of a scheme is measured by whether it blends in with the surrounding countryside. The desire to imitate nature, albeit in a small setting, is as strong today as it was in the eighteenth century.

Capability Brown (1715–83) was the most famous and prolific designer of the Landscape Garden style and his name is the one most associated with landscape parks. However, it was his successor Humphry Repton (1752–1818), in his book *Observations on the Theory and Practice of Landscape Gardening* published in 1803, who clearly set out the aim as 'the perfection of landscape gardening consists in the fullest attention ... to Utility, Proportion, and Unity or Harmony of the Part to the Whole.' He said:

> ... the chief beauty of a park consists in uniform verdure, undulating lines contrasting with each other in variety of forms; trees so grouped as to produce light and shade to dis-

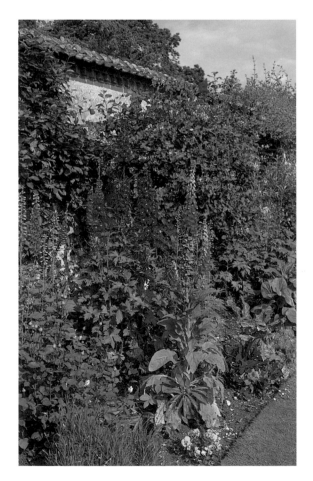

ABOVE LEFT
The delicate tracery of the Gothic temple at Painshill frames a spectacular view.

ABOVE
The columned portico of the small temple at Stourhead, perched above the lake.

LEFT
The foxgloves and delphiniums at Heale House are planted as in a typical English flower garden.

OPPOSITE
Two views of the garden at Sheringham House, Norfolk, from Repton's 'Red Book'. Above is the site before his proposed design for an English flower garden; below, the design, with its randomly placed flower beds, shows the style of growing plants to different heights.

Trees were trained to grotesque shapes, to add humour to gardens.

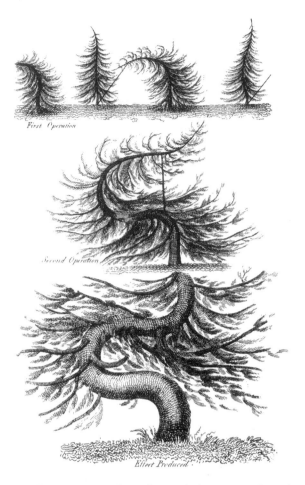

First Operation

Second Operation

Effect Produced

play the varied surface of the ground and an undivided range of pasture. The animals fed in such a park appear free from confinement, at liberty to collect their food from the rich herbage of the valley and to range uncontrolled to the drier soils of the hills.

Even though today many parks are in a state of decay, they still create much of the beauty and variety of the countryside.

The English Flower Garden style is very similar to the Theatrical Garden. Both are inspired by art and in this case by poetry. This style is based on the garden created at Nuneham Courtenay by William Mason (1725–97) and George, 2nd Earl of Harcourt (1736–1809). The inspiration came from the epic novel *La Nouvelle Héloïse* by the philosopher Jean-Jacques Rousseau. In this style the intimacy of flowers is used instead of the grandeur of the wider landscape.

It is a small garden, full of annual, herbaceous and perennial flowers. The aim is to grow as many colourful sweet-smelling flowers as possible in a picturesque layout. The shape is flexible and the design can be enlarged or reduced. But it must not all be revealed at first glance. The interest and features should be discovered as the visitor walks around.

The Villa Garden uses all the design ideas of the three styles already mentioned in this section, but in a much smaller area. It developed in response to the prosperity of the merchant and professional who needed attractive year-round gardens to set off their new villas built on the outskirts of towns. These gardens were miniature landscape parks and flower gardens. The distinctive style developed during the early part of the nineteenth century, when interest in the plants became as important as the design. Plants were grown to show off their shape and habitat. Frequently, individual specimens were grown on the lawn, where each plant could be clearly seen.

The famous horticultural journalist John Claudius Loudon (1783–1843) beautifully described Villa Garden design in his books and gardening magazines. This style was intended for small areas around detached or semi-detached houses and so can be easily created today. Its beauty lies in the variety of the design and the plants.

Two influential commentators summed up the quality of the eighteenth-century natural garden. One, William Marshall (1745–1818), said that 'our idea of natural is not confined to neglected nature, but extends to cultivated nature – to nature touched by art, and rendered intelligible to human perception.' And Horace Walpole (1717–97), usually more caustic, said that 'succeeding artists have added new master strokes of these touches and the introduction of foreign trees and plants ... contributed essentially to the richness of colouring so peculiar to our modern landscapes.'

5

The Theatrical Garden

THE theatrical garden is a garden to walk through and experience. It titillates the senses and captivates the eye. Built on a series of images which spark off the imagination, it can be compared to a theatrical piece – a play in which the acts unfurl and scenes are performed. The principal difference is that at the theatre the audience remains seated but in the garden people move through, viewing the performance.

The play can be as long or as short as there is space available for it. So today an act or even one scene can be re-created in quite a small area using the theatrical style, but in the eighteenth century many acts were woven into pleasure gardens around farmland and woods. The scenery used was large enough to fit in with the scale of the garden.

The essence of the theatrical garden is to imitate nature or natural conditions. It is an artificially contrived style because the aim is to experience all aspects of the countryside in one garden. Many different elements may be crammed into it: wild mountain crags, noisy cascading waterfalls, open moorland meadows, dense mysterious woodland, open pastoral fields, exotic woodland garden and colourful shrubbery. As it is rare for all of these elements to be naturally present on one site, those missing have to be created in the most suitable place in the garden, whilst those features that are present must be exaggerated.

This style is very visual and is designed to provoke a reaction in the viewer. It is fun, amusing and enjoyable. The theatrical garden is based on a desire to realize in three dimensions, if not four, the magic qualities of the famous seventeenth-century landscape paintings of Claude Lorrain, Salvator Rosa and Nicolas Poussin. The designers wished to interpret scenes of these classical images in their gardens so that they could walk through them and experience the sensations as though the images were reality. In actual fact these 'classical' pictures of Claude, Rosa and Poussin were painted from the artists' imaginations and they were not true scenes of ancient Greece or Rome at all. However, the skill and amusement of re-creating these pictures out-

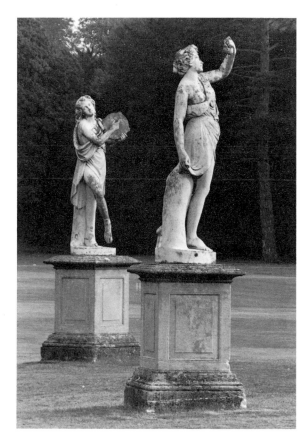

Two large statues are placed to add drama to the landscape of a glade.

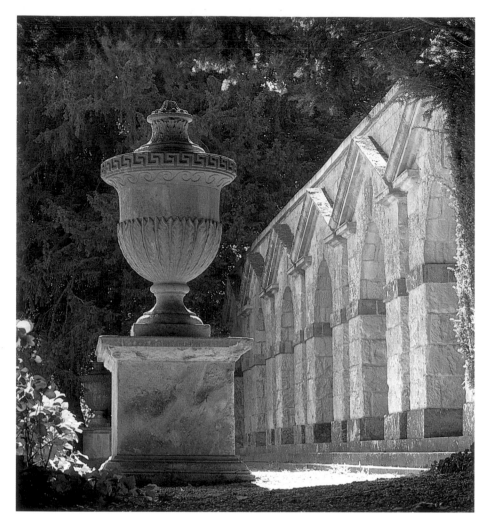

A theatrically placed urn before a dramatically lit colonnade creating the illusion of a stage set.

OPPOSITE
The stunning effects of the grotto at Painshill, with its exaggerated stalactites made of soft render, imbedded with quartz, shells and other glittering material.

to time during a walk. Very often there were buildings or follies known as 'eyecatchers'. The placing of these buildings, statues, bridges, water and all the other elements which made up the garden was so contrived that, together with the planting, they created the scenes within the acts of a play. Some of the buildings were made out of timber or even papier mâché and painted to look like stone or stucco. Some might be constructed very simply and inexpensively, or be similar to glorified summer-houses. Others might have a romantic facade built in front of a more substantial structure such as a barn or cottage. Of course some were beautifully made, designed by the most influential architects of the period.

These gardens could be appreciated on various levels either simply for their sheer beauty and the satisfaction of the experience or for the enjoyment of puzzling over some obscure classical reference depicted by a statue or by the siting of a group of figures implying a classical tale or allegory. A set-piece mystery could only be solved by knowledgeable friends who understood the nuances. Sadly, many of these references are difficult to understand today as we no longer have the classical education necessary to interpret the Greek and Roman world.

One of the early theatrical gardens is at Painshill, Surrey, and much of the information in this chapter is comes from research into its restoration. The designer Charles Hamilton sought to produce a series of dramatic events and set out to confuse the visitor, particularly over the size and scale of individual features. This was accomplished by creating set pieces where future episodes could be glimpsed or where a past spectacle could be re-viewed from a surprising and unexpected angle.

Charles Hamilton was a master at this form of design. Horace Walpole described Painshill in his influential essay, *A History of Modern Taste in Gardening*: 'all is great; foreign and rude; the walks seem not designed, but cut through the woods of pines; and the style of the whole is so

side took hold of the imagination of the intellectuals of the mid-eighteenth century, who considered 'Gardening is more antique, and nearer to God's own work than Poetry' (Alexander Pope to the Earl of Oxford, 1724).

Some of the most famous British gardens were designed in the theatrical garden style. These include Stourhead in Wiltshire, laid out by Henry Hoare; Rousham near Oxford by William Kent; Hagley Hall near Wolverhampton by Richard Lyttelton; Hawkstone Park near Shrewsbury, and Painshill near Cobham in Surrey by Charles Hamilton; Taymouth Park near Loch Tay by the Earl of Breadalbane; and many others which sadly do not exist today.

The aim was to devise ways of using the site to its best advantage, working out which views should be seen and which features should be hidden. Some features might remain always hidden whilst others might reappear from time

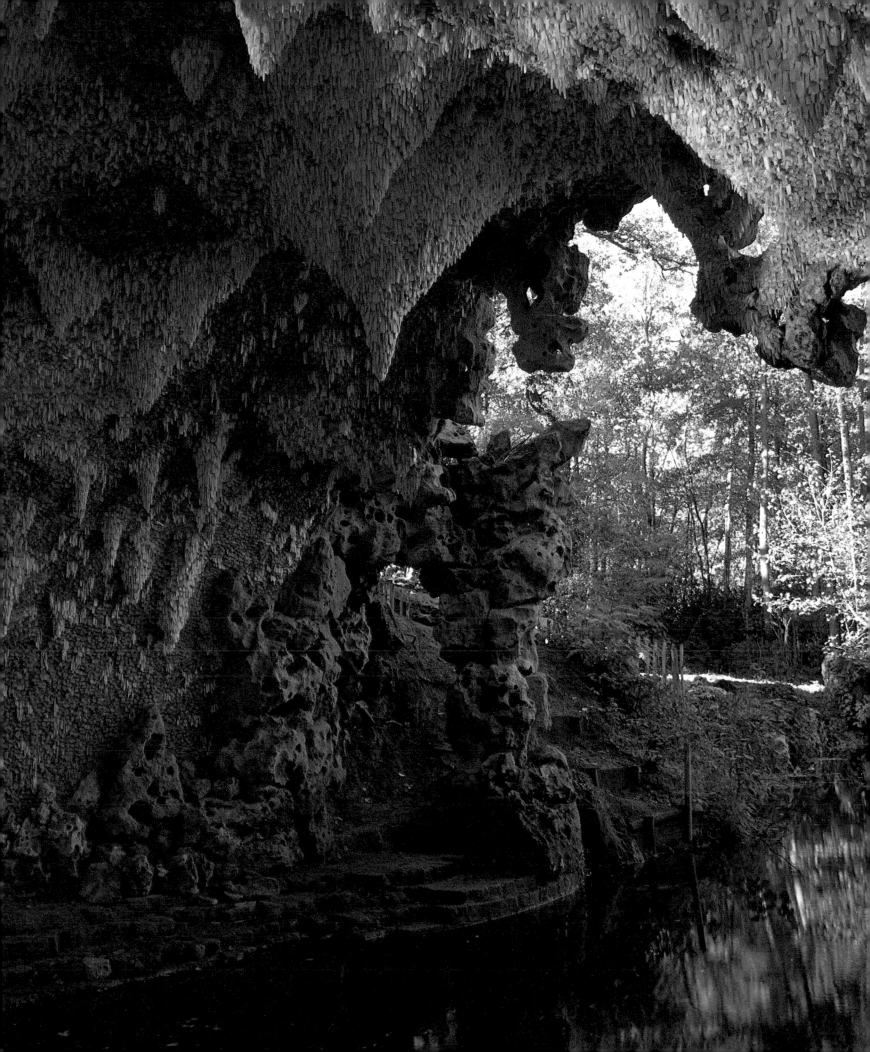

Follies and Eyecatchers

The Turkish or Venetian Tent

The Turkish tent at Painshill looked over the lake at the end of the circuit walk. It was designed to hold picnics or simple outdoor parties. Most other tents were moved around the garden and were taken down during the winter but the one at Painshill was more permanent.

Tents are made from canvas, which may be either sown in stripes or painted and supported on a frame. At Painshill this frame is quite substantial but more usually it is constructed of wooden or cast-iron poles. Light wires can be stretched between the poles to decorate the tent with plants.

The Painshill Turkish tent was oval inside and measured about 16 ft (4.8 m) long by 12 ft (3.6 m) wide. The floor was made from tiles and brick on edge set in a decorative pattern, and the canvas was fixed to a plastered back wall. The colourful pediment and ornate finial was made from painted papier mâché.

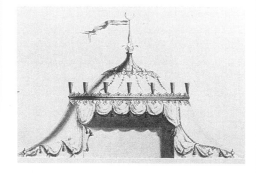

The Hermitage

A hermitage is supposed to represent the isolated retreat of a contemplative philosopher and it must be made out of simple materials. At Painshill even the path to the hermitage helped to reinforce the seclusion and was overshadowed by a dense wood of Scots pine, Norway firs and other conifers. The door opened into a small room which led into a second room where, from the small window, there were spectacular views of the garden. The frame was made from rustic and twisted logs with their bark left on, and the walls were made from upright logs or portions of large roots. The roof was thatched and the furniture was as simple and primitive as the outside.

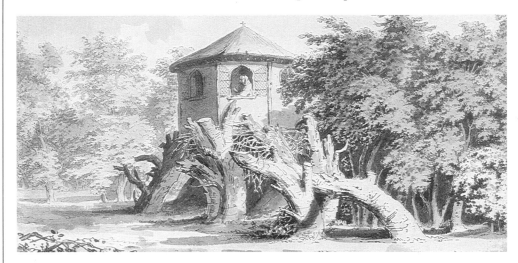

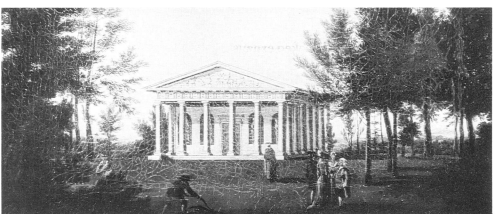

The Temple of Bacchus

This fine temple at Painshill was modelled on the Temple of Concord at Stowe and was built as a miniature of an ancient Greek temple. On a pediment above the entrance is a basso-relievo of a drunk Silenus supported by six columns of the Doric order. Under it are niches for statues and the side walls are supported by pilasters. The temple was only 25 ft (7.6 m) square. It was built from brick covered with stucco and painted white.

grand, and conducted with so serious an air of wild and uncultivated extent that when you look down on this seeming forest, you are amazed to find it contain a very few acres.'

In order to appreciate the variety of the theatrical style it is worth considering the many different experiences that Hamilton managed to evoke. A contemporary visit to Painshill is described here.

The prologue began even before the visitor arrived at the garden, as there were glimpses into the site from the road, from across the river, and at the entrance, where there was a long vista across grass meadows to the tall Gothic tower.

The first episode in the play took place in the more or less conventional garden adjacent to the house. Lying along a flat plateau overlooking the winding river, it was filled with an array of exotic plants and a formal parterre. It was a garden of beauty, intimacy and enclosure, which was relieved by views over the woodland belt to the steeple of Cobham church. All very peaceful and unexciting, so where was this revolutionary landscape which everyone raved about? All that could be seen was a pastoral scene of the open valley floor below, grazed by sheep and enclosed by woods. The route led down and up a steep hill which looked exhausting. Was the effort worth it?

With the descent into the valley, an enchanting tiny Gothic temple could be glimpsed peeping over the trees. But the path led resolutely onwards into the dark and overshadowing trees covering Wood Hill and up a steep bank towards a glimmer of light, which suddenly turned into a spectacular view across water to the Surrey hills at least twenty miles away – all rather unexpected.

Through an avenue of strange conifers the path turned sharply into an oval lawn edged by shrubs, with a view back to the flower garden. Close by was a large and rather startling statue of the *Rape of the Sabines*, which scandalized some commentators. When curiosity about the statue had been satisfied, the visitor turned round to view the shrubbery, and again the delightful white Gothic temple was silhouetted against the sky, at the end of a long glade. A false perspective made the temple look further away. However, its graceful charms beckoned the visitor on. When the temple was reached through the amphitheatre, as the oval lawn was called, there was a spectacular view over the lake below to an arched Chinese bridge, and beyond in the middle distance to the Temple of Bacchus lying in the trees and a brilliant Turkish tent glittering in sunlight. In the distance was the castellated top of a Gothic tower.

The third episode began by following the winding walk down to the lakeside and through exotic shrubberies, where the mood changed from light glades with sunlight filtering through the delicate leaves of the robinia to the sombre darkness of conifers. The views across the lake were short, intimate and domestic. The quiet water was crossed by a humped-back bridge and the path led down to a contemplative peaceful lagoon. Entering a small dark door, the route penetrated into the earth in a pitch-black tunnel with low overhanging stalactites bearing down around blind corners. Darkness engulfed the visitor except for a distant shimmer of light, which gradually grew nearer as one proceeded down the tunnel, eventually arriving at an enormous chamber with water cascading through it. This was a

The white Gothic temple glistens against the sky, the climax of a vista in a garden, but which also cleverly suggests that the garden extends well beyond. The use of such features serves to enhance a garden visually and spatially.

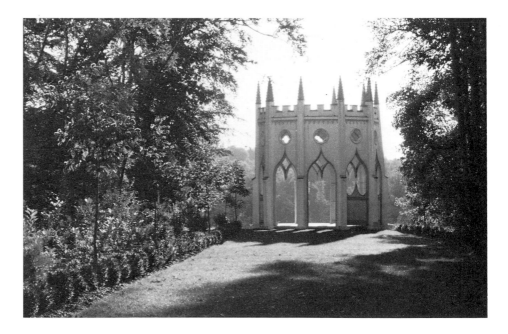

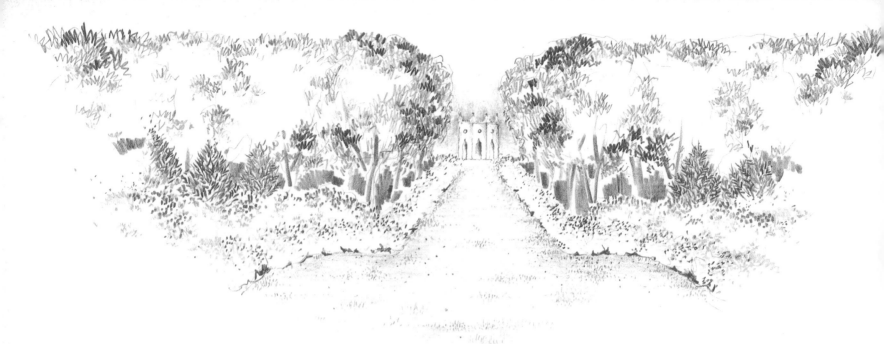

A sketch of a Gothic temple. It is emphasized by two lines of box, which skirt the glades of trees. In the foreground is the stepped planting of an amphitheatre.

The fantastic folly of the Ruined Abbey at Painshill reflected in the lake. It is a brick-rendered facade, constructed to hide a derelict brickworks in about 1770.

OPPOSITE
The long vista of a ride or allee, leading to a statue silhouetted by the evening sun.

most magnificent man-made grotto.

From the grotto the path led over two bridges and along the tranquil lake before passing the dramatic and antique ruined mausoleum tempting the visitor to view its remains. Through the broken arch a gigantic waterwheel might be spied far away across the river.

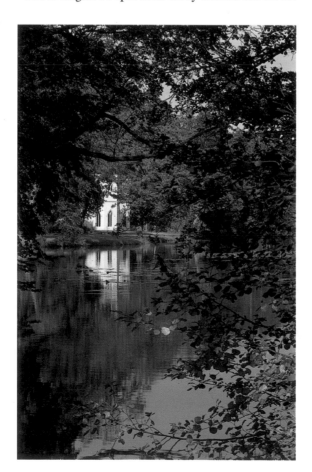

The way across the five-arched bridge was barred and so the route turned towards the gurgling, splashing noise of tumbling water spilling over a large stone cascade fed by the waterwheel. From this point the mood changed from the more manicured pleasure ground to the wild and rugged woodland. Here the visitor had to walk along a narrow path cut out of a steep and overhanging sandstone cliff, passing through a wild forest of dense conifers. Suddenly, around a corner, there was an open 'alpine' valley where the trees rose up from the meadow at the bottom of the sloping banks.

The path then proceeded through a dark and gloomy wood and led to a tree house and hermitage. The open doorway of the hermitage revealed spectacular views over the River Mole to the Surrey hills. Once there was a real hermit to welcome visitors, but he spent too much time in the local public house and spoilt the effect.

There followed a climb up the tall Gothic tower, which revealed the most amazing views to London on one side and Windsor on the other. However, views over the garden were prevented by a little turret.

The return journey meandered through open shrubberies filled with exotic plants, producing a more cultured and domestic mood after the rigours of the Wild Wood; this was a garden of colour and texture, of open glades

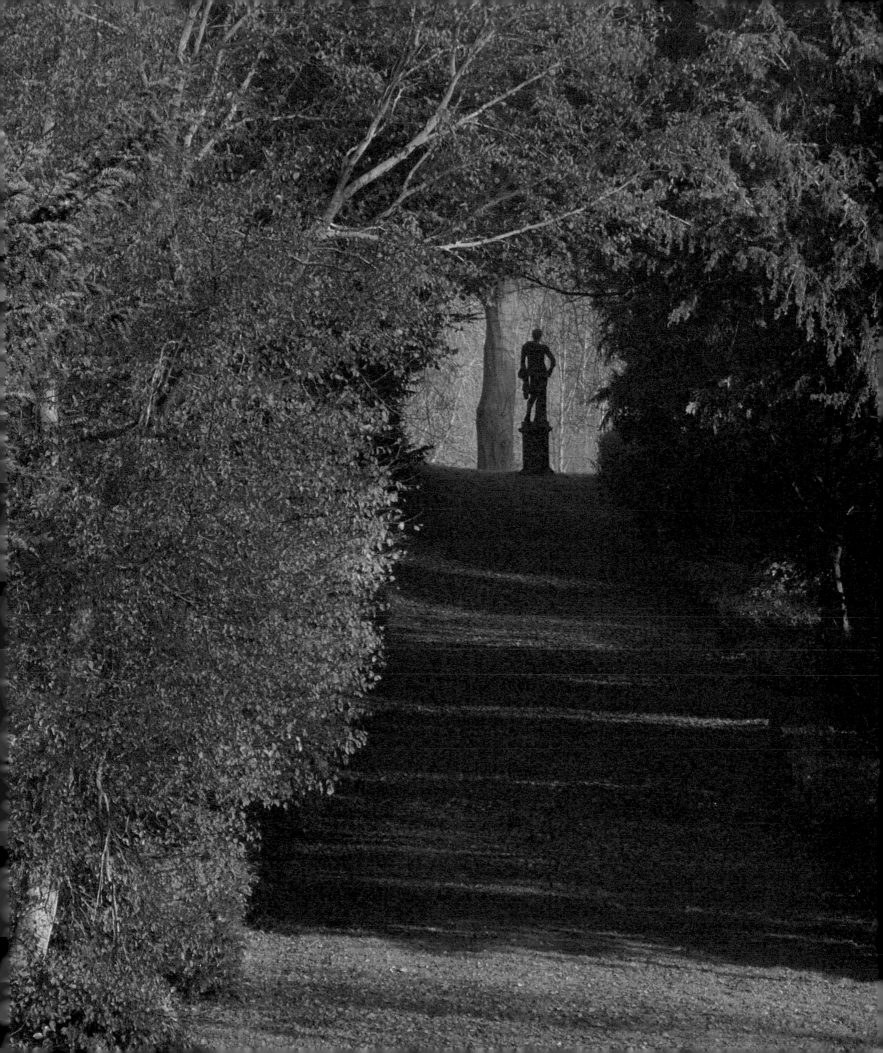

The stepped planting shows the precision of the planting, which is clipped to create the effect of an amphitheatre in a flat woodland glade. At the back are evergreen trees, at the front deciduous trees and flowers edged by box hedging.

and smooth lawns. Framed in the middle of a lawn was a small temple with a delightful portico. Inside the door was a huge, nude statue of Bacchus and beyond him were more startling views across the broad sweep of meadow far below: from darkness into light!

At the end of the garden, the emotionally and physically exhausted visitor was allowed to rest, to sit in the extraordinary Turkish tent, made of brightly painted and heavily decorated canvas, and to admire the sensational view over the lake back towards the grotto and the Gothic temple.

The route returned across the tranquillity of the pasture with peacefully grazing sheep. There were occasional glimpses across to the lake but soon the lodge gates appeared and the adventure was complete.

This brief description of the many effects that Charles Hamilton created at Painshill illustrates the rich variety of these theatrical gardens. But Hamilton had one more trick. He was a very skilled and knowledgeable plantsman and this garden was created mostly by planting exotics. Many had been recently introduced from America, and they added to the fantasy, as few visitors recognized them.

Although the layout of these gardens is unique, some of the contrasts at Painshill were created by the shrubberies. This can be clearly seen in the amphitheatre on the top of Wood Hill, where the shrubs were used to form the sloping sides. This stepped planting was recommended by Batty Langley in his book *The Principles of Gardening* (1728) and by Philip Miller in his *Dictionary of Gardening* (1731).

Miller describes the stepped planting and recommends that:

> Roses, Honeysuckles, Spirea frutex, and other kinds of low flowering Shrubs which may be always kept very dwarf and may be planted pretty close together; and at the Foot of them, near the Side of the Walks, may be planted Primroses, Violets, Daffodils, and many other Sorts of Wood Flowers, not in a strait Line but rather to appear accidental as in a natural wood. Behind the first row of shrubs should be planted Syringa, Cytisus, Althea frutex, Mezerions, and other flowering Shrubs of middle Growth, which may be backed with Laburnums, Lilacs, Guelder and other flowering shrubs of large growth; these may be backed with many other sorts of Trees, rising gradually to the Middle of the Quarters, from whence they should always slope down in every way to the walks.

He suggests the front three rows of the border should follow the line of the meandering path and that in the rows behind, the planting distances should suit the plants used and should not be in straight lines. These plants should gradually rise to form a 'handsome slope'.

Even at this time, despite the development of natural gardening, shrubs were not planted in groups of one kind to look natural but were planted singly. A plant of one variety would generally be planted next to one of another sort. The smaller shrubs in the first rows were planted close together, probably at about 1 ft (0.3 m) apart, and the middle-size ones were planted further apart at about 3–4 ft (0.9–1.2 m) distance. The taller shrubs and trees were planted quite close together at about 6–9 ft (1.8–2.7 m) apart, making a dense barrier fairly quickly. Several contemporary books suggested that when the trees in the last section grew too big they could be moved and used as standards in the park.

The depth of the shrubbery depended on the situation, but in one plan the front section, called the border, was only 30 in (0.75 m) wide and contained three rows of perennial plants. The second part, known as the 'plantation', was 5 ft (1.5 m) deep and included three rows of medium-size shrubs; and the final section was the 'old hedge rows'. If there was a path behind the shrubbery then flowering shrubs could be planted to line the grass paths. In larger shrubberies it was suggested that the paths should be 5–6 ft (1.5–1.8 m) wide, but in smaller ones the grass paths could be only 4 ft (1.2 m) wide. Their edges were scattered with wild flowers.

There was quite a mixture of planting in the border, and individual plants included lilies, hollyhock, golden rod, columbine, honesty, crown imperials, stocks and roses. The second section, or plantation, contained larger shrubs such as syringa, rose, laurel, lilac, holly, honeysuckle, Spanish broom and laburnum. The final section contained trees such as beech, balsam poplar, hornbeam, alder, chestnut, hazel, and crab apple.

Evergreen and deciduous shrubs were not planted together but were kept separately. They were also planted in slopes, and Miller suggests that the first line should be planted with:

Laurustinus, box, spurge, juniper, savin and other dwarf evergreens; behind these may be placed laurels, Hollies, Arbutus's and other evergreens of a larger Growth; next to these may be place Alternus's, Phyllyrea's, Yews, Cypress's, Virginian Cedars, and other Trees of the same Growth; behind these may be planted Norway, Silver Firs, the true Pine and other sorts of the like Growth and in the middle should be planted Scotch Pines, Pinaster, and other largest growing Evergreens.

In smaller gardens rising clumps of evergreens could frame the view or mark the edge of the

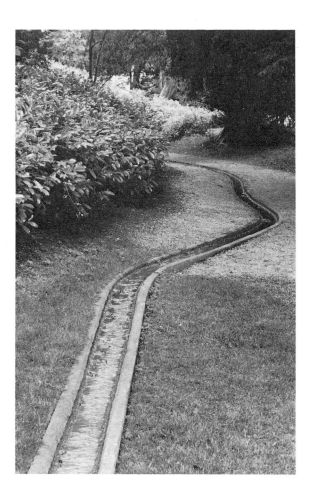

The rill snaking through a woodland ride at Rousham. The noise of bubbling water was intended to create the illusion of a stream flowing somewhere in the background.

shrubbery. Behind this slope of evergreens several kinds of flowering shrubs could edge the serpentine grass paths, adding variety. The grass paths were kept mown and the edges kept free of weeds. Miller was very keen on keeping the shrubberies weed-free and suggested hoeing them at least two or three times a year. The shrubs were to be pruned so that the branches did not cross and once a year the ground between them was lightly dug.

The delight of the theatrical garden is that parts or acts of it can be created in any size of garden. Much of the detailed layout is derived from the ground itself, but as many dramatic experiences as possible can be packed into the scenes. Strong contrasts can be created with light and shade, or with feathery leaves of deciduous trees and solemn conifers, with tall trees and low shrubs, or by framing and hiding views to an eyecatcher. This garden should be fun, and the theatrical garden style is an intellectual forerunner of many of today's popular theme parks such as Disneyland.

6

The Landscape Garden

THE landscape garden is gardening on a grand scale. The inspiration for the design is drawn from the place itself by exaggerating the natural form to add variety to its shape and size. Using the simple ingredients of land, trees, water and grass this style creates landscapes of magnificence and vision.

The gardens range in size from one or two acres to enormous landscape parks of over a thousand acres. They very often provide the setting or frame for country houses both large and small. Without these resplendent surroundings some of these buildings would look small and insignificant.

For example, the drive with its entrance gate from the road identifies the beginning of the visit. It sets up responses from the visitor, who anticipates pleasurable experiences as the drive curves through the landscape. A glimpse of elegant chimneys or a glance at a columned portico through a break in the trees indicates the house. Often there are more delightful views of the surroundings before the facade of the house is suddenly presented to the visitor.

The first sight of the house is carefully designed to show it off at its most impressive. A backdrop of trees can help to emphasize the profile of the architecture; or a line of trees may lead up to the main front of the house, the outline of the roof is silhouetted against the sky, making the building appear larger.

These gardens developed from the theatrical style but the landscape garden is simpler and the experiences are less intense and on a larger scale. The ground available for a landscape garden was greatly eased by changes in farming methods which advocated large fields

sheltered by plantations for raising cattle, sheep and deer. The style became highly fashionable at a period when prosperity encouraged many landowners to 'improve' their grounds aesthetically as well as economically. Large tracts of common land were enclosed and fenced by their new owners, under Acts of Parliament. Workers' cottages lying adjacent to the outbuildings of a large house were demolished and rebuilt further away so that the landowner's home could stand surrounded by its beautiful landscape and not by a clutch of run-down hovels.

One of the greatest exponents of the landscape style was Lancelot Brown known as 'Capability' because he frequently enthused that 'this place has "Capabilities" to become a "beautiful" landscape.' He developed a series of principles which could be used in most sites, and he designed over 210 landscape gardens throughout Britain.

Although he is credited with sweeping away most of the earlier formal gardens, research shows that many of his new designs included trees from earlier formal avenues. In some of the large formal landscapes only a few trees had to be removed and others were even transplanted to achieve the sweeping and curving shapes of the more 'natural' effect. He was also a champion of tenants who had to be moved, and he helped to resettle them in superior housing.

Later in the eighteenth century the style developed from the softer and smoother lines of Brown to the wilder and more grotesque shapes of the Picturesque school led by Richard Payne Knight and Uvedale Price. They advocated the imitation of the more 'sav-

OPPOSITE
A clump of limes in the park at Belsay serve to establish the middle distance between the garden and the woodland beyond, thereby exaggerating the space of the landscape.

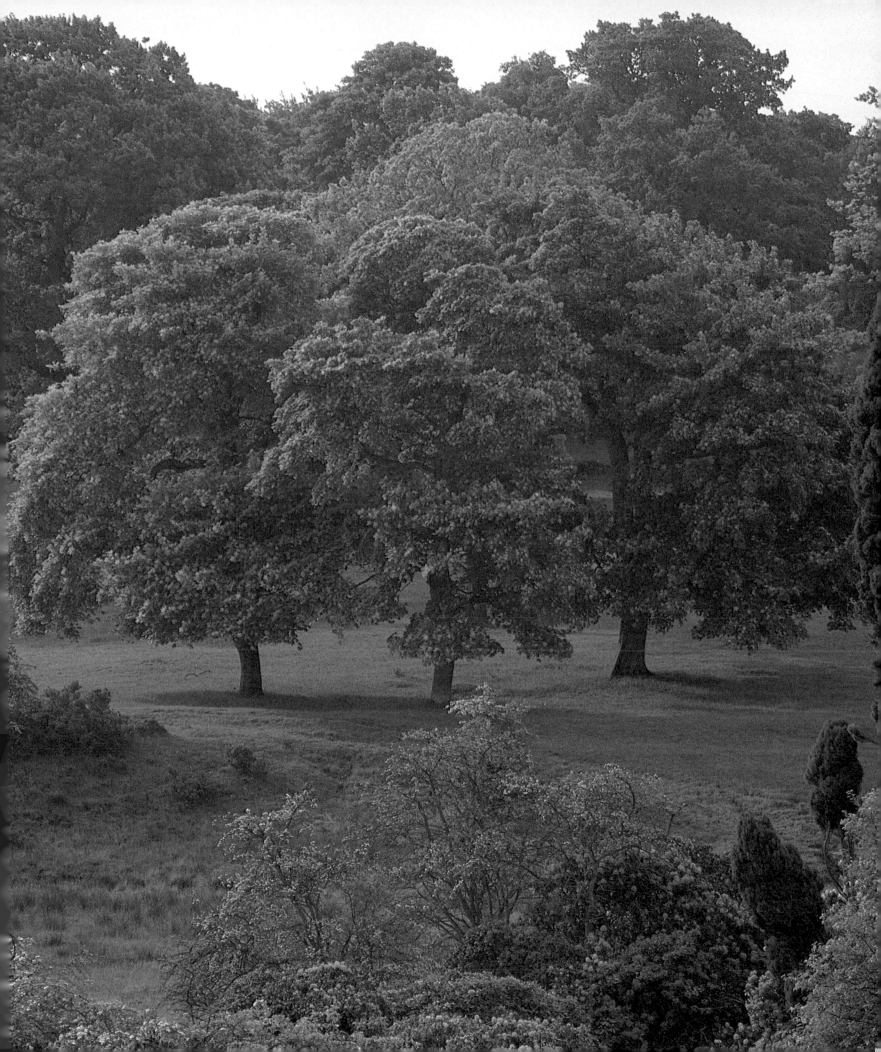

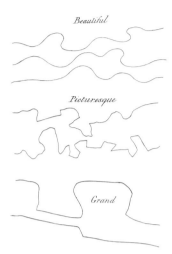

Outlines of New-Made Plantations

Beautiful

Picturesque

Grand

This drawing from J. C. Loudon's Observations, *1804, illustrates the different pattern lines for growing woodlands around a park, according to whether the desired effect is to be 'beautiful', 'picturesque' or 'grand'.*

Different types of tree planting in a landscape garden: (1) is a grove, (2) is a coppice wood, (3) is a grove underplanted with a thicket, and (4) is a clump.

age' elements of nature and were particularly impressed by the rugged scenery of the Wye valley and Welsh Marches.

Humphry Repton subsequently developed a more practical approach which incorporated Brown's principles. He also wrote several books describing the form, composition and scale of landscapes. He was particularly interested in the way in which viewers saw the landscape garden and how certain perspectives could fool them. Repton realized that the extravagances of the style – which advocated that browsing deer or grazing sheep be allowed up to the windows or doors of the house – were not very convenient for ladies in their light slippers, and so he introduced the terrace in front of the house. Farm animals were kept at a distance by a ha-ha or sunk fence, which gave the impression that they were allowed to roam freely up to the front door.

Early in the nineteenth century William Gilpin romanticized the park and introduced 'cloud' plantations of trees instead of the more straightforward clumps laid out by Brown nearly fifty years earlier.

Landscape gardens were created until World War I. There are many examples of the style and in Britain these gardens or parks constitute much of the variety in the mainly agricultural countryside. Sadly, due to age and changes in farming practices, many are very decayed and have lost much of their aesthetic value. Some have been recently replanted and a

few still display their original magnificence. The following gardens demonstrate features of the style: Blenheim Park, Oxfordshire; Woburn Park, Bedfordshire; Weston Park, Staffordshire; Petworth Park, Sussex; Highclere, Hampshire; Bowood, Wiltshire. Recently, some of the concepts have been used in major landscape projects, such as the reclamation of derelict land and in the settings of new industrial parks.

By the nineteenth century landscape gardening had developed into three recognizable styles, which are described by John Claudius Loudon in *Observations*, published in 1804. He says that 'wherever ornament is the principal consideration, there must be a particular effect which the artist intends to produce.' This will either be 'a beautiful variety, a picturesque variety, or a degree of grandeur and sublimity'. He also recommends that these styles can be mixed together but that the designer should be aware of 'attending to the qualities which produce these [effects] in trees and shrubs'. These styles were described in detail in contemporary books and are discussed at length in current garden history literature.

The 'beautiful' style refers to Brown's designs of graceful or serpentine curves sweeping in broad strokes around plantations or clumps. It should be harmonious, suave and smooth. This effect can be produced, according to Loudon, by 'neat gravel walks, winding easily through smooth turf, among

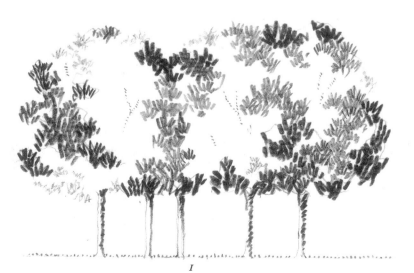

1

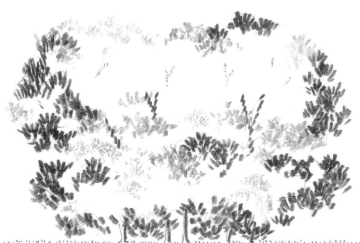

2

varied groups of trees' such as lime, beech, ash and robinia.

The Picturesque style advocated by Uvedale Price is produced by irregular, striking and forceful lines contrasting with the pastoral scene. Typical of this type might be 'a path in a rugged dell, forcing its way through irregular groups and thickets of oak, elm, thorns, elder'.

The 'grand and sublime' depends more on a bold outline of 'deep incisions, forming large bays and promontories', and was portrayed by Loudon, Gilpin and other nineteenth-century designers. It is a grander and more sombre style, using larger, more definite shapes. The 'grand forms' of 'oak, chestnuts [both horse and sweet] and pines' with their 'grave and solemn colours' were much favoured.

The first rule when laying out a landscape garden is to consult the 'genius of the place', that is to say, to identify the special characteristics which can be used in the design, for example, where the most attractive views are or where such a view can be made by framing with trees or by adding a building such as a bridge or summer-house. The aim is to emphasize as many impressive spectacles as possible. Sometimes this may be a folly or a beautiful tree; even chimney-pots of a distant cottage viewed from an angle can be pleasant; or the feature can be outside the park, such as a church spire or tower. Sometimes a farm building may have a decorative facade built onto it so that it can act as an eyecatcher.

The second and obvious aim is 'to correct or to conceal any particular object that is disagreeable'. Woodland trees can be used to hide unsightly buildings, although today these are often larger and more obtrusive than they were in the eighteenth century.

Landscape gardens are made from trees, grass, water and sky. They are edged with plantations containing trees 'so grouped as to produce light and shade to display the varied surface of the ground'. The presence of water exaggerates shapes by reflection and the grass is grazed by animals 'at liberty to collect their food from the rich herbage of the valley'.

Lakes or serpentine rivers were an important feature of Brown's landscapes. He skilfully dammed small streams, and created shapes with curving lines, giving the impression that the river or lake glided round the corner for ever instead of returning to the small stream or spring. The lake was usually formed in the lower-lying ground but if the land was too hilly several smaller lakes could be divided by either a broad waterfall or a bridge covering a dam.

The stillness of the water reflecting the brightness of the sky, or the ripple of waves on a breezy day, produced the much desired variety and constantly changing scenery. In some sites, particularly on steeper slopes, the nose of the bank could be removed so that more of the water could be seen. As Repton stipulated, the banks of a river should never be 'equidistant, the water in some places will spread to more

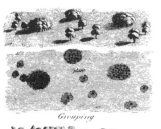

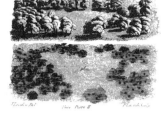

This drawing from J. C. Loudon's Observations, *1804, shows different ways of placing trees, according to the effect desired, either of 'clumping and dotting', or of 'grouping'.*

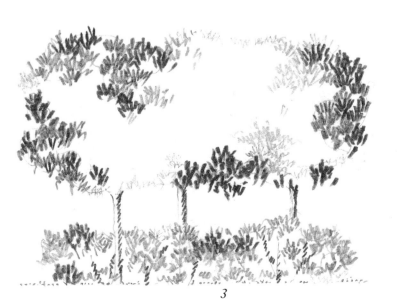

3

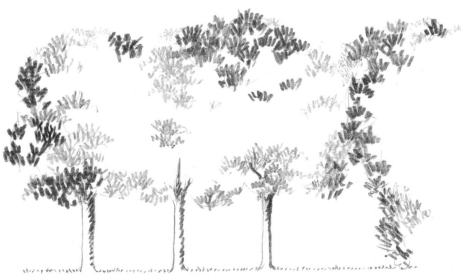

4

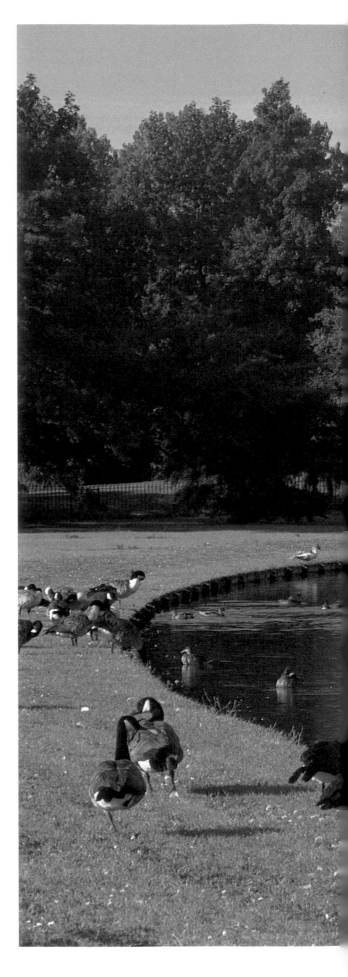

than twice the breadth it does in others . . . a river seldom proceeds far along the middle of a valley, but generally keeps on one side, or boldly stretches across to the other, as high ground resists, or low ground invites its course: these circumstances in natural rivers should be carefully imitated.' A bridge was often designed to feature in the garden but it was important that the crossing should look natural and be in a place that would be likely to be spanned.

Most landscape gardens were enclosed by trees, which could be planted in a thin strip called a belt or as a much larger wood. This outline created the frame of the garden and the edge exaggerated the 'prominence or recesses' of the ground. Often the woods accentuated the higher ground and the pasture the lower and more fertile areas. The woodland boundary was often made by a hedge or thicket, which could be quite a harsh line, so this was softened and made more beautiful by planting a few trees standing out from the wood in the park and 'belonging to or seeming to belong to the wood'.

Views from the house should not be interrupted by any line or fence in the foreground, so a sunken fence or ha-ha can be used to keep the farm animals away from the house. The lawn runs from the building to the top of a retaining wall or very deep ditch. From the base of the wall a steep bank can rise up to the same level as the top of the wall, but the width of the

OPPOSITE
The splendid bridge at Audley End, over the sweep of the river Cam, which was widened by Capability Brown in the mid-1760s into a lake for the garden.

The pretty decorative charm of the Chinese bridge over a stream at Wrest Park is typical of the features of 18th-century landscape gardens.

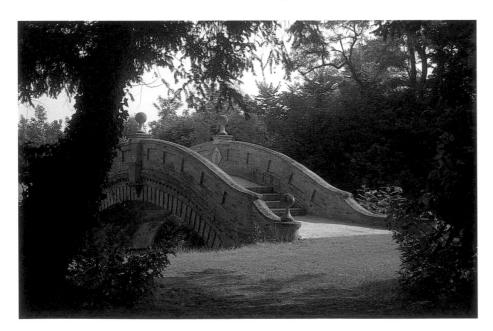

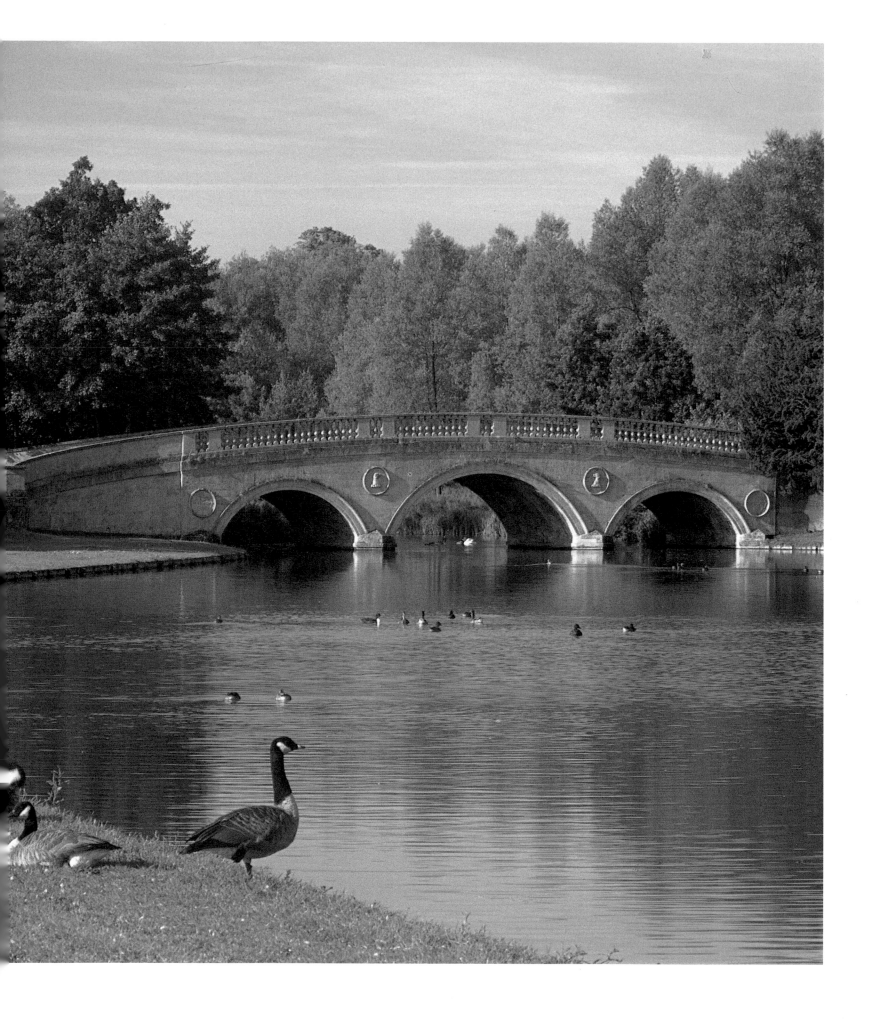

Examples of Tree Guards

Paling, Rustic and Modern Guards should be made from pressure-treated poles or sawn posts. The paling guard is made from half sawn poles fixed with stout twine. The rustic guard is made from poles fixed with galvanized nails and protects the tree from sheep only.

Stone Guards are lumps of stone packed close together with the points facing upwards in a circle of about 4 ft (1.2 m) in diameter. This will protect the tree from cattle but for sheep and deer netting will be required around the trunk. The stones protect the tree for a long time, and hold it in place as well as mulching it during the summer.

Black Wrought-Iron Guard This circular guard has fourteen uprights and is overall about 6 ft 10 in (2 m) high. It is painted black. The uprights are made of 1/4–1 in (0.0005–0.025 m) iron bars and are fixed top, centre and bottom to an iron band with a diameter of approximately 2 ft 4 in (0.7 m).

ditch ensures that the animals can neither leap across it nor climb up the wall. This barrier is used to provide an unimpeded view from the house to the fields and possibly to a lake beyond. There are several techniques for constructing ha-has, depending on the type of animals grazing the field as well as on the land form.

Three different types of tree plantations were traditionally used in landscape gardens: 'a grove, or a collection of trees without undergrowth; a wood or forest, or a collection of trees with undergrowth; and copsewood [coppicewood], undergrowth alone'. Clumps or groups in the park were planted as groves, and should appear when 'walking through them as a large collection of single trees', with grass growing under them. They were planted either as single trees in their final position or as a group in which the seedling trees were thinned until the selected ones remained. If the group required fencing for protection, this was removed when the trees were large enough. The outline was then varied so that the shape appeared more natural, and grass was sown between the trees.

Repton stated that small clumps should not be planted in an odd number of trees and that 'no group . . . can be natural in which the plants are studiously placed at equal distances.' He advocated that trees should be planted more randomly so that some branches overlap and so that 'two or three trees are placed very near to each other, whilst the perfection of the group consists of the combination of trees of different age, size, and character.' In fact the planting of two or more trees in the same hole was recommended to create a more natural effect.

The larger plantations were protected from grazing animals in various ways and these had an effect on the design. A common barrier was a ditch topped by a hedge of prickly plants such as hawthorn, gorse or blackthorn. A second method was to use a wooden paling fence, but this was thought too obtrusive so a more invisible fence was recommended by Repton and Loudon, made from strands of wire strained against narrow wrought-iron posts. In the nine-

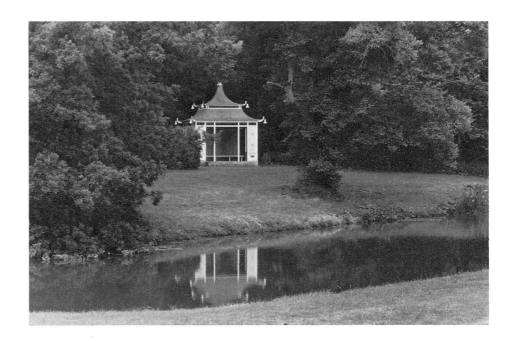

teenth century this soon developed into iron park railings. Sometimes individual trees were protected by different sorts of guards or cradles.

The main varieties of trees planted in clumps were oak, elm, beech, ash, sycamore, horse chestnut, sweet chestnut and lime. Scots pine, larch and cedar were used sparingly to accentuate the group. In the nineteenth century many of the more exotic varieties were used, usually clumped together in family groups, such as all the limes (or the genus *Tilia*), ash (*Fraxinus*), horse chestnut (*Aesculus*) and oak (*Quercus*). In these clumps, the browsing line grazed by the cattle or deer, up to about 6 ft (1.8 m) off the ground, is often unconsciously used as a scale by the viewer to judge the size and height of trees at various distance. So if there are no animals to graze the trees it is important to prune the lower branches to a similar line.

The woodlands around the perimeter could also be planted in several different ways, some of which related to the economic value of forestry but they also added variety to the landscape garden. Narrow belts defining the outline could be planted with standard trees in the same way as the larger clumps but were underplanted with 'thickets' of scrub such as hawthorn, coppiced oak and sweet chestnut so that the belt could not be seen through nor could the viewer judge its size The main trees were spaced 15–30 ft (4.5–9 m) apart.

The Chinese pagoda at Wrest Park is a theatrical and dramatic feature in the landscape garden, adding ornament and colour to a green landscape garden.

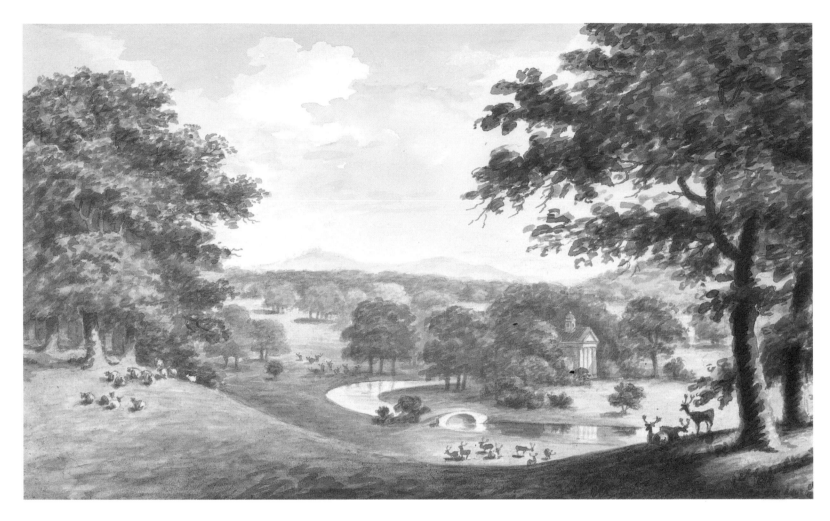

Prospect towards the River, Langley Park *(1790) by Humphry Repton. The sweep of the landscape emphasizes the clever placing of the clumps of trees. A small stream has been widened to create the effect of a large lake. The bridge and temple add viewpoints to the landscape and bring it together.*

Woodlands were planted in much the same way as they are today but in the eighteenth century the foresters were very concerned about keeping the ground clean and weed-free between the rows and even went to the trouble of growing vegetables between them. The first three or four rows of trees on the outside of the plantation followed the curving line of the fence to emphasize the shape of the wood. The fence line was not broken by rows of trees planted at right angles to it.

Most of these plantations were planted as forestry. For example, one-year-old or two-year-old trees were planted in rows about 4 ft (1.2 m) apart and with 2 ft (0.6 m) between each plant. In more difficult conditions, such as exposed chalk downs, seeding in rows was recommended and, for example, if an oak woodland was sown an acorn was included in the seed mix at every 6 in (0.15 m).

In Repton's words, 'The perfection of landscape gardening consists in the fullest attention ... to Utility, Proportion, and Unity or harmony of part to the whole.' The landscape garden expresses the simplicity of nature and imitates in miniature larger expanses of natural countryside. The style beautifies and accentuates the ground form and provides an inspiring setting for a building. The 'English landscape garden' was copied all over the world, and it is claimed that this style is one of Britain's great contributions to world art. It can easily be recreated today, either for a country house or for some other building such as an office.

7

The English Flower Garden

THE English flower garden is full of flowers and sweet smells. It is the earliest distinct style where the emphasis is on flowers growing 'naturally'. The garden is small, intimate and colourful. The flowers can be seen and appreciated by walking around it, when a sequence of views is arranged to show secret vignettes contrasting with longer and broader vistas. It is designed to display flowers all year round.

Enclosed by thick plantations, the flower garden is inward looking and should be shut off from the outside world. Once in the garden, the visitor moves in an isolated and yet protected world, full of beauty and solitude. The layout uses many of the design ideas described in the more dramatic theatrical garden and the grander landscape garden (Chapters 5 and 6) but they are here reproduced in miniature.

This style is ornamental rather than 'useful' and, unlike many earlier enclosed gardens, the kitchen garden is completely separate. In the eighteenth century, trees sheltered the flower garden and isolated it from its surroundings, which were usually a landscape garden or park. The garden itself was hidden and mysterious, a surprise contained within a landscape garden.

Although some flowering plants were grown in the pleasure grounds or shrubberies of many of Capability Brown's landscapes, until the late eighteenth century most of the tender and exotic ones were grown in the walled garden amongst the fruit and vegetables. Almost the first and certainly the most influential garden of the new style was the English flower garden at Nuneham Courtenay in Oxfordshire. This charming flower garden was designed with a 'poet's feeling and a painter's eye', by William

Mason and George, 2nd Earl of Harcourt.

Both men were enthusiastic followers of the 'divine' philosopher Jean-Jacques Rousseau, and it was his description of Julie's garden in his novel *La Nouvelle Héloïse* which inspired the creation of the significant garden which epitomizes this style. In the same way as contemporary designers such as Charles Hamilton and Capability Brown, Mason and Harcourt wished to imitate nature, but they used the intimacy of flowers instead of the grandeur of the wider landscape. Symbolically, the love of nature was to inspire feelings of virtue as well as

The flower borders of English flower gardens were distinguished by plants of bright colouring and contrasting heights, and contained within box or other low-grown hedging.

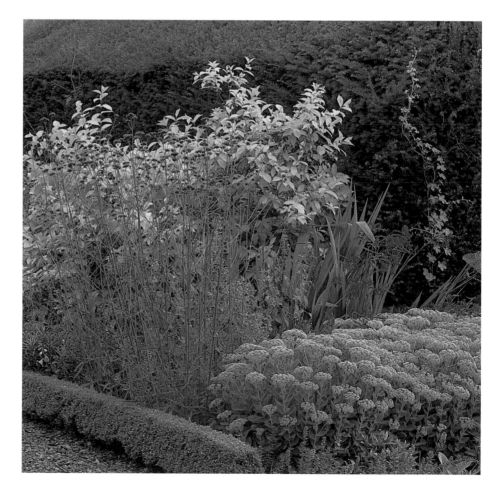

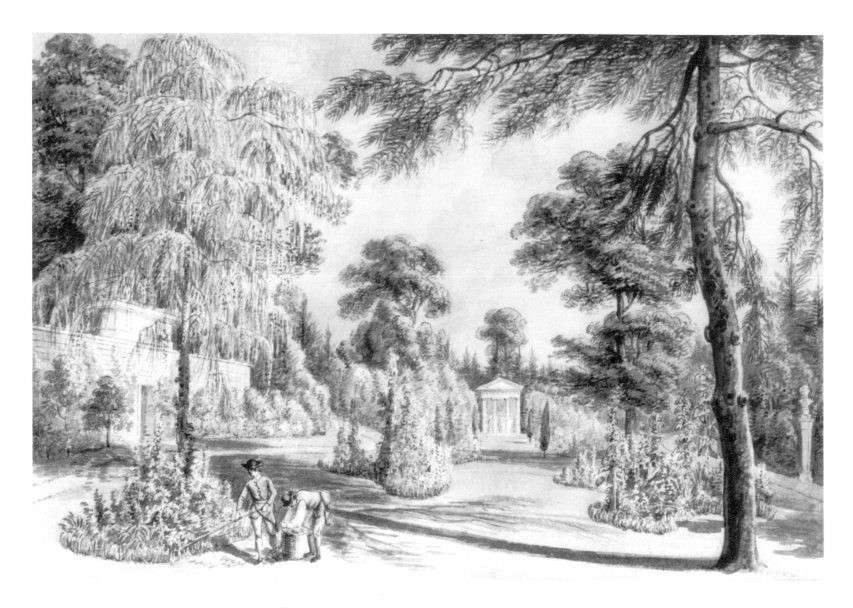

Gardeners at Work,
Mason's Garden,
Nuneham Courtenay,
c. 1777, by Paul Sandby,
two watercolours of the
famous flower garden
near Oxford, designed by
the Reverend William
Mason for Lord
Harcourt in about 1775.
This view depicts a broad
sweep of the garden,
encircled by the
meandering path, with
the orangery on the left,
and the temple at the far
end. Set in the closely
mown grass are the
undulating-shaped
flower beds.

pleasure. Flowers were seen as being able to raise the soul and the 'study of botany will detach us from ourselves and lift us up to its Author.'

The English flower garden at Nuneham was much admired by contemporaries and many visited it. The style was copied at other places, including Strawberry Hill. Horace Walpole even tried to steal Lord Harcourt's gardener to make a similar garden for him! Other examples included Mount Edgcumbe in Cornwall; Blickling Hall in Norfolk; and Culzean Castle in Ayr. As the style is essentially ephemeral no original garden remains today, but both Nuneham Courtenay and Mount Edgcumbe are currently being restored.

Some years later in 1804 J. C. Loudon in *Observations* aptly states that the flower garden 'should contain such a variety of trees, shrubs, flowers, etc. as that a number of each will be in perfection every month of the year'. He goes on to explain 'that they should be placed in irregular groups and thickets, of different sizes, gliding into one another on smooth lawn, beautifully varied, and broken into small, confined scenes, by trees and shrubs of the most elegant sorts. Throughout the whole, smooth gravel walks should wind in a graceful, easy manner.' This beautifully describes English flower garden style.

Flowers are the most important feature in this garden, and the way in which the visitor walks through the garden and looks at them forms the base for the design. The sinuous curves of the path entice the viewer to discover more and to find out what is around the sweeping corner or behind the thick bushes. The aim is to create experiences and stimulate the emotions as in the theatrical garden, but on a smaller scale.

At Nuneham the entrance path leads through a narrow and dark passage enclosed by evergreen yew and laurel. In front stands the tall statue of Flora framed by more gloomy laurels. Here the path splits into two but the long view to the church, built as a classical temple, beckons onwards and the other path is forgotten. As the visitor rounds the corner the statue of Hebe stands on the lawn in greeting. Opposite it, dramatically placed is the Temple of Flora, framed by delightful and colourful flowers. Here is the flower garden.

The walk continues around the garden and its circuit exaggerates the length. By following it the visitor encounters many experiences, not only sweet-smelling flowers but also occasional glimpses of some object, a temple, seats, statues and vases. Sometimes these may be hidden from the path and only visible from the opposite side of the garden. The small grotto is concealed under vegetation until it suddenly appears in front of the walker.

'Patches of flowers and clumps of shrubs of unequal dimensions and various shapes' – this was Lord Harcourt's offhand description of the planting. But the shape of each bed was contrived to frame or hide views of the objects. Mason drew a schematic plan to show these borders and they are illustrated in watercolours by the eighteenth-century artist P. Sandby.

The free and natural form of the small flower beds at Nuneham is created by curving lines, and their shape can be likened to a kidney. These beds are carefully laid out so that each one is different, but despite this 'natural' form

Gardeners at Work, Mason's Garden, Nuneham Courtenay, c. 1777. A view of the garden looking in the opposite direction, out from the temple. It shows well how the edges of the beds curve, how dense the planting can be, and the effect of growing plants, shrubs and trees together, particularly the small upright conifers. In both pictures the large trees are pruned high to ensure light reaches the flower beds.

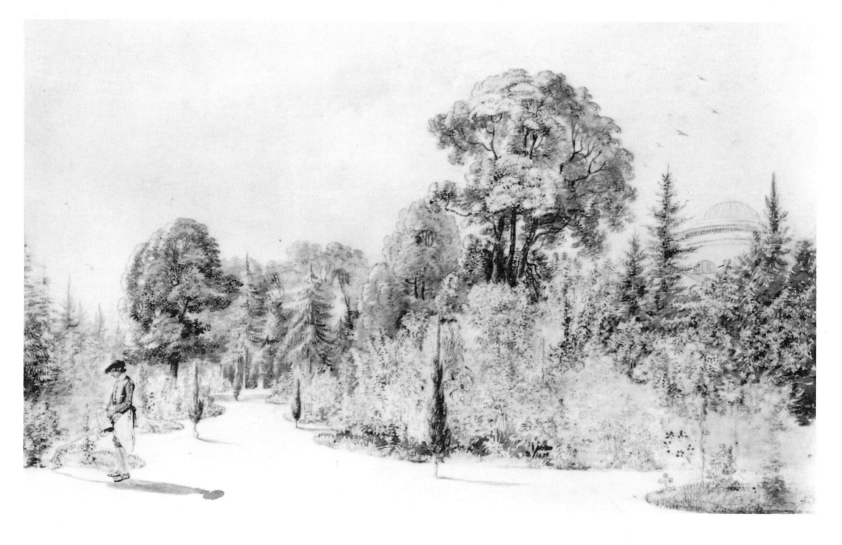

OPPOSITE
This sketch shows the effect of curving and undulating beds and the variety of planting and height found in the English flower garden. Height is not concentrated at the centre, and is created by plants such as honeysuckle and convolvulus, grown on posts, and which also give colour and smell to the beds. Though they are intended to look natural and 'unstructured', these plants are actually heavily pruned to keep their shape.

BELOW
Section across the flower garden. A path set in the grass runs between a shrubbery on the left and a flower bed on the right. The drawing reveals clearly the contrasting different heights of the plants, which emphasize the unexpected and undulating shape and three-dimensional quality of the bed. The graded levels of the shrubbery, edged by flowers, create the enclosure for the garden.

they are used to frame the main views. The vista to the Temple of Flora from the statue of Hebe is framed by the borders, with only one small portion of each bed making up the line. The curving shape is also designed to encourage the visitor to investigate, and the grass paths between the beds beckon and entice exploration. The effect is like a maze designed to confuse, confound and entrance.

In an English flower garden, the width of the lawn between the serpentine path and the borders constantly changes to exaggerate the line of the path, which frequently swings from one side of the grass area between the flower beds to the other, magnifying the extent of the curve. The path, measuring about 30 in (0.75 m) wide and covered with fine gravel and coarse sand, can be used to highlight particular areas or smaller secondary paths. Low-growing wild flowers such as daisies, clover, violets and primroses can grow in the lawn, but for most of the year it should be kept smooth and well mown.

This style of garden features many objects. At Nuneham they are classical images through which a story unfolds, adding a touch of mystery and evoking a sense of drama. Unlike the theatrical garden style, however, the objects are on the whole smaller and less complicated. For example, they might include a small bust, an urn or vase raised on a plinth and perhaps some broken antique stones casually lying on the ground, or a wooden summer-house with an added columned facade, such as the Temple of Flora. In places not requiring classical symbols, wooden tubs and brightly painted terracotta vases filled with flowering plants are used.

Although marble statues and objects have always been much admired, even in the eighteenth century many gardeners could not afford them so they used cheaper materials such as wood or lead and painted them to look like marble or stone. It is intriguing to consider how they would have used some of the modern materials to create their objects! Today, reproductions of this type of classical vase or urn and their

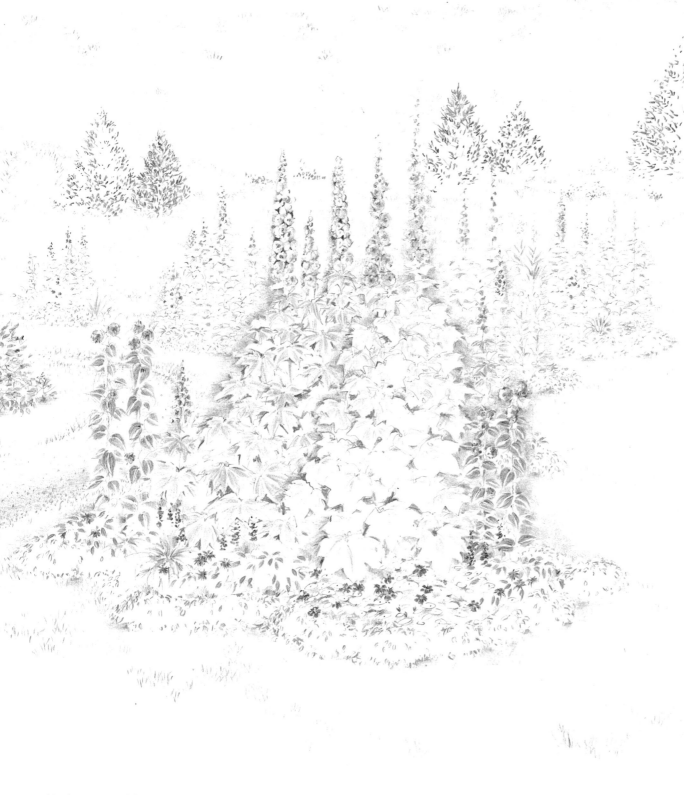

plinths are readily available in cast stone. Some more complicated designs have been cast in fibre glass, but this technique must be very well done as otherwise this material is inclined to become brittle and crack, particularly when it is outside in all weather conditions.

One of the aims in an English flower garden is to grow as many exotic plants as possible. In

*Plan of the structure of
the English flower
garden. The enclosed
garden is explored by
wandering along the
meandering path
through the lawns and
discovering amidst the
shrubs the many different
flower beds and features
like statues, a summer
house or grotto.*

the eighteenth century there were far fewer plants to choose from than are available today; even so, in an important catalogue by W. Aiton, *Hortus Kewensis* published in 1789, the author noted that there were over 6,000 plants growing at Kew Gardens. This catalogue forms an excellent reference for anyone seeking to re-create this style on an historically accurate basis.

In the late eighteenth century the introduction of many species from abroad meant that gardeners had more plants to choose from than their forebears earlier in the century but most of the flowers were quite small, delicate and paler in colour than those we are now used to. The flowering season for most of the herbaceous plants was much shorter but gardeners then were more concerned about scents and textures than we are now.

The English flower garden is enclosed, and from the outside in its landscape setting it appears to be just an ordinary wood or copse. To create this effect at Nuneham tall trees were scattered in small groups around the outside of the garden and a very thick undergrowth of yew, laurel, box and other evergreens surrounded it. Thus the trunks of the trees were shown up by the dark green hedge behind which actually enclosed the garden.

When creating such a garden it is important to give a sense of enclosure, of moving into another world. A plantation can be used to mask unsightly views or to hide more modern objects or buildings. From inside the thick outer plantation exotic and textured evergreens should be used to blend in with the dark green background of trees so that the junction between shrubbery and shelter-belt woodland cannot be seen. These are arranged so that the tall shrubs are planted at the back and the lower ones in front, creating a gradual smooth slope. The twisted, prickly and colourful leaves of hollies are much favoured, especially as they contrast well with the smoother and more bland Portugal laurel. Occasionally feathery and delicate pale green leaves of the locust tree float over the dark textured, mass adding lightness and variety. Texture and different shades of greens play an important role and should be carefully chosen and mixed together.

Within the evergreen border inside the flower garden a single flowering shrub can be planted such as a lilac, viburnum, philadelphus, or a larger rose 'to appear as if escaping from the dark bosum of the evergreens'. Smaller conifers may also break up the thicker shrubs, and more vigorous climbers such as clematis can be encouraged to grow through them. These plants should be planted singly and not in large groups or clumps.

0 1 2 3 4 5 6 7 8M

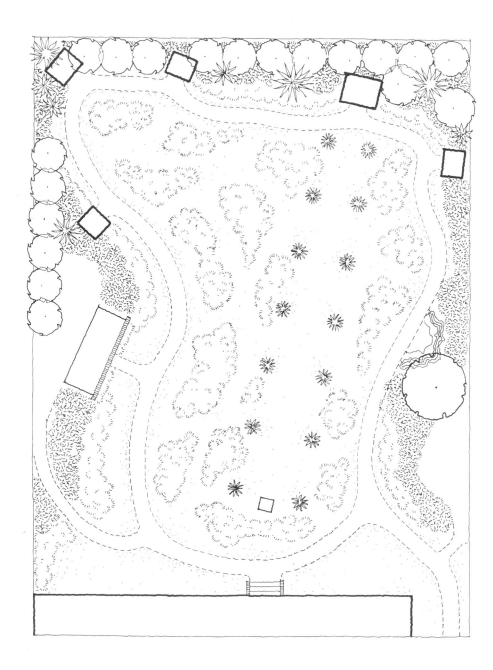

Examples of Decoration

Statues and Other Artifacts sited in the English Flower Garden are just smaller versions of those that feature in the Theatrical Garden. They are carefully situated to make the garden look as large as possible. They can be used as eyecatchers to accent the longer view or they may be placed quite close to the path to distract the attention of the viewer away from another feature. The objects are very varied and are often modest priced and so they can be obtained easily today.

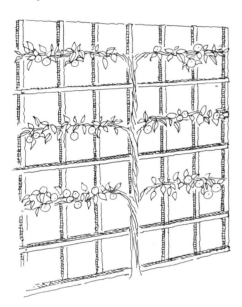

If there is a wall or building on one side of a garden it can be covered with fruit trees such as apples or pears, or if it faces south, it can support the finer fruits such as peaches or apricots. These can be espaliered or fan-trained and attached to a stout trellis made from timber lattice, 3 x 2 in (0.075 x 0.05 m), fixed at 1 ft (0.3 m) squares. Alternatively, the trellis can be made in a special pattern and will provide decoration during the winter.

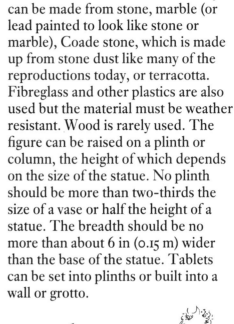

Simple wooden summer-houses or garden sheds can be faced with a wooden portico supported by Doric columns. These can be painted to look like marble or an off-white colour to look like stone. Papier mâché may also be used to make the decorations, which can be either classical, as in this sketch, or Gothic, with arched windows and arrow-shaped finials. Windows and openings are better hidden on the sides.

Garden seats can be very decorative and there are many eighteenth-century patterns now reproduced which are suitable for the English Flower Garden. Circular wooden seats made to fit around a large and magnificent tree were very popular throughout the eighteenth and nineteenth centuries. Here you can sit in the dappled shade and appreciate the tracery of the branches.

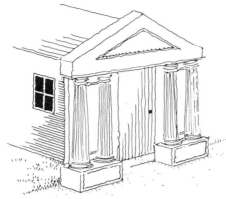

The most common objects in these gardens are statues, vases, columns, tablets and other monuments. They can be made from stone, marble (or lead painted to look like stone or marble), Coade stone, which is made up from stone dust like many of the reproductions today, or terracotta. Fibreglass and other plastics are also used but the material must be weather resistant. Wood is rarely used. The figure can be raised on a plinth or column, the height of which depends on the size of the statue. No plinth should be more than two-thirds the size of a vase or half the height of a statue. The breadth should be no more than about 6 in (0.15 m) wider than the base of the statue. Tablets can be set into plinths or built into a wall or grotto.

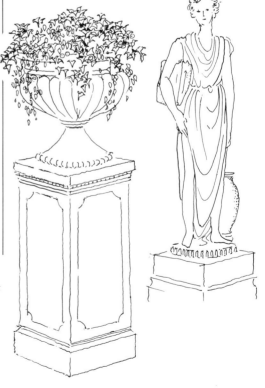

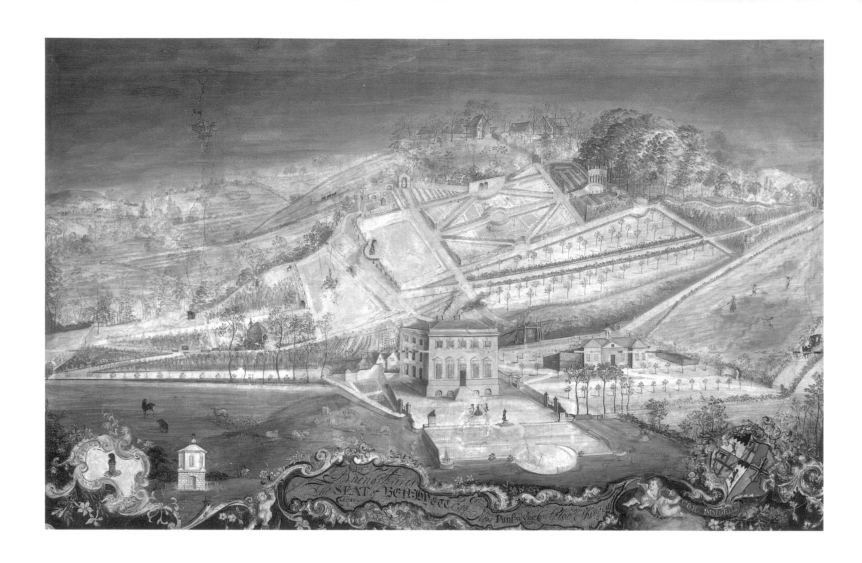

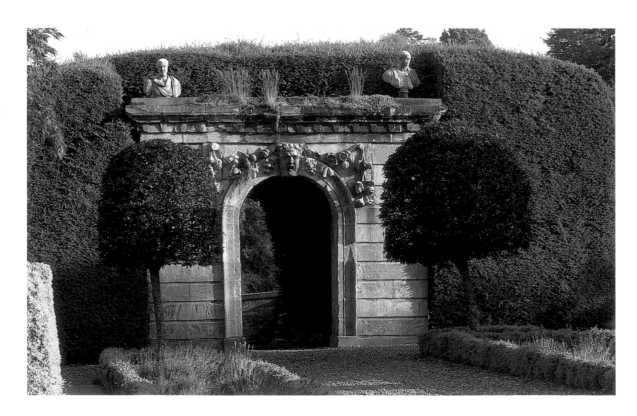

ABOVE
Painswick House,
Gloucestershire, *1748*,
*by Thomas Robins the
Elder, with its little
temples, summerhouses
and attractive planting of
flowers, beautifully
illustrates the transition
between the theatrical
garden and the English
flower garden.*

*In the English flower
garden, an arch, as here
at Drummond Castle or a
temple often featured at
the end of the garden. But
such a facade can also be
used to disguise a simple
shed or provide shelter for
a garden seat.*

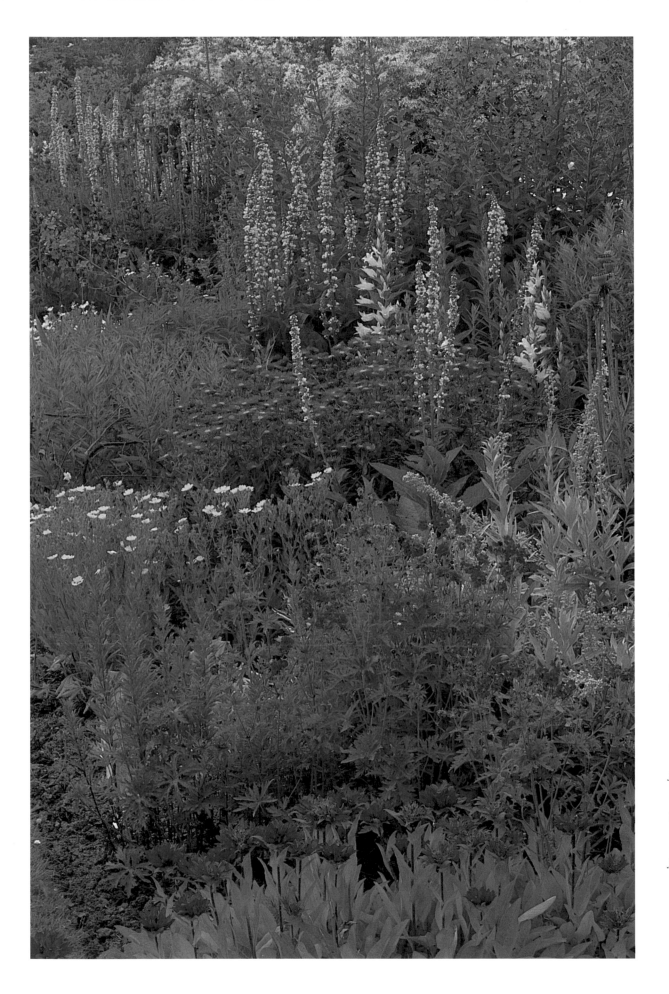

A part of the border at Hergest Croft shows how attractive and surprising are the different gradations of flowers, as found in an English flower garden. Flowers are grouped in 'mounds', with tall spikes of colour shooting upwards. Low clipped box between the grass and flowers holds up the more extravagent flowers as well as keeping a tidy edge between the plants and the grass. Usually, the taller blooms are at the back but occasionally a higher flower spike breaks up the smaller plants along the outside of the beds.

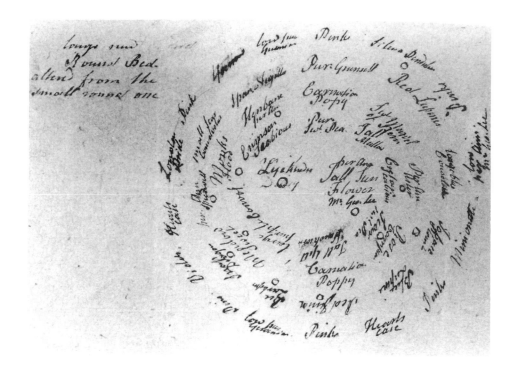

A planting scheme, from the Harcourt papers, of individual plants set in a round bed. On the outer ring, single pinks alternate with other plants such as heart's ease and mignonette. Next is a ring of red and blue plants such as lupins, snap dragons, tobacco plants and convolvulus. The third ring contains carnation, poppies, purple asters, henbane; the fourth, crimson scabious, purple sweet pea, large purple convolvulus, tall mallow. The centre is filled with even taller flowers.

In the eighteenth century the desire for variety and texture produced a rich and spotted effect. This was particularly noticeable in the flower beds, where 'irregularity' of shape, and brightness and freshness of the plants was much admired. Horace Walpole remarked of Nuneham that the 'flowerbeds would hurt the eye by their littleness.'

In order to create such an irregular effect each plant is placed next to a different kind and not in a group. Although the varieties are mixed, the planting pattern is quite regular and the flowers rise gradually towards the centre like a pyramid. Beds can be edged with low-growing plants such as box, pinks or daisies. Usually these are planted alternately, such as a pink next to a mignonette followed by a pink and so on.

In some beds tall plants are planted next to smaller ones, such as a hollyhock next to a phlox. Clematis or sweet-smelling honeysuckle are twined around straight hazel sticks giving the same upright effect. The more vigorous climbers should be pruned close to the support each year.

Colour is of course important. By using blue and grey tones it is possible to exaggerate the size of the garden. Bright reds and oranges can be used to accent or foreshorten certain parts.

In the smaller beds, herbaceous or annual plants should be planted in concentric rings towards the centre, where one or two larger plants such as hollyhock or guelder rose are placed. The same variety of plants may appear in the same bed but not adjacent to each other. In the larger beds where more shrubs are used, at least the first three rows should be planted to follow the outline of bed. However in the middle area the larger plants can be planted in rows, with the tallest in the centre. The edging can be planted in the same way as for the smaller beds.

Seasonal planting is also important. The central beds can be planted out for spring and then replanted for the summer. Flowers in pots can be plunged in the ground so that they look as if they are growing there naturally. The pots are removed when flowering is over and the plant can be grown on in the nursery for use the following year.

A selection of spring flowers used in the eighteenth century includes snowdrop, Christmas rose, crocus, daisy, primrose, violet, wallflower, daffodil, cowslip, anemone, hyacinth, tulip, lily of the valley, periwinkle, iris, crown imperials, gentian, trillium, London pride and cyclamen.

A similar selection of summer flowers includes delphinium, lupin, foxglove, honesty, tobacco plant, heart's ease, columbine, campanula, larkspur, hollyhock, sunflower, yarrow, stocks, pinks, sweet william, carnation, day lily, martagon lily, peony, thrift, St. John's wort, monarda, mignonette and valerian.

The English flower garden is rich and full of experiences 'which beautifully harmonize with that profusion of flowers and curious plants' (Repton). The colour and delicacy of this garden can easily be created and its intricate form is a delight to look at. Flowers require some maintenance, as with any herbaceous borders, but the design can easily be modified to almost any garden and can be a source of joy.

8

The Villa Garden

THE villa garden is romantic, colourful and practical. Flowers spill everywhere, even in baskets amongst other flower borders. Beautiful trees are planted as individual specimens on the lawn to be admired for their handsome shape as well as their botanical interest. Shape, colour and beauty are the essence.

Flowers are planted around the house and curl up ornate tracery of the overhanging veranda. Decorative pots adorn the balcony. The garden blends gradually from the graceful flowers set in the lawn to a shrubbery and rugged wild garden beyond. On the other side of a ha-ha or sunk fence lies a meadow or paddock sheltered by a belt of trees framing a distant view of, for example, a church spire.

These gardens were serious displays of their owners' status and they were occasionally pre-

A circular bed brimming with bedding of low-growing plants at Shrublands, surrounded by a ring of vases on plinths.

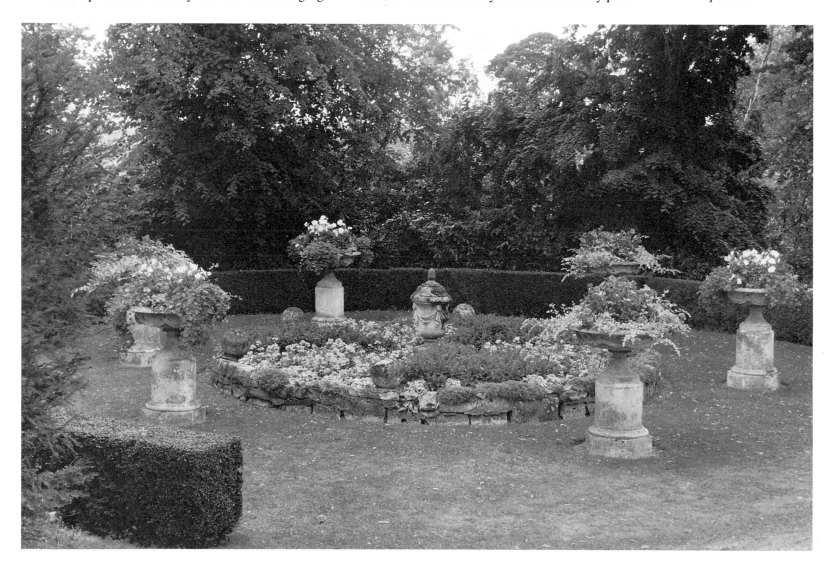

A feature characteristic of the villa garden, an Italian alabaster vase framed by a pair of Irish Yews.

The gaudy blue of the garden bench at Shrubland Hall with the blue metal garland above is typical of the villa cottage garden furniture and colours.

tentious. The villas were properties to be lived in all year round and so the gardens were intensive and filled with flowering plants to give an effect throughout the seasons. Many were designed by professional landscape gardeners and there are several contemporary books devoted to describing how to lay out these gardens (see Bibliography). Humphry Repton described them in 1816 in *Fragments on the Theory and Practice of Landscape Gardening* as 'giving the impression of informality and naturalness [when they are] actually very contrived and conform to strict rules on "taste". He elaborated some of the methods of designing these

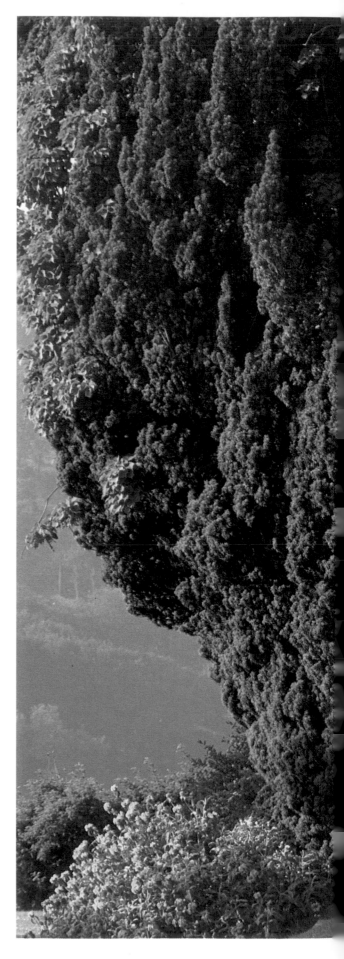

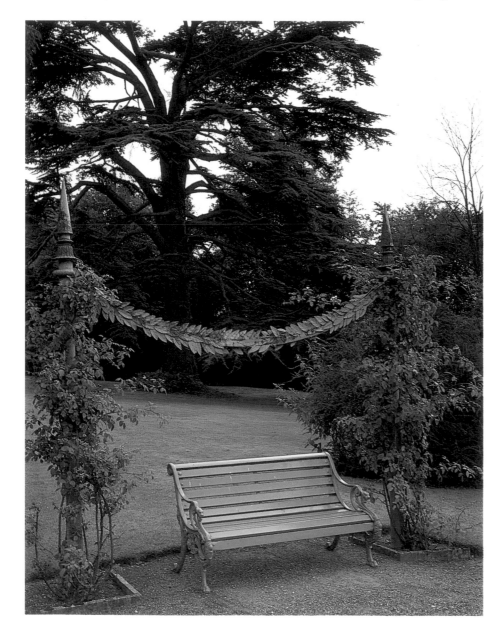

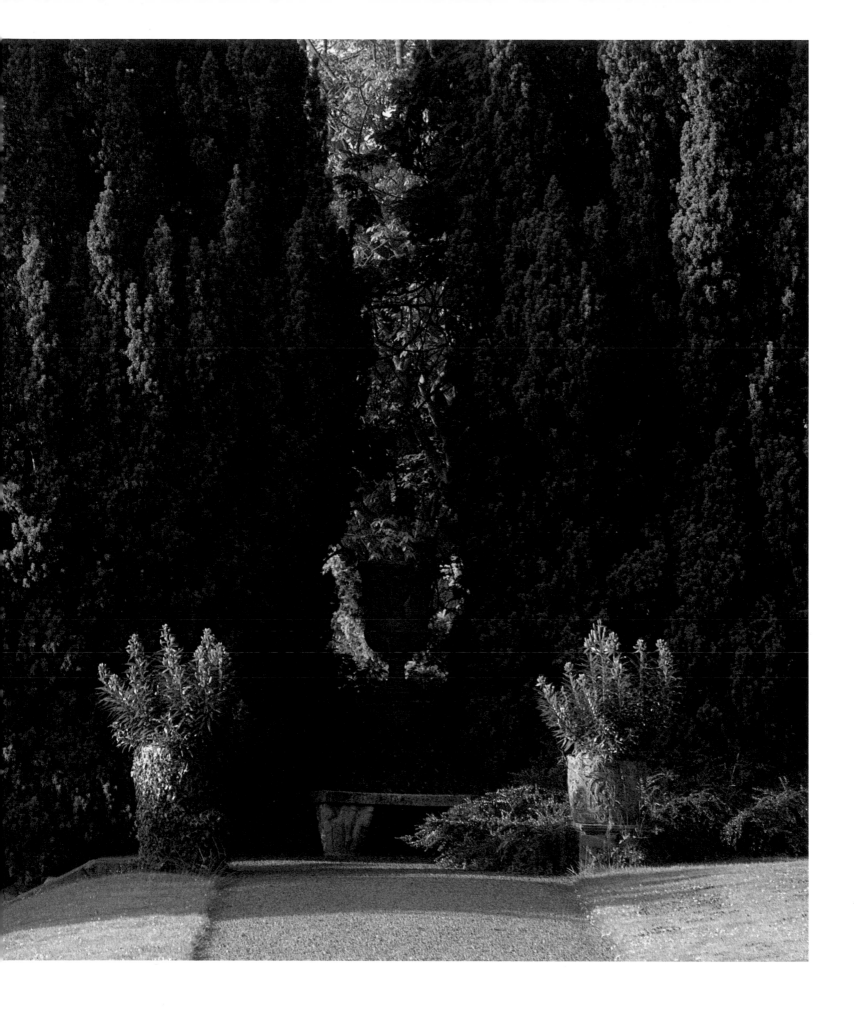

The plan of a villa garden. A path meanders from the verandah around the lawn, which, edged by shrubberies, displays single trees grown as specimens and circular beds of flowering plants. The different sizes of the beds are determined by their distance from others and from the path. Growing plants in a circular bed makes them easy to look at and to care for.

gardens by saying 'it is not by adding field to fields or by taking away hedges, or by removing roads to a distance, that the character of the villa is to be improved; it is by availing ourselves of every circumstance of interest or beauty within our reach, and by hiding such objects as cannot be viewed with pleasure.'

Although relatively modest in size, villa gardens packed in most forms of gardening. By the beginning of the nineteenth century the rise in prosperity meant that many more people were able to afford to garden and Repton explained that 'in the neighbourhood of every city or manufacturing town, new places and villas are daily springing up; and these, with a few acres, require all the conveniences, comforts, and appendages, of larger and more sumptuous, if not more expensive places.' Around their elegant Georgian and Regency houses, gentlemen wished to display all aspects of a much bigger property, including shrubberies, plantations, woodlands, parks, lakes, rivers, pleasure grounds, extensive kitchen gardens and all kinds of flower gardens as well as a conservatory adjacent to the house.

This 'gardenesque' style was cherished by Jane Austen and many other writers. Many of her characters discuss the 'taste' required in laying out these gardens. John Keats also was passionate about gardening and several of his poems recount the delights of his own garden in Hampstead, which is currently being restored. However, it was probably J. C. Loudon who did most to promote this style, which is described in detail in many of his books.

Examples can be found on the outskirts of most large cities and spa towns such as Bath, Brighton and Clifton near Bristol, but few remain today as they were laid out. The garden in front of Brighton Pavilion, designed by Humphry Repton for George IV, the Prince Regent, is currently being restored. The garden of the Admiral's House in Chatham Docks is also under restoration. Many villas and gardens were designed by John Nash, and those he planned within the circle at Regent's Park, London, are of the period though most have been radically altered.

Villas were built in response to the need for fresh air, clean water and healthy living and were very often placed just below the brow of a hill. This elevated position was able to provide good views over the surrounding countryside and across to a new lake or down to the river. Distant views framed by large trees were most prized.

The pursuit of painting and botanical study, particularly by the ladies of the house, opened up interest in the individual shape and growing habits of special trees and other plants. Thus it became important for these plants to have sufficient room to display their natural form and so

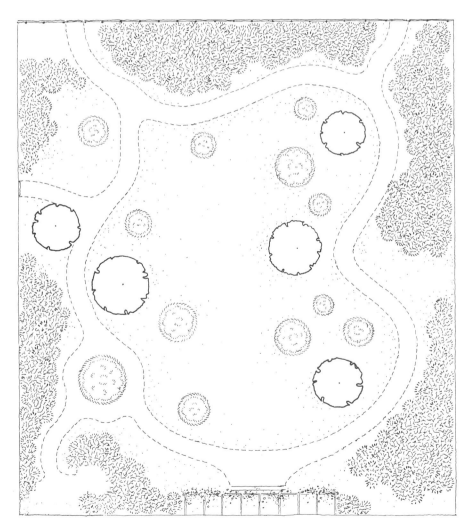

0 1 2 3 4 5 6 M

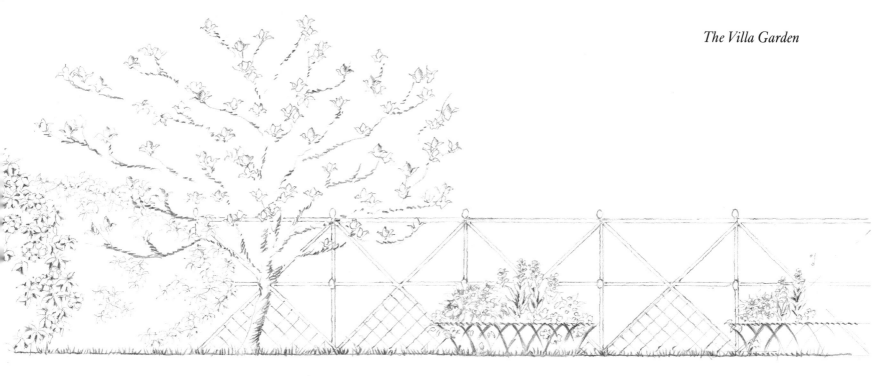

many were planted as single examples on the lawn.

The scene was set for the visitor on arrival at these villas. Space was usually limited and a turning circle was needed in which to turn round. Its shape and decoration provided the first impression of the property, and much emphasis was given to it. A large and stately fountain with a basin echoing the circular or oval shape of the drive was very popular. This might be replaced by an imposing statue or simply a 'cedar, or other evergreen'. Baskets of delicate iron tracery might edge the entire circle with bright flowers. The importance of the entrance was such that Loudon recommended that two or more houses should share the same drive so that it could be more impressive.

He also stated that, 'the classical pine or cedar should accompany the Greek or Roman architecture; the hardy fir, the oak, or the lofty ash, the baronial castle.' These should frame the house and separate the front and public facade from the secluded and private pleasure garden. An evergreen specimen of yew or laurel strengthens this barrier, which can be softened with flowering shrubs.

Stepping out of the principal rooms, a paved or gravel area provides a dry and comfortable approach to the garden. A south-facing facade can be shaded from the bright sun by a delicate wrought-iron canopy supported by light columns decorated with lacy tracery. Exotic climbers such as wisteria, grapes, climbing roses and passion flowers can be twined around painted wooden trellis attached to the walls. This veranda may be painted, the favourite colours being blues and dark greens but seldom white. When it is really hot, brightly striped blinds can be lowered.

Sitting out on these verandas or on the paved terrace was a favourite pastime of the Victorians and they covered them with extravagant displays of plants in ornate vases, baskets, urns and other decorated containers. These were filled with all kinds of exotic plants, many of which were brought out from the nearby conservatory for the summer. Urns and vases might be placed along the edge of the terrace, set at least 1 ft (0.3 m) above the ground on a retaining wall or a balustrade.

Walls or fences close to the house were festooned with greenery, and conventions developed that, for example, the 'water closets' should be covered with ivy and the pigsty with sweet-smelling clematis! Views from the terraces opened out onto wide expanses of lawn edged by shrubbery. More distant views to the countryside beyond were devised where possible by using a ha-ha and by framing the opening with trees from the shrubbery.

An exotic tree and flower beds in front of a decorative fence in a villa garden. The sketch shows the height of the beds related to those of the tree and the fence.

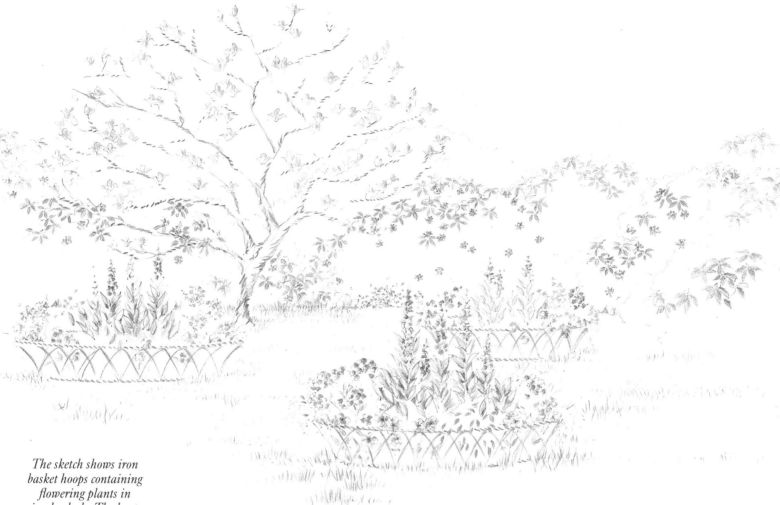

The sketch shows iron basket hoops containing flowering plants in circular beds. The hoops also serve to add decoration to the garden and to visually distinguish the flowers from their grass setting. In the background are flowering shrubbery and an exotic tree grown to display its natural form.

OPPOSITE
A view through a decorated verandah of a villa garden. In the foreground is a tripod with the favoured dried pampas grass, and flowerpots in the form of baskets. Note the delicate tracery of the verandah, covered with roses and fruit trees. Villa gardens are small but densely packed with colour and ornament.

Walking through the shrubbery was an activity frequently enjoyed by the ladies of the house and, according to Jane Austen, much of the social intrigue took place amongst the bushes! Connected to the house by a wide sweeping walk, the serpentine path bordering the shrubbery was covered with gravel and was at least 6 ft (1.8 m) wide. Where necessary the path was sunk below the level of the lawn so that the gravel could not be seen from any of the principal rooms.

Charles McIntosh in his influential *The Book of the Garden* (1853) writes that 'the great art ... depends on judiciously directing the winding of the walks, and varying the views of natural and artificial objects, so that the spectator may not always be aware that he is at times nearly retracing the ground he has previously passed.' Smaller paths leading to other parts of the gar-

den should meander from the main path past shady and leafy shrubs.

For winter and summer effect the shrubbery can be planted with 'an abundance of evergreens' mixed with exotic flowering shrubs and broad-leaved trees. Today there are many such shrubberies growing where the evergreen, especially yew, holly and both laurels, have taken over and swamped the more delicate flowering shrubs.

Around the edge of the lawn in front of the shrubbery and often on the other side of the serpentine path, trees are grown to 'stand free and distinct from each other'. The trees sometimes exhibit the shape and habit of a family or genus, for example rhododendrons, or plants from one part of the world, such as the west coast of America, so that the characteristics can be studied. These may be planted in groups of

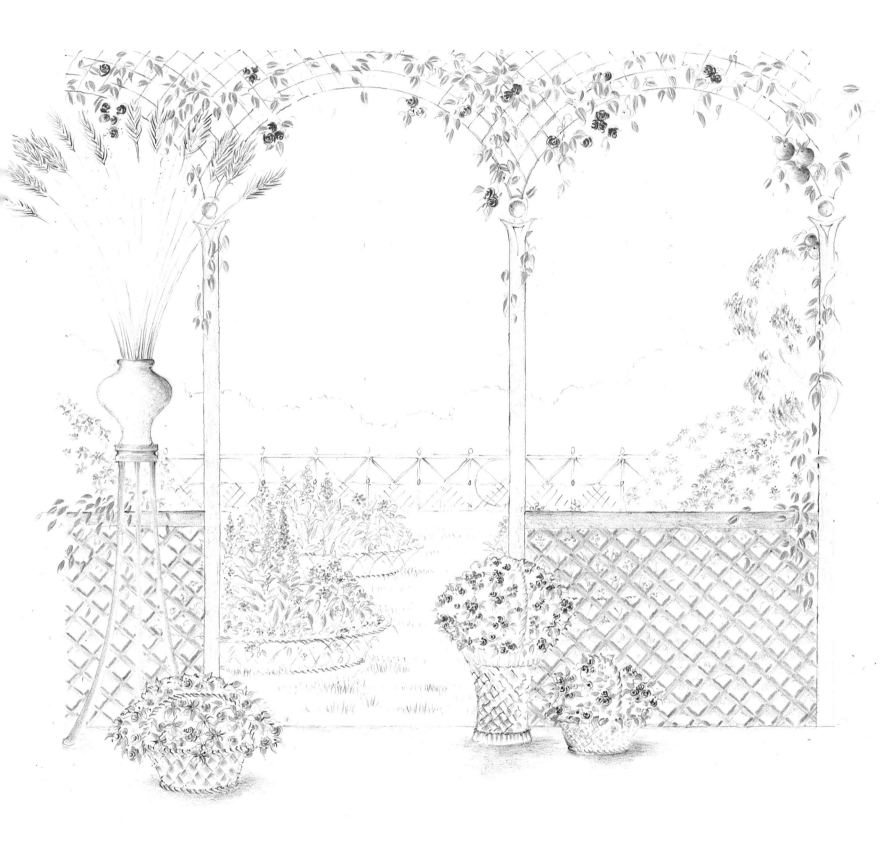

Baskets of Flowers

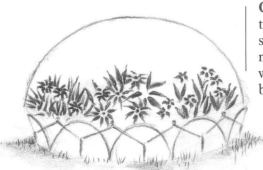

Basket Work 'A bed of flowers and shrubs within a basket looks like a bouquet of flowers' explained J. C. Loudon in 1824. He continued, 'they give a finished and enriched appearance to highly polished scenery and help to keep children and dogs off the beds.' Basket-work edging runs around the circular borders close to the house, along rectangular beds or even around the large pattern of a flower parterre. These edgings are low, 6–12 in (0.15–0.3 m) high. Basketwork can be woven out of willow or hazel shoots, and either left plain or painted. The design can be rather rustic, similar to a simple wattle pattern, or more delicate like basket work. The canes can be painted to match the colour scheme of the veranda or house. Ornate handles may be woven into the edging on either side like those at the side of a laundry basket or over the flowers like the handles of a carrying basket. Delicate basket work should be stored inside during the winter. This edging is fixed into the ground with a stout cane of about 12 in (0.3 m) woven into the basket at about 18 in (0.45 m) intervals.

Cast-Iron Wirework The delicate tracery of cast-iron wirework fills the same function as basket work and is much more durable. The strands of wire can be bent into many patterns but the simple half circle and diamond

patterns shown here were very popular. The wire is about 1/4 in (0.005 m) thick, and is bent into hoops about 1 ft (0.3 m) in diameter, which stand 9–18 in (0.23–0.45 m) high above ground level, with 9–15 in (0.23–0.38 m) stuck into the soil.

Each hoop can be placed adjacent to another one, or they can overlap each other by as much as two-thirds of the width, creating an attractive and tighter pattern as shown in the sketches. The diamond-shaped hoops can be used in the same way. Both patterns can also be used together, the

one alternating with the other. Individual hoops can be set into the ground, forming a portable and temporary edging, or they can be fixed on to a larger single strand of wire cast to look like rope. This can also be used to provide a basket 'handle'. Wirework is usually painted either black or dark green but, like willow baskets, it can be painted to match the colour of other woodwork.

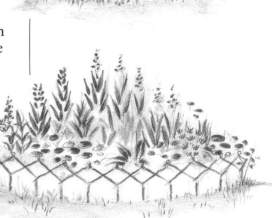

three, five or seven. The trees may be selected to demonstrate contrasting forms, such as an upright beech growing next to a pendulous one, or to display a particular characteristic such as thorns or variegated leaves.

On the manicured lawn between the specimen trees circular beds overflow with colourful flowers. These are placed on the lawn in artistic clumps and in the smaller garden 'the size of the circle should vary from 18 in to 10 ft (0.45–3 m) in diameter and be at least 3 ft (0.9 m) apart and thrown into groups or constellations as the stars are in the firmament' (McIntosh). In larger gardens the circles may increase to 15–20 ft (4.5–6 m) and 'ovals may be adopted but squares and polygons should be avoided.' Each bed should not be more than 12 ft (3.6 m) from either the gravel walk or each other.

McIntosh recommends that these circular beds should be 'of greater or lesser size: the former of these should be planted with flowering and evergreen shrubs only: and if each bed be limited to either different varieties of the same species, or to different species of the same genus, the effect will be enhanced. The smaller beds should be in like manner planted chiefly with flowering plants, either of one species or variety, or with different species or variety of the same genus.' He also advocates that some circles can be seasonally bedded out with bulbs and annuals but that 'no herbaceous, annuals or other flowering plants' should be used as edging plants to the shrub beds.

The layout should be simple. McIntosh explains that 'the difference in the sizes of the beds and the disposal of them on the turf, will produce a pleasing variety of outline that cannot be attained by any other means whatever.' While Loudon remarks that 'Flowering plants in beds, bounded with trellis work, on grass plots, will have the appearance of flower-pots, or baskets of nosegays, rising out of the ground.'

The Victorians took up this idea of baskets of nosegays, and many colourful circles were edged with either wicker work or cast iron

hoops rising 6–12 in (0.15–0.3 m) above the grass. Elegant handles could be fixed on the side or over the centre to reproduce the effect of real nosegays in delicate baskets. Loudon states that 'these wicker-work frames may be used with or without verdant edging ... they help to keep off small dogs, children etc.'

Intricately shaped delicate iron hoops may also be used to edge the beds. Each hoop is interlaced with another, producing a light edging about 12 in (0.3 m) tall. They may be placed individually or welded together in sections.

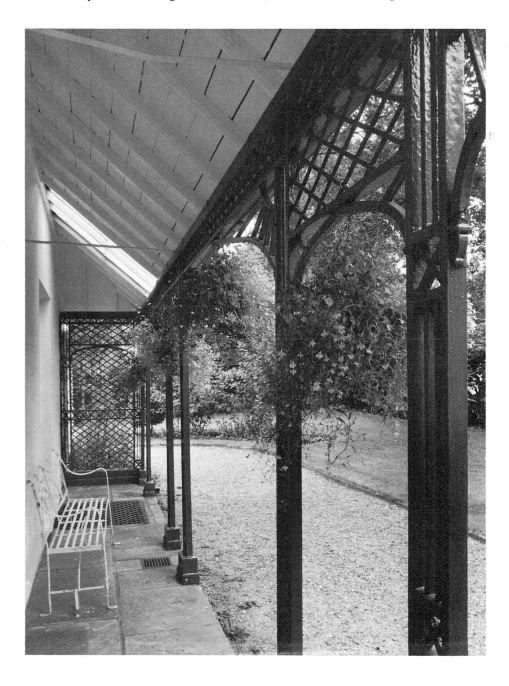

A pretty wrought-iron trellis forming a tiny verandah at Keats House, for surveying the villa garden.

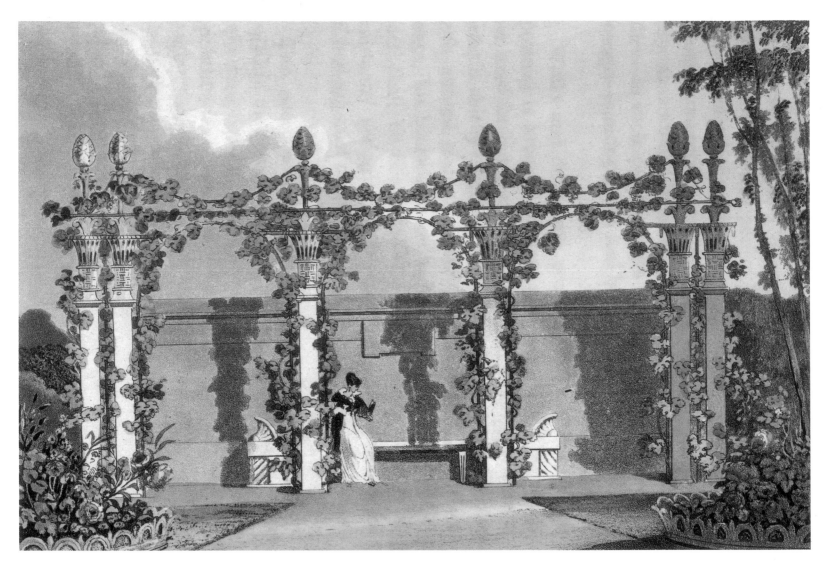

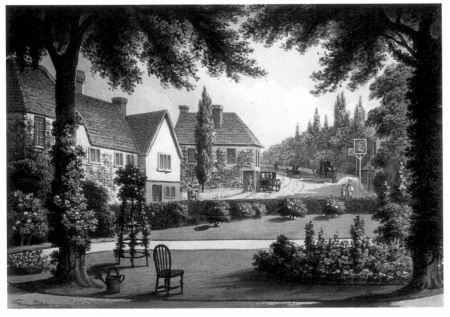

Edging plants can also be used, and the 'best is dwarfish box, thrift is the neatest.' The daisy, pink, London pride, primrose, violet, and periwinkle are all recommended as suitable edgings, and even the strawberry 'with the runner cut close during the summer will have good effect; the wood strawberry is suitable under the spreading shade of trees.'

'The flowers', according to Loudon, 'may be florist's flowers or herbaceous perennials with a mixture of dwarf shrubs . . . such as are showy, of brilliant and distinct simple colours, as white and scarlet lilies, red and white roses, nasturtium, candytuft, daisy, larkspur etc. They admit few yellows, or small scattered flowering plants; but study to have masses of the same colours and forms, contrasted by different colours in masses.'

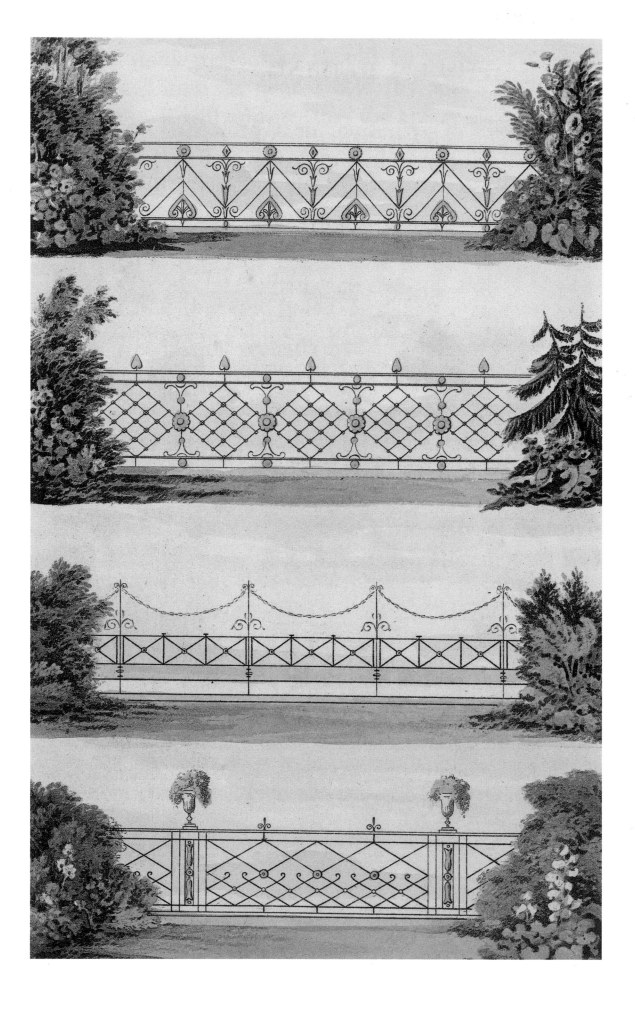

This engraving from John Buonarotti Papworth's Hints on Ornamental Gardening, *1823, shows four different examples of delicate and pretty garden fencing. Often made of wrought iron, the fences can be painted in any colour.*

OPPOSITE TOP
An illustration from John Buonarotti Papworth's Hints on Ornamental Gardening, *1823, showing a villa garden seat at the end of the garden, with very ornate rose-entwined columns. In the foreground are the circular flower beds edged by decorative wrought-iron hoops.*

OPPOSITE
BOTTOM
View from my own Cottage, in Essex *by Humphry Repton, from* Fragments, *1816, the plan for the improvement of his Villa garden. There are many different styles of growing flowers: within a circular bed, surrounded by hoops, are flowers of varying heights; climbers clamber up a simple frame placed on the lawn and up the trunks of trees; sweet-scented flowering shrubs grow individually in the grass. A basket-shaped flower pot is placed on the lawn.*

9

The Walled and Flower Garden

THE walled and flower garden is enclosed, sheltered and warm, where plants are intensively grown for admiring, for picking and for eating. In a small area, vegetables line up next to fruit bushes; flowers grow under the sanctuary of the limbs of apple trees; and herbs mingle with the roses. This style mixes flowers with vegetables and fruit and it aims to be both attractive and productive.

Sun and warmth permeate this garden. As it is usually screened by walls or hedges, it is like a 'secret garden' and most views are contained within it. Sheltered from the wind and protected from the cold frosts, here is 'one of the greatest comforts and even luxuries of a country residence' (Repton). All the senses are delighted and much pleasure is gained by looking at orderly rows of delicious vegetables; by examining the ripening of such delicacies as strawberries, redcurrants or raspberries; by appreciating the colour of tasty tomatoes or the heavy scents of flowers wafting on the warm evening air, or the taste of a perfect peach freshly plucked from the tree.

The style can be adapted to the space available and can be copied in the smallest of gardens if there is sufficient sunlight to ripen the vegetables. Not all of them need constant sun and some varieties can be grown in the shade but this restricts the range. Carefully planned, a small plot can provide fresh flowers and vegetables at every season.

In Britain, growing vegetables, fruit and flowers sheltered by walls has been going on for the past two thousand years. Until the mid-eighteenth century, when the 'natural' style became fashionable, the garden was close to the house, the walls of which were often used as shelter. However, since the eighteenth century the walled kitchen garden has usually been sited away from the house in the most favourable place, for example in a gently sloping south-facing and frost-free area.

Towards the end of the eighteenth century, Humphry Repton did much to popularize the pleasures gained from this style and emphasized not just its functional necessity. He saw that the walled garden could be used for the 'comfort and utility' of the family all year round. He suggested, in particular, the addition of evergreen plants to create dry, sheltered winter walks.

This garden required sunshine and shelter and from now on the site of a new garden was chosen with great care and skill. This was very noticeable in the less favoured climate of the northern regions, particularly in Scotland where without the warming walls the range of fruit would have been drastically reduced. Here, by necessity, the walled garden was sometimes sited some way from the house and might be attached to the stables or other outbuildings.

As science advanced and provided more ways to generate heat and power so the skills increased of growing exotic fruit such as pineapples and bananas, or tender vegetables such as melons, aubergines and peppers. Throughout the nineteenth century much time and effort was lavished on producing the widest available variety and on lengthening the ripening season.

The walled garden is usually laid out on a rectangle, with gravel or grass paths dividing it into four sections. The longest axis should run east to west so that the largest area faces south, preferably on a gentle slope. More ornamental shapes such as octagonal, oval or circular can be used. At least one side, usually that facing south, should be faced in brick.

The paths delineate the shape of the beds and usually meet in the centre at a circular feature, which may be a pond, well or fountain, or even a flower bed. A border bed runs around the perimeter, with a path next to it, which should be gravel if fruit is grown on the wall as this will reflect the heat. The border can be from about 4–8 ft (1.2–2.4 m) wide. If more depth is available for the border a service path can run along next to the wall in front of the fruit for easy access.

The walls on the north and east sides are usually taller and measure at least 8–12 ft (2.4–3.6 m). Along the south side the wall in smaller gardens can be lower, about 5–6 ft (1.5–1.8 m) to allow more light in and cast fewer shadows. The long blank walls of a house or stables can be used but often need to be extended to create a free-standing wall. Potting sheds and other offices can abut the rear of a wall.

Hedges, espalier-pruned apple trees, open trellis covered with vines, sunflowers, runner beans or other climbing plants can form the enclosure of the garden. Shelter from the wind is essential and tall trees are not favoured as their long shadows reduce the sunshine and thus the heat available. Throughout Britain there are many regional variations in climatic conditions and it is necessary to discover what these are. For example, in the north of Scotland where gales constantly lash the coast the walled garden is subdivided with additional hedges made from plants such as fuchsias, gooseberries and blackcurrants. In southern areas where the wind is not so strong or cold north-facing walls can be used for growing figs, blackberries and loganberries.

Brick absorbs heat during the day and gradually releases it during the night, and because

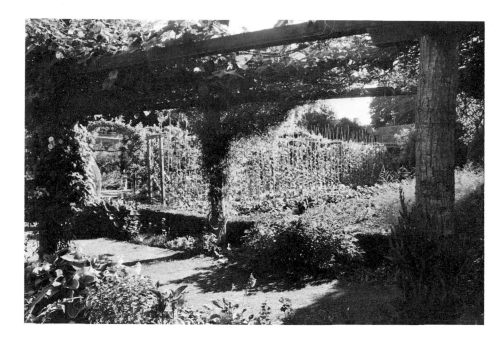

of this it is the favoured material for constructing the walls. Even in areas where the building material is stone, an inner skin of brick is often used, and back walls of fruit glasshouses are always built of brick.

Specialized walls were developed for growing certain fruit and for ripening cherries, apricots, peaches and nectarines. 'Hot-walls' were built from special heat-absorbing bricks, and lengthy boiler flues carefully wound their way through the wall, gently heating it and keeping the frost off the fruit. In quite a few larger kitchen gardens these can still be seen, particularly at Belsay Hall in Northumberland and Weston Park in Staffordshire. The type of brick bond indicates the use of the wall and its age. Detailed knowledge of the construction of specialist walls and more information about the many different types used in a Victorian walled and flower garden can be found in *The Book of the Garden* by Charles McIntosh, published in 1853.

It is important to protect the fruit tied to the walls, and various trimmings can be added, such as copings from which nets are hung to prevent birds and insects from eating the fruits, and hessian to shelter them from winter frosts. Grapes, peaches, nectarines, plums and figs may be grown in special glasshouses, but these are costly to maintain.

The width of the main path depends on the

A view at Heale through the flower-laden pergola onto the vegetable garden. Whereas the plants in the flower beds and growing over the pergola together form a rich, heady mixture of colours and textures, each vegetable, by contrast, is neatly displayed in a separate row, or tidily fastened to growing frames. The low box hedge serves partly to keep away white fly.

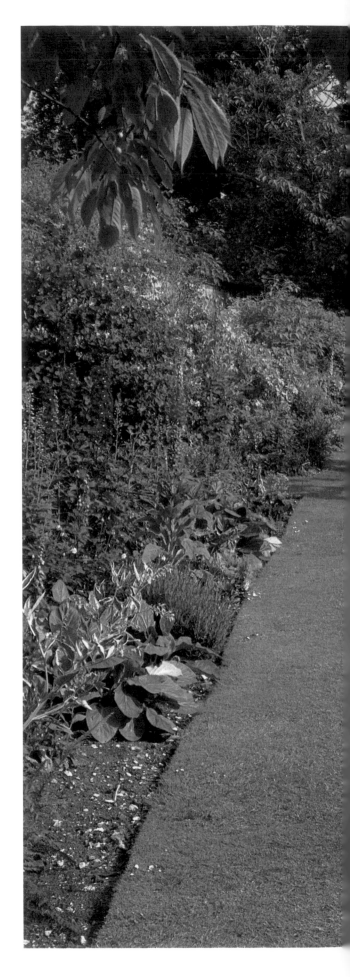

OPPOSITE

OPPOSITE
Heale garden, where growing vegetables and flowers decoratively together produces wonderful combinations of colours, textures and even smells.

At Brent Eleigh, rows of different vegetables create a pattern of varied greens and textures.

size of the walled garden and whether there are colourful flower borders on either side of it. If there is no border, then the path can be as narrow as 3 ft (0.9 m) but if there are broad borders on either side then it should be at least 6–8 ft (1.8–2.4 m) wide. The subsidiary paths are usually made with grass and must be wide enough for a wheelbarrow. The main paths are usually dressed with fine gravel, but narrower ones can be laid with an interesting brick pattern such as herring-bone or Flemish bond. In

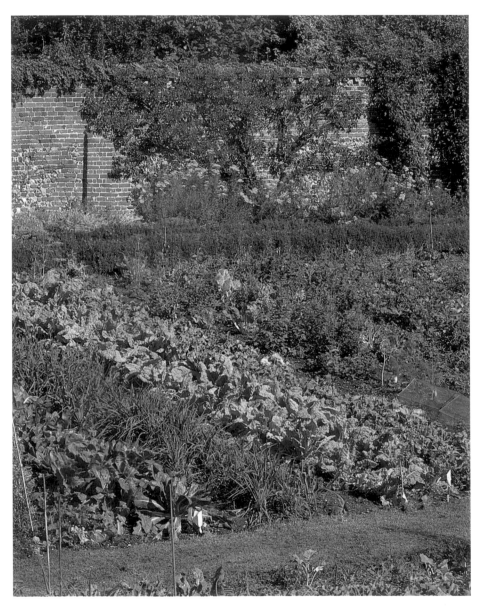

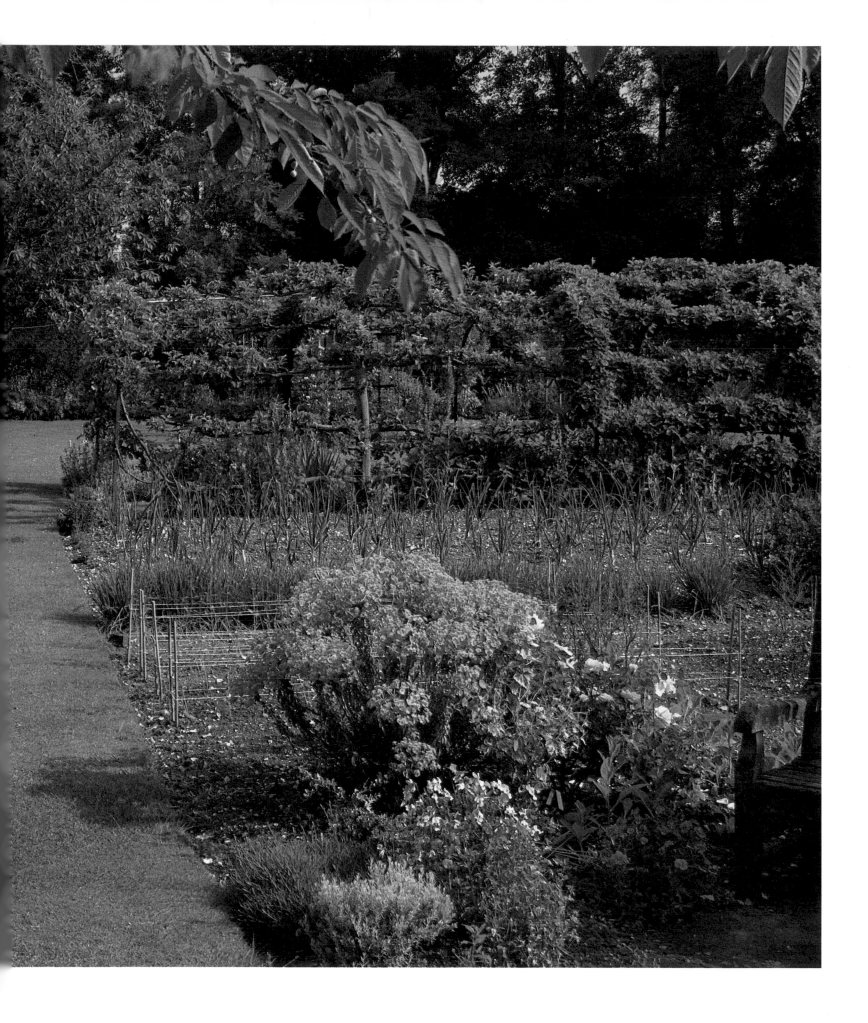

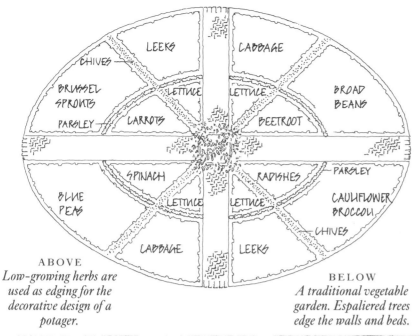

LEEKS · CABBAGE · CHIVES · BRUSSEL SPROUTS · LETTUCE · LETTUCE · BROAD BEANS · PARSLEY · CARROTS · BEETROOT · SPINACH · RADISHES · PARSLEY · BLUE PEAS · LETTUCE · LETTUCE · CAULIFLOWER BROCCOLI · CHIVES · CABBAGE · LEEKS

ABOVE
Low-growing herbs are used as edging for the decorative design of a potager.

BELOW
A traditional vegetable garden. Espaliered trees edge the walls and beds.

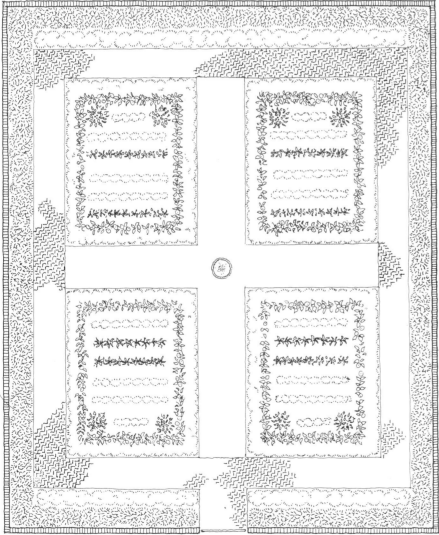

0 1 2 3 4 5 6M

the eighteenth century crushed cockle shells were very popular as path dressings. All the paths should drain well and be laid with suitable cambers and falls.

Good drainage is essential and much effort should be placed in making sure this is correct for all the plants grown. For example, peaches, nectarines and especially apricots thrive on well-drained soil. The soil itself requires to be constantly improved and dug over, with manure or mulch added in order to ensure healthy and delicious produce. A source for watering is crucial and stand-pipes should be placed at various points in the garden. Many older walled gardens contain a central ornamental fountain which splashes into a lily pond, or a decorative well-head to supply the water, if laboriously.

The paths can be edged with various borders such as brick, stone or terracotta tiles, or delicate wire hoops. These help to keep the edge firm, especially on well-trodden paths.

Many flowers can be grown in wide borders stretching on either side of the central paths. These cross borders can be planted in a similar way, such as four matching herbaceous beds, or each quarter can be different from the other: for example, a pair of herbaceous borders on one side; a pair of spring borders filled with primroses and bulbs; a border of one or two types of plants such as catmint and roses; and a narrow border of mixed hostas or lady's mantle. Flowers can also be grown over arches, doorways, tunnels and up the walls. Garlands of clematis may festoon the brickwork, or sweet peas may climb over light wrought-iron arches, creating sweet-smelling arbours over grass paths. Roses may drip over the wooden doorways, creating a romantic entrance to the enclosed and 'secret' garden. The variations are endless.

In larger gardens these borders may be backed by fruit trees fixed to a wire frame. These can be pruned into various shapes. Behind this line of fruit, are rows of vegetables carefully chosen to display their colourful foliage and assorted shapes. For example, a row of

Methods of Training Fruit

Pruning fruit trees ensures better fruit, as most require air and sun to ripen properly. Many beautiful shapes can be created which will suit the particular needs of different fruit. Apples are the most versatile and fruit will grow on smaller spurs on all ages of wood. Apples can be trained in almost all of the shapes shown except the double-mitre or pergola.

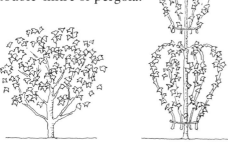

The espalier shape is formed by selecting a pair of shoots on either side of the main stem. Cut down the main stem to about 1 ft (0.3 m) from the base of the other two. The distance between the shoots depends on the pattern and can be between 9 in (0.23 m) and 15 in (0.38 m). The horizontal branches are trained on wires or supple willow stakes. In following years the pruning procedure is repeated until the desired height and pattern have been obtained.

Pears can also be trained as espaliers, cordons or fans and will fruit on spurs in the same way as apples, but they grow more readily on young wood than old so the older branches need to be removed regularly.

Peaches and apricots grow on the previous year's shoots and so their branches also need regular pruning. They can be trained in all forms of espalier, cordon and fan shapes. In Britain they usually need the warmth of a west or east wall in order for the fruit to ripen. Plums fruit on one-,

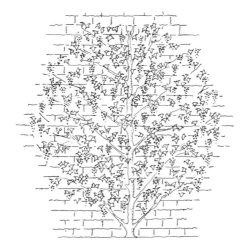

two- or three-year-old spurs and thus prefer to be trained in the fan shape. However, some varieties can be trained as espaliers or cordons.

Cherries bear fruit on first- and second-year wood and are usually trained in the fan or vertical fan shape.

Gooseberries produce fruit on all ages of wood but the younger branches bear larger berries. Most bushes just require thinning but they can be trained in a fan shape up a wall, or over pergolas or arched trellis. For this, gooseberries should be planted in rows 5 ft 6 in (1.7 m) wide about 3 ft (0.9 m) apart.

Black and red currants bear fruit on all ages of wood and can be grown as bushes or up walls, pruned in the vertical fan shape, or as the double-mitre shape, where the young shoots are tied to a metal frame. The brightly coloured bunches of fruit dangling from this figure are most attractive.

Raspberries bear fruit on last year's wood and all the old and weak stems must be removed. They can be trained up a pergola or as a bushy fan but are not suitable as an espalier.

Medlars and quince can be trained in all the espalier shapes or grown as a standard bush. Mulberries can be pruned against a wall, which improves fruiting in the colder regions.

Grapes can be trained up the wooden frame of a pergola, and vegetables, such as runner beans, and flowers, such as sweet peas and nasturtiums, can be grown up the supports.

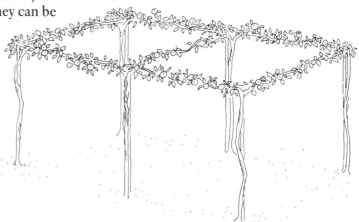

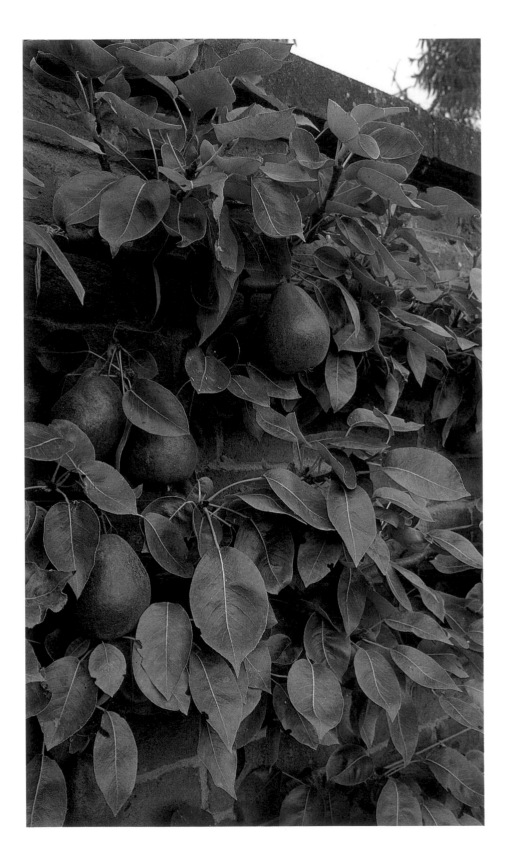

dark blue 'January King' cabbages may be placed next to a row of leeks; or different lettuces – the red leaf, curling leaf, and heart lettuce – make a striking pattern when planted together.

Today there is an enormous range of vegetables, most of which are known as 'separate cropping', which denotes those grown from seed in neat rows for ease of cultivation. 'Single variety' denotes varieties planted in patches at regular intervals for successive cropping such as beds of globe artichokes. 'Secondary crops'

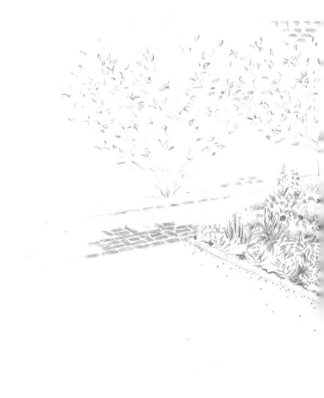

are those which are underplanted beneath a main crop, for example, summer spinach between rows of peas or beans. Traditionally, triangular glass cloches have been used to warm and protect young seedlings just pricked out. Today the more unattractive polythene tunnels have taken their place.

The varieties of vegetables grown depends on the needs of the cook but there are some delicious ones which can only rarely be obtained in the supermarket and which are worth growing, such as blue runner beans, blue peas,

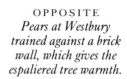

OPPOSITE
*Pears at Westbury
trained against a brick
wall, which gives the
espaliered tree warmth.*

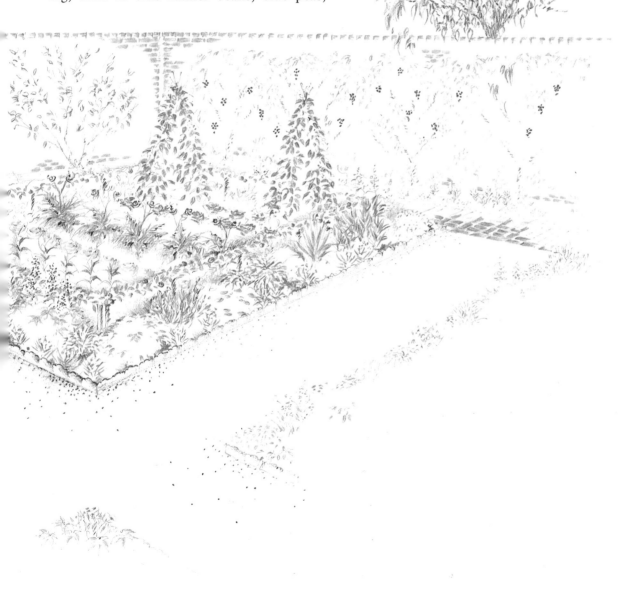

*A compact flower, fruit
and vegetable garden.
Low-trained apple trees
separate the vegetables
from the outside border,
which mixes flowers and
herbs. In the background
are runner beans trained
on poles like a tee-pee.
Against the wall grow
espaliered fruit trees and
bushes – they can be
apples, pears, plums,
peaches and even red
currants. The brick walls
generate warmth for the
espaliered trees, and
further warmth, against
frost, comes from the
brick path which runs
around the garden close
to the brick wall.*

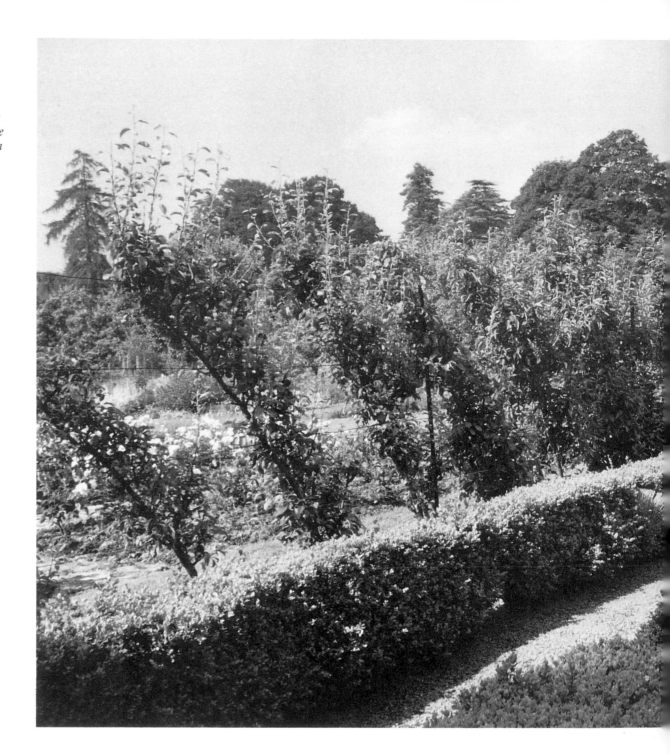

Rows of pears trained as cordons, with a box hedge beneath, are used to form a high hedge to a flower garden. The espaliered trees give shelter to the garden, but also form a decorative 'wall'.

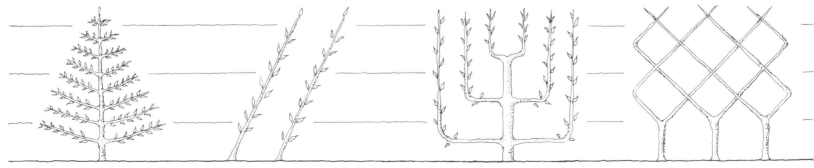

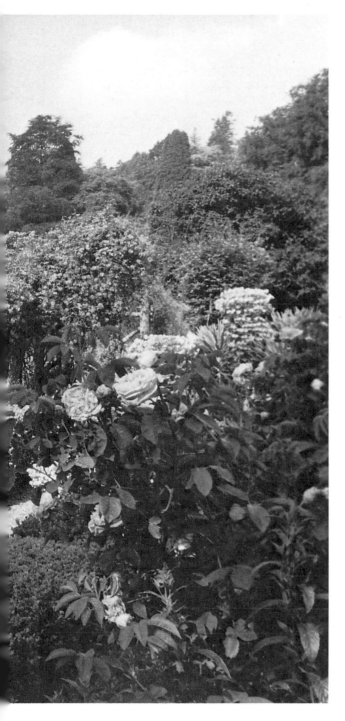

mange tout peas, and others which are easy to grow and much tastier if picked fresh, such as globe artichokes, all salads and courgettes. The delight of the taste of truly fresh vegetables is one of the greatest culinary treats, particularly if they are grown organically.

Vegetables can be grown in a pattern known as a *potager*. The tall stakes of runner beans act like spires and are placed at the four corners of a square. A small stone or brick path leads from each corner to a central feature, which may be either a seat or flower bed. Each path is edged with a herb such as thyme, parsley, chive or chervil. Behind these the vegetables are planted in rows around the perimeter or in lines towards the centre. A potager takes one of the patterns in the knot garden or pleasaunce garden and uses vegetables instead of flowers.

Even within an 'ordinary' kitchen garden there are more interesting ways of growing vegetables, such as training the red-flowered runner bean over arches of hazel sticks or bordering the paths with herbs, or using globe artichokes in a decorative way.

Special borders can be devoted to growing flowers for arranging in the house or for drying or pressing. Rows of irises, roses and delphiniums particularly may be grown in attractive and colourful patterns.

Fruit can also be grown in delightful shapes. For example, a double-tiered raspberry frame produces two festoons of berries. Red and black currants can be trained like a fan to cover a whole wall and clusters of bright berries are easier to pick as well as being decorative all year round. Gooseberries and black and red cur-

Fruit trees can be trained into quite stunning shapes. Here are eight examples showing how attractive they can look. From left to right they are: fan, cordon, upright espalier, lattice, low espalier, espalier, two branched espalier, and vertical fan. For all their differences, the aim is the same – to prune the buds to reduce the quantity of leaves so that the sun can bake the ripening fruit. Espalier patterns are best for apples, and cordons for pears, but all the shapes can be used for other fruit as well, such as plums, cherries, apricots, damsons and peaches.

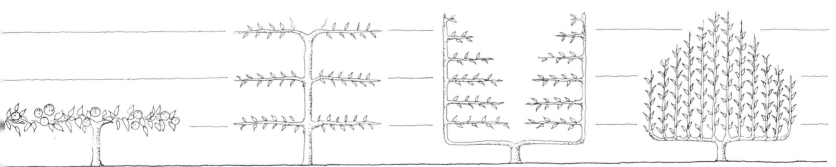

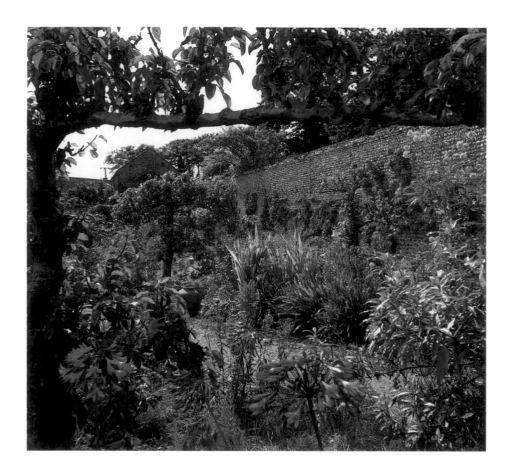

The walled garden at Wiverton Hall, Norfolk, looking through an espaliered pear tree across to the peach and pear trees on the wall.

tional buildings necessary for the workings of a kitchen garden, including a potting shed, tool shed, fruit room, apple store, boiler room, onion and seed room and a gardener's cottage. This can have an attractive facade, such as the portico at Yester, East Lothian; or a cottage orné covered in thatch and rustic timbers such as the one at Culzean, Ayrshire.

Ornamental pots can be used for growing lilies and other special flowers. These may stand out near the glasshouse or decorate one of the central paths. Large terracotta pots may be placed at regular intervals along a sheltered walk growing colourful flowers, some of which may be edible, such as nasturtiums or pansies. Others may contain invasive herbs such as mint, or herbs used all year round such as parsley, which can be moved into the greenhouse in the event of cooler temperatures. Rhubarb forcing pots are used to grow thin and delicate stems of this vegetable. Traditionally, many walled gardens contained beehives so that bees would pollinated the fruit. There have been many varieties of hives, such as the early straw beehives in the Tudor Garden, Southampton, or the Gothic beehouse at Chevening in Kent.

The walled and flower garden is a delighful place to sit. It is warm, sheltered and colourful. Rustic bowers swamped in roses tucked into a quiet corner have always been very popular and can be easily made from rough posts with their bark left on, of Douglas fir, sweet chestnut or oak. Alternatively the design may feature wooden seats or more ornate wrought-iron seats on which to sit and enjoy the prospect of the appetizing and plentiful treats in store. The garden is rewarding in many ways – not only to look at but also to enjoy the produce in gourmet dishes. It is also a pleasure to be able to walk around the walled area and bask in the warmth of the early spring sun when the rest of the garden is windswept and bitterly cold. The only requirement for treating this type of garden is a sunny site, as the design is adaptable to any size and can be created in any pattern. It is a garden of many pleasures.

rants make thick hedges and can be used to divide up the garden. However, the birds also enjoy the delicacies of ripe fruit so most should be grown in a fruit cage. These can be made from netting supported by wooden posts but they can be more ornamental if slim metal pillars are used. The cage should be high enough to allow the plants to stand erect and the netting should be black or brown, not green.

A working kitchen garden may well require a glasshouse to give the seeds an early start. There are many shapes of glasshouse, each with a specific purpose, such as a fruithouse for peaches, nectarines and cherries; another for vines, which require as much heat during the summer as possible; a melon house; tomato house; forcing house; orchid house and so on. The choice is wide. The glasshouse should be placed where it is warm and sheltered in winter. Around it can cluster some of the func-

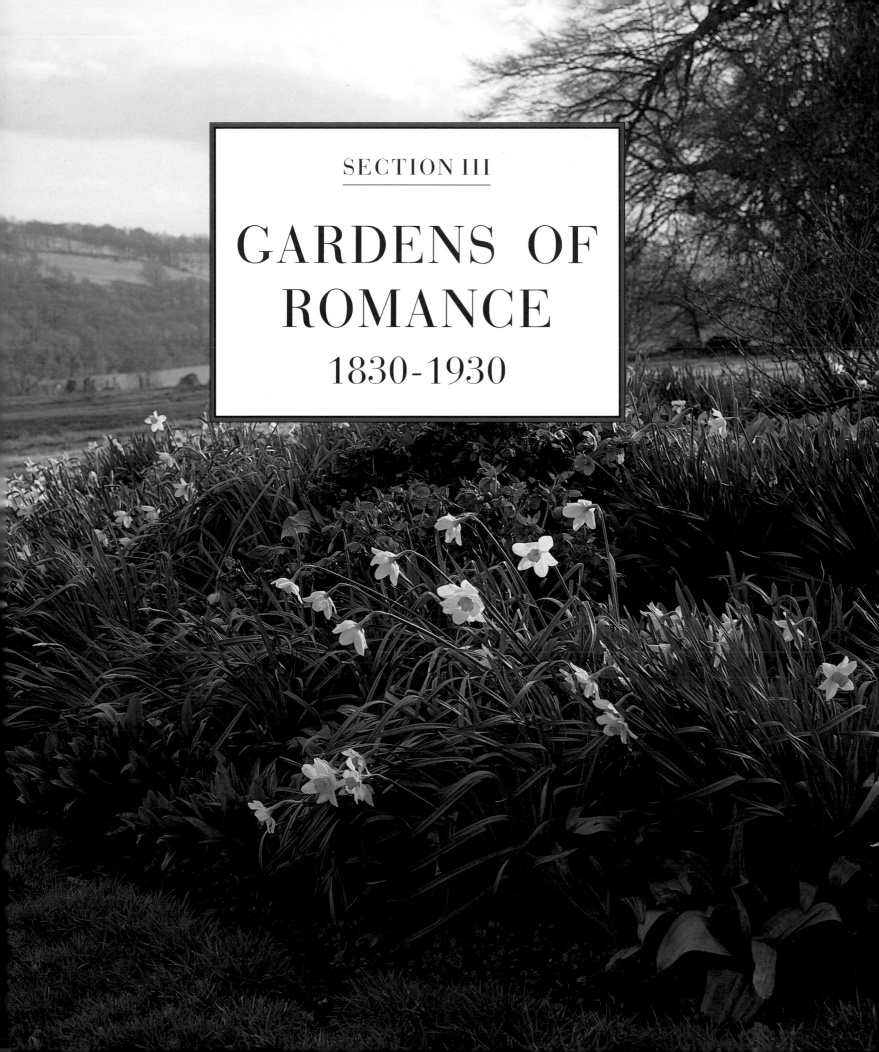

SECTION III

GARDENS OF ROMANCE

1830-1930

Introduction

PREVIOUS PAGE
The daffodils and the deep red hellebores at Hergest Croft dance in the spring light on the edge of the wild and woodland garden, against the spectacular view of distant hills.

Jets of water splash in the tropical conservatory, containing an enormous variety of exotic plants, including bananas, palm trees and orange trees in tubs.

THE Victorians gardened with enthusiasm. They enjoyed the flamboyance of spectacular displays. They were fascinated by scientific botany and stimulated by the romance of history, especially the chivalry of the medieval and Tudor periods. These interests combined to create large gardens of great confidence and scientific merit. They also created many formal ornamental gardens using designs copied from early eighteenth-century pattern books.

The Gardens of Romance were created in an atmosphere of rising prosperity generated by an explosion in technology and the growth of trading around the world. Science, engineering, education and the arts developed, producing professionals skilled in each particular area. This specialization of skills also occurred in gardening and led to the creation of gardens for particular types of plants, such as roses, or with certain habitats, such as the Rock and Quarry, Wild and Woodland and the Exotic Conservatory gardens. Gardeners and horticulturists developed expertise in one field.

The division of the garden into specialist areas is as attractive today as it was to the Victorians. By concentrating on the unique qualities of a plant, colour or season the result can be much more effective, the colours more intense and the variety more interesting. The Victorians loved all these special areas and habitats, and most large gardens contained examples of as many different kinds as possible, using an increasing palette of colours as many more varieties were being produced by hybridization.

Most Victorian gardens were laid out by professional designers, ably assisted by highly skilled head gardeners. The owner merely orchestrated the whole project, which often accompanied massive refurbishment to the house. Some of the most famous designers were architects, such as Sir Charles Barry (1795–1860), whose garden designs included Trentham, Shrublands and Cliveden. Other designers were professional gardeners, such as Sir Joseph Paxton (1801–65) and Charles McIntosh (1794–1864). Sir Joseph began as a humble gardener at Chatsworth in Derbyshire and rose to design the Crystal Palace for the Great Exhibition in London in 1851. McIntosh supervised the enormous Scottish gardens at Dalkeith Palace, Drumlanrig Castle and Bowhill for the Duke of Buccleuch and Queensberry; he also wrote a very influential book, *The Book of the Garden* (1853). William A.

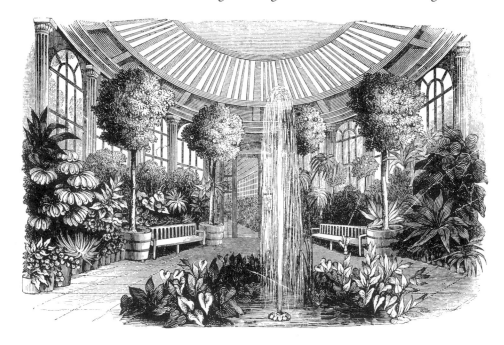

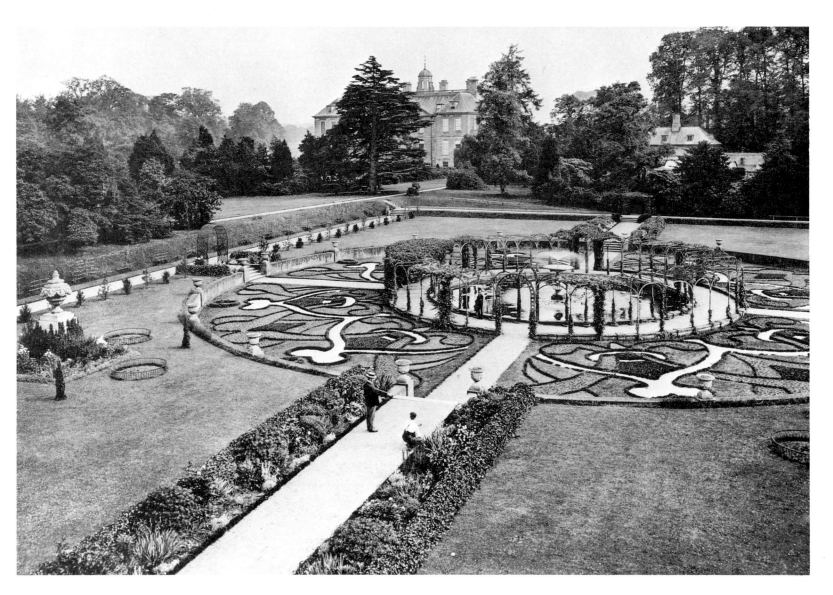

Nesfield (1793–1881) started as a painter and became an influential garden designer. He usually worked with his prolific brother-in-law, the architect Anthony Salvin (1799–1881). These four designers laid out many gardens in the Ornamental Garden style.

By the end of the century attitudes towards the vast ornate and artificial displays of the Ornamental Garden had begun to change. This was partly due to the influence of the Arts and Crafts movement led by William Morris (1834–96), which championed the use of natural materials such as wood and stone instead of man-made concrete and iron; and it was also partly due to the cost of upkeep.

In gardening, this resulted in the desire to naturalize plants, to encourage them to grow naturally in the Wild and Woodland Garden style. William Robinson (1838–1935) was the greatest publicist of this style and wrote many influential books. His garden at Gravetye Manor, Sussex, where he experimented with his ideas, is now being restored. Gertrude Jekyll (1843–1932) was greatly influenced by Robinson's ideas and added her extraordinary artist's skill to the colour mixes of planting.

Whilst Robinson took the romance of nature to heart, the romance of history, in particular the admiration for the controlled, symmetrical designs of the great formal eighteenth-century landscape, was advocated by another influential designer Sir Reginald Blomfield (1856–1942), and these two were great protagonists of their opposing theories.

The head gardener at Belton House, Grantham, directing the planting in about 1900. Outside the central rosarie is an elaborate broiderie parterre with swaths of intertwining colourful bedding and pale gravel.

OPPOSITE
In 1832 Lewis Kennedy laid out the dramatic parterre at Drummond Castle, in the shape of St Andrew's Cross – over 150 years later it is still stimulating and a model for inspiration to gardeners.

In the early part of the twentieth century two other designers stand out from many others in their influence on garden design. They are Harold Peto (1854–1933) and Edwin Lutyens (1896–1944). Both were architects and were primarily concerned with structural layout, such as walls, steps and terraces. Lutyens was concerned with using natural material and was deeply interested in historic buildings, so much so that their influence can be seen in much of his work. He worked closely with Gertrude Jekyll, and together they formed one of the most famous partnerships in garden design – Lutyens designing the layout, walls and so on and Jekyll the planting.

Throughout the nineteenth century, interest grew in plants as scientific specimens and much attention was given to developing them as economic crops. This impetus encouraged plant collecting as a sideline to the trading exploits of enterprising merchants in all corners of the world. Many sent plants back, but until the invention of the Wardian Box, only a few survived the rigours of the voyage home.

The recently formed botanical institutions such as the Royal Botanic Gardens at Kew and the Royal Horticultural Society in London saw the importance of collecting plants systematically, especially from the Far East, in particular Japan and China. So they sent out many collectors specifically to collect plants. Robert Fortune (1812–80) was one of these, and he introduced rhododendrons, tree peonies, deutzias, *Cryptomeria japonica* and many others. These intrepid travellers survived some quite hair-raising experiences and returned with vast collections of plants. Several nurserymen also recognized the opportunities and sent collectors abroad to bring back garden plants. James Veitch & Son was one of the most renowned.

We have all grown accustomed to the plants introduced at this period. Is there a single garden which does not have at least some of the varieties of rhododendrons, magnolias, primroses, clematis, roses, maples and conifers collected during the nineteenth century? Whilst this great influx of plants was arriving in the gardens, enormous strides were also being

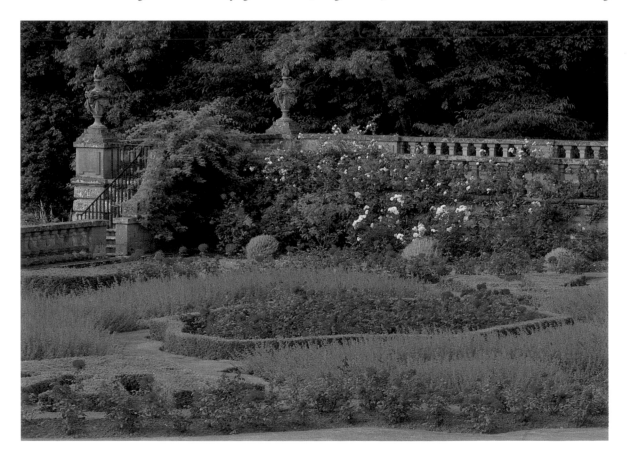

The parterre at Mellerstain shows the romantic effect of contrasting two strong colours – purple lavender and scarlet roses.

taken in breeding plants. Pansies, primulas, stocks and many stalwart annuals were hybridized to produce the brilliant technicolour of Victorian carpet bedding. They transformed seasonal planting by producing longer-flowering plants of a more uniform size. Plant breeding became an economic science. This huge increase in the range of plants available, whether they were new species from abroad or new hybrids, facilitated the growth of specialist gardens.

In the Ornamental Garden style brilliant displays were laid out on terraces close to the house. The parterres were designed to be seen from above or to walk through. Broad terraces provided space to entertain in and the low carpet bedding produced colour all the year round. Elegant pots filled with flowers decorated balustrades or emphasized grand flights of steps. It is a style of exuberant decoration, bright colours and intricate patterns, set on stylish terraces that evoke the grandeur of Italian gardens. The vitality of these designs can be easily re-created today.

The romance of the rose with its chivalrous symbolism sparked off the Victorian fashion for the Rosarie or rose garden. New skills of breeding produced many more varieties so that Rosaries could be filled with the delicate blooms and sweet scent. Protected and secluded, the Rosarie was often surrounded by an attractively shaped yew hedge, which created a sanctuary separate from the rest of the garden. This style is easy to create, and is breathtakingly pretty for its season, with the profusion of scents and colours of massed roses.

The Rock and Quarry Garden is another specialist style which first began in the late eighteenth century and became very popular with the Victorians. The arrival of many exciting alpine plants from abroad and the influence of the Japanese and Chinese styles inspired many gardeners to create wild and savage landscapes in miniature. Mountain screes, alpine meadows, rocky crevices were all carefully imi-

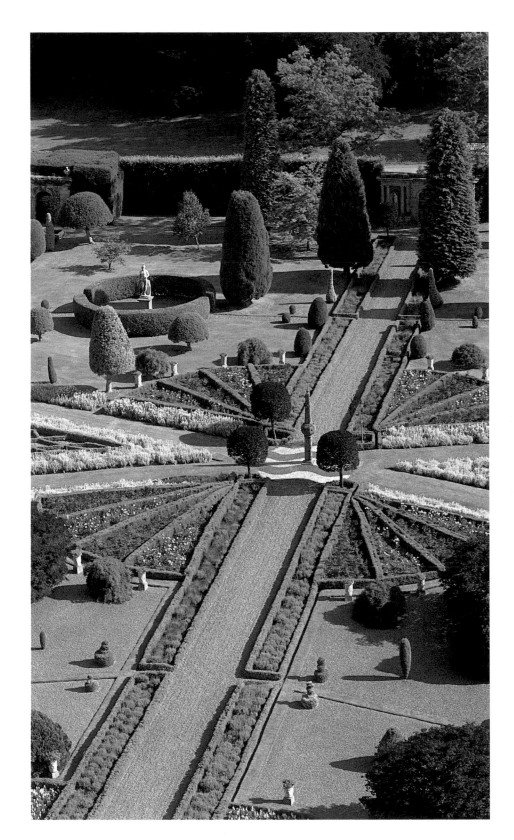

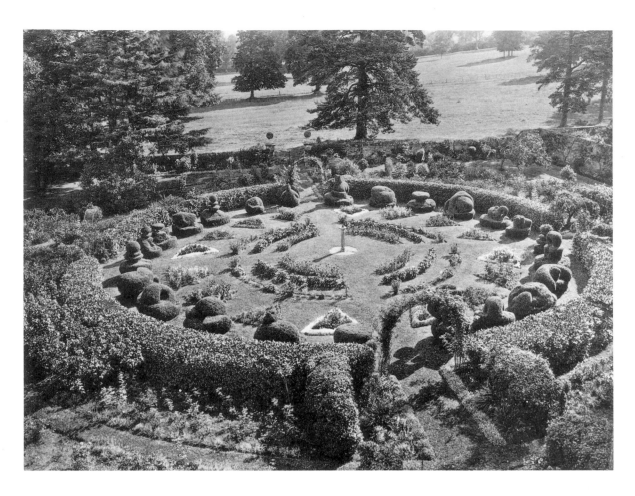

The circular garden at Chastleton, Oxfordshire, in about 1900 is a mixture of beauty and the absurd.

tated and planted up with a wide range of exquisite and delicate alpines. This style presents a challenge – it requires skill to grow the specialist plants, but it is rewarding when successful. It is possible to have different special flowers in bloom at all times of the year.

The Wild and Woodland Garden meets the desire to grow trees and shrubs in a natural wood. The Wild Garden is carefully created to grow as many plants as possible in a beautiful and apparently wild setting. Trees show off their unique shape whilst shrubs thrive and clamber together in organized disorder. These are attractive gardens and easy to create.

The Sheltered Garden is the style made famous by Gertrude Jekyll and Edwin Lutyens. The design harks back to the formal shapes popular in the early eighteenth century. The garden is made from natural materials and

planted with stunning designs. It is a garden of changing experiences, of small rooms, one leading off another. The soft and delicate colour tones of the planting combined with the strong shapes of the architecture make this an exciting style to re-create.

The Exotic Conservatory style is self-explanatory. It is a garden within the protection of a glasshouse attached to the house, where gardening can be enjoyed in all weather. It is a place in which to examine the latest plants or just to appreciate the feathery effect of luxurious foliage. Bright colours sparkle in the tiered displays and special plants can be grown in the borders. It is a place of contrasts, full of dark foliage, with scatterings of luscious flowers, and it can be used for year-round entertainment, an attractive extravagance providing many pleasures.

10

The Ornamental Garden

THE ornamental garden is bright, gaudy and decorative. It is usually near to the house and is laid out on terraces connected by steps. The exuberant and colourful patterned borders are filled with a wide variety of plants. Designed in all shapes and sizes based on a geometrical pattern, the beds can be filled with herbaceous flowers providing colour all year round, or bulbs in spring or annuals throughout the summer. Stunning shows can be created with this style of bedding, which rose to staggering displays at the height of its popularity in the late nineteenth century.

The ornamental garden augments the architectural style of the house. For example, a Gothic, mock-Tudor or medieval castle style might have 'geometrical' patterned parterres in keeping with the period. While for a classical Italian or Grecian Revival building the ornamental garden can be slightly softer and more 'gardenesque'. However, Victorian enthusiasm ensured that few of their ornamental gardens were historically accurate, and although most were based on seventeenth-century patterns they developed a style of their own.

In the ornamental garden spacious terraces

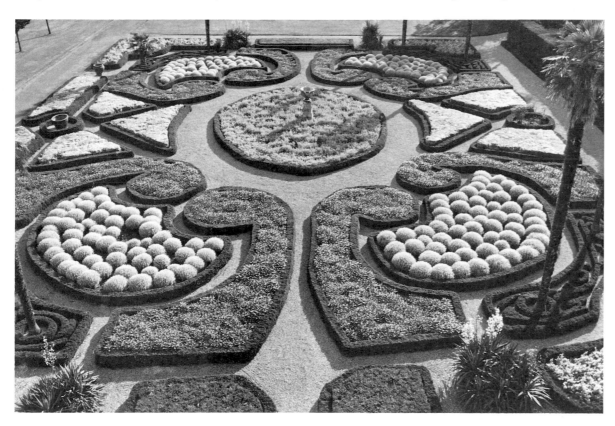

The highly decorative and exciting cutwork parterre at Chevening. It was formerly filled by a paisley pattern of bedding plants and is now planted with coloured herbs to give effect all the year round. The dark green box hedging gives a strong definition to the beds of different colours and leaves against the pale even texture of the gravel.

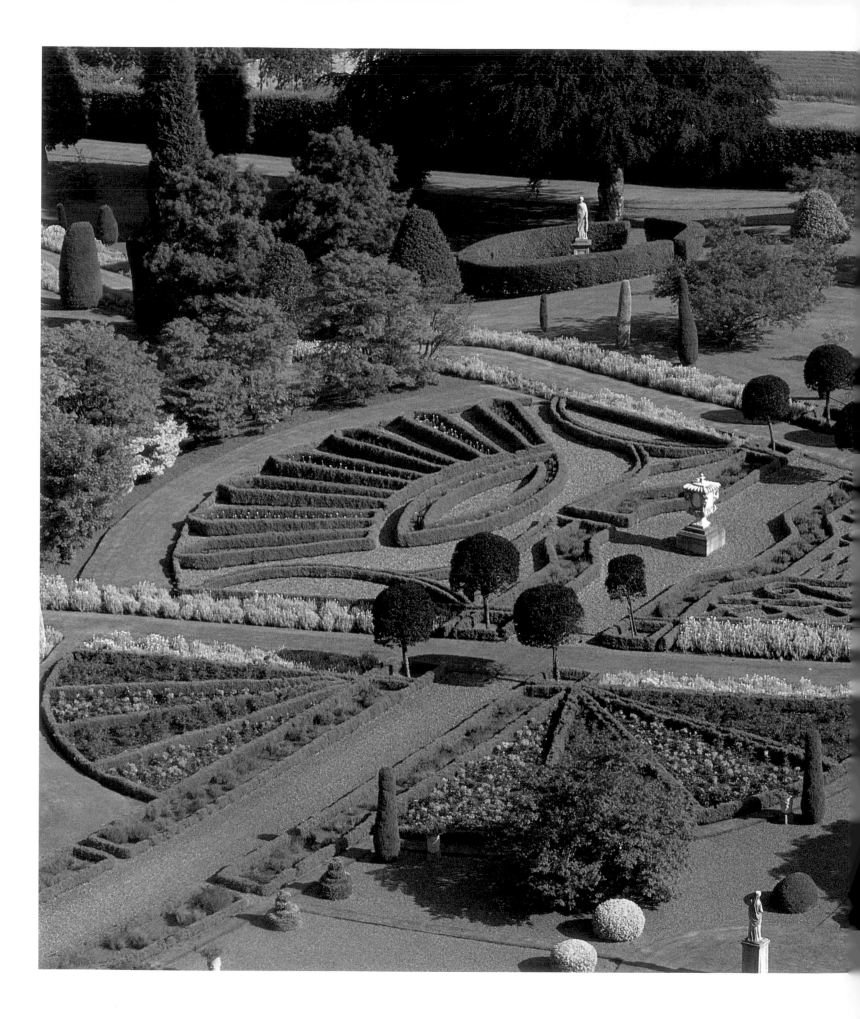

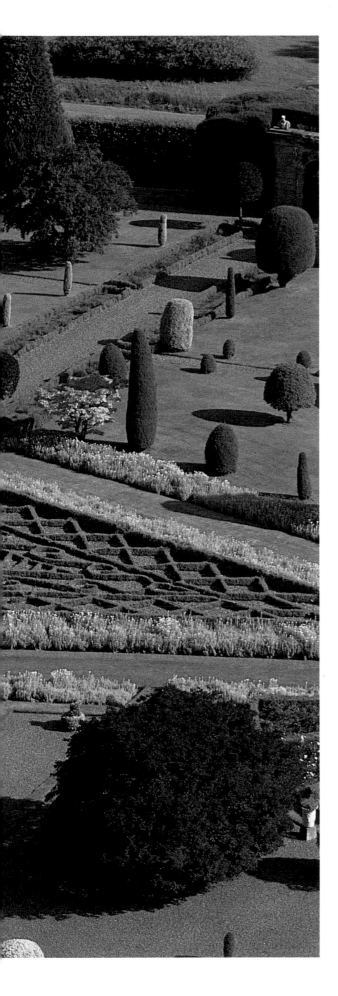

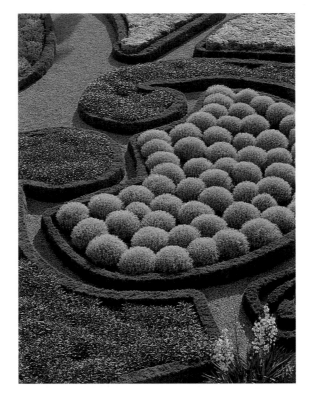

Part of the magnificent and breathtaking parterre at Drummond Castle, laid out in the shape of St Andrews Cross, and filled with plants of rich colours.

A detail of the parterre at Chevening showing the very strong and simple abstract pattern created by balls of grey Santolina chamaecyparissus, yellow shrub honeysuckle – Lonicera nitida 'Baggesen's Gold', grey leafed senecio – Senecio greyii, and purple sage – Salvia officinalis Purpurascens, all edged by low dark green box.

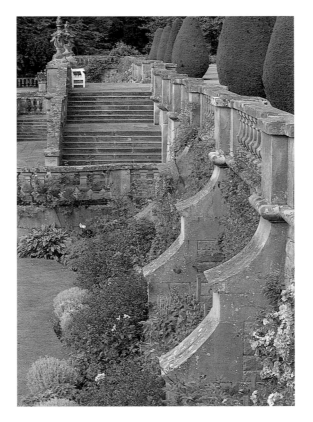

The dramatic sweep of the decorative buttresses supporting the high upper terrace at Mellerstain, and separating the richly planted borders beneath. Roses and Santolina grow in profusion and riot over the walls and up towards the balustrade. The architecture has an impressive presence in the atmosphere of the garden, as have the formal line of sentinel-like clipped yews.

border the house and are joined together by straight paths. Avenues of trees or shrubs can frame longer views or entrances. Rows of flower beds are set in symmetrically shaped lawns. The changes of levels between two terraces or different garden areas are decorated with all kinds of ornaments such as walls, balustrades, flights of steps, banks, statues and vases filled with shrubs or flowers. In the words of Uvedale Price: 'The more magnificent the mansion, the richer it is in architectural details, the more symmetrical and highly adorned with works of art the garden around it should be.'

The ornamental garden originated in the early nineteenth century to amplify the new style of architecture which harked back to the chivalrous medieval period for its inspiration. The style was the basis for most of the gardens around many new houses until William Robinson, a landscape gardener and writer, began objecting to the uniformity of its shape. Towards the end of the century, it combined with the softer and more artistic style created by Gertrude Jekyll and her followers to develop into the Sheltered Garden.

Improved gardening skills produced an explosion in the range of plants available and much effort was poured into hybridizing them. This resulted in the spectacular carpet bedding schemes so beloved by the Victorians. Many of the magnificent displays in public parks today are based on these schemes. At the height of their popularity, weekly articles appeared in the *Gardener's Chronicle* magazine extolling the magnificence and praising the intricate patterns of these carpets of flowers.

Most houses built or renovated in the later part of the nineteenth century sit on the terraces made for ornamental gardens, and so there are many examples of the style through-

out the country. One early example is the terrace garden at the Greek Revival house at Belsay Hall in Northumberland. Another is at Drummond Castle at Crieff, where the parterre is laid out as a St Andrew's cross; this style of parterre is typical of those attached to Gothic buildings, in this case, a ruined castle. The terraces and gardens of the seventeenth-century house at Weston Park in Staffordshire were created in about 1850. Those at Mellerstain House were designed later, in 1902 by Sir Reginald Blomfield, a renowned designer of the formal ornamental style.

In order that the magnificence of the garden – especially the decorative parterres – can be seen from the house, the main terrace should be set about 3–4 ft (0.9–1.2 m) below the ground floor. The house should be on a grass platform, with a straight walk running parallel to it above the main terrace. Narrow beds covered in a ribbon of low flowers can be laid out on the top terrace but only if it is wide enough. If the facade of the house has a broad bay window or a large projection then the top terrace should echo its shape.

The change of level between the upper and lower terraces can be taken up by a sloping grass bank with a low balustrade or clipped hedge along the top, or a low retaining wall capped with an ornamental balustrade. It can be adorned by vases or urns filled with flowers, or by other statues set on the piers. One or two flights of steps should be broad and straight, or narrow dividing into two flights which curve around a feature such as a fountain or bower. Or they may be at the ends of the terraces, where they may zig-zag like a staircase in order to take up a large level change.

The walks should be either straight or 'some segment of a circle. Their width must be ad-

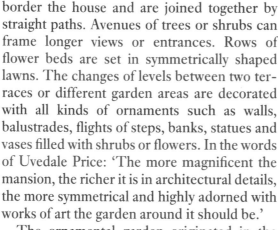

A section through an ornamental garden. It reveals the many contrasts that are found in such gardens: the height of the balustrade with its plinth and elaborate vase on top; the low-planted ribbon border below; the width of the border to the thin, narrow balustrade; the clear determined outline of the balustrade and vase to the natural growth of the border. The latter has stone edging, and on either side is a grass path.

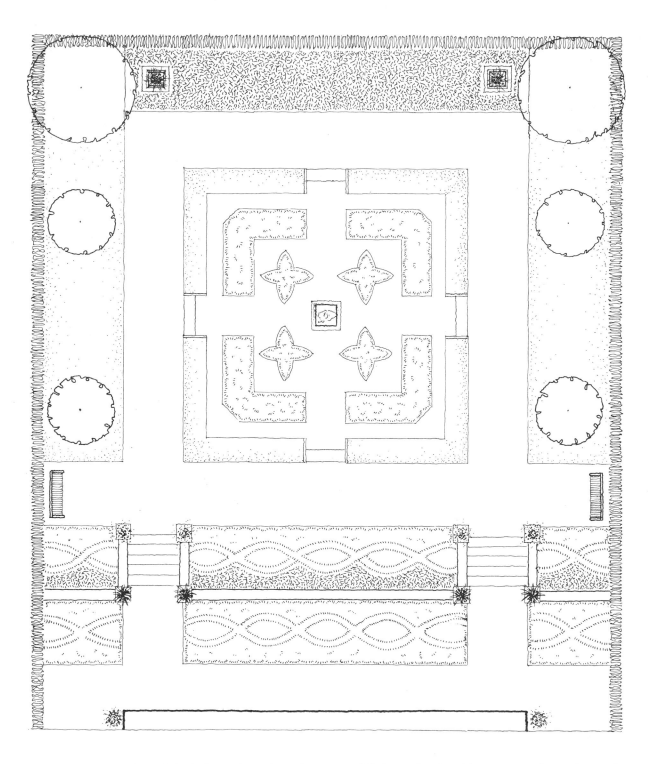

Stepping out of the house the guest is dazzled by the narrow border of brightly coloured annuals. The simple pattern is repeated from one end of the bed to the other and flows like a 'ribbon'. Hence its name, 'ribbon border'. Behind it is a low balustrade of stone or brick and each column can be adorned with an ornate vase. Two larger ones can emphasize the flight of steps leading down to the lower parterre. Laid out symmetrically, it is designed to be seen from the upper windows or as a surprise when an unsuspecting guest walks out onto the terrace and is startled by the riot of colour below. More subdued herbaceous borders frame the centre bed and the magnificent garden is enclosed by a yew hedge.

0   1   2   3   4·M

justed to their length.' A long broad path should end in a feature some way beyond the terrace, giving the impression of a much larger garden. For example, ornaments such as statues should not be placed at the centre crossing of long walks because they disrupt the scale, but a group of shrubs planted at the crossing can mask a shorter length.

All the paths should cross at right angles and the end outside the terrace should lead to objects such as vases, statues, seats, alcoves, temples, urns, sundials, ornamental pedestals or evergreen shrubs. These can be clipped into topiary, particularly if associated with a Gothic style of house. Otherwise rhododendrons were the most favoured shrubs, but Portugal laurel, bay and holly can also be used. In larger gardens, a yew grown as a tree, a cedar, hemlock or Douglas firs may terminate the path, but these must be planted as individual specimens. Stone ornaments will stand out better if they are framed by an evergreen group. Not all walks should end in planting particularly if a pleasing view can be highlighted.

Enclosed by gravel paths, the ornamental garden is filled with mass plantings of different shapes. Some of the parterres are copies of those given in John James's *The Theory and Practice of Gardening* (1712), and have been described in the Knot Garden (Chapter 3). Other shaped borders cut out of the grass and filled with flowers are uniquely Victorian.

Circular flower beds are still the most desirable shape especially for growing single specimens or clumps of shrubs. But 'oval figures or oblong shapes with circular ends or numerous combinations of curved lines uniting at an angle will, if symmetrical, be more garden-like than purely angular ones. Their chief require-

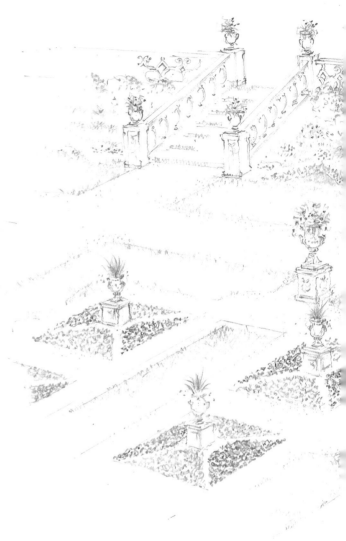

The very striking pattern of the strapwork parterre at Shrubland Hall – filled with brightly coloured annuals, foliage, and pale shades of gravel, and all held within the simple geometric lines of box hedging.

OPPOSITE
View from the Upper Terrace, Shrubland Hall, Suffolk, *by E. Adveno Brooke, 1856. Designed by Sir Charles Barry from 1849 to 1854, the garden and terrace was the peak of drama, romance and ostentation – a 19th-century Hollywood film set, and one of the greatest gardens of the century.*

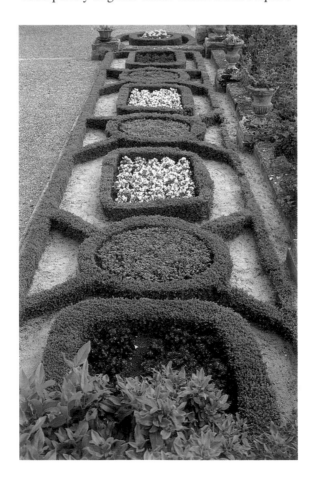

ment is that they should be regular; that is that their several parts should balance and correspond.'

Ribbon-like patterns repeating a simple design can run along the top small terrace directly in front of the house and usually contain short bedding plants so that the lower garden can be seen over them. In the lower garden, beds of different shapes can be grouped together to form one geometric pattern.

In his influential book *The Practical Gardener*, first published in 1817 and reprinted in many editions, John Abercrombie states that 'either a

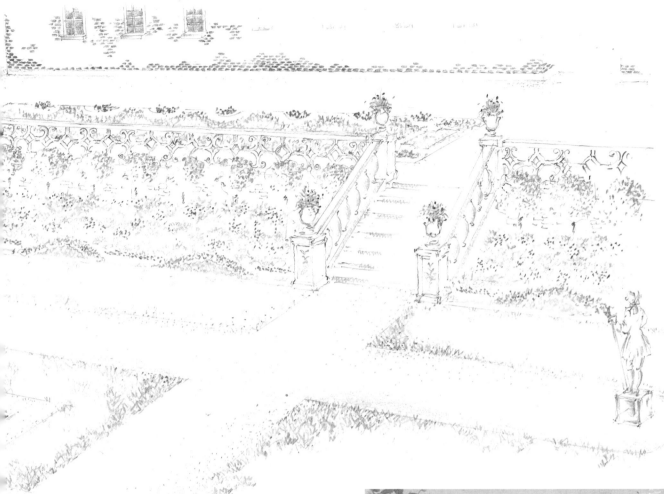

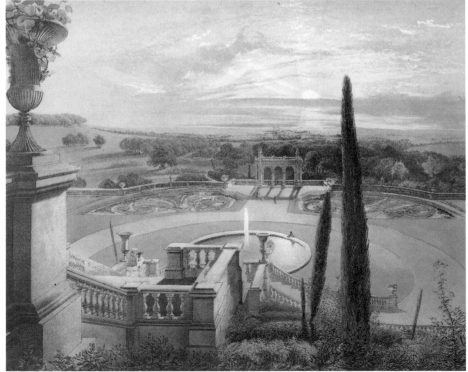

The plan of an ornamental garden outside a house. On the top terrace is a ribbon border of bright and colourful plants. It is important that the level of the border is kept low and the height of the plants does not interfere with the stone pattern of the balustrade. Formal steps lead down to the lower garden, with its bright herbaceous borders and path-edged formal parterres. The colouring of the latter should be extremely strong and dazzling, against the grass setting.

square or oblong ground-plan is eligible; and although the shape must be adapted to local circumstances, it is desirable that it should be of some regular figure.' Mrs Jane Loudon in the *Florist's Manual* explains 'the difficulties of disposing of a few borders in turf ... to form a connected glow and ... when viewed from the windows of the house or from the principal entrance of the garden, one border should not intercept the beauties of another ... that the vacancies between the borders, forming small avenues ... by which the whole is separated into broken parts and the effect is lost.'

Balustrades and Wall Decorations

can be fixed with mortar on top of each plinth and pilaster. The vase can be made from cast stone, stone, lead, concrete, cast-iron, fibreglass or terracotta but it is important that the latter two materials are strong enough to withstand the weather.

Statues, pilasters with balls and other decorations can also be placed on the piers instead of the vases. However, the more decorative statues should be seen in relationship to the house or

Balustrades, parapets, vases and statues are used to add decoration as well as uniting the architecture of the house with the garden. The patterns must emphasize the style of the house, for example, if the house is Grecian or classical then the balustrades should reflect this style, with the columns and plinths made from stone or cast stone. If the architecture is more Gothic or Tudor and uses bricks and tiles then the balustrade should copy this and be constructed of the same materials.

other built feature and not on their own. Busts and urns are often best seen in niches or adjacent to a wall.

The balustrading sets out the proportions of an ornamental garden and outlines its shape, particularly during the winter months.

Balustrading can be made from moulded materials, cast stone or clay tiles. A simple balustrade can be made from brick with large drainage tiles used for the columns. The coping can be made with a paving tile which is then covered with stucco and painted.

The columns are supported by pilasters about 3–5 ft (0.9–1.5 m) apart, and a larger pier finishes off the wall bordering steps or other breaks. A vase

The herbaceous plants and shrubs filling these patterned borders can be divided into five classes. The types are: the general or mingled flower garden; the massed flower garden; the select flower garden; the changeable flower garden; and the botanic flower garden. These are clearly explained by J. C. Loudon in a later edition of his *Encyclopedia of Gardening* published in 1878. He states that the mingled flower garden 'is to mix the plants so that every part of the garden may present a gay assemblage of flowers of different colours during the whole season'. Loudon explains how a border in the mingled style should be planted. He suggests that the plants should be divided into four colours – red, white, blue and yellow; the flowering period is divided into six times; and the bed divided into four rows, the 'lowest plants placed nearest the walk and the tallest at the back in regular gradation'. Most plants are spaced about 18 in (0.45 m) apart and planted in concentric rows in circular beds or in straight rows in borders on either side of a walk. By the mid-nineteenth century, the mingled style was not as popular as the other classes.

In the massed flower garden 'the flowers are planted in masses of one kind, either in separate beds, or in separate divisions of the same bed'. The effect of 'arranging the flowers in masses of one colour . . . is striking and brilliant . . . intended to produce the effect of a Turkish Carpet in which the pattern is defined by masses of colour strongly contrasted with each other: each bed presenting a different colour, and being filled with one kind of flower.'

Colour is very important in these borders and the Victorians really enjoyed quite garish mixtures. Contrasting colours and the effect of different colours on each other became a study in itself and several influential books were written about colour composition.

Colour can be divided into two classes: warm ones, including reds, oranges and purples; and cold colours, including blues, greens and yellows. The warm colours complement cold ones and vice versa. White complements all colours.

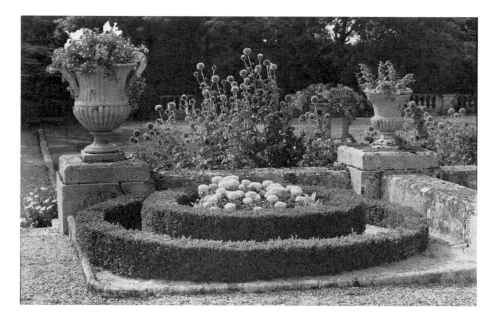

For example, cold colours can be placed next to gravel, which is buff and a warm colour. On the other hand, grass being green and therefore a cold colour complements warm ones such as red. Then there are recognized colour opposites. For instance, yellow complements purple and orange complements blue because they are opposite to each other. Thus the colour composition of a border might be red followed by white, then yellow by purple, or orange by blue.

A compound colour such as purple should never be used between the two primary colours that create it, i.e. blue and red. Two primary colours can be placed near to one another but only in small quantities, such as a speck of yellow or red adjoining a mass of blue. The same can apply to compound colours such as a speck of yellow or red next to a mass of purple.

The best effect is when single plant types are massed together and the colour contrasts with those of neighbouring beds. Sometimes a band around the edge is needed in order to set off the main colour. For example, 'cold' flowers (blue, yellow) growing on grass might be contrasted with a strip of flowers of a warm colour such as red, orange or purple.

There are further refinements of these colour combinations. The combination of a pair of primary colours is better than that of a primary and compound colour, especially if the latter contains the primary colour of its pair. For example, red and yellow blend better together

A corner of the garden at Shrubland Hall showing an ornamental garden in miniature. The two bold circles of hedge are separated by gravel, while densely planted bright-coloured marigolds fill the centre. Behind two vases overflow with flowers, while a bed of Echinops rises up between them.

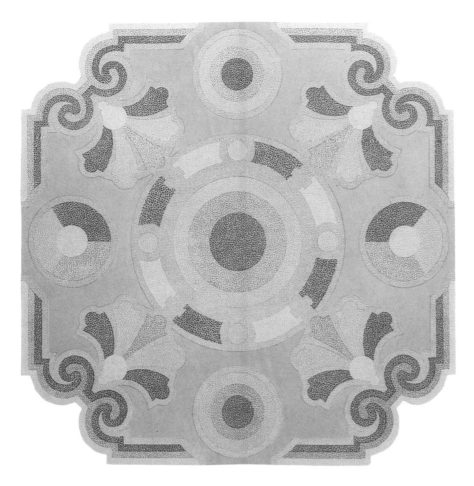

Engraving from Charles MacIntosh's The Gardener. *The primary colours of red, blue, yellow and green set in pale gravel form a range of contrasts, juxtaposing strong reds and yellows to weaker blues and greens.*

Scheme of colour relationships in an ornamental garden

The most intense colours in the massed flower garden should be placed at the centre, gradually softening towards the margins of either the parterre or an individual bed. As McIntosh explains, 'Hence bright scarlet makes the best centres, and whites the best margins.'

In order to intensify the colour in such gardens, the plants were kept as near the ground as possible by pegging them down, 'so as to display the plants without showing any of the leaves or stems'.

The third class is the select flower garden, limited to so-called 'florist's' flowers, American plants, annuals, bulbs and so on. Sometimes this type can be mixed, such as bulbs and annuals together, but the best effect is obtained by limiting the borders to one sort.

The fourth class is the changeable flower garden in which all the flowers are kept in pots and plunged into the beds in succession or whenever the last flowers are over. Hyacinths, pinks, dahlias and chrysanthemums are particularly suitable.

The final class is the botanic flower garden in which the plants are arranged for study and not for a 'rich display of blossoms'.

The ornamental garden exemplifies the Victorian exuberance and confidence. It is 'the most capable within a given space for more grand and magnificent effect than any other ... a greater profusion of richly sculptured and highly artistical decorations'. Pattern, colour and simple shapes mix together to create a panoply of decoration and ornament. Parterres of the earlier periods were copied and fantasized into more grotesque and larger-than-life shapes. Although requiring some care and attention, these gardens are gorgeous displays of pomp and vitality.

than red and orange. Similarly, if a primary colour is blended with a compound colour it is better if the compound one is brighter than the primary one. For instance, red and violet contrast better than blue and violet. Another way of arranging colour in the larger and simpler patterns is by using the principle of a rainbow, thus red next to orange followed by yellow, green, blue and violet.

For example

dark blue	orange	sapphire blue	black	green
dark brown	scarlet	pea-green	violet	salmon
black	sea-green	scarlet	dark green	buff
violet	green	scarlet	dark blue	

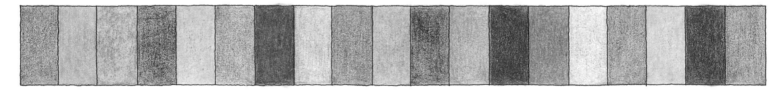

11

The Rosarie Garden

A ROSARIE is a garden filled with roses either festooning as garlands or freely flowering as bushes. Enjoyed only in the summer when at perfection, this garden is a collector's paradise displaying all kinds of roses. Romantic, fragrant and secluded, the delicate blooms are sheltered by tall evergreen hedges.

Roses are symbolic. They are celebrated in legends, given as tokens of passion, esteem and fidelity and used as emblems of allegiance. In the fifteenth century, the red rose of Lancaster and the white rose of York were the symbols for the two sides in the Wars of Roses and were used to decorate many Tudor buildings.

Roses have been grown for at least the past three thousand years. The first cultivated roses came from Persia, and by the sixteenth century four varieties – *Rosa gallica, R. moschata, R. damascena* and *R. alba* – were widely grown. By the late eighteenth century the number had increased to about a hundred varieties and in 1799 Empress Josephine created the first col-

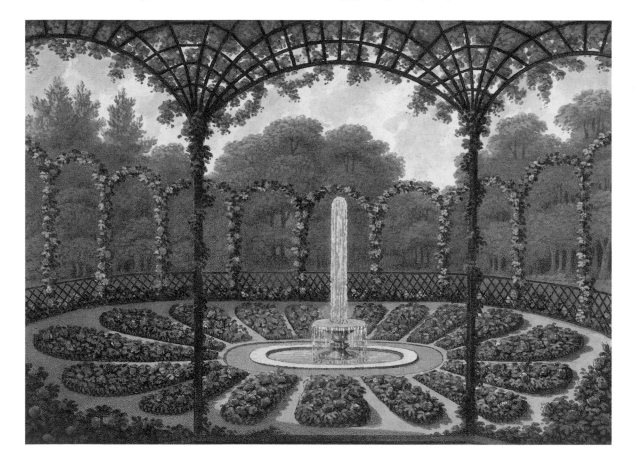

Humphry Repton's 'The Rosary at Ashridge' from Fragments on the Theory and Practice of Landscape Gardening *(1816). It shows a wooden trellis supporting climbing roses which wind round the post and are trained to flower on the trellis above. The petal-shaped beds, edged by basket work, surround a central fountain.*

lection of roses at Malmaison in France. Her garden devoted solely to roses laid out in small beds was an entirely new idea and instantly established a fashion which quickly spread to Britain. By 1816 Humphry Repton had designed a rosarie in his garden at Ashridge, but as most of the roses only flowered once a year and the colours were restricted to white, pink and red, his garden was severely limited and restrained compared to those of today.

By Victoria's reign most gardens had a rosarie, rosarium or rose garden. This was partly due to the romance of the rose, particularly its heraldic symbolism from the Middle Ages, an era which the Victorians loved, and partly because of the desire to collect botanical orders systematically.

Several rosaries still exist today and there is a particularly good early nineteenth-century circular one at Rockingham Castle, Northamptonshire. The walled garden at Mottisfont Abbey, Hampshire, contains the National Trust's 'old-fashioned' rose collection formed in the 1960s by their adviser Graham Stuart Thomas. At Polesden Lacey, Surrey, there is a good Edwardian rose garden. The National Rose Society's garden at Chiswell Green,

Hertfordshire, displays a wide collection of all kinds. The Royal Horticultural Society has planted two rose gardens at Rosemoor in Devon, showing the modern roses such as hybrid teas and floribundas in one, and the old-fashioned roses in the other. A rosarie has recently been planted in the walled garden at Castle Howard, Yorkshire. There are, of course, many other rose gardens open to the public.

Rosaries are gardens in which to display roses and to delight in the beauties of a single bloom. So 'the nearer these can be brought to the eye the better' states William Paul, a noted Victorian rose grower, in his influential book *The Rose Garden*, published in 1848. He continues 'in the formation of the rosarium, it appears to us that the simpler the forms of the bed the better ... and parallelograms, squares, ovals, circles and other regular figures are in perfect harmony with the character of the plants, admit of the most perfect arrangement, and display the roses to the greatest perfection.' Later he recommends that the rosarie 'should be formed of a few beds and sizes suitable to the space at hand, with gracefully-curved outlines and few points or angles, as Roses do not fill these angles satisfactorily'.

Rosaries can be circular, square or rectangular in shape. As Charles McIntosh said, the paths should 'bring the visitor close to the object to be viewed and ... enable him to reach the flowers without going off the walks'. The main cross walks should be made from gravel or, in smaller gardens, from patterns of brick such as herring-bone. Fresh green grass sets off the colour of roses so the beds are often bordered by grass strips at least 1 ft (0.3 m) wide. McIntosh recommends planting bulbs and annuals in the rosarie 'so that there would be, first a show of early bulbous flowers, then a grand display of roses, and lastly, the show of annuals'. As roses today flower for much longer it is not so necessary to plant annuals to prolong the colourful flowering period.

The rose garden at Rockingham Castle is an

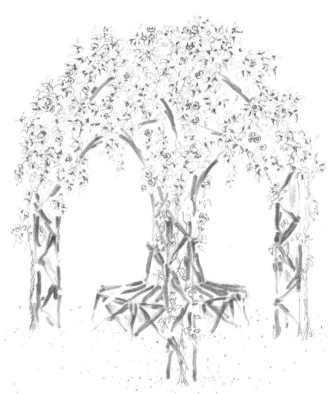

A wooden rustic arbour with a round circular seat supporting roses cascading romantically down from above.

excellent example of a circular rosarie laid out in the 1830s. It can be viewed from the high mount which was formerly part of the castle keep, where the circular shape and concentric pattern can be clearly seen. Entering through a 12 ft (3.6 m) hedge under curving arches of yew, the four cross paths meet and enclose a large circular feature in the centre. This used to be a fountain, but it has recently been replaced with a statue. Garlands of roses supported on delicate wrought-iron pillars linked together with swags of lightly twisted wire rope used to surround the central beds in which the finer noisettes and hybrid perpetuals were grown. These were not replaced when they disintegrated in the 1950s.

All the individual rose beds are rectangular, but as they are laid out in concentric rings following the circular yew hedge they are smaller along the inner side than the outer. At the outside the beds are about 6 ft (1.8 m) wide, narrowing to about 3 ft (0.9 m) wide. The length depends on their position in the rings of beds. Taller roses should be planted at the back in the longer outer rings, with the smaller ones in the shorter beds nearer the paths.

A rosarie is usually enclosed by a tall evergreen hedge about 8–12 ft (2.4–3.6 m) high. Clipped yew was most favoured and could be pruned into fantastic shapes using different coloured yew such as the yellow and variegated forms as well as the upright Irish variety. These shapes could be most amusing, with hedges clipped to look like elephants or castellations around the garden. In the later part of the nineteenth century this kind of topiary became an art form and some of the figures were pruned into twisted corkscrews, arbours shaped like temples or, more extravagantly, huge crowns, using the different colours of yew and box to form the shape. There is a good example at Megginch Castle, planted in the rose garden to celebrate Queen Victoria's Golden Jubilee in 1887.

In some gardens topiary itself became predominant and yew was clipped into the figures

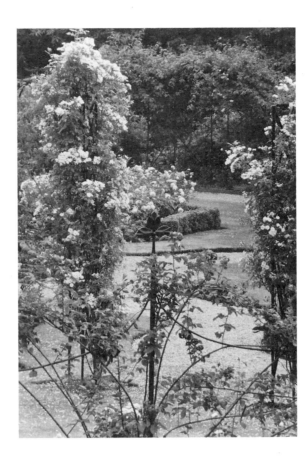

Warwick Castle rose garden showing the delicate tracery of the wrought-iron frame for rambling roses. Behind are two tall upright pole roses framing another bed of bush or dwarf roses, edged by a low box hedge.

in a game of chess or to depict a nursery rhyme or children's story such as *Alice in Wonderland*. These figures are made by fixing a wire frame firmly into the ground outlining the grotesque shape. It should be just slightly smaller than the finished figure and the plant is trained, tied and clipped to its support, which thus becomes the guideline for pruning it.

Common laurel and Portugal laurel can also be used for hedges or topiary in more informal situations but they are not as good as yew. In more open areas a rosarie can be surrounded by a shrubbery of mixed evergreens such as laurel, holly, yew and box. Quantities of the native Burnet rose or Scotch rose can be planted amongst the shrubs to soften them.

Roses are rich feeders and enjoy warmth and sunlight, so avoid overhanging trees which will cast too much shade and with large roots which will absorb all the goodness. The soil should be constantly improved, dug over and well prepared. Well-rotted manure is still much favoured but more modern substitutes are available. If fertilizers are used make sure that additional organic material is added.

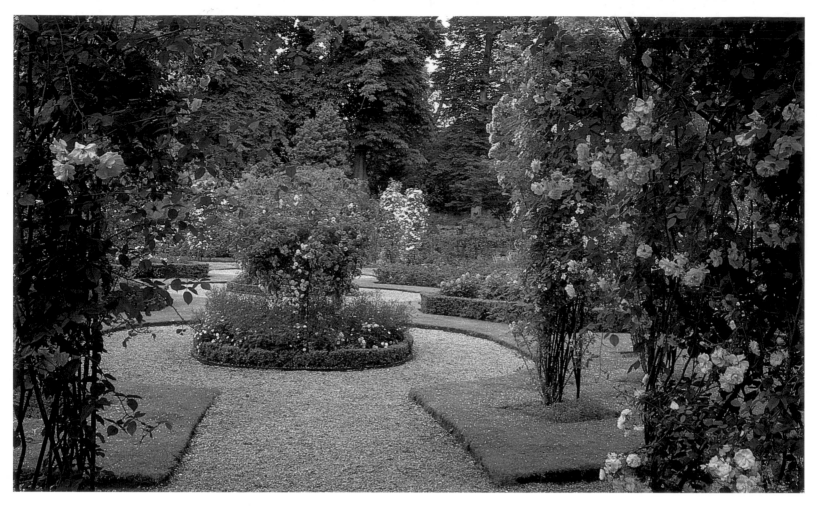

ABOVE
*The rose garden at
Warwick Castle – a
circular arbour of roses
surrounds a bed of
weeping standard roses.*

LEFT
*At Levens Hall the won-
derful range of forms and
colours possible in a yew
topiary is emphasized by
bright annuals.*

FAR LEFT
*Ways of training pillar
roses at Warwick Castle.
The foreground roses are
on metal frames, the pair
at the back on pillars.*

OPPOSITE
*Roses scramble over the
pergola of stone pillars
and wooden beams at
Hestercombe.*

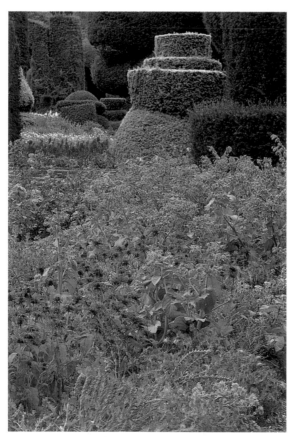

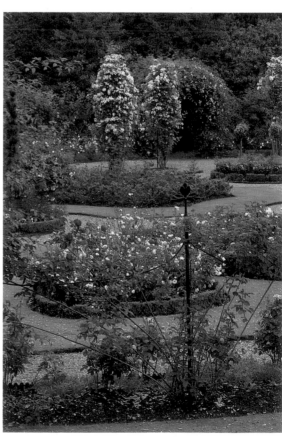

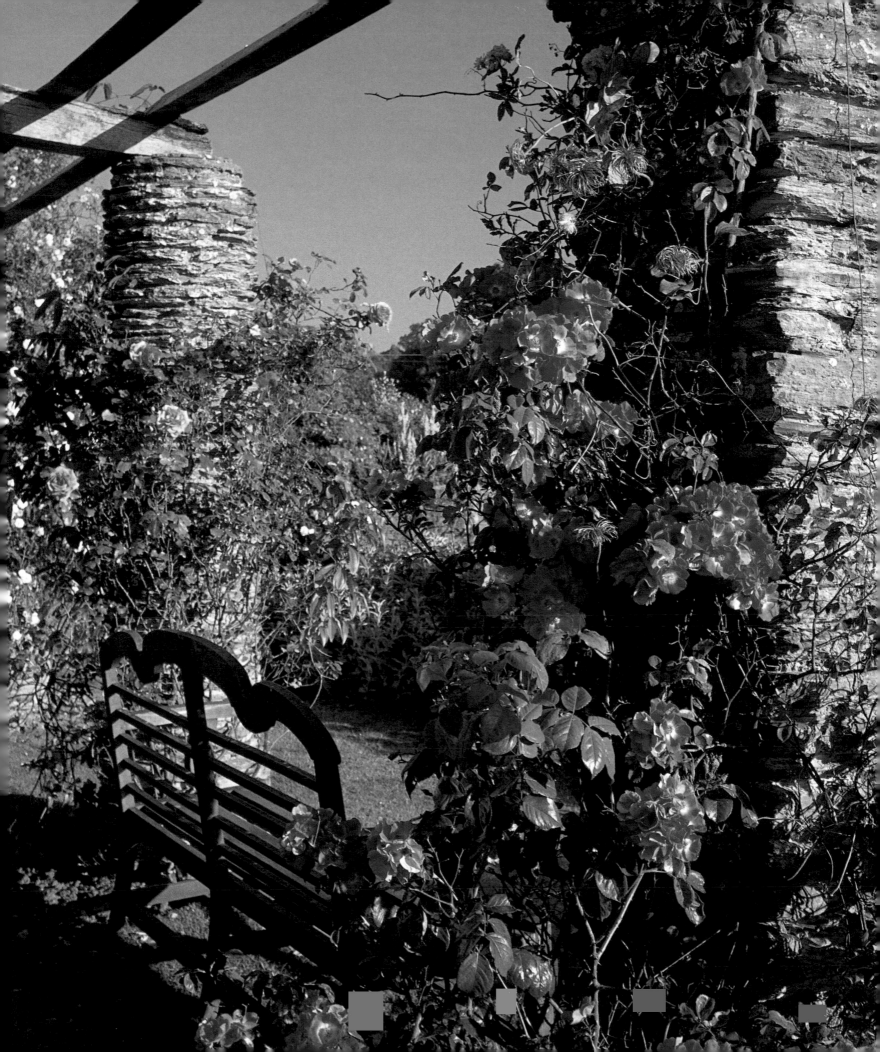

Topiary and Hedging

Topiary is the method of clipping yew or other hedging to look like a living wall of realistic or fanciful shapes – vases, columns, balls or obelisks. The result has the effect of living sculpture.

Rosaries are often enclosed by tall yew hedges of 8–12 ft (2.4–3.6 m) high. These hedges can be clipped to have straight sides or may be decorated with shaped piers topped with balls. More decoration can be added by using

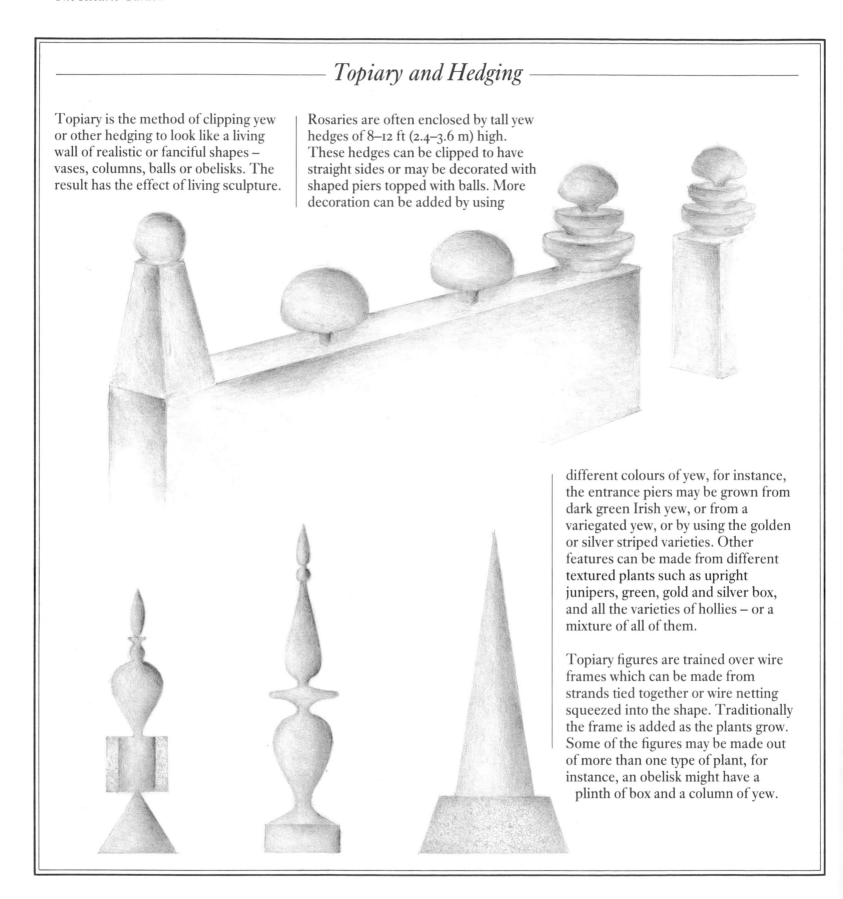

different colours of yew, for instance, the entrance piers may be grown from dark green Irish yew, or from a variegated yew, or by using the golden or silver striped varieties. Other features can be made from different textured plants such as upright junipers, green, gold and silver box, and all the varieties of hollies – or a mixture of all of them.

Topiary figures are trained over wire frames which can be made from strands tied together or wire netting squeezed into the shape. Traditionally the frame is added as the plants grow. Some of the figures may be made out of more than one type of plant, for instance, an obelisk might have a plinth of box and a column of yew.

In smaller gardens, especially where there is not enough room for grass, other edgings can be placed between the paths and beds, such as knobbly tiles on edge, slate, or small wire hoops such as those used in the circular basket beds described in the Villa Garden (Chapter 8). Wicker-work edging up to about 12 in (0.3 m) high can be woven from hazel or willow sticks and filled with sweet-smelling roses. Box grown to 12 in (0.3 m) high is popular as an edge, especially in the geometric patterned rosarie (such as the 'compartiment' parterre described in Chapter 3. In this type of rosarie beds are only filled with one variety of rose and should be separated from others by gravel paths.

A rosarie may incorporate features in a rustic style – decorative fences festooned with sweet briars, ramblers and tall Bourbon roses around the outside of the garden, or rustic wooden pillars supporting one or two varieties of roses to add height and colour. Cascades of the more vigorous climbing roses such as *R. filipes* can cover small rustic arbours or thatched-roof summer-houses. These can be made from bark-covered grotesquely shaped branches of softwood, and can be infilled with panels of different kinds of moss, lichens and bark set out in diamonds, crowns, stars and other patterns. Fir cones can be used as a cornice or to highlight a pattern. Knobbly stumps of larch or pine may support the wooden seats in such an arbour. The floor can be made from small round wooden blocks or bricks. If a rustic feature is used in a rosarie, all the other features should be in the same style. For example, wrought-iron pillars do not blend well with heavy rustic posts.

The delicacy of light cast-iron pillars can decorate the more formal rosarie. Placed about 3 ft (0.9 m) apart, these pillars can be linked by swags of rope, twisted wire or light chains, creating spectacular garlands of roses around the garden. Wooden trellis may also be used to create lattice-work arches, bowers, arbours and tunnels covered in roses.

Occasionally these features were even grander and more ornate. Mrs Beeton in her *Book of Garden Management*, published in the 1890s, records a rose temple made from galvanized wire, festooned with sweet-smelling roses. She suggests that it 'forms a suitable embellishment for the garden in any conspicuous part where two paths meet and cross . . . it consists of a domed structure in wire lattice work surmounted by an ornamental pinnacle . . . and entered on each side by a highly ornamental

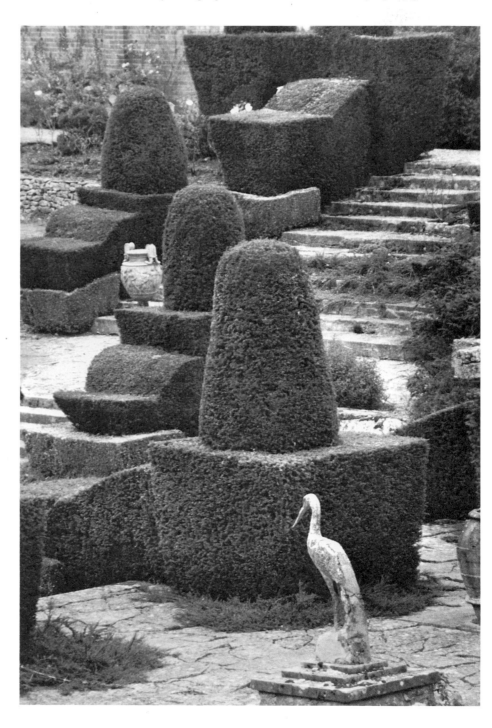

The extraordinary and eccentric range of clipped shapes and heights of hedge found in a 19th-century topiary garden

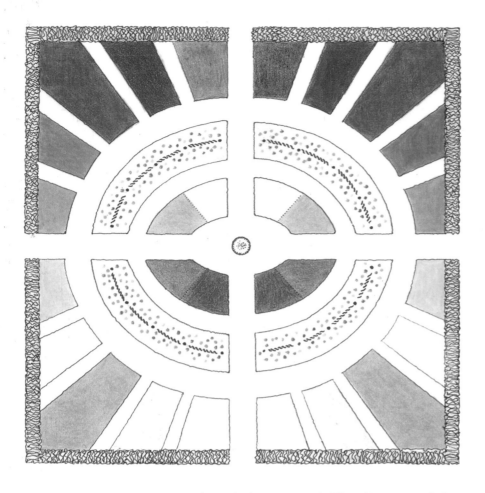

ABOVE
A traditional rosarie with its radiating dramatically-coloured rose beds. Bush roses are on the outside, dwarf at the centre, and separating them a circle of garlanded rambling roses above dwarf roses of mixed colours.

arch, styled an annex.' The diameter of the central section was 8 ft (2.4 m) and each of the four entrances was 30 in (0.75 m) deep. Thus the overall size of the structure was 13 ft (3.9 m) square. It was painted in two shades of green, and even in 1890 it cost £45!

Of course, smaller versions of the rose temple can be made to suit the size and width of the paths. The width of the wire trellises supporting the dome can vary from 9 to 15 in (0.23–0.38 m). One, two or three of the arched openings can also be filled in to form an enclosed summer-house.

A simpler form of the rose temple is the galvanized wirework arch made in several styles – the flat arch, the recessed arch and the high arch. These form 'admirable supports for roses or any other climbing plant that is desired to train over a garden path'. They should be 7 ft (2.1 m) above the ground in the centre, 4 ft (1.2 m) wide and 18 in (0.45 m) deep.

It was not until the mid-nineteenth century that the modern hybrid tea and hybrid musk roses were bred from *R. moschata* and the recently introduced 'perpetual' flowering China rose. Throughout the nineteenth century much effort was put into breeding roses and many of the 'old-fashioned' roses were raised. Since then, these have been continually hybridized to obtain a longer flowering season, hardiness to the climate, disease resistance and variety of colour, scent and habit. All the main classes of roses that we grow today come from just a few varieties. The development of the modern rose is clearly described in several recent books listed in the Bibliography. For example, *R. multiflora* came from Japan in 1862 and is the parent of all the floribundas. The China rose and musk rose produced the noisettes. The China rose and the Autumn Damask are the parents of the Bourbon rose, named after the Isle de Bourbon where they were raised. The Bourbon rose and the Portland rose produced the hybrid perpetual much loved by Victorian gardeners, and the hybrid

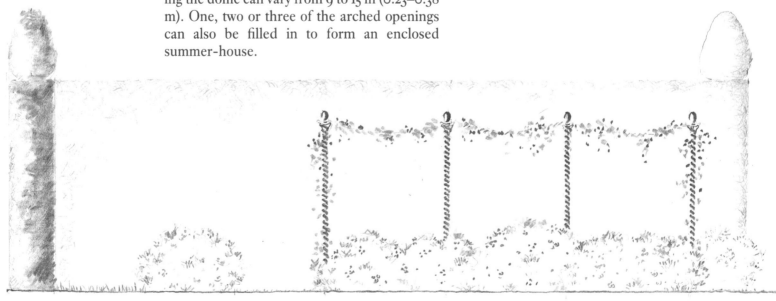

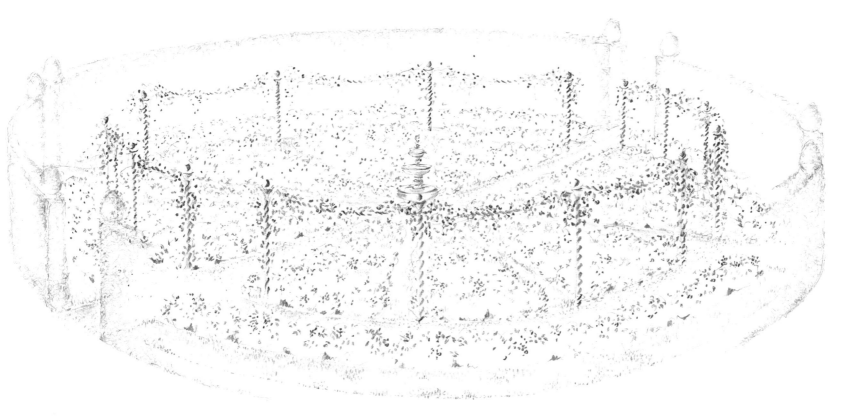

perpetual and the China tea rose produced the hybrid tea rose in 1867, but it was not bred to any great extent until the twentieth century.

These crosses resulted in four main types of roses: the standard rose with its clear stem about 2–6 ft (0.6–1.8 m) high where the rose cascades in a loose ball around it; the shrub rose which grows naturally up to 15–20 ft (4.5–6 m) or creeps about as a ground cover; the bush or 'dwarf' rose, either floribundas with clusters of smaller blooms flowering throughout the summer or the hybrid tea which usually has one much larger bloom on each shoot. All the climbers and ramblers make up the fourth group.

According to William Paul in 1848, choosing a selection of roses to fill the rosarie can be a 'mathematical brain teaser'. It is much more difficult now, as there are many more varieties. The style of a rosarie and whether it is to be planted as a period garden or with more modern breeds may depend on the location, the climatic conditions and what maintenance is

A tall hedge encloses an oval rose garden, 'garlands' of roses accentuating its shape. Small beds allow the roses to be examined individually. The arbour makes both a spectacular display of different rose varieties and an enclosed room of powerful and heady scents.

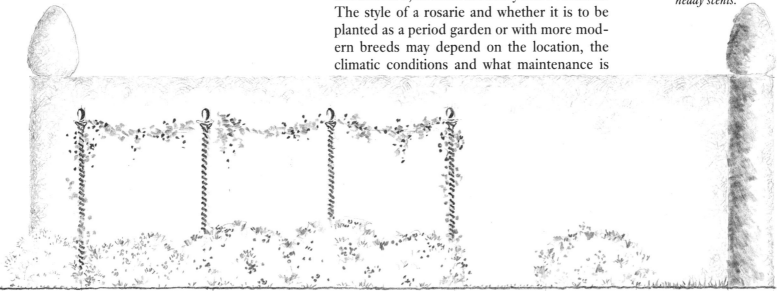

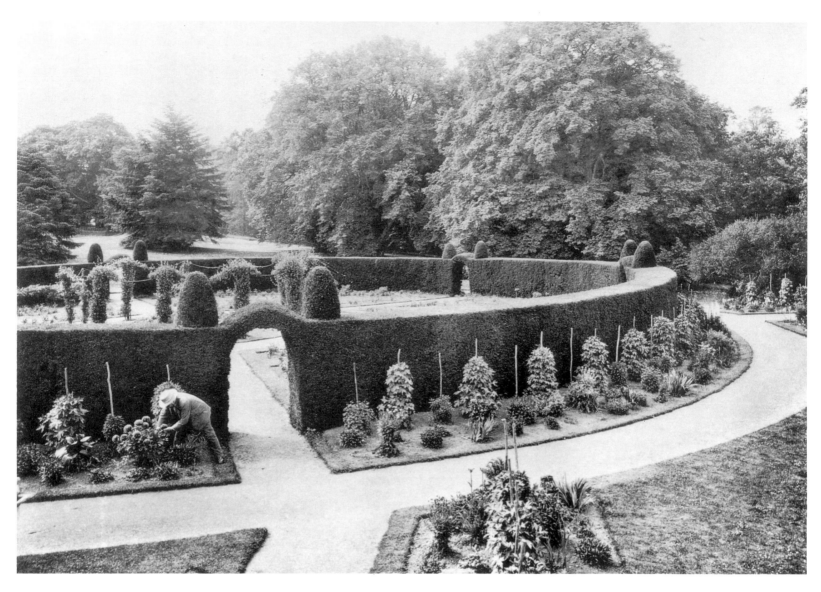

The rose garden at Rockingham Castle, in 1900 Established in 1835, it is encircled by a topiary hedge. Within are garlanded roses and low rose beds, on the outside a border filled with delphiniums and herbaceous plants.

PAGES 146–7
An elevation showing the height of the bush roses and garlanded rambling roses against the yew topiary hedge. The fountain is a dramatic central feature.

available, as many of the older varieties require more care.

Colour combinations are also important, and during the nineteenth century certain theories developed about them (see Chapter 10). Very often, colour can have more impact if there is an emphasis on one colour in particular sections of the garden. Stronger colours are more powerful, but they need to be softened with gentler hues and, likewise, pastel shades need to be heightened by stronger accents. The plan for the new rosarie at the Royal Horticultural Garden at Rosemoor combines a collection of nineteenth-century varieties with some of the newer 'old English' roses, producing a colourful and vigorous selection which will grow in the heavy Devon clay. The colours around the garden are graded from the dark purples through pinks to whites and running from yellows through to oranges and buffs back towards the pinks, with the hotter colours in the less sunny part.

Rosaries are colourful, scented and secluded and make summer gardens full of beauty and delights. They are ideally placed in sunny situations and the size of the rosarie can vary from the very small, with festoons of roses climbing over a simple arch, to the more complicated circular gardens so beloved by Victorians. Roses can be dried and sprinkled with oils to make pot-pourri or condensed to make lotions for the skin; or they can be distilled to form rose water, which flavours sweetmeats such as Turkish delight and other culinary delicacies.

12

The Rock and Quarry Garden

DELICATE alpine flowers creeping over stones, rugged branches clinging to rocks, and long tendrils tumbling over cliff faces decorate rock and quarry gardens. The aspiration is to create alpine meadows, imitate high rock screes and reproduce chunky peaks of mountain tops and cliffs adorned by dripping ferns or exotic orchids.

Within a rock garden many fascinating and enchanting plants can flourish. Around miniature mountain peaks nod the flower heads of creeping alpines. Tiny daffodils, irises and fritillaries sway in the wind on the pebble scree. Carpets of gentians, field orchids and pinks fill the more open ground. From a small tarn or alpine pool springs a mountain rill, dripping and splashing over rocks, under stones, falling over boulders and cascading over waterfalls through the rock garden. The water eventually finds its way into another pool, where it drips over the ledge to seep into a bog garden inhabited happily by the more luscious plants.

Rocks of different shapes and sizes have long fired the imagination of gardeners. Many eighteenth-century gardens contained 'savage' features of rock work – masses of rocks or groups of stone placed to look as if they were natural outcrops. Many grottoes imitated rocky caves, especially those with stalactites, such as the caves around Cheddar Gorge.

Towards the end of the eighteenth century, the picturesque style advocated by Uvedale Price used dramatic forms of rocks, cliffs and boulders to create terror and awe in the viewer. Inspiring these emotions was an important part of the experience in these gardens, and the effect was achieved by grotesque distortions of size. The horror of stumbling to the edge of a sharp precipice or stepping over a deep cleft or split in the cliff face were all part of the 'fun'. A rock garden like this was created at Hawkstone Park near Shrewsbury, with a sombre entrance leading to dark and damp tunnels, where a flickering candle beckoned on into a huge chamber. Here an ancient hermit welcomed the visitor to his rocky fastness. This garden is being restored.

This style of rock garden had little to do with growing alpine plants and more to do with providing startling and terrifying experiences to thrill and excite (not unlike the Theatrical Garden, see Chapter 5). In the romantic spirit of the time, early-nineteenth-century gardeners were enchanted by the notion of creating their own savage mountain scenery. Cliffs were carved with ledges for plants. Pinnacles and tall islands were left as features. The walls zigged and zagged and were cut and shaped to join together to form an arch or frame a secret door. In the 1820s Sir Charles Monck designed his

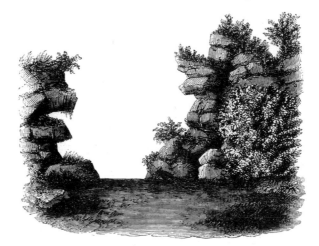

This illustration from How to Lay Out a Garden *by Edward Kemp, 1858, shows that the earliest rock and quarry gardens were intended to be of 'zigzag, broken, and rugged lines', recognizing no symmetry and abhorring 'everything allied to law and system'. Kemp selects as special features of the gardens, 'wildness, ruggedness, broken ground, straggling and bold herbage, dashing water, fantastic groups of vegetation, the cracked and discoloured stems and tortuous branches of trees, ruins nearly dismantled, except of the Ivy and the Fern.'*

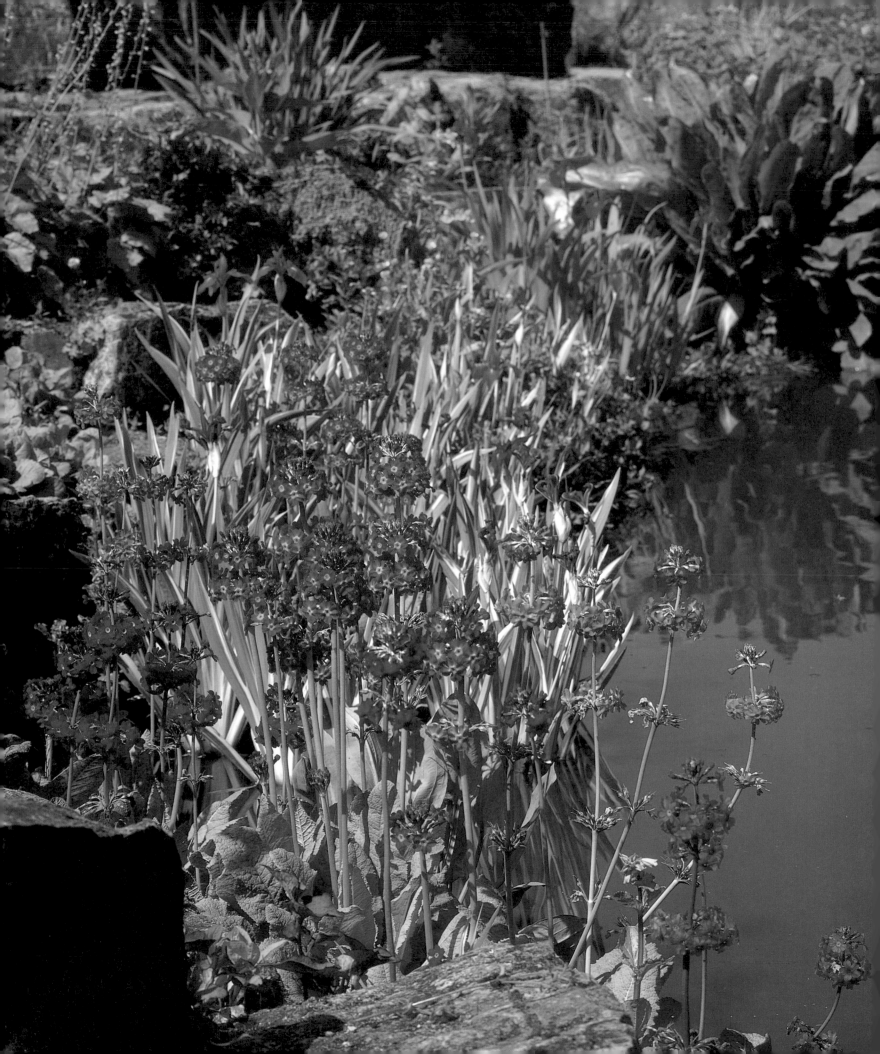

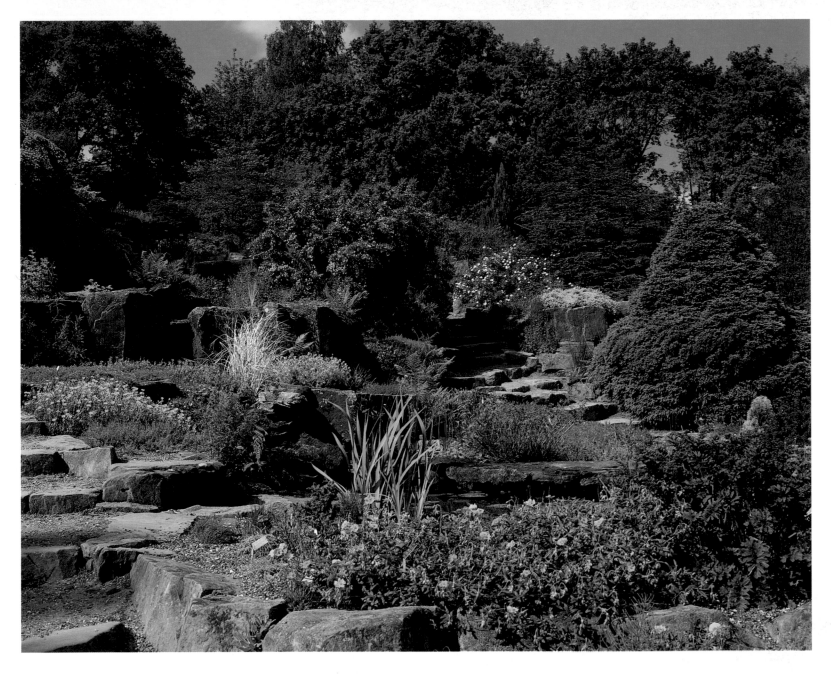

quarry garden at Belsay in Northumberland like this and his grandson subsequently filled it with species rhododendrons and other trees. It is an inspiring garden to visit.

The Victorians continued to be fascinated by such 'mountain' landscape, but were also increasingly absorbed by the botanical interest of the delicate plants. As the nineteenth century progressed many fabulous alpine plants arrived from expeditions exploring the Himalayas, and rock gardens were built especially for these plants. The extensive rock garden at the Royal Botanic Gardens at Kew, Surrey, was one. And in about 1850 James Pulham Jun. created the huge rock garden tumbling down a man-made hillside in Battersea Park, London.

By the beginning of the twentieth century most large gardens had a secluded rock garden for growing alpines, and a fashion developed for copying the dramatic summits of famous mountains, such as the top of Mont Blanc reproduced at Hergest Croft Gardens, Herefordshire. The craggy peaks were actually painted white to represent the snow cap.

The Rock Garden at Wisley. The dry alpine conditions are necessary for the cultivation of the plants. The placing of stones to resemble an outcrop and the scattered planting is deliberate. Water in the rock garden imitates a hillside pond (opposite), where primulas and irises grow on the water's edge.

A doorway at the end of the quarry garden of Belsay. The stone was quarried to establish a dark, overpowering, narrow ravine where the sheer cliff faces rise from the floor of the valley. The dominating size of the rocks at Belsay create romantic and awe-inspiring moods in the visitor.

A rock and quarry garden can be made out of a natural feature such as an old quarry, a small valley with an outcrop of stones, or a cliff face. Or it can be completely artificial, made from rocks brought to the site. These can be laid on a bank or knoll on either side of a sunken path.

The rock garden will be decorative and will aim to imitate natural conditions suitable to grow a range of alpine plants, but it should also show the grandeur and magnificence of mountain scenery. This might not always sit naturally at the front of a house, in which case the rock garden can either be in a separate area hidden from the rest of the garden or to one side, in a sunny place.

Sun and light are essential. Alpine plants do not mind the wind, however they dislike overhanging trees which may drip on them. Southeast facing slopes are the most appropriate and a north aspect is the least suitable. A sloping site with a slight dip is the best so that a path can wind through a natural 'pine' valley or rocks can rise up beside the path. The size of the garden can range from a few stones to an acre or two. Whatever the size, 'big bold masses of rockwork are essential . . . to give it that natural appearance'. But this effect can also be obtained by using comparatively small rocks.

In *The Book of the Garden* (1853) Charles McIntosh explained the principles for con-

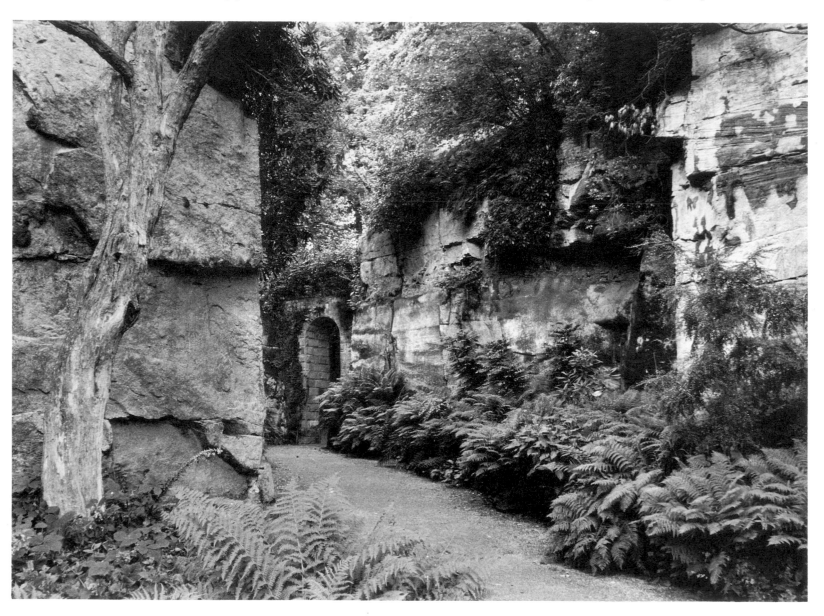

Dry-Stone Walls and Screes

One of the best and simplest ways of growing rock plants is in a loose wall. Any change of level requiring a retaining wall can be used as a home for rock plants. A dry-stone wall is built without mortar and can be made from brick or stonc. Shaley or crumbling sandstone is the best. Behind each course the earth must be compacted and firmly rammed to support the wall and every three courses or so, some extra long stones should be laid front and back to tie the wall into the bank. A thin layer of soil is used in the same way as mortar and provides a bed for the next course as well as enabling the plants to grow in the joints. The face of the wall should slope inwards, and the stones incline towards the bank so that the rain is caught and carried through to the soil behind. The wall should be planted as it is built, for example, with hardy ferns.

If larger rocks are used or natural rock exposed it may be necessary to provide an artificial pocket to hold the soil and moisture. Made from a cement mixture to which has been added a third part soil or peat instead of sand, the pocket will support the growth of moss or lichens and blend into the rock.

The moraines on top of the mountains where many delicate alpines grow can be imitated by making screes out of stones of all different sizes from boulders to gravel. Set into a gentle south- or west-facing slope, the stones provide sharp drainage in winter and act as mulch in summer.

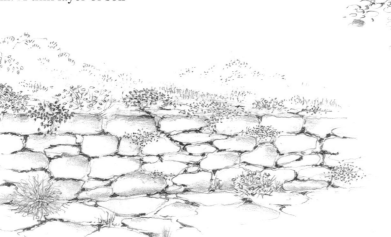

Many of the large-flower alpine primulas love these conditions, especially the sky-blue *Primula marginata*, with its light dusting of white which looks like a coat of flour. In their original habitat these plants are covered by snow during the winter, and in Britain they may need to be kept artificially covered because they do not like damp winters.

Plan of a rock garden, surrounded by low trees and with a pebbled scree at the bottom. A stream, which is not a necessary component, slips over the rocks. The rocks are separated by steps made from the scree or smaller stones.

structing rock gardens. 'When the culture of rock plants is an object, the rockery should present two or more aspects, one damp and shaded, the other fully exposed to the sun. Ferns and plants of the shade should occupy the former, while sun-loving plants should inhabit the latter.' The layout should 'imitate natural rocks, cascades and alpine rivulets'.

As the aim is to reproduce an alpine hillside, the best way of copying them, nineteenth-century gardeners were told, is to look at the way the rock lies naturally on top of a mountain. However, there are some simple rules which can be followed without climbing up some high and distant peak.

One of the most important is to ensure that all the rock or stone comes from the same source or, if not, that the different types can appear together naturally, such as granite with intrusions of marble. If sandstone is used, it is most important to ensure that the striations or grain of all the rocks run in the same direction, or if they dip or slant they should look natural. All the exposed rocks must look as if they are only a small part of a large outcrop, most of which is hidden by the soil.

Some plants grow better on limestone and others on neutral sandstone. It is usually better to use the local stone or the nearest source of similar stone. For example, in the Cotswolds yellow sandstone should be used, and in Cumbria grey granite. Similarly, if the garden is on gravel, a buff sandstone would look more like a natural outcrop than would a grey granite.

If a natural outcrop is available, the rock face should be opened up and all the weeds and debris thoroughly cleared out. Cascading plants will cling to crevices on the cliff face; if such crevices are not naturally present they can be especially made for the plants. These pockets should be made to slope inwards in order to retain some moisture, but most of the water must drain from them. If necessary, this slope can be achieved by raising the side artificially with a cement mix tinged with soil to make it look natural, leaving small holes for the drainage. Sufficient soil to hold the plants should be wedged into these crevices with either small stones or more cement. Many rock plants have long and tenacious roots so it is important to give them enough room to grow.

When creating an artificial rock garden the scope is enormous but it can be quite difficult making introduced rocks look natural. An attractive way is to lay a narrow path winding around a knoll of gently sloping banks, grad-

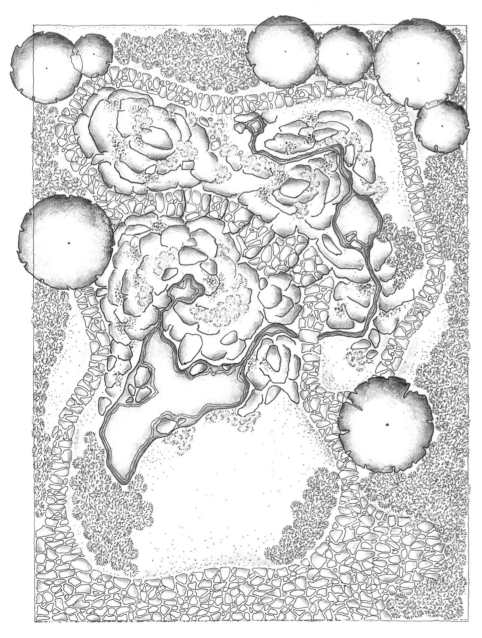

0   1   2   3   4   5M

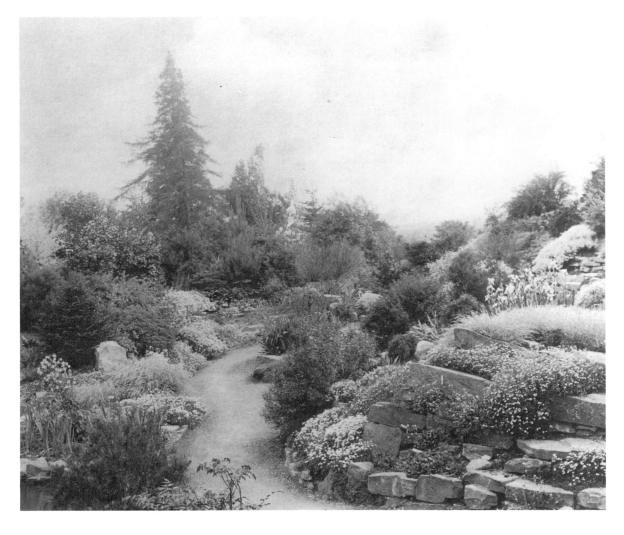

A rock garden of 1904 at Hergest Croft, about four years after it was made. Its construction and appearance were based closely on photographs of famous Rock gardens – the section in this picture was inspired by the Rock Garden at Kew. The foreground structure exhibits well the tilting of the rocks to encourage rain water to spread amongst the rocks. What is impressive is that, although typical of rock gardens, the carpeting of the plants and flowers is so luxuriant.

ually rising up low steps. If possible the path should run from one part of the garden to another. If the winding path needs to be sunk lower than the surrounding ground, the topsoil should be stripped before the rocks are laid on the subsoil. This can be used to fill the pockets for the plants.

On entering the rock garden the rocks should be gradually introduced, in the same way as a rocky outcrop usually has a few stones lying randomly near it. The slopes forming the bank should vary as much as possible. In some places the bank should slope gently whilst in others it will rise quite sharply. The path can skirt around a large boulder before passing a low and relatively flat plateau. Large bold rocks make natural sharp corners to the winding path, which should contrast with the gentler and more open curves of the wider areas. If the rock garden is in a natural or artificial basin,

the gradient of the slope need not be more than 1:4, but a small area of cliff face does add interest.

In a sufficiently large garden it is most effective if the rocks at the centre can tower above the viewer to reach to about 8–9 ft (2.4–2.7 m), however 5–6 ft (1.5–1.8 m) serves almost as well.

If rocks are placed one above another on a sloping bank, the one underneath should project in front of those on top so that falling rain can soak the plants growing in the fissures of soil created between them. When using larger stones, at least one third should be buried, leaving two thirds exposed. This provides sufficient soil to hold the moisture if the stones slope towards the bank behind but it will also permit drainage to prevent waterlogging the plant roots.

One of the ways of keeping the soil in position and preventing it from being washed out

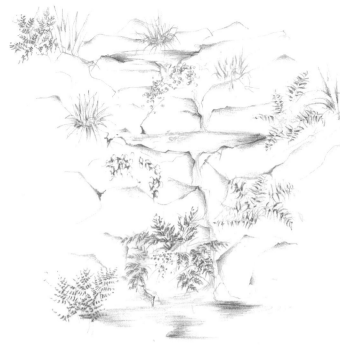

A sketch showing how to place stones around a little stream in a rock garden, with the water dripping over the stones from one level to another, in imitation of the source of a mountain stream. Low plants grow in amongst the crevices.

A section through a typical rockery, showing how the stratification of the rocks is arranged in a natural way. It is important that most of the garden is bathed in sunlight throughout the day and year. Note that the rocks are tilted so that rain water rather than splashing off, slides back into the crevices where the plants are growing.

by heavy rains is to form a series of terraces. These should vary in height, width and outline, and a gradient of about 1:4 will allow the moisture to percolate into the soil without making the ground waterlogged. These terraces should also merge and separate at different levels varying the width. The more gentle the gradient the wider the terrace can be. The largest rocks should be kept for the steeper gradients, which can be almost perpendicular. In a wider terrace an odd rock appearing here and there is quite sufficient.

The paths can be as narrow as 2 ft (0.6 m), widening in places to between 6 and 7 ft (1.8–2.1 m). Small stones can be set on edge to border the path and can also be used as treads for the larger flat stones acting as steps. Sedums, saxifrages and alpine campanulas can be planted between each step so that in a short time the steps cannot be seen.

'Moraines' and screes can be made for alpines which require these special habitats. Small stones or large gravel pebbles should fill a bed about 1 ft (0.3 m) deep on top of a layer of coarse stone about 4 in (0.1 m) deep.

The growing conditions for these high mountain plants has to replicate the climate and soil conditions of their natural habitat. Many plants growing in the Alps or Himalayas spend the winter under a thick blanket of snow which keeps them dry and warm, protecting them from sudden changes of temperature or extremes of cold. For example, the delightful blue primroses with downy grey leaves must be protected in winter in order to survive, especially in England. However, these grow well in Scotland, where they are likely to have snow cover during the winter. Himalayan blue poppies also need to be kept dry during the winter, which can be done by placing a sheet of glass over them from November to April.

At the top of a natural mountain range water drips down the rocks and slowly builds up into a sparkling stream splashing down the hillside, and this magical effect can be reproduced in a rock garden. The water can emerge from under a rock where all the workings are easily hidden, or from a wishing-well where it can drip over the basin into a narrow rill. From here it can gather speed and cascade into a small pool or tumble over stones into a larger water garden before seeping into the bog garden.

Aubretia tumbling down drystone walls or sweet-smelling pinks clinging to the stones

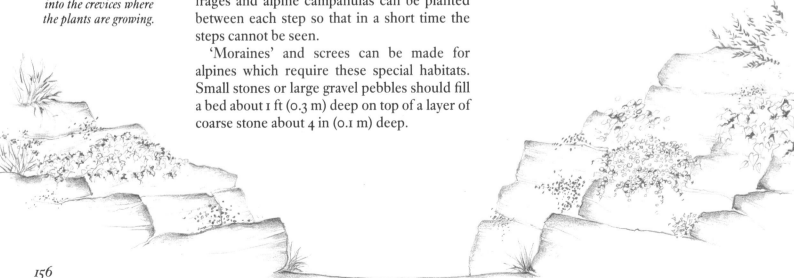

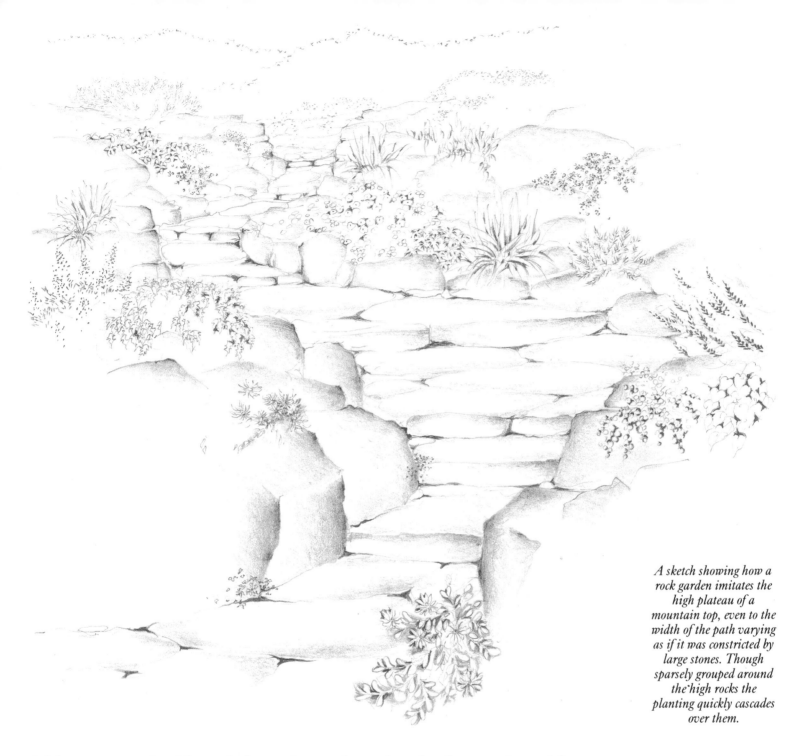

A sketch showing how a rock garden imitates the high plateau of a mountain top, even to the width of the path varying as if it was constricted by large stones. Though sparsely grouped around the high rocks the planting quickly cascades over them.

brighten up any garden. Most rock plants enjoy warmth and sunlight, but as they also require moisture they grow more happily on a retaining wall than a free-standing one. These retaining walls should be constructed so that very little, if any, mortar or cement is used to hold the stones together.

Rock plants include alpines and any plant which is of a suitable habit and height to grow in a rock garden. Some can be used for a mass effect, such as rock roses, arabis, campanulas, some saxifrage, whilst others such as alpine pinks are too small or diminutive to provide a splash. These little treasures should be planted separately from the brighter and coarser plants which could easily smother them. With certain varieties it can be more impressive to plant the same genus together, particularly if they require the same conditions. Bold cascades of thyme and alyssum should contrast with small tufts of mossy saxifrage, and each group should vary as much as possible. For example, carpets of the blue, low-growing *Gentiana acaulis* can be dazzling next to rocks covered with *Thymus serpyllum alba*.

Many special bulbs such as the tiny daffodil *Narcissus bulbocodium* grow happily protected by the rocks. Some will naturalize to create carpets of colour, such as the blue *Scilla siberica* or species crocus. As the leaves die down during the summer, it is worth planting the bulbs under some low-growing perennials such as thyme, sedum or saxifrage.

Ferns and mosses love the damp and shady corners and their feathery foliage can also be used to highlight flowers of other plants. Dwarf shrubs or miniature trees emphasize shapes of rocks. Dwarf conifers are particularly appropriate, although some of the varieties introduced at the beginning of this century have grown much taller than expected and now tower over many rockeries. Varieties of small trees, such as the low-growing bearberry willow, planted at the foot of a rock give the impression of a much bigger cliff. Colour combinations are a matter of choice but as many of these plants require special conditions the choice may be restricted by their needs. The basic rule that taller plants should be grown at the back and the smaller ones in the front can be applied, but with variety, as it is in the wild.

Rock gardens can be dramatic and magnificent. From the arch joining two cliffs together in an old quarry to the diminutive plant just introduced from the Himalayan peaks, it is a garden of contrasts, rugged shapes and exciting profiles. Creating a rocky mountain landscape can be challenging and rewarding.

At Hazelbury Manor, Wiltshire the rock garden was made in the last five years, and through the massing of dense planting snakes a meandering path. Rock gardens, as here, can often be made on steep banks that are left from excavations.

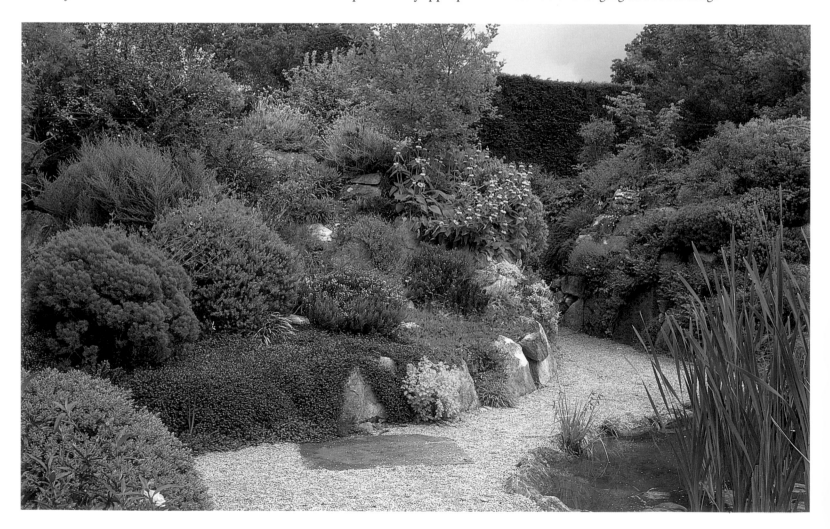

13

The Wild and Woodland Garden

IN THE wild and woodland garden plants from many exotic regions of the world grow happily and naturally together in great profusion. Planting exotics in wild places in a contrived fashion is easy but the skill is in creating the natural effect. In 1899 Gertrude Jekyll warned 'wild gardening is delightful, and in good hands a most desirable pursuit, no garden is so difficult to do well, or is so full of pitfalls and paths of peril.'

During Queen Victoria's reign, gardeners, obsessed with the beauty and botanical interest of plants, acquired more and more exotic trees and shrubs as soon as they arrived from abroad. The warm, soft and wet conditions of the west coast of the British Isles suited many of them, especially rhododendrons. The aim was to grow a range of extraordinary plants, such as the pocket handkerchief tree, wellingtonias and magnificent rhododendrons and camellias in conditions where they could flourish and look natural.

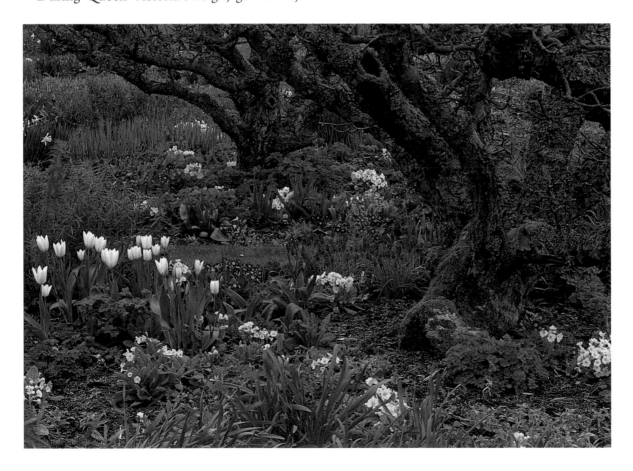

A Spring flower meadow underneath woodland. Tulips are only successful in such gardens if planted, as here, on the edge of a glade, or beneath well-pruned apple trees, so that the tulips can enjoy the heat of the summer soil. Miniature daffodils, grape hyacinths and lots of primroses benefit from dappled sun throughout the year – they become blind if grown in the shade and die in full sun.

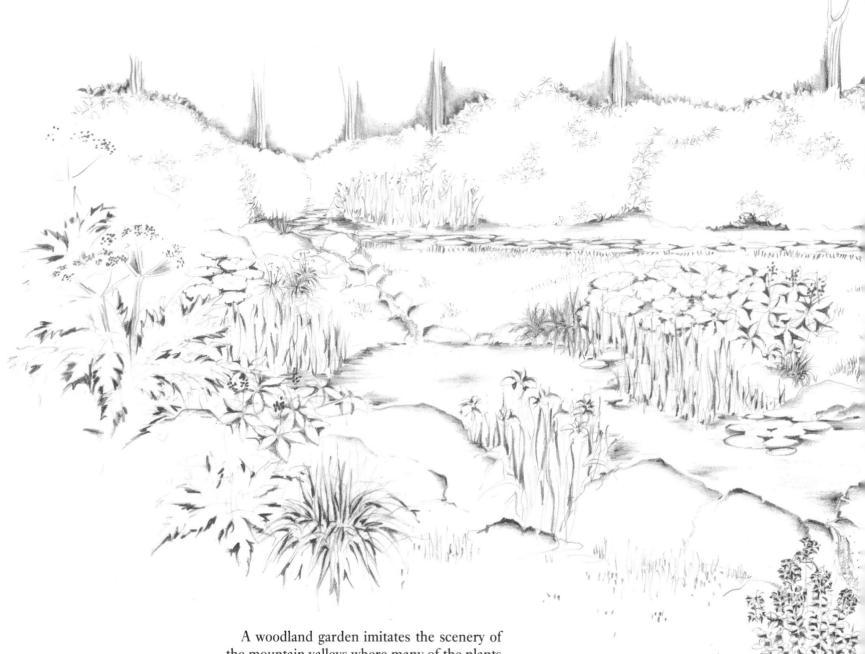

A woodland garden imitates the scenery of the mountain valleys where many of the plants originally grew. However, many more kinds of plants are grown in these gardens so the real resemblance to an actual Himalayan or alpine valley is very slight. Most such natural valleys are isolated from each other, so that perhaps only four or five species of rhododendron may grow together – very different to the remarkable panoply of varieties that are on show in the modern wild and woodland garden.

Sheltered valleys usually provide the most suitable conditions and here the gardener can experience the thrill of nurturing these novel plants and watching them grow to create a gar-

den of texture and colour. Bronze bark sparkles in low sunlight, shiny leaves flutter in the breeze, whilst the spectacular trusses of rhododendrons glow pink, white, scarlet and crimson in the dappled shade cast by the tree trunks. The garden condenses all the sensations of a Himalayan walking tour into one small space and removes the visitor into a rich and colourful mountain fantasy.

When this style was in its infancy, Japan was

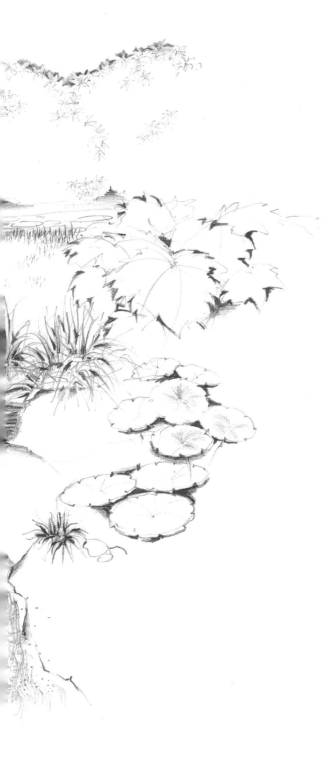

garden. In some nineteenth-century gardens Japanese-style artefacts were used, such as the bleached wooden tea-houses, delicate latticed bridges and stone lanterns. These were often placed around lakes edged with large stones.

The Victorian passion for exploration and the invention of the Wardian case in which tender species could be transported from one hemisphere to another spawned an immense increase in the numbers of fascinating plants to grow. The rich supply became available through the heroic efforts of missionaries and other ambassadors, such as traders exploring the Far East, especially Japan, China and the Himalayas. Imagine the excitement on the arrival of the sensational pocket handkerchief tree, which had only been described and never seen. These intrepid plant collectors had managed to penetrate into the remote high mountains of southern China, and their adventures were quite amazing and often dangerous, but it was their perseverance which gave us so many of our treasured garden plants. Their knowledge and skill in recording and describing the circumstances in which these plants grew made it possible for the gardener to reproduce these conditions in the wild and woodland garden.

Many of Britain's famous gardens illustrate this style. In the 1850s James Hooker sent back large-leaved rhododendrons to his friends on the west coast of Scotland. Some can still be seen at Stonefield House on the Mull of Kintyre. Osgood Mackenzie was an early pioneer at Inverewe on the north-western tip of Scotland. Shortly afterwards the Loders at Leonardslee and High Beeches on the greensand of West Sussex started to collect them and to hybridize them, creating many of the colourful varieties we have today, such as all the *Rhododendron loderii* crosses. Many of the renowned Cornish gardens were planted at this time.

The aim of the woodland garden is to grow as many different plants as possible as naturally as possible in a small area and the skill is to provide a range of different habitats to cater for them. The design has to be tuned to the

A woodland stream broadens into a small pond. Around the edges and between the stones flourish bog plants such as irises, primulas, kingcups and royal ferns. Most of these plants are more effective if planted in large, isolated groups.

opening up to foreign visitors for the first time in over two hundred years. For many centuries Japanese gardeners had been imitating nature in a small space and their designs were influential in emphasizing the naturalness in a small

*Sketch of a glade
showing a woodland
meadow surrounded by
shrubs. Rhododendrons,
azaleas, viburnums,
lilacs, philadelphus,
ferns, and hellebores lead
to the trees behind.*

amount of space available. In larger gardens it can extend from a dark wood, where the myriad textures of the tree trunks are only stroked with shafts of light, to the open and sunny edge of a wild garden meadow. And yet even in a small garden it is possible to use at least some of the ingredients of the style.

The woodland garden is usually within or adjacent to an older wood so that the mature trees can provide shelter and protection for the exotic trees and shrubs. Many of the 'exotic' plants like the summer coolness and winter warmth found under trees. The trees and shrubs should be planted quite close together

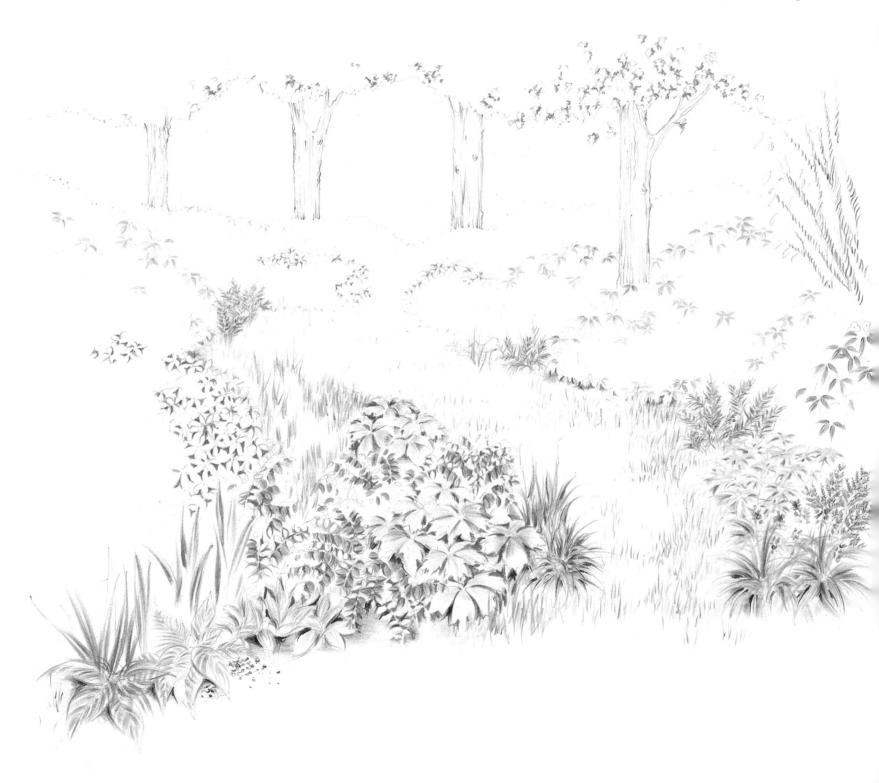

Sketch of a glade showing a woodland meadow surrounded by shrubs. Rhododendrons, azaleas, viburnums, lilacs, philadelphus, ferns, and hellebores lead to the trees behind.

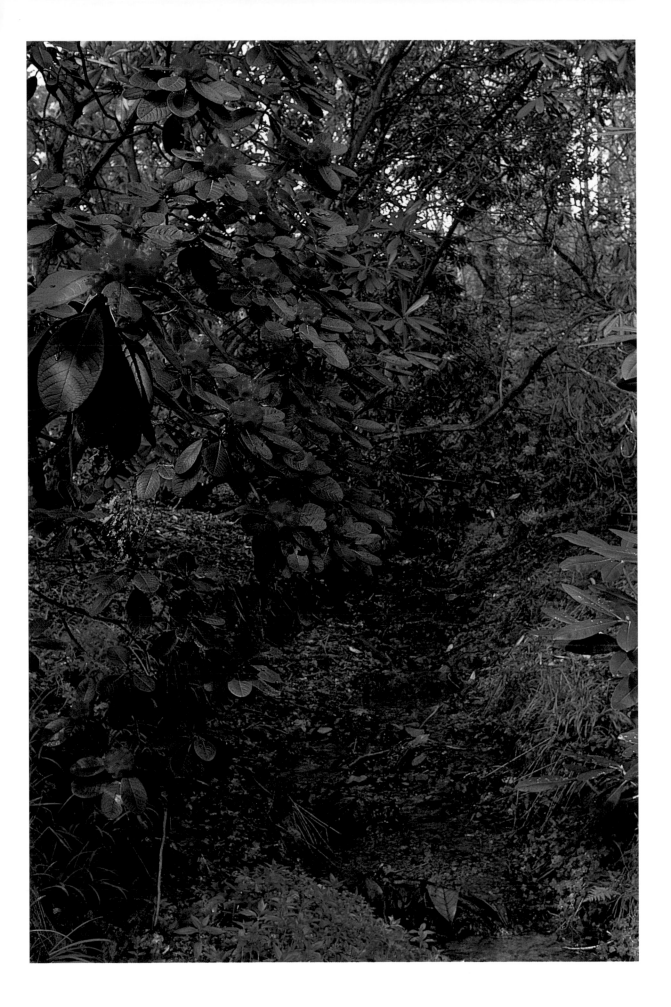

Rhododendron Mallotum protected by a canopy of trees, grows over a gentle stream.

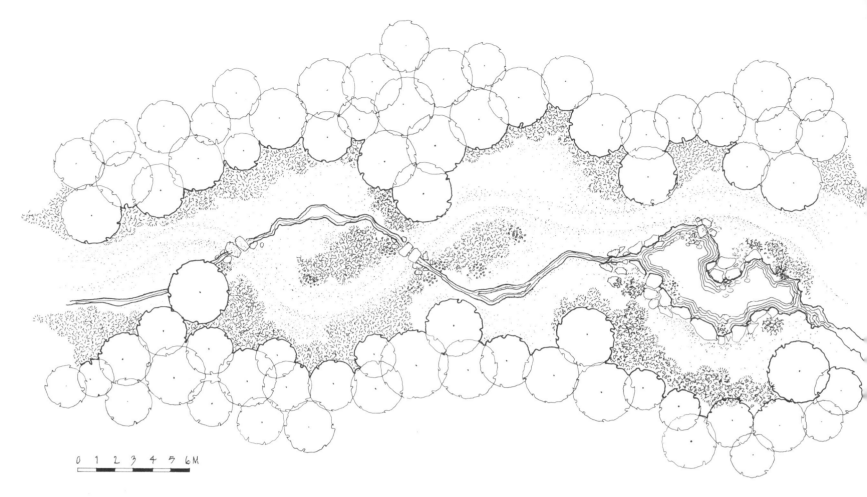

0 1 2 3 4 5 6M

The plan shows the shape of a garden established by woodland trees and the natural flow of the stream, which is widened to form a still pond. The grass path meanders through the garden, crossing the stream by stepping stones. Within each grassy area, the shrubs and smaller trees are clustered together by colour or variety to establish places of different atmosphere and character.

to imitate the wildness of their natural habitat. As most of the plants originally grew on the sides of high mountain valleys, these conditions should be copied, for instance, by forming an alpine scree or opening up glades to create meadows surrounded by lower shrubs blending into the wood.

The noise and movement of water emphasize the mountain scenery. Springs can be transformed into tumbling streams mimicking moorland rills, flowing past stones and swirling over gravel until they cascade into still reflecting pools. In larger gardens the water can also splash over waterfalls or fall through rocks, run through stepping stones or open out into a small pool. Most of these effects can be made by diverting an existing stream or by using a pumped system. Clean sparkling water copies fresh mountain streams and is preferable to a cloudy, slimy pond.

A smaller pool can be sited on higher ground so that it holds the water to flow down the waterfalls. The channels can be emphasized by using stones, with the larger ones placed as close to the path as possible so they can be seen. The splashing water can be slowed up by running over gravel and smaller stones and the banks planted with damp-loving plants such as celandines, rodgersias and sedges. Water may seep out making a boggy area and in the damper spots bright primulas and gawky kingcups may flourish in cool March skies. In summer the larger pools can be covered with waterlilies.

Special plants should be sited where they can be seen at a distance across clearings or close to from meandering paths. A rustic summer-house acts as an eyecatcher across a glade or it may overlook a valley from a promontory which offers spectacular views over a carpet of rhododendron blooms. These shelters can be made out of grotesquely shaped tree trunks with panels of woven heather or moss decorated in intricate patterns.

A twisting and turning path meanders around the plants, the larger the garden, the longer the path. It can be a narrow mud track cut out of the slope and covered by leaves or a bark or sawdust mulch, emphasizing the upland character and imitating the paths that cling to steep mountains. Turf steps or ramps made with rustic posts can ease the climb. The route may go around large plants or the plants may be pruned so that they arch over it; but should never go in a straight line, even when crossing a glade.

Before planting, the ground should be prepared by cleaning out and removing the undergrowth, especially brambles, thistles and other invasive weeds. As most of the exotic plants like growing under dappled shade but not in the darkness of a dense forest, it is often necessary to thin out the existing trees to provide just the right canopy of leaves to protect but not starve the delicate plants. The trees may be chosen for their attractive shape or because their canopy lets in the right amount of light. In most conditions larch and oak provide the best shelter. Oaks are especially beneficial to rhododendrons as their acid leaves mulch the ground.

In the woodland garden many different conifers can be set out in groups as in a forest. Deciduous trees can be planted close together to form copses or mixed with one or two varieties of conifers but masses of different sorts should not be planted together. One plant of each kind does not look very natural planted in a group, so it is better to plant groups of similar kinds, such as one family or genus or one rhododendron group (just as one kind of plant dominates an area in the wild).

Specimen trees and shrubs can be planted around and in open glades but they should not fill them up. In the wild, trees may grow very close to each other or a beautifully shaped single one may stand alone in a meadow. The mountain scenery effect is created by massing shrubs together so that they look as if they are tumbling down a hillside or edging a forest glade or bordering an alpine clearing.

When planting it is important to vary the distance between the trees to imitate nature. In wooded situations they may be only 6–9 ft (2–3 m) apart but at the edge of a glade they can be 15–30 ft (5–10 m) apart. Contrast is essential and nothing should be symmetrical or regular. Knowing where the plants come from and what conditions they require helps to plant them in a suitable place. There are many reference books which can give this information: the habit of the plant; the shape of its leaves; the colour of the flowers; when it flowers; how tall it grows and so on. These details will all assist planting in the best position.

The number of different varieties of rhododendron is enormous and they range from tree rhododendrons growing up to 30 ft (10 m) or more, with large flower trusses cascading all the way down to the ground, to tiny alpine shrubs growing no more than 6 in (0.15 m) high. Many have enormous and brightly coloured flowers of all shades, especially pinks, scarlet, deep reds and rich purple. Most varieties have large green leaves which look very similar to each other but some of the species have quite beautiful leaves and coloured bark.

Shrubs can be planted in large groups of one sort, groups of one colour, groups of mixed varieties in one planting and as single specimens. The distance between them should be varied but does depend on their ultimate size. In the wild, the stronger types swamp the smaller ones and they can be maintained to give a similar effect but with careful selective pruning which in fact favours the smaller ones. Tender shrubs require protection from cold frosts and so should be planted under trees near a glade where sunlight can fall on them.

It is essential to consider the blending of colours and contrasting of texture. Colours can be emphasized by mixing, or one can create a massed effect by blending them together.

Wherever the woodland floor is open to sunlight it can be sown with wild flowers – in spring, bluebells, white garlic and dog's mercury, and in summer succeeded by the more delicate ferns and woodland grasses. However, it is essential to control invasive weeds such as

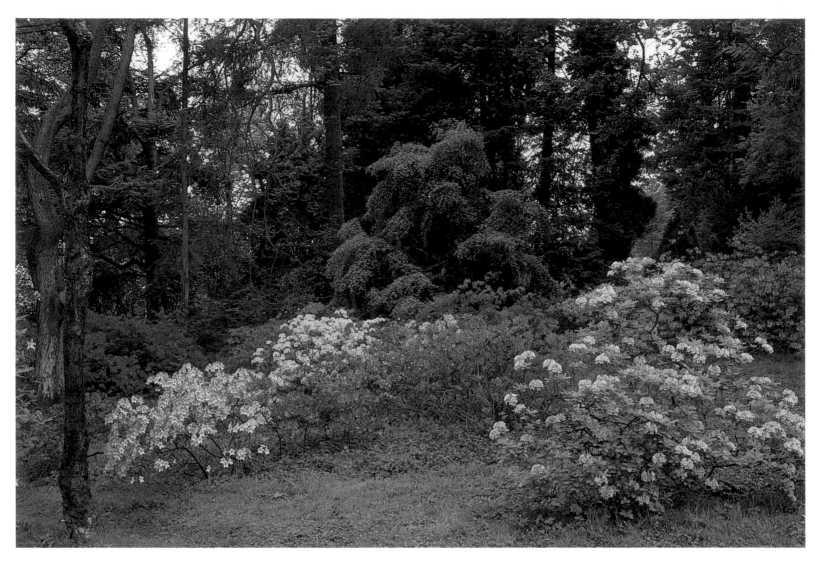

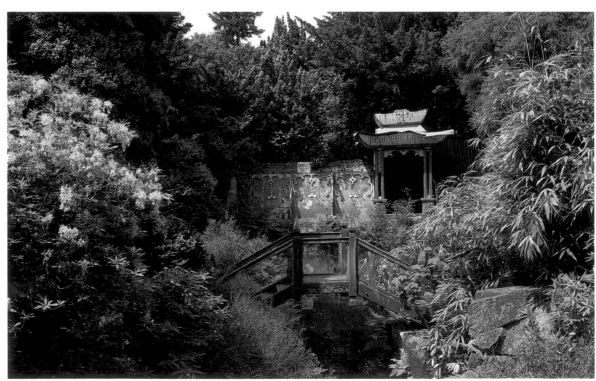

ABOVE
*Rhododendrons and
azaleas grown in an open
glade, sheltered by trees.*

*The garden of Biddulph
Grange shows the
Japanese influence upon
the development of the
wild and woodland
garden style – in the use
of pagodas and bridges as
decorative features and
the planting of brilliantly
coloured rhododendrons
and azaleas.*

Wild Flower Meadows

Wild flower meadows can flourish in the undergrowth in open glades amongst the trees. They may also be sited in open lawns or rougher grass, emphasizing the natural character of the wilder parts of a garden. However, all types of meadows require careful management to succeed: it is not enough just to stop mowing the grass as this alone will not produce wild flowering plants.

Spring Woodland Meadow
Under the open canopy of a broad-leaved wood of oak, ash, lime or beech, primroses, snowdrops, scillas, bluebells, grape hyacinths, oxalis and other spring bulbs flourish in the winter sun. The thicker undergrowth needs to be cut down or removed in the autumn so that the flowers grow above the ground cover.

Summer Woodland Meadow The ideal situation is along the edge of a wood or in open glades where occasional shafts of sunlight hit the ground. Foxgloves, martagon lilies and cow parsley flower throughout the summer amongst the shade-tolerant grasses. Remove vigorous undergrowth. Once the seed has set about the end of July or early August the area should be mown or trimmed.

Spring Lawn Meadow This contains small bulbs, especially crocus, species of iris, daffodils, snowdrops, narcissus, scillas, grape hyacinths and tulips. The grass must not be cut until the leaves of the bulbs have died and it is better to keep the bulbs that flower in February and March separate from those that flower later. Thus a lawn with February bulbs can be mown in late May whereas a lawn with daffodils should wait until mid-June.

Summer Lawn Meadow Daisies, buttercups, violets, speedwells and other wild flowers which grow about 3 in (0.075 m) high can flower in the lawn all summer long. Mowing should be reduced to once every two weeks in May and every three weeks for the rest of the season. All the mowings must be removed. If special plants such as orchids are grown the grass should not be cut until the middle of July.

Autumn Meadow This contains flowers and ornamental seed heads which look best in September or October. Cut the grass in November when the seeds have dispersed, and twice in April or early May to control the more vigorous grasses and allow the flowers to dominate. Remove the mowings because an unsightly thatch of grass builds up and stops the wild flowers from growing.

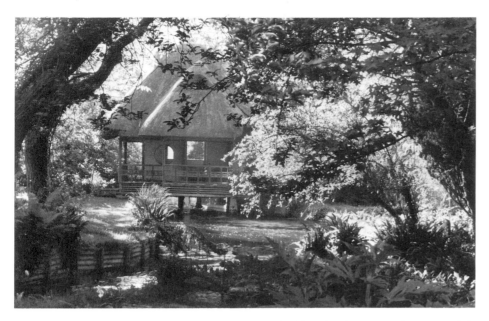

A thatched 'roofed' Japanese teahouse on stilts straddles a stream – a feature or 'eyecatcher' in a woodland garden that also provides shelter.

brambles and willow herb so that the more delicate wild flowers can survive.

The wild garden lies on the edge of the woodland garden where the trees give way to shrubs and meadows and where bulbs and wild flowers are naturalized. Many smaller, more delicate shrubs can be planted here, especially around the meadows. The larger varieties which enjoy sunshine should be grouped nearer the trees, leaving the meadow open.

Plants such as azaleas, hydrangeas, philadelphus or viburnums are often used. Gertrude Jekyll was very fond of species roses and recommended growing the spinossima types here as well as the other varieties. Seedlings and suckers can grow so long as they do not compete with other and more precious plants. Specimens of the smaller and showier exotics such as the snake bark maples and white-stemmed birches can also be planted to show off the beauty of their barks.

The naturalizing of flowers, whether bulbs, herbaceous or wild flowers, makes the wild garden. Violas, primroses and even wild orchids grow through delicate grasses carefully sown to look as if they are in the wild. Flowers are planted in grass, along streams and in woods. Spring meadows can be created by planting bulbs in grass. Drifts of daffodils may be planted but each variety should be grouped together. As the bulbs increase the groups will blend. New daffodil varieties can be added as they become available, but different types such as trumpets or double should always be planted in separate clumps. Smaller species bulbs such as irises, jonquils, crocuses and miniature daffodils can be naturalized in shorter lawns. Great swathes of the blue-flowered *Scilla siberica* have been know to run riot in March.

Summer meadows can be made from two different types of wild flowers, and they do not mix. One is composed of the annual weeds of cultivated soil such as the red poppy and blue larkspur; the other is the flowers from permanent pasture such as the ox-eye daisy, clover, buttercup, campion and foxglove. For the first, the soil has to be dug over and exposed for the seeds to germinate. The second has a permanent sward but the grass must consist of the slower growing varieties otherwise it will swamp the flowers. Usually these meadows cannot be made out of improved pasture unless the grass is burnt off and reseeded with less competitive varieties. When sowing meadows in woodland, special grasses which grow in the shady conditions should be used.

Autumn meadows grow larger and more decorative wild flowers such as teasels, thistles, arching stems of tall grasses. These can usually compete with a normal grass sward.

Mowing also affects the meadow. The foliage of spring bulbs should be allowed to die down before cutting. Short summer meadows of buttercups, violas and daisies can be mown every three weeks. Other summer meadows should be mown in July and again in October or March. Autumn meadows should be mown in April and October to control the grass and allow the flowers to set seed.

The beauty of these plants – the infinite variety of shape, texture, colour and smell – is a joy. Nurturing and succeeding with them is a great pleasure, and there is place for a small wild and woodland garden in almost every garden.

14

The Sheltered Garden

THE Sheltered Garden is enclosed, subdivided, protected and sheltered. Linked to the house by terraces, each division delights in a speciality – a white garden, an iris garden, a water garden, a Dutch garden, a rose garden or a great 'plat'. Paths run through arches or down flights of steps joining these gardens together. Walls, fountains, pergolas and flagstones create strong architectural forms providing the shape. Filled with riots of flowers contrasting with the lawn, they are colourful and packed with textures and seasonal changes.

The formal architecture and the style are a frame for the informality of the planting. Flowers cascade down walls, clamber over pergolas, froth over paths, creep over steps or cling to crevices. Plants produce the decoration whilst the structures provide the shape.

This is the style made famous by Gertrude Jekyll and used by Lawrence Johnston when creating Hidcote, Gloucestershire; by Vita Sackville-West in her renowned garden at Sissinghurst, Kent; and today by Christopher Lloyd at his family garden at Great Dixter, Sussex. This style, and those gardens which represent it, is still the most influential of all styles today.

The ideas evolved from a reaction against gaudy carpet bedding which completely disregarded the growing habits of the plants and was only interested in their brightly coloured flowers. William Robinson in his influential book *The English Flower Garden* (1883) attacked this desecration of the plants particularly as they were thrown away as soon as they had finished flowering. He advocated letting plants grow naturally, but this has certain disad-

vantages, not the least being that most of the time they are not very colourful, as few plants flower all summer long. So he recommended that special parts of the garden should be set aside for particular varieties, either based on type or colour, and that when flowering was finished these garden rooms did not necessarily form part of the circuit walk.

At the same time the powerful Arts and Crafts movement was promoting the use by craftsmen of natural materials as opposed to materials that were man-made and mass-produced in a factory. For instance, they advocated the use of wood instead of metal, stone or brick instead of concrete. They were also influenced by the stylized and abstract forms of plants and their parts. This influence was

Looking down the pergola at Rousham, showing the mixed border under the tumbling climbing roses. The planting is a riot of smells and rich colours – a very heady experience.

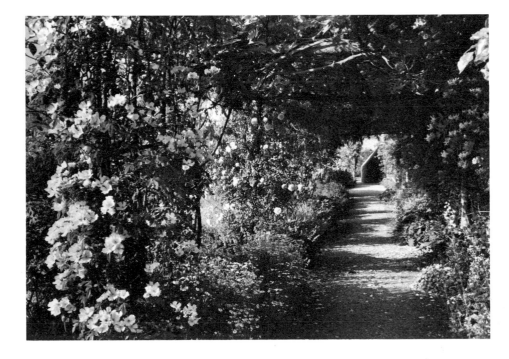

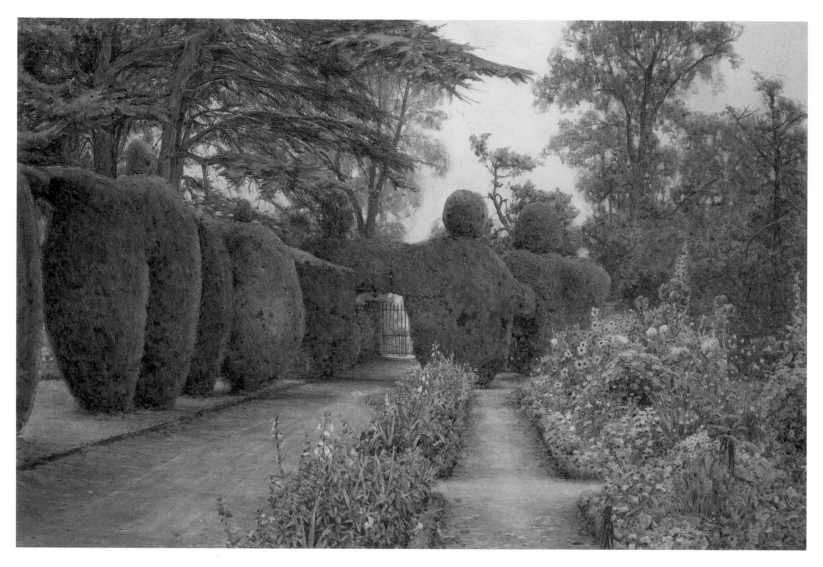

E. A. Rowe's watercolour of Campsea Ashe, Suffolk, showing the informal planting of perennials enclosed by a topiary yew hedge. The great bushes of michaelmas daisies, highlighted by gigantic red hollyhocks, together with yellow helenium daisies, and riots of yellow and red nasturtiums all show the brilliance of a late summer border. Colourful summer annuals pack the two ribbon beds in front.

based partly on the study of Gothic or medieval works of art and partly on the recently discovered and completely novel use of natural materials and abstraction of form apparent in Middle Eastern and Far Eastern design, particularly Japanese.

These concepts had an enormous impact on garden designers, who by the end of the nineteenth century had split into two camps – those who championed William Robinson's natural style and those who followed the more traditional formal style of Sir Reginald Blomfield. Early in the twentieth century these two styles generally came together: in England in the designs by Edwin Lutyens and Gertrude Jekyll; and in Scotland in those by Sir Robert Lorimer.

Other designers followed, such as Thomas Mawson and Sir Harold Peto. Later, in the 1920s, came Percy Cane and much more recently, particularly since World War II, John Codrington, Lanning Roper and Graham Stuart Thomas, who designed many of the National Trust gardens.

Many of these sheltered gardens are situated around smaller houses built for professional owners who were often personally interested in plants and gardening. This style is particularly suitable for the gifted amateur because, once the structure is laid out, the planting can easily be changed and, for instance, the latest plant introduction added. This is borne out in the number of influential gardens designed by accomplished people who were not professional gardeners: Lawrence Johnston at Hidcote; Vita Sackville-West at Sissinghurst; Margery Fish at Lambrook, Wiltshire; Leonard

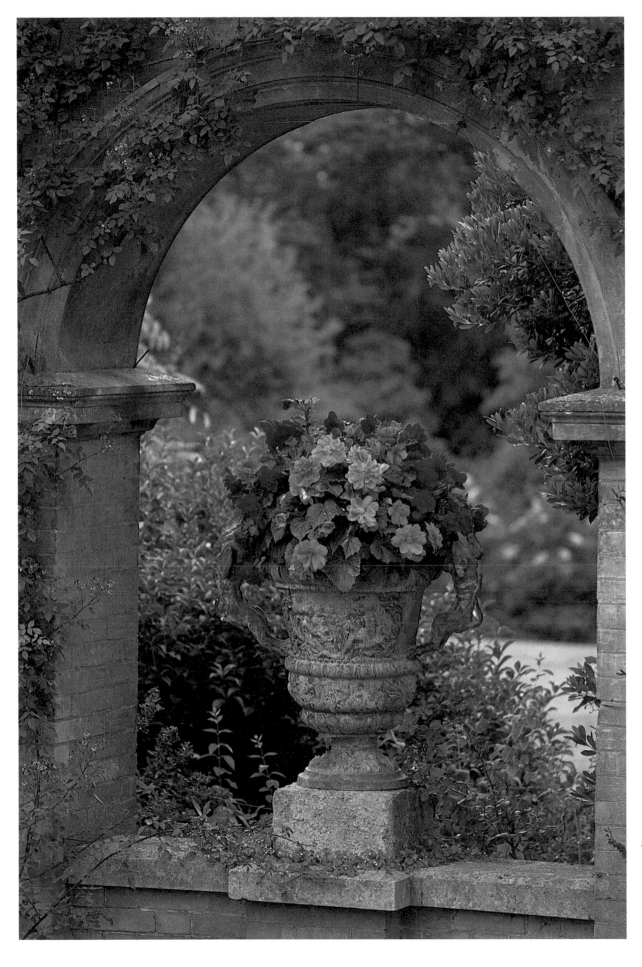

A garden vase spectacularly placed under an arched pergola and filled with clashing red and pink begonias.

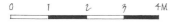

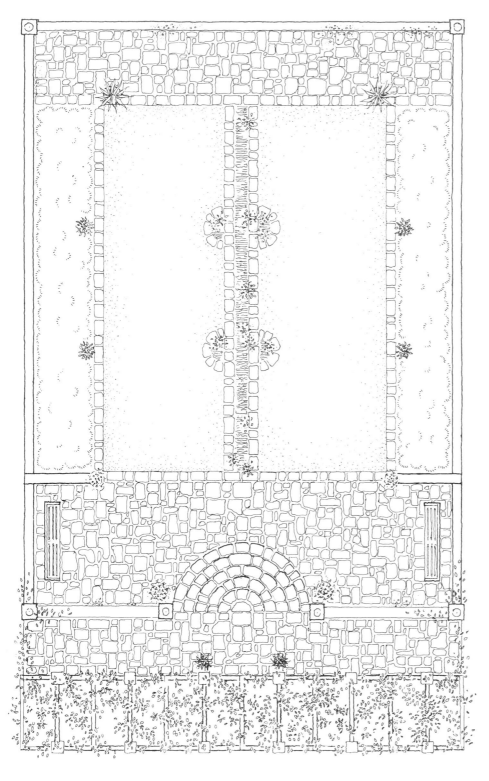

Messel at Nymans, Sussex; the Loders at Leonardslee, Sussex; and the Banks at Hergest Croft, Herefordshire.

Thus the sheltered garden is a 'mixed' style. Generally the shapes are taken from the formal styles of the seventeenth and eighteenth centuries, but they are planted with a much wider range of materials using more subtle colours.

The structure of the garden is often laid out by the architect who has designed the house. In 1927 Percy Cane explained in an article that 'the architectural character of the house must be the keynote for any architectural treatment in the garden.' Between the house and its terraced garden there should be a sense of harmony and proportion devised by a skilled use of perspective contrasting with enclosure, as well as the use of stone or brick matching those in the house. Circles are balanced with squares and rectangles, producing beautifully controlled and precise designs.

This style can be used in many different situations as it is very versatile and flexible. Its character depends on the space available and it can be laid out with one, two or more outdoor 'rooms' linked together with a strong, formal axis. This axis is frequently, but not always, aligned with the house. Many of the smaller gardens or courtyards open out from this central line, joined by paths.

The shape of each room depends on its type and its relationship to the whole layout. For example, a secluded rose garden can be a square divided into many geometric-shaped beds enclosed by a high yew hedge. The water garden can be long and narrow with a rill running down the centre or on either side, enclosed by low rubble stone walls. The summer herbaceous border can stretch along the brick wall of the kitchen garden using the mellow colour to display the plants.

On stepping out from the house, a broad paved terrace, preferably facing south, is typical of this style. It should be generous, and certainly large enough to sit and eat out on, with room enough for deck chairs and wooden tables. Often overlooking the main garden, this raised terrace provides enticing views.

The change between one type of garden and another should be immediately apparent. Stepping under tall yew arches, down steps or through narrow gates in the wall clearly indicates the beginning of a new scene. Glimpses through one arch and past another to an eye-catcher at the end of a vista or enfilade will arouse curiosity and lead the visitor on to explore further.

Steps link these gardens and the treads can be circular, oval, rectangular or square. Many of the patterns are variations of the ones shown in books published early in the eighteenth century. At Great Dixter there is a series of circular steps where each small flight joins and separates from another flight. At Hestercombe a double flight links the upper terrace to the 'great plat'.

Walls come in all shapes and sizes. Tall ones swoop down in dramatic curves to join lower ones. Others retain high banks whilst some stand free. The mixture is endless, but the line of the coping usually links the 'rooms' together and accentuates the shape, for instance, a curving sweep can be emphasized by bricks on edge or the flatness of the terrace by stone blocks. Most walls are made of rubble stones or bricks

which are lightly mortared together.

Balustrades edge the terraces and flights of steps, acting as handrails. Many of these designs are also taken from the eighteenth-century design books. Balls, acorns, urns, vases, pineapples and other ornaments decorate the plinths of the stone or reconstituted stone balustrades. These can occasionally be substituted by wooden railings.

Narrow paths can be made from gravel or brick. Grass should only be used on broad paths as it will not tolerate much wear. Countless patterns can be created using two colours of brick, or stone with brick, or flagstones edged with brick. The combinations are endless. Large rectangular flagstones can be laid on the terrace near the house but in smaller areas such as the paths or, for example, between the flower beds in a rose garden, the stones can be placed in a more random pattern known as 'crazy paving'.

Within a special garden the pattern of paving should be consistent throughout the whole area. This unity increases the scale and size of the garden. The materials and patterns used in the paving can also be repeated in the enclosing walls or their copings. Thus red tiles used as a decoration in the brick paving might also appear as decorative protection on a brick wall.

Carpets of sweet-smelling thyme or mats of

OPPOSITE
The plan of a sheltered garden. Down the centre is a stone edged rill with semi-circular beds for water plants, such as irises. On either side of the lawn are two broad herbaceous borders, and at either end, broad paved terraces. In the lower part of the drawing, a flight of semi-circular steps leads from one of the terraces to an upper terrace on which is a pergola covered by climbing plants.

Close-up of the rill. The rill and semi-circular beds for bog plants have broad stone edging. The water in the rill flows over a series of shallow stones to break the reflection and make the sound of tinkling water.

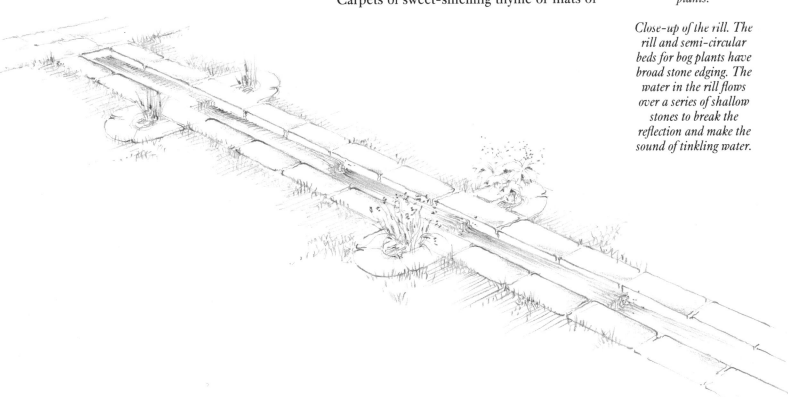

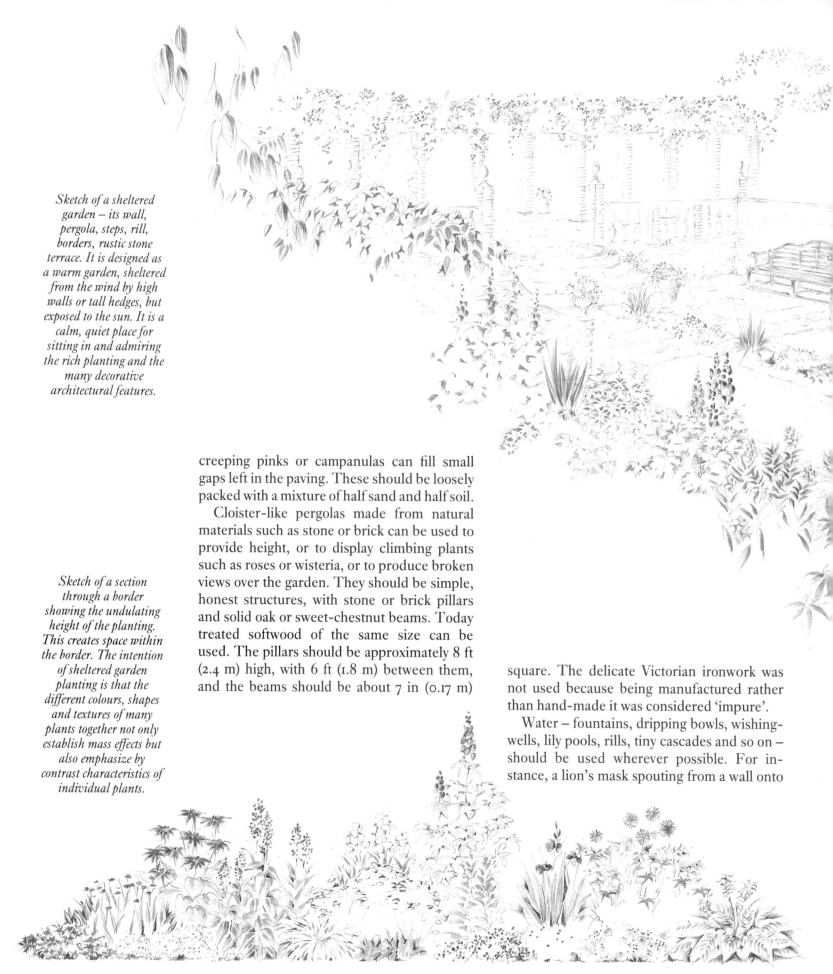

Sketch of a sheltered garden – its wall, pergola, steps, rill, borders, rustic stone terrace. It is designed as a warm garden, sheltered from the wind by high walls or tall hedges, but exposed to the sun. It is a calm, quiet place for sitting in and admiring the rich planting and the many decorative architectural features.

Sketch of a section through a border showing the undulating height of the planting. This creates space within the border. The intention of sheltered garden planting is that the different colours, shapes and textures of many plants together not only establish mass effects but also emphasize by contrast characteristics of individual plants.

creeping pinks or campanulas can fill small gaps left in the paving. These should be loosely packed with a mixture of half sand and half soil.

Cloister-like pergolas made from natural materials such as stone or brick can be used to provide height, or to display climbing plants such as roses or wisteria, or to produce broken views over the garden. They should be simple, honest structures, with stone or brick pillars and solid oak or sweet-chestnut beams. Today treated softwood of the same size can be used. The pillars should be approximately 8 ft (2.4 m) high, with 6 ft (1.8 m) between them, and the beams should be about 7 in (0.17 m) square. The delicate Victorian ironwork was not used because being manufactured rather than hand-made it was considered 'impure'.

Water – fountains, dripping bowls, wishing-wells, lily pools, rills, tiny cascades and so on – should be used wherever possible. For instance, a lion's mask spouting from a wall onto

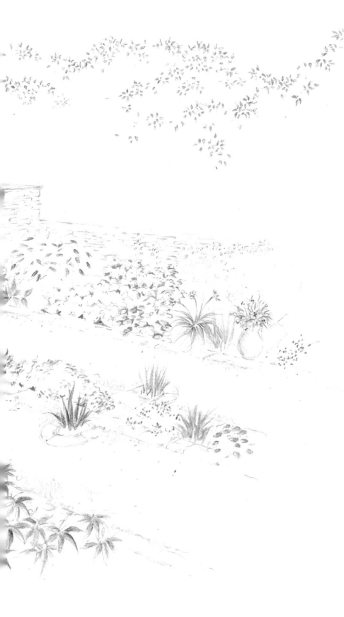

or with colourful flowers cascading over them. Set in sheltered arbours or on the terrace near the house, these stone basins copied a Japanese tradition as well as providing special conditions for alpine plants.

'While the plan may be compared to the drawing of a garden picture, planting is the painting of it,' states Madeline Agar in 1911 in her book *Garden Design*. She continues, 'a knowledge of colour, habit and season of plants is needed ... and besides this the designer should have an eye for effective planting and the fit disposal of trees and shrubs.'

The inspiration of Gertrude Jekyll lies in her skill as an artist and designer. She was one of the first designers to make the use of colour the primary feature of her designs and her ideas are still in use today. She painted many influential 'pictures' with plants, and introduced the idea of blending subtle colours to create a satisfying theme and to heighten features. She used a mixture of perennial plants to make her renowned herbaceous borders.

Describing the colour composition of a long border, she wrote:

> it means the arrangement of colour with the deliberate intention of producing beautiful pictorial effect by means of harmony and of contrast ... It begins with flowers of tender and cool colouring – palest pinks, blue, white and palest yellow, and passing on to deep orange and rich mahogany, and so coming to a culminating glory of the strongest scarlet, tempered with rich but softer reds, and backed and intergrouped with flowers and foliage of dark claret colour. The progression of colour then recedes in the same general order, as in its approach to the midmost glory, till it comes near the further end to a quiet harmony of lavender and purple and tender pink, with a whole setting of grey and silvery foliage.

Colour harmony extended into the garden 'rooms', producing the famous 'white' garden at Sissinghurst, where only white flowers are

a semi-circular pool might act as a source. The water bubbles over coloured tiles along a rill or narrow shallow channel down the centre of the garden. The channel is often edged with stone to reinforce the shape. At Hestercombe this rill feeds four circular lily pools on either side before rushing underground. Sometimes the water reappears further down the hill, where it bursts out of a 'spring' tumbling and splashing through the wild garden or shrubbery like an alpine stream. This can be seen at Coleton Fishacre Garden, Devon.

Stone sinks, basins, lead cisterns and other artefacts are often planted with alpines, herbs,

Steps and Walls

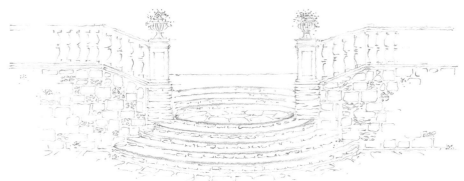

wall and planted up with ferns, thymes, pinks and other plants which enjoy these conditions.

Steps are built as features and these sketches show three different patterns. Where there is room, a platform between the runs provides more character and can be made in a decorative pattern using different materials to the walls, such as this one of brick tiles shaped in a hexagon.

Most sheltered gardens are enclosed by walls or hedges and are joined to other parts of the garden by steps. Their character adds to the atmosphere of the garden and Gertrude Jekyll was very fond of growing plants in the walls. The height of the wall depends on whether the garden is to be totally enclosed or whether there are particular views to be seen over it. Sometimes the top course can be built like a dry-stone

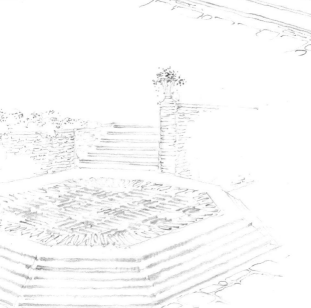

Oval steps which rise to a platform at the junction of the wall and rise again on the other side are very typical of this period. This design and several others are copied from examples built in the early eighteenth century and can be seen in John James's book *The Theory and Practice of Gardening* (1712). Walls and steps can be made of local stone blocks, or as a rubble wall using more shaley stone or with brick. The stones can be of any size but the quality should be checked because some stone and brick will disintegrate when frosted.

mixed amongst a variety of green foliage, and the 'red' borders at Hidcote. Rooms or borders can be filled with one or even two colours such as greens and variegated plants, yellow and blue flowers.

Other rooms can be specialized to create a scented garden, or herb garden; or they might provide one habitat such as a water or bog garden; or to be planted with seasonal flowers such as bulbs for spring or winter; or they might be gardens for just one variety such as irises, roses, lilies or Michaelmas daisies. As Madeline Agar said, whatever theme is chosen make sure that 'the groups are bold – never less than three plants together – dovetailed into one another'. Gertrude Jekyll herself advised, 'Aim for informal feel, luxuriant, billowing, softening lines and hard edges. Plants are found on walls, in paving, in borders, on almost every surface and in profusion. Don't be mean with planting.'

When planning a border the tallest plants should generally be placed at the back or, if the border is seen from both sides, in the middle, but it is essential to create soft and billowing lines and this can be done by bringing some of the taller plants forward and pushing certain medium-size ones to the back.

A border solely of catmint or a hedge of rosemary creates a subtle effect in a small area. Lilies or other delicate plants can grow out of carpets of pinks or other plants with grey foliage. Rare flowering trees can be planted as a background to the borders, while dark green yew or holly hedges may enclose these gardens. The evergreen Irish yew or upright juniper can be used to mark formal paths or long axes.

Large expanses of grass are to be avoided except where they are needed for games of croquet or lawn tennis but grass can be used as a cool restful contrast in a busy parterre. Natural meadows with small, delicate spring bulbs and early orchids growing between fine grasses is very much part of the soft look so highly prized but is perhaps the most difficult to cultivate as the soil condition must be just right – that is, very poor. Christopher Lloyd treasures one

outside the front door of Great Dixter.

Colour, harmony, seclusion and peace pervade the sheltered garden. Attractive and colourful, these garden rooms can be created in a small courtyard or as part of a larger area. The style enables masses of one kind of flower to fill a border or endless varieties to be mixed and blended in a unity of design to create a beautiful herbaceous border. This style is familiar to most gardeners and thus easy to re-create.

The architectural features of a sheltered garden are epitomized at Hestercombe, designed by Gertrude Jekyll and Sir Edwin Lutyens together in 1906. It is the fusion of strong shapes and outlines with the soft, billowing luxuriant forms of plants.

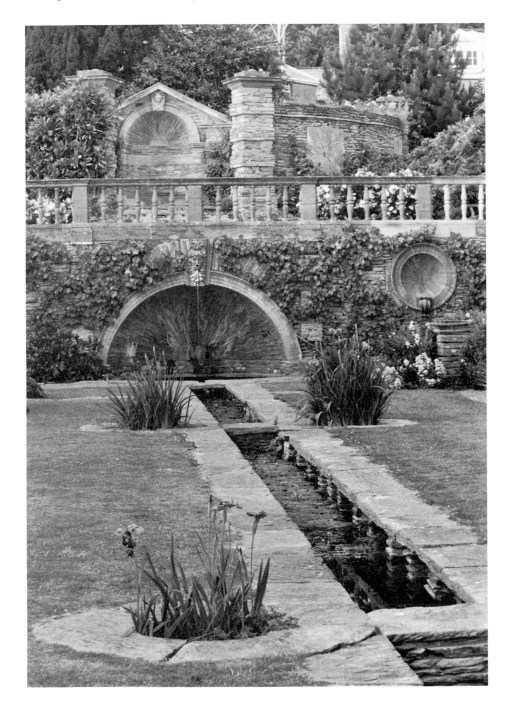

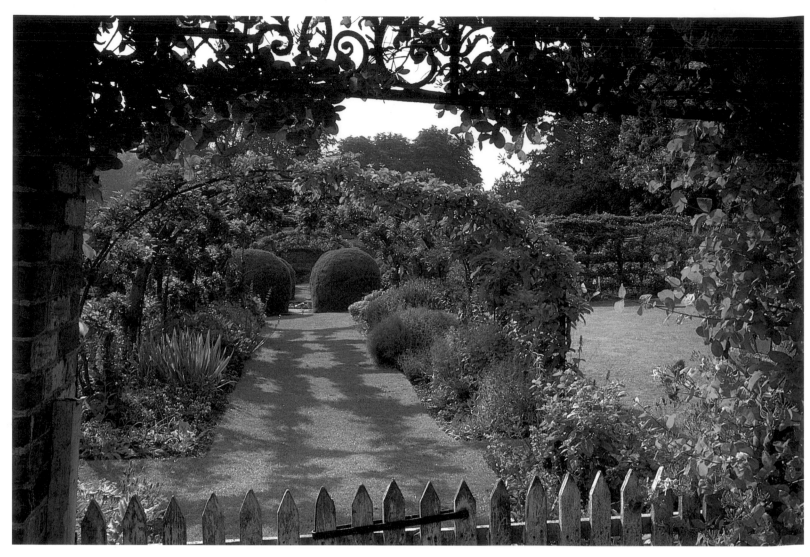

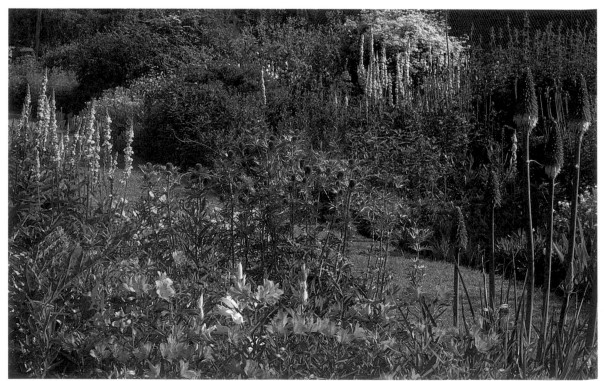

ABOVE
At Heale, a view past an herbaceous border in a sheltered garden through to an apple orchard. Note how the narrow borders emphasize the variety of height and colour of the plants.

An herbaceous border in Jekyll's most colourful style, using plants of different heights and colour. At the back is a tall white herbaceous clematis, at the front Peruvian lilies and upright red hot pokers.

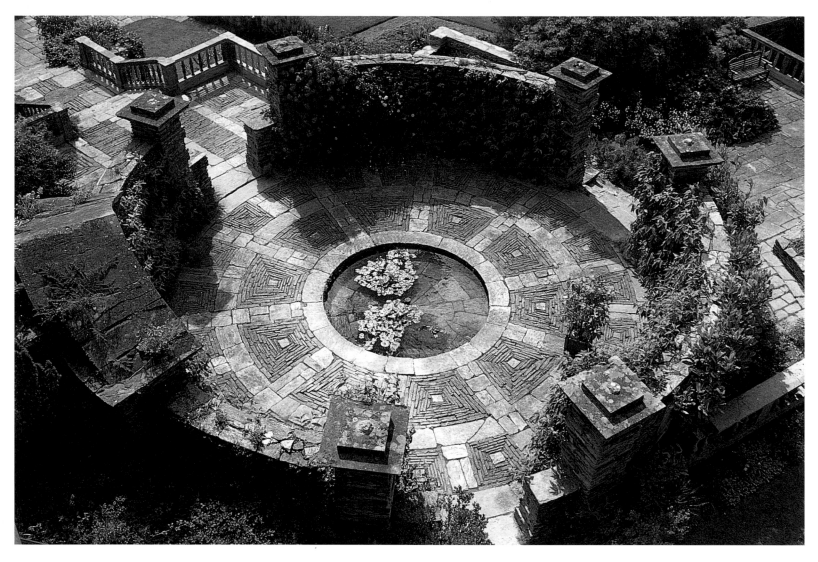

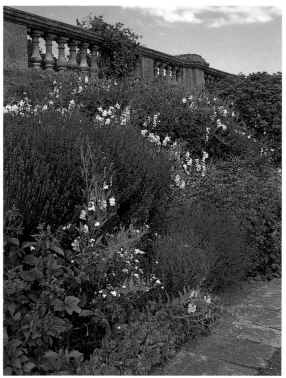

The subtlety of this style of Jekyll border lies in using only two contrasting colours – purple lavender and purple fennel set against white campanula. In the front are the grey-green leaves of the purple-flowering sedum. The stone wall behind acts as a backdrop, protects the plants and sets off their colour.

The dramatic form and radiating lines of a circular staircase 'landing' in the garden at Hestercombe. The exaggeration of the mosaic pattern by the mixture of stone tiles and cobbles is typical of Lutyens' work.

179

15

The Exotic Conservatory

TENDER and exotic plants grow in the exotic conservatory protected by glass from the cold. Many strange and tropical plants can thrive inside this delicate and ornate garden room. Luxuriant and bold, textured foliage gives height and interest to magnificent displays of colourful blooms billowing and cascading from floor to ceiling. Their scents and aroma fill the air. These exotic species can be accompanied by other tender plants such as geraniums, fuchsias and begonias. Bathed in warmth and sunlight, these will give a rich array of flowers up until Christmas.

Sweet scent, glowing colours and fantastic shapes combine within the lacy glass structure to create this architectural garden room. Separated by a small alcove, lobby or corridor, the exotic conservatory can be attached to the house on the south-eastern or south-western side or it can be free-standing in its own garden. A conservatory is ideal for entertaining in, for walking about in bad weather and for dining in. Eating under the clusters of grapes on a vine, or drinking amongst the camellias and gardenias is an enjoyable experience.

Exotic conservatories for tender plants evolved from the seventeenth-century orangeries which sheltered prized citrus fruit such as oranges, lemons, limes and grapefruit from winter frosts. As the skill of glassmaking developed, the dimensions and style of the glasshouse improved, but until the manufacturing technology of the Victorians, conservatories were only built by the very wealthy. The revolution came with the production of cast iron, which created a light and airy structure, and the invention in 1848 of plate glass, providing larger panes which could stretch between the delicate iron pillars and their finials.

During the nineteenth century exotic conservatories became the rage and variations can be found in the most unlikely places, such as perched on a rooftop like a covered roof-garden, or as an enlarged bay window or tacked on the front facade as an entrance hall or foyer. Ferns and mosses can grow in deep shade in conservatories facing north and an east-facing corridor provides perfect conditions for camellias. As interest in horticulture and plants grew, even more conservatories were built and at the height of their popularity they were erected in any available situation.

Exotic conservatory gardening was given an enormous boost in 1851 by the Great Exhibition housed in Sir Joseph Paxton's Crystal Palace glasshouse, which became a symbol of Victorian technology. Mrs Beeton in *The Book of Garden Management* explains the difference between the various kinds of glasshouses. A conservatory is for growing plants that 'are too tender to stand the severity of the winter'. It may be without heat, in which case it is known as a cold house, or it can be heated to between 40 and 45 degrees Fahrenheit (5–7 degrees Centigrade) during the coldest nights. Plants can grow naturally in borders as well as in pots on staging. In a greenhouse 'all the plants by which it is tenanted are in pots or tubs, and platforms and stages are erected . . . in order to bring them as near to the glass, so that they may have the benefit to full exposure of the light', and the winter temperature should not fall below 50 degrees Fahrenheit (10 degrees Centigrade). A hothouse or stove is the warmest

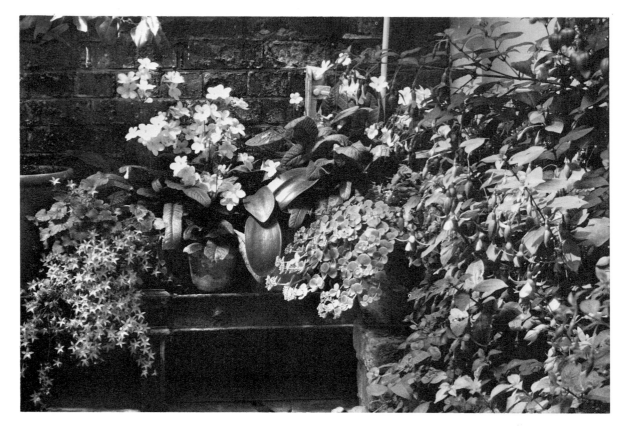

A great variety of plants can be grown in a conservatory. Here Streptocarpus blooms in pots alongside yellow-leaved ivy, fuchsia, campanula and amaryllis.

and is designed for growing tropical plants or forcing fruit. 'A higher temperature must be sustained within it and a moisture atmosphere must prevail' and the heat should average about 75 degrees Fahrenheit (24 degrees Centigrade) and not fall below 60 degrees Fahrenheit (15 degrees Centigrade). In a Victorian kitchen garden there were many other types of glass-houses designed especially for growing fruits and vegetables such as melons, tomatoes, grapes, peaches, pineapples, mushrooms and so on, and for particular functions such as propagation, standing out or growing on. These are not included in this chapter but are well described in many of the nineteenth-century books listed in the Bibliography.

The architectural style of the exotic conservatory 'should, at least, be in harmony with that of the house: if ornaments are permitted, they should be Gothic, Tudor, or Grecian ... congruity is to be studied.' Designs were published for conservatories, porches and verandas in various styles. The catalogues of the famous suppliers such as Messrs. Messenger & Co., Loughborough, are the basis for many of the conservatories reproduced today.

When building a new conservatory, there are certain requirements of aspect, heating, ventilation and drainage which should be considered as well as the growing conditions for the type of plants chosen, such as the soil and humidity. Specialist advice on all these matters is probably useful. However, if the conservatory is to be used for entertaining this can conflict with the most suitable conditions for growing many of the exotic tropical plants, as they will require a much greater humidity than would be comfortable for the guests.

Once the style has been chosen, the conservatory 'might be rendered both picturesque and interesting, apart from the actual brilliancy of the flowers, the principal feature being to relieve the spectator, as far as possible, of the idea that he is walking under glass' explains the Victorian expert, Mr Noel Humphreys, quoted at some length by Mrs Beeton. He continues, 'I propose to do this by making the frame-work for the glass of some irregular form, resembling the branches of trees or ribs of large leaves, such as palms.' He also recommends planting large ferns and palms between the pillars and climbing plants trailing over the arches so that

The conservatory at
Wallington Hall.
Conservatory planting
is spectacular and
colourful, and here
tree ferns clamber
up supports to
wrought iron tracery.
There are a great
range of ferns, varying
in colour through greens
and mauves. There are
palms in front, and
pelargoniums.

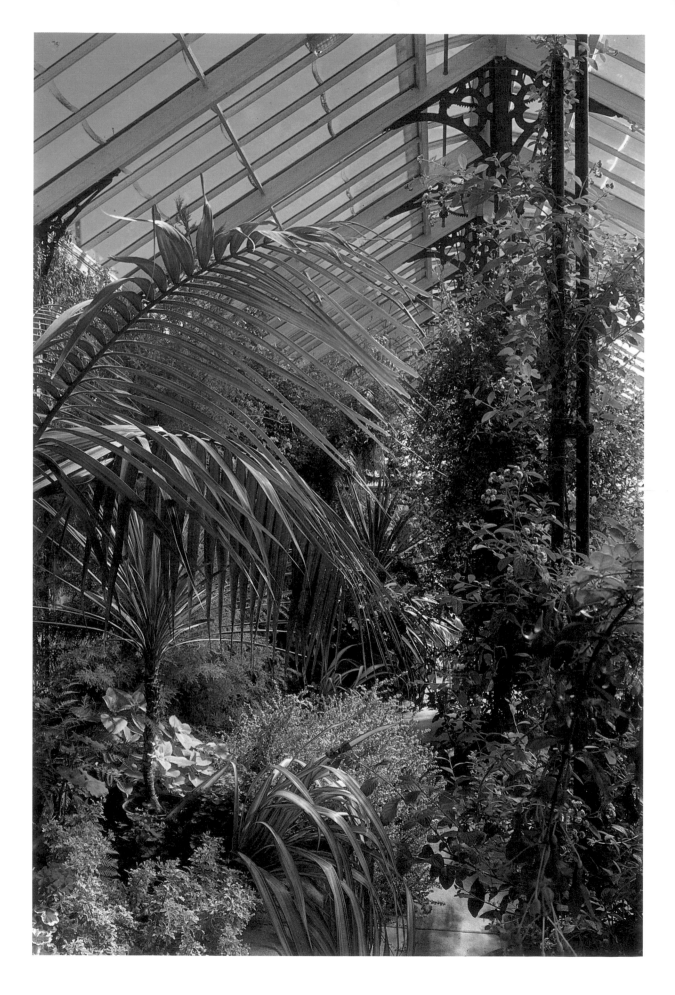

182

the line of the arches is half hidden and broken by the plants.

Most conservatories are based on a rectangle or square, and the size depends on the aspect and position. However, it is the decoration, the pattern of iron work, the shape of the beds, the stands, benches and platforms used for displaying the plants which give them their romantic character.

Humidity and water for the plants are essential. The supply can be either decorative, such as a dripping 'stream of tepid water' flowing through the darker and more shady parts, 'amid fragments of rock and boulders, in which aquatics and rock plants from the tropics might be displayed', or it can be more practical, such as a tank under the staging filled with rainwater from the roof.

In a dark and shady place a fernery can add a touch of the tropics to a cool exotic conserva-

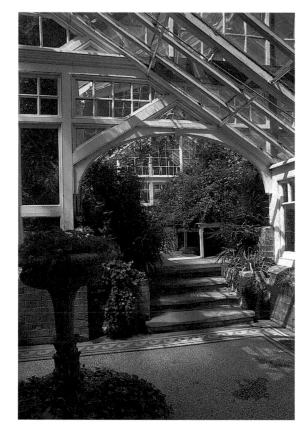

The conservatory as a room, as at Hergest Croft. There is a magnificent display of fuchsias up the steps. In the foreground is an indoor fountain, now filled with flowers. The flooring is an elaborate pattern of mosaic tiles.

BELOW
The marvellous and exotic fernery at Rousham, with its extraordinary rock work. The wall is made of imitation stone, with pockets designed for growing special ferns. Pots of brightly-coloured plants on the black-and-white mosaic floor further emphasize the dark, romantic rock face.

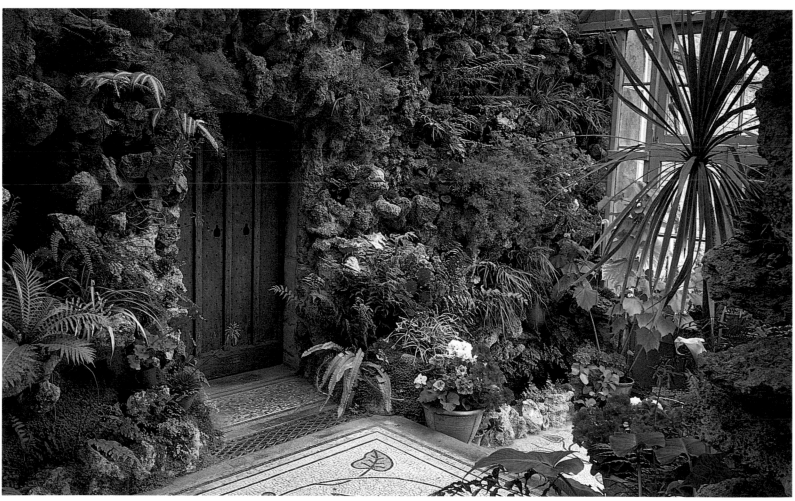

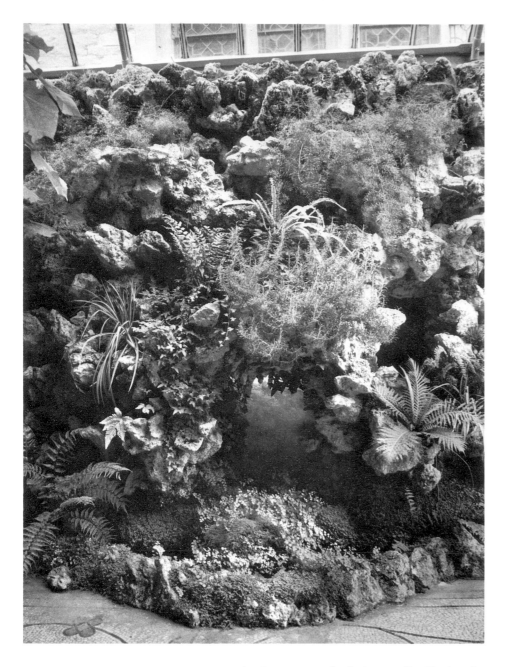

A semi-circular conservatory grotto of tufa rock, filled with different ferns and ivies.

mosses, lichens and some orchids. Under the filmy decaying bark, stone and gravel provide the sharp drainage needed for many ferns.

Most plants require greater humidity during the hot summer months and this is done by hosing down floor or paths between the beds and staging. Brightly coloured tiles of red, blue, terracotta, black or white, or patterned stone, polished marble, slate or terrazzo can be laid in attractive designs to emphasize the layout, and this flooring can easily be washed down. The level and falls of the floor control the water dispersal, which can be into either a flower bed under the staging or decorative grating covering a drain.

Pillars, arches, plinths and other structural braces supporting the benches can be beautifully and decoratively patterned. They can be made in modern materials but based on nineteenth-century cast-iron structures. Ornamental panels or colourful ceramic tiles can be used to cover ugly or bare surfaces, for instance, unsightly sides of raised beds. These tiles may be based on the patterns of William Morris, William de Morgan and other Arts and Crafts designers.

In the nineteenth century the favourite colours for the rendered walls were white, cream or stone. Shades of green and blue with darker shades or black were used to highlight the shape of the cast-iron pillars and arches, especially the pillars holding up the staging and benches. Lead-free paint without fumes to damage the plants should always be used.

The layout of an exotic conservatory may vary considerably. The main display can be in the centre with a walk around the outside. Or if the conservatory is to be used for entertaining, this central area can be laid out as a patio, with a fountain or plants in pots separating it from the path. Or if changing displays of colourful plants in season are desired, such as brilliant geraniums, weeping fuchsias or sweet-scented lilies growing in pots, they can be shown on raised staging made from narrow wooden slats. This central area can also be designed as a bor-

tory sited on a north-facing wall. Curiously shaped feathery ferns will grow out of specially made pockets or brackets fixed to the wall and concealed by rocks or cork bark. Drips of water oozing over stones or dribbling along bark-covered branches into tiny pools can help to create the effect of an exotic tropical rain forest and provide the humidity required by the ferns. The facing of the wall can be formed to look like the tangled branches of the forest and can be covered by a render of weak cement mixed with peat and soil. These damp dark conditions are also suitable for other plants such as

Staging of Plants

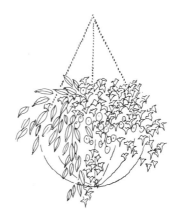

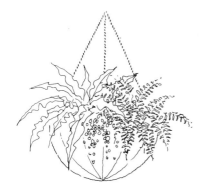

Staging allows for the plants grown in pots to be arranged artistically in groups according to the conditions they require. Some plants like more sun while others prefer shadier conditions and so can be displayed at the back of the house. Staging can be level or tiered and made out of cast-iron grating or timber slats, but not of stone or slate as they do not allow the heat to circulate properly.

Plants on the staging are carefully placed to create the effect of a flower border. If displaying a seasonal show it is better to let the plants grow up together because, as they grow into one another, the foliage of the plant below will hide the pot of the one above. This also prevents the pots from being scorched by the sun. Most plants should be grown in terracotta pots, which allow the air to circulate freely and the water to drain better than plastic ones.

Baskets hanging from the ceiling can be colourful and attractive and suit some plants better than others. Geraniums, petunias, heathers and verbenas all enjoy growing in baskets. Certain orchids grow better when suspended from the ceiling, as long as there is sufficient humidity. Most plants like some humidity and it can easily be provided by placing a cistern below the staging and filling it with water either supplied directly from rainwater spouts or from the mains.

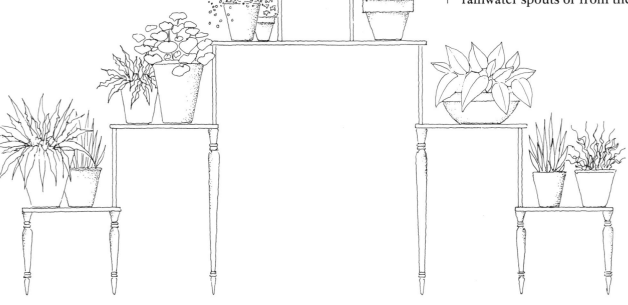

der with, for example, the taller and more permanent plants in the middle and the smaller and more temporary ones, such as those in pots, around the outside.

Staging raised in layers assists the grouping of plants so that they appear to be growing as if they are in a border. If the shelves are correctly spaced, the flower pots can be kept out of sight. The stage should be at least 26 in (0.66 m) from the floor and can be attached to the walls.

Another nineteenth-century design uses 'neat cast-iron staging' constructed as circular or square tables with flanged edges. Drainage from any table is important, and most stages are made from treated timber slats which allow the excess water to drip through to the floor.

Other smaller ornamental tables constructed in cast iron, slate or wood can be moved from the conservatory into an alcove or hall. Such tables can also be made from mod-

The sketch of the interior of a conservatory. The black-and-white mosaic floor is laid out in a diamond pattern. The metal staging echoes the pattern of the floor tiles. The indoor fountain is shaped like a table. Plants are placed on the staging, with ferns and other shade- or moisture-loving plants underneath.

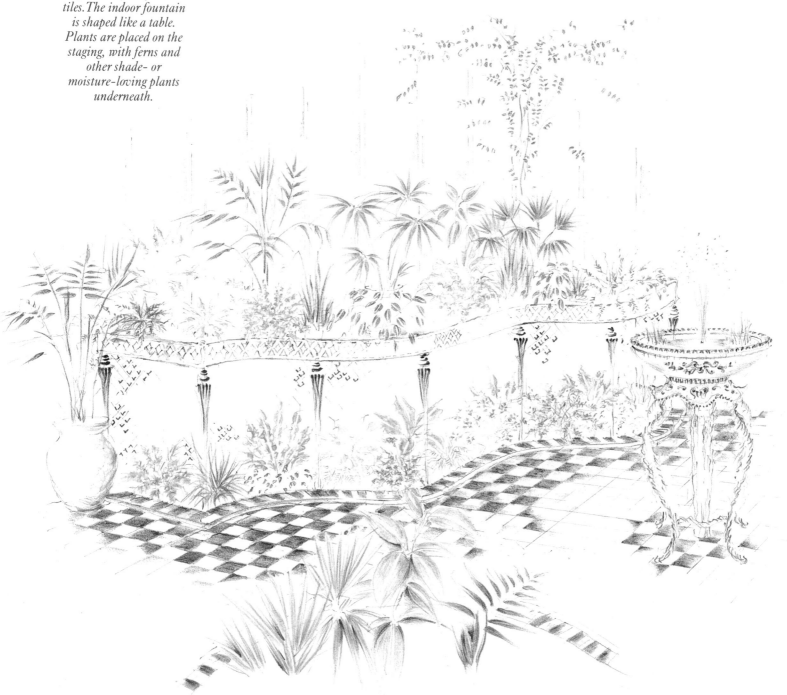

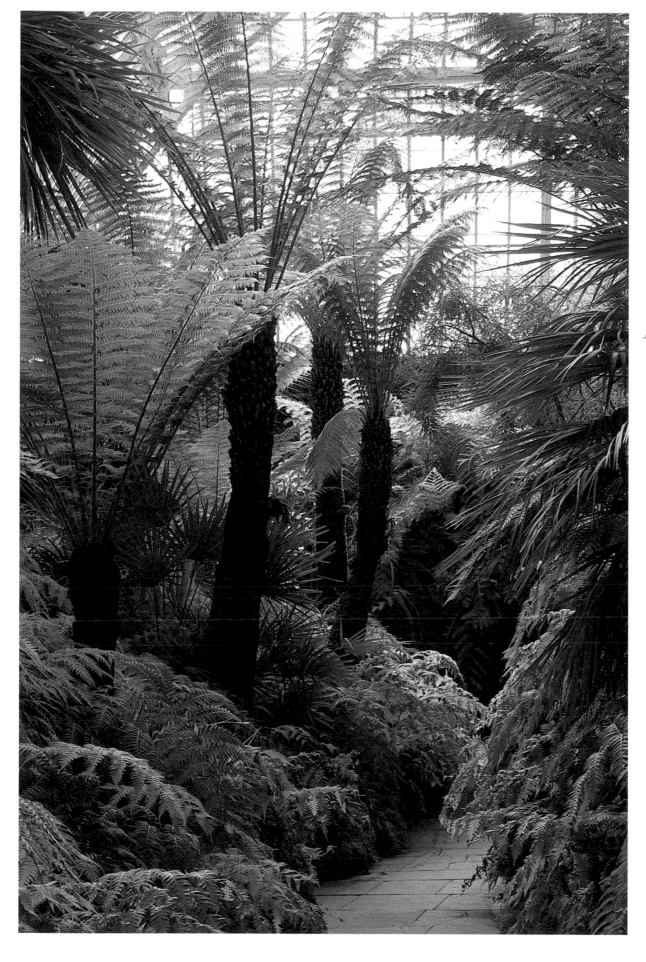

The magnificent 'hothouse' at Tatton Park, evoking the humidity and heat of a tropical garden or even jungle, and filled with ferns including the huge tree fern dicksonia.

ern materials but they must be strong enough to hold plants. The top recess should be deep enough to cover the plant pot and it should be lined with a waterproof material. The plants should stand on a layer of gravel. They should be placed like a flower arrangement and the pots covered with moss. In more elaborate tables, small fountains can play, the water pipe possibly camouflaged by a decorative tree trunk. Other tables may be covered by a highly ornamented glass cover like a Wardian case, which keeps the humidity in. These enable many plants to survive in the drier conditions of the sitting-room.

Exotic orchids can be grown in wooden baskets covered in cork bark and suspended from the ceiling. Alternatively they can be staged on wooden slats placed over water either in basins or in the rainwater tank, which should be kept at a constant temperature. Humidity and free drainage are necessary, as are heat in winter and light in summer, to promote flowering.

Climbers growing in the ground or in pots can twist and curl around the pillars and their flowers festoon the walks. Taut wire frames can be provided for many flowering climbers especially annuals such as black-eyed Susan, nasturtium and blue or white morning glory. These plants were very popular in Victorian conservatories because their foliage provided a screen from the hot sun during the summer whilst in the winter it died back.

Delicate *jardinières* made from elaborate wirework are very decorative and provide another way of displaying plants in a small area. These can be shaped like baskets or layered like staging or attached to a pillar like a flower stand. They are usually white, but can be painted any colour to suit. Wirework can also be used for hanging baskets suspended from the high ceiling. Brightly coloured ivy-leaf geraniums, trailing lobelia and many verbenas and other sun-loving plants can create a riot of colour. The variation of planting is endless.

Wrought-iron seats decorated with suitable motifs such as ferns or oak leaves may be placed in alcoves or around small tables. There are many fancy patterns for them which can be

The ground plan of a conservatory. A dominant feature is the very pretty black-and-white mosaic floor, around the outside of which is erected the raised curved staging, echoing its shape. Plants are grown in the raised staging, in beds below it, in the two large circular beds and in pots on the floor. At the centre is a small fountain.

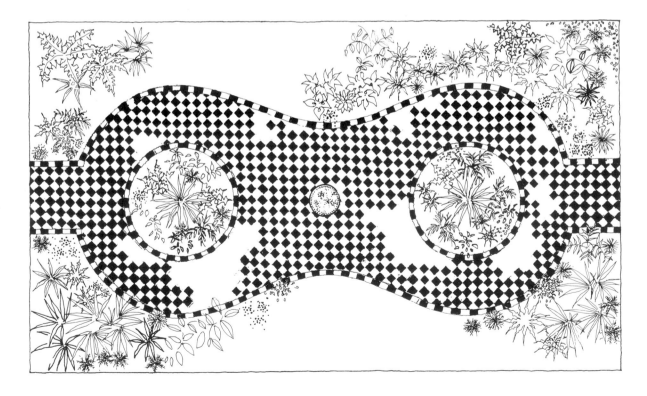

0   1   2   3   4M

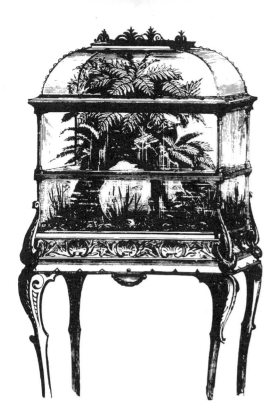

viewed at the Ironbridge Museum library. They can be painted to tone in with the colour scheme of the rest of the conservatory. Alternatively rustic seats are made from bark-covered branches of grotesque shapes and set into an alcove surrounded by tropical plants. Whatever style is chosen, it must not be mixed with others.

In his book *How to Lay Out a Garden*, published in 1858, Edward Kemp is very keen on sculpture, particularly in alcoves or along the passage between the conservatory and the house. He explains that 'sculpture of a high order, in marble or marble vases, urns, tazzas, &, can be most fittingly accommodated in architectural conservatories, whether on pedestals, or in niches and recesses. Nothing throws out and relieves marble statuary so well as dark-foliaged plants, such as Camellias.'

Orange trees are always grown in square boxes whose sides come apart so that when necessary the plants can easily have their roots pruned or be transplanted into larger boxes. Elaborate motifs can be painted on the sides to fit in with the other decorations but in early orangeries the boxes were painted plain white or green.

The exotic conservatory 'may be considered as a covered or exotic garden' and the plants grown can range from an ornate display of flowers to a tropical jungle. Swaying palms, feathery ferns and fanciful cycads growing permanently in beds imitate the hot humid tropics, whilst the flowering season of tender garden plants such as geraniums, plumbago and bougainvillea can be extended to display brilliant colours from June to January. Exotic climbers such as the pink lapageria or the cerise passion flower can festoon the house and the overpowering scent of *Jasminum polyanthum* can pervade the conservatory and the rooms beyond.

As a 'garden' room the exotic conservatory is an enchanting addition to any house and is marvellous for any gardener who wishes to grow more exotic and unusual plants. Exciting and colourful, it is a wonderful luxury as a warm garden on a cold winter's day and gorgeous on a summer's evening when entertaining guests amongst the sweet scents and brilliant flowers.

A Victorian plant case and aquarium, decorated with metal filigree, which is placed on an ornate table. The ferns and water plants flourish and create oxygen for the fish within the sealed system of the case.

A narrow but very imposing indoor conservatory built in a drawing room. The ingenuity of its late Victorian design lies in incorporating a large window as a glass wall.

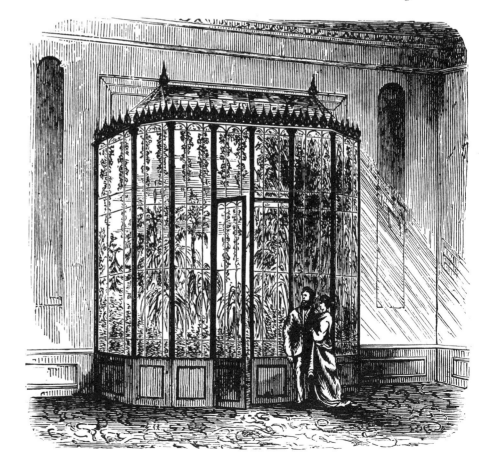

Parterres and Borders

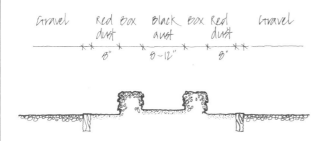

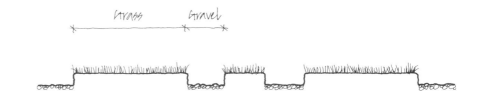

This shows a section through one of the scrolls or tendrils of an **Embroidery Parterre**. Red brick dust or crushed stone is placed next to the box hedge and is kept in position by a narrow timber board set about 1 in (0.025 m) above the level of the gravel. Between the box hedges blacksmith's dust fills in the detail of the pattern. This can be substituted by crushed coal or finely ground dark stone.

In order to achieve the maximum effect this parterre needs to be beautifully maintained and all the litter and debris must be picked up. The hedges should be clipped twice a year to keep them trim.

This section shows the **Formula** for setting out the compartments of a parterre in the Fantasy and Knot Gardens. The width of the compartment B must be either twice, three times or four times the width of the central path A. It should not be any measurement in between, nor should it be more than four times the width of the path. If it is, then the width of the path should be changed in order to conform to the formula.

This section through the heraldic **Knot Parterre** shows the spacing between the hedges and gravel. The hedges should all be clipped to the same height and width. When trimming the hedge, the sides should be slightly battered so that the top is narrower than the bottom. This will ensure a uniform shape as the top of the hedge, which receives more sunlight, will grow more quickly than the base.

The section through the **Grasswork in the English Manner** shows how the pattern is cut into the lawn. Gravel is laid about 2 in (0.05 m) below the level of the grass and the turf is carefully cut to keep the shape. The pattern should be set out at least once a year and string can be used to mark the straight lines but wooden templates should be made for the curves. If the lawn has recently been disturbed and the grass is not vigorous enough to hold the edges then the pattern can be set out with narrow timber boards pegged into the ground. In the eighteenth century the grass was cut with a scythe and in order to keep a good sward the turf was changed every four years.

'Plattes Bandes' Borders

There are four different types of narrow borders around a parterre. They are usually raised in the middle and are 'set out with Flowers, Shrubs and Yew'. The width of the band

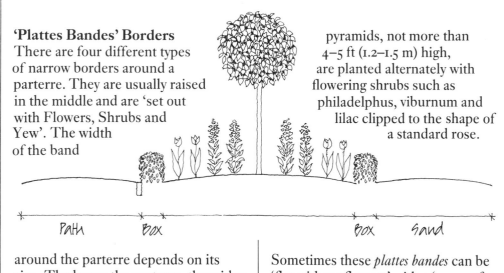

pyramids, not more than 4–5 ft (1.2–1.5 m) high, are planted alternately with flowering shrubs such as philadelphus, viburnum and lilac clipped to the shape of a standard rose.

around the parterre depends on its size. The larger the parterre, the wider the borders. However, the normal width is about 4 ft (1.2 m) but it can be as much as 6 ft (1.8 m) wide.

This section shows the border filled with flowers. It is edged with a low box hedge. The flowers are planted in rows, with the middle rows kept for plants that are bedded out according to the season. The type of plants should not be mixed, for example, bulbs should not be planted with herbaceous plants. If the border is 6 ft (1.8 m) wide then there are four rows on each side of the centre line making eight altogether. If the border is only 3–4 ft (0.9–1.2 m) wide then there will be just four rows altogether, two rows on either side of the centre.

The larger clipped shrubs are placed at regular intervals along the middle of the border. Yew or box pruned into topiary shapes such as balls on poles or

Sometimes these *plattes bandes* can be 'flat without flowers' with a 'verge of grass in the middle bounded by two small paths raked smooth and sanded – sometimes garnished with yews, flowering shrubs with vases and flower-pots set regularly along the middle of the verge'. These narrow paths should be raked and not rolled. John James recommends using vases of 'Dutch ware'.

As a variation of this type of border orange trees grown in boxes may be used as decoration instead of the vases. During the summer these can be set out evenly spaced along the raked path. A low box hedge marks the outer edge of the strip but there is no hedge on the inner grass verge. Sometimes clipped yew is planted between the cases so that there is some shape during the winter when the oranges are stored in the greenhouse.

Here the borders are planted with bulbs in a 'chequer' pattern. If there are four rows the first two rows might be planted with tulips and the other two with hyacinths. If the border is much smaller and there are only two rows, then the row next to the hedge could be planted with a tulip and the other one with a hyacinth and a daffodil alternately.

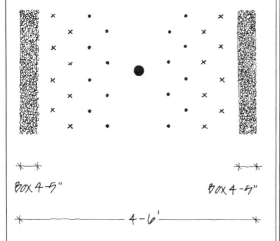

Borders

Flower borders can be as long as there is room in the garden but they should be fairly narrow. Their shape can be 'straight, circular or in cants turned into volutes, scrolls, knots' and they can be either detached or set along walls. The 'choicest borders' should 'not run next to the house'. A path usually runs along the front of the border and it can be edged in various ways, for instance, with a box hedge, bricks on edge, flat stones or boards painted green. The soil is usually raised about 2–3 in (0.05–0.075 m) above the edging. Larger borders can be 'filled with great trees such as limes and horse chestnuts between which sets yews, shrubs and flowers of a large kind' like a primitive shrubbery!

Avenue and Woodland Planting

Avenues John James established a formula for the setting out of an avenue or single walk or a double avenue or double walk. The proportions he specified ensure that the perspective of the feature will be most effective. If an avenue is too narrow for its length, it will lose the dramatic effect. For double avenues, the outside or counter walks should be half the width of the central walk. In spécial circumstances the width of the outer walks can be slightly reduced.

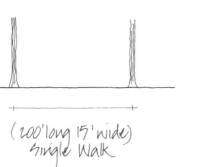

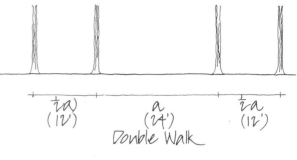

(200' long 15' wide)
Single Walk

½a)
(12')

a
(24')

½a
(12')

Double Walk

Woods planted in Rows This style is very similar to forestry practices today. Either conifers or broad-leaved trees are planted but not both together. The trees are planted as whips or transplants, in rows about 6 ft (1.8 m) apart. The ground is kept clean and even cultivated as if a 'Kitchen Garden'. The trees should be high pruned to leave a clear stem of 20–30 ft (6–9 m) with no fork in it. From the second year the young trees should be pruned to a single leader and regularly thinned. Using this treatment some trees, such as limes or beech, can grow to 15–20 ft (4.5–6 m) in five to six years.

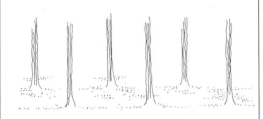

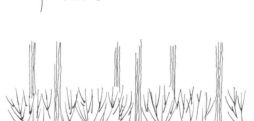

Coppice Wood The coppice is made up of young vigorous shoots sprouting from stumps of sweet chestnut or hazel that are cut down every ten to fifteen years. These small trees usually grow amongst standard trees such as oak. The young coppice forms a dense undergrowth and screen in the woodland.

Groves of Middle Height These woods form the background to paths, rides and allées as well as to the more exotic halls, cabinets and galleries. The trees are not allowed to grow much higher than 30–40 ft (9-12 m) and they are either pollarded or have their crowns drastically reduced.

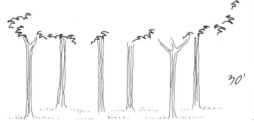

30'

Groves in Open Compartments These also form the background for allées but they have fewer trees in the centre so that flowering shrubs and woodland bulbs can be planted along the narrow winding paths amongst the trees. This was sometimes called a wilderness.

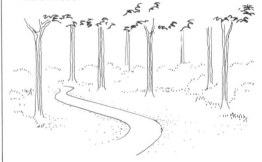

Groves in Quincunx are planted without any hedges or understorey, either 'checker-wise, right angles or parallel lines' just like an orchard today. The ground under the trees is either raked and rolled or mown. Sanded walks can cross the middle of the planting. By the 1720s they were planted in a 'perfect square not in a Five of Cards shape'.

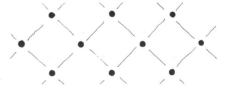

Arbours

'Natural' Arbours These are formed from the branches of trees 'artfully interwoven' and tied with wire or strong twine to a wooden or iron frame supported by narrow battens, which can be shaped into hoops or circles. All the supports must be covered by the vegetation.

Colonnade The trees are grown to resemble cloisters running around a close or a Roman circus. Each column

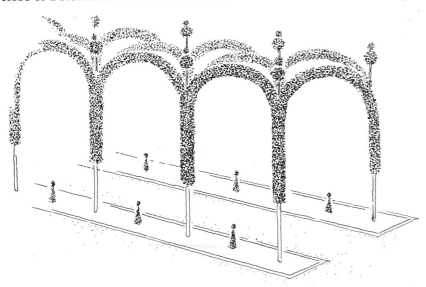

is about 10 ft (3 m) high and about 3 ft (0.9 m) in circumference. The base, capitals, cornices and fillets are each about 1 ft (0.3 m) high. The plinth is about 18 in (0.46 m) high. At the top of each column the trunk of the trees is exposed and above the leaves are clipped into another feature such as a vase or finial. Each column is fastened to the adjoining palisade hedge with wooden cross-beams made from branches clipped square to look like timber beams.

Gallery The delicate tracery of clipped trees trained over arches to resemble the Gothic vaulting in a cathedral. In this sketch the two rows of trees are set in a border with flowers and clipped yew. The trunks (the pilasters or columns) are bare to about 6 ft (1.8 m), above which the branches are closely clipped. The main part of the tree is trained over a wooden or metal arch, with a small branch left to create a vase or finial. The gallery is best made from elm or lime but beech and hornbeam can be used.

Arcade Similar to the colonnade but the lower hedge is used to create windows rather than columns. This lower part can be made from hornbeam but the piers are usually grown as elm or lime.

Portico Like the colonnade, but much more extravagantly shaped, like a grand entrance to a building, with columns, cornices and other decorations.

Ball of Elm A simpler decoration which can be used as a column. This can be made from lime, elm or beech. The stem should be clear to about 6–7 ft (1.8–2.1 m) high, topped with a clipped circular head of about 3 ft (0.9 m) in diameter. It can be finished off with a square plinth around the base made from hornbeam.

Ha-Has and Cascades

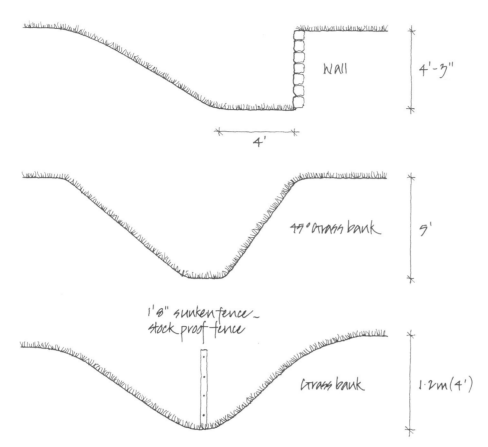

Wall

4'-3"

4'

45° grass bank

5'

1'8" sunken fence –
stock proof fence

Grass bank

1.2m (4')

Sunk Fence Ha-Ha An agricultural fence is erected at the bottom of the ditch. The top of the fence must be below ground level on either side of the ha-ha. The gradient of the ditch should not be more than 30-35 degrees to allow the stock to graze it.

Cascade An artificial rocky waterfall that noisily breaks the water as it flows over the stones. The cascade can be constructed from the overflow of a lake or it may be a small waterfall in a river or stream. In the eighteenth century cascades were designed so that the water splashed evenly over a stepped sloping stone wall with a slight lip on the top of each course; or they might fall over each tread of a flight of steps. Nineteenth-century cascades were more likely to fall over randomly placed stones.

Wall Ha-Ha This should be used if the ground falls away and is most appropriate where lawn meets meadow. The wall should be about 4 ft 3 in (1.3 m) high and faced in local stone. The ditch at the bottom must be about 4 ft (1.2 m) wide.

Ditch Ha-Ha This relies on the steepness of the banks to keep out the stock and can be used to divide arable land from pasture. It will restrain cattle, sheep and most horses except for those trained to jump! The bottom of the ditch should not be wider than 18 in (0.45 m).

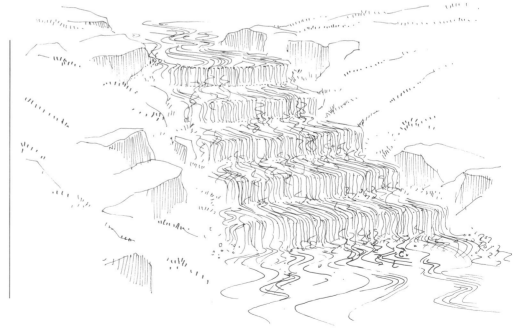

Rustic Fence Patterns

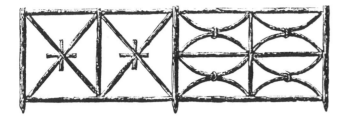

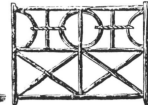

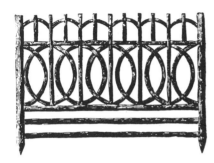

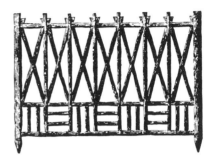

There is a huge variety of fence styles designed to suit every situation. Many of the styles protect the garden from rabbits or stop visitors from walking over the flower beds. These illustrations show a range of rustic fence patterns. Almost all of the styles should be made with the bark retained.

The fences are made from the straight rails of larch, sweet chestnut or oak thinnings or coppice. The curved stakes are fabricated from the more supple hazel, willow varieties, ash and mountain ash (rowan). If the post is stripped of its bark it can be painted but the colour should closely resemble the bark; it should not be painted green or red. The fences can either be joined together or used as movable hurdles, with the side posts made from larger stakes. The cross-rails and little

decorative pieces are taken from the smaller ends of the trees.

Most joints should be mitred but they can also be bolted or nailed. Knots tied around the joints can be made from the very thin shoots of willow or from moss rope.

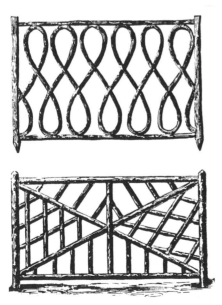

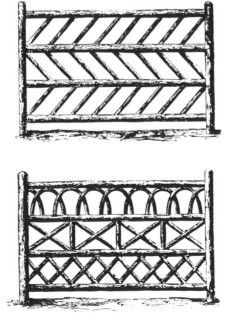

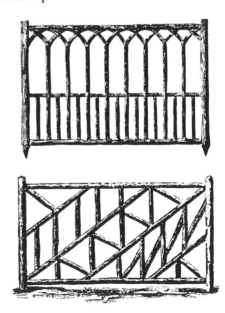

Vases

Ornate classical vases fixed onto pedestals, plinths or parapets of walls decorate Ornamental Gardens. The shape of the vase should reflect the architecture of the house. The size of the vase and pedestal relates to the size of the garden. If the garden is less than a quarter of an acre (0.4 ha), the vase and plinth should not be more than 4 ft (1.2 m) high and 22 in (0.55 m) diameter. If the garden is over an acre (0.4 ha) the vase and plinth height should be increased to at least 6 ft (1.8 m). The proportions of the two vases illustrated here are correct for a small garden. They might also decorate a conservatory, entrance hall or low terrace wall. These were made from white terracotta imitating stone and were fired by Doulton and Watt of Lambeth.

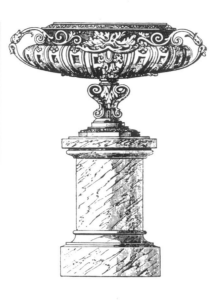

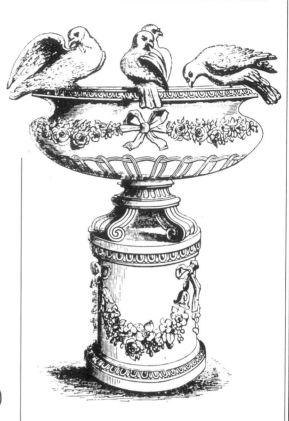

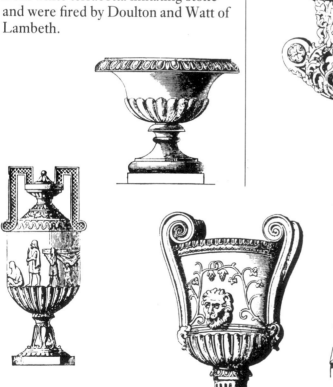

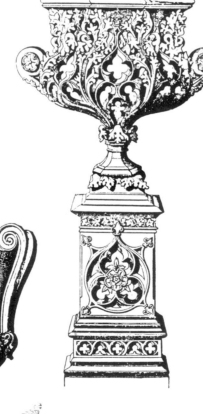

High Victorian sentimentality enjoyed this rich vase on which rest models of cooing doves. It was made by Copeland and Minton. The vase should be sited, according to Charles McIntosh, in a 'conspicuous place on a Terrace' or in a conservatory.

This clay urn might decorate a Grecian, Roman or Italian Ornamental Garden. It could also be made from cast-iron and painted to look like marble or bronze.

Rose Shapes

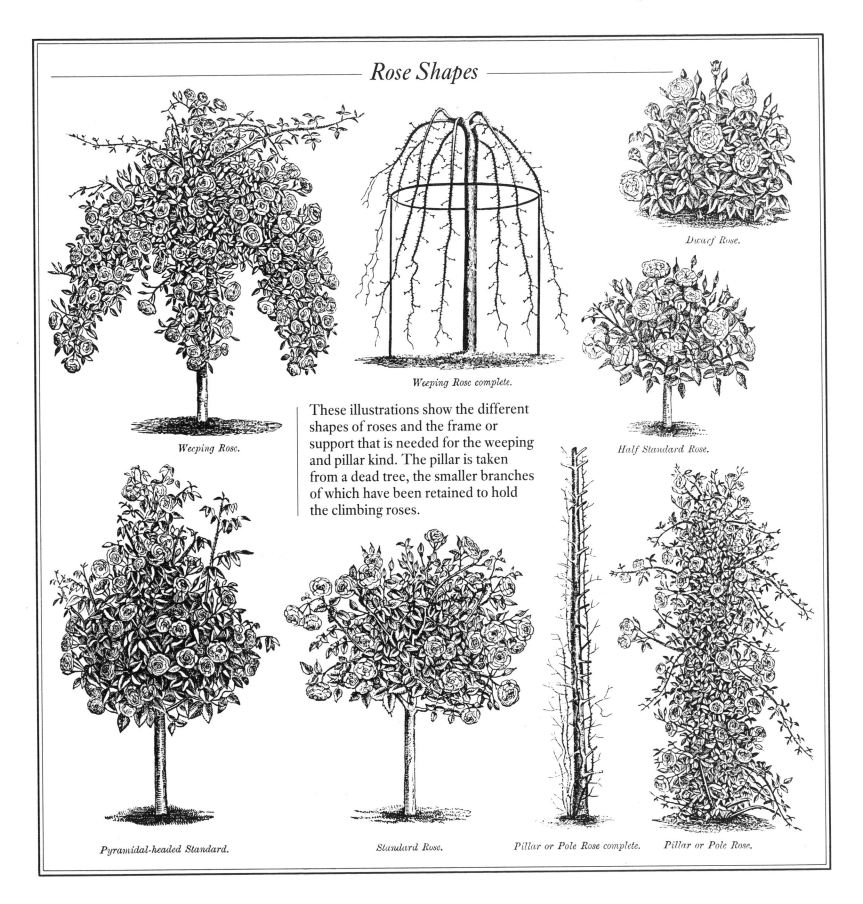

Weeping Rose.

Weeping Rose complete.

Dwarf Rose.

These illustrations show the different shapes of roses and the frame or support that is needed for the weeping and pillar kind. The pillar is taken from a dead tree, the smaller branches of which have been retained to hold the climbing roses.

Half Standard Rose.

Pyramidal-headed Standard.

Standard Rose.

Pillar or Pole Rose complete.

Pillar or Pole Rose.

Rustic Bridges

A stream can be crossed by stepping stones or by an attractive rustic bridge made from treated timber covered with bark. Most bridges are strong enough to carry pedestrians but for a bridge that is to carry vehicles the construction must be checked by an engineer or other specialist.

The span of a timber bridge can be 10–20 ft (3–6 m) and the path will be 3–5 ft (0.9–1.5 m) wide. The main timbers that stretch from one side to the other can be supported by a stable bank or on stone-faced abutments. For a

longer bridge, an additional batten or supporting beam can be added at the centre of the span to increase the strength. Rustic struts supporting the bridge are very attractive and add strength. The more twisted and artistic they are, the less strength they will provide.

The path over the bridge can be made from small round logs no more than 4 in (0.1 m) diameter cut from the top of larch trees. These are laid across the battens end to end in a straight line across the width of the bridge. If the

logs are larger they should be sawn in half and the straight side fixed downwards. In damper climates this log path can become slippery and should be covered with wire netting.

If a more formal path is desired, deal or oak boards can be placed on the battens and covered with a layer of asphalt. The battens, parapets and handrails for rustic bridges should either be made from posts with their bark on, such as oak or larch, or pieces of bark should be fixed onto any exposed wood.

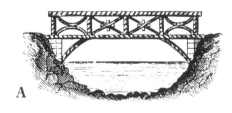

A

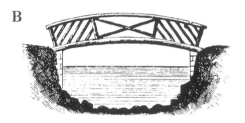

B

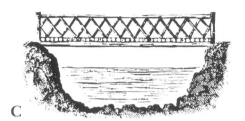

C

A has a stone abutment and ornate parapet and handrail. The decorative struts are not structural.

B has a slight curve. The parapet uprights can be double the size of the diagonal ones.

C is similar to **A** and **B** but is decorated with twisted ropes of the moss *Polytrichum commune* neatly wound round and nailed to the posts.

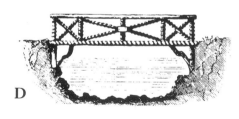

D

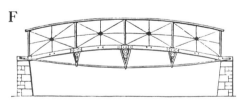

F

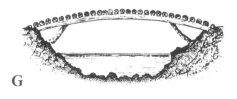

G

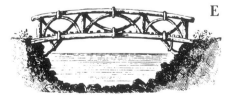

E

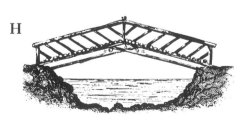

H

D and **E** are decorated with rustic branches.

F is a very simple suspension bridge. It is much stronger than the other styles and can be used to cross wider spans.

G is a simple bridge with no handrail. It is slightly curved and is surfaced with wooden stretchers.

H is a simple bridge using the principles of the arch to provide greater strength.

Paths and Steps

Paths in the Wild and Woodland Garden wind through the woods past overhanging shrubs, squeezing by the trunks of trees or clinging to the sides of steep banks. Their character emphasizes the natural and wild effect and they provide a dry surface to walk on throughout the year.

The width of the path should vary throughout the garden. It should never be less than 1 ft (0.3 m) wide – enough to allow one person to use it. Where there is room, it can be extended to 6 ft (1.8 m).

Usually the path is made of compacted earth but in the damper and more boggy places it will need to be strengthened with a stone base covered with coarse bark mulch, fine wood chip or sawdust. This will rot down quite quickly and so it will need to be replaced occasionally.

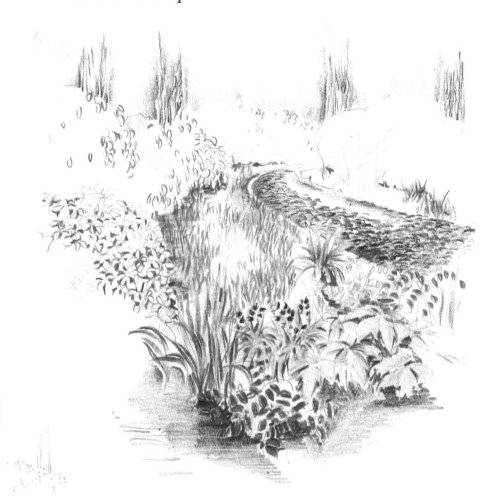

The path may rise up a steep slope either as a ramp or as steps. The steps should be made out of timber and each should be no more than 8 in (0.2 m) high. Logs cut in half lengthwise and fixed in position by two stout posts on either side make good steps or risers. The treads should be made of the same material as the rest of the path. If the path rises gradually it can be made as a step ramp. In this case the step should be a maximum of 4 in (0.1 m) high and the ramp should be 4–6 ft (1.2–1.8 m) deep. The ramp can also rise but the slope should be no more than 1:8. The path should be laid with a camber or fall to one side so that rainwater will drain off and not erode the path.

Rustic Seats

In small gardens, seats act as eyecatchers, and to anyone sitting on them they should offer attractive views. In very large gardens there is more room for them to be scattered about.

A   Designed in four sections which are joined together around the trunk, this seat is shaded by the tree and it also protects it like a tree guard.

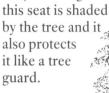

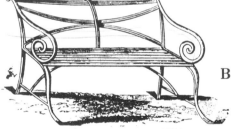

B   This light cast-iron seat is simple and elegant and should be placed near the house.

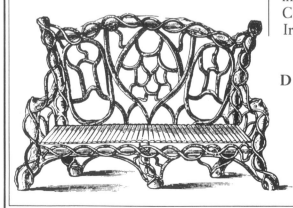

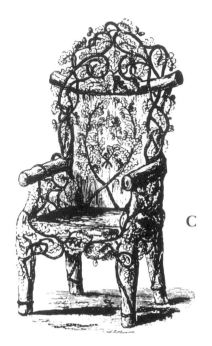

C   Charles McIntosh considered this rustic chair to be 'truly artistic'. It is made with rustic posts covered with bark and with a pattern of woven stems such as twisted ivy.

D   E   F   These rustic seats are all made from timber with the bark left on or with pieces of bark fixed as decoration. **D** is supported by larger branches, while **F** is made with smaller and more twisted stems. These patterns were also reproduced in cast-iron by Coalbrookdale Ironworks.

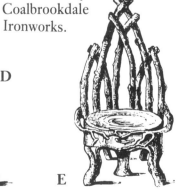

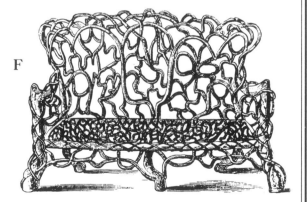

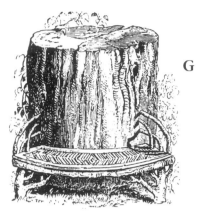

G   This seat makes good use of an old stump and is constructed to look as if it has grown out of the tree.

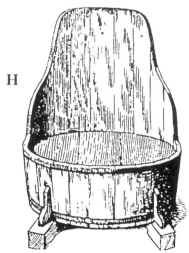

H   A seat cut from a cider barrel with one end reduced and the other shaped to make the back rest.

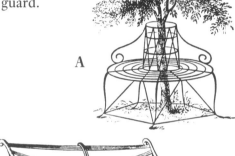

Moss Summer-Houses

A

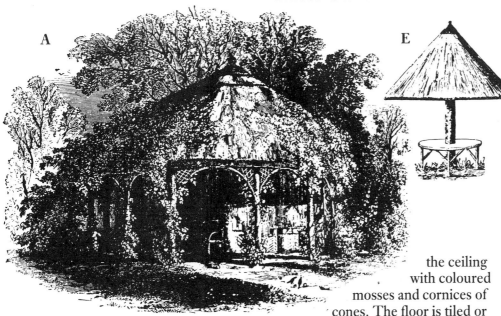

E

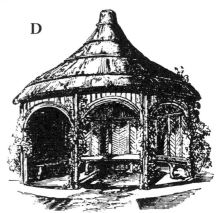

protect them from rot, with the panels fixed between five of the supports. Hazel rods about 1 in (0.025 m) thick are laid in a herring-bone pattern. Thatch the top part with reeds and board the lower section over and cover with rods. The floor is of coloured pebbles set in a diamond pattern.

C is more rustic, with supports of larch or oak without any plinths or pediments. The roof is thatched with reeds or heath and covered with a rose or clematis. Common mosses decorate the ceiling and panelled walls, and the floor is compacted clay.

the ceiling with coloured mosses and cornices of cones. The floor is tiled or laid with blocks of wood, or decorated with cobbles, shells or flints.

Moss summer-houses and rustic covered seats provide rest or shelter in the romantic and wild scenery of a Woodland Garden. They are often placed to act as eyecatchers, beckoning the visitor through the shrubs. The rustic columns frame attractive views across the garden.

Construct the summer-house from trunks with the bark left on. Decorate the inside with patterns of mosses, cones and shells. Thatch the roof with reeds or dried heather and decorate

Using natural materials many shapes and sizes can be created – from a rustic seat below a simple roof to an elaborate summer-house with several rooms and seats outside in an open colonnade, sheltered from rain and wind. Creepers twine up the columns and cover the thatched roof.

These three designs show how to make an oval or round house and vary the design. Design **B** is made from eight supports set on stone plinths to

D is more elaborate. The roof is thatched with reed or heath and secured with ropes of the common moss *Polytrichum commune*. The seat is supported by rustic legs and the roof by arched columns.

In **E** the thatched roof is supported by hazel rods fixed like the ribs of an umbrella to the tree in the centre, which can be either a dead stump or alive and growing out of the roof! Moss is firmly fixed between the ribs. The seat is made in four sections and supported by rustic legs.

B

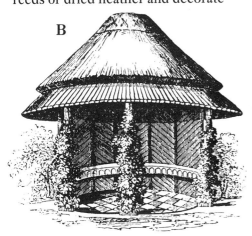

C

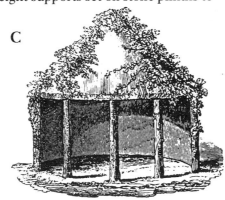

D

Planting Plan for an Ornamental Garden

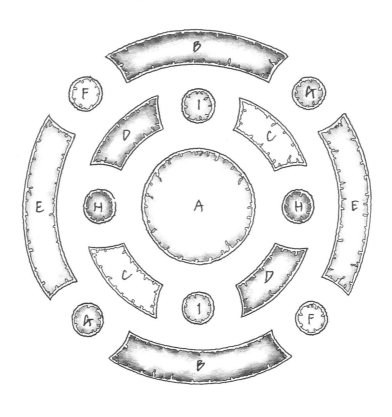

A 10 ft in diameter — Collection of China roses, including R. semperflorens, sanguinea, and all the varieties of Noisettiana. The gaps are planted with a mixed collection of bulbs. There may be a standard purple Noisette rose in the centre, and the marginal line should be of mixed hyacinths.

B Red–flowering herbaceous plants and red flowering bulbs, the border of Amalde Rosette hyacinths.

C White–flowering herbaceous plants and white–flowering bulbs, the border of white crocuses.

D Blue–flowering herbaceous plants and blue–flowering bulbs, bordered by blue or purple crocuses.

E Yellow–flowering herbaceous plants and yellow–flowering bulbs, bordered with yellow crocuses.

F Variegated horse–shoe pelargoniums, alternating with mixed hyacinths, and bordered with mixed crocuses.

G Variegated ivy–leaved pelargoniums, alternating with mixed tulips, and bordered with mixed crocuses.

H Fuchsia coccinea, or any tender annual or greenhouse plant alternating with mixed Narcissi, and bordered with mixed dog's-tooth violets.

I Heliotropes, or other tender annual or greenhouse plants, alternating with mixed Iris Xiphium, and bordered with mixed Scilla sibirica and bifolia, the latter in its blue, white and red varieties

The beds are raised a little in the centre.

Step Plans

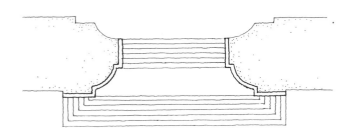

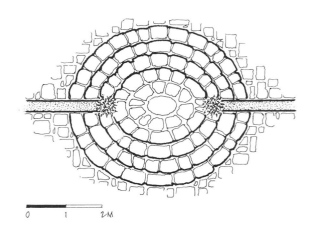

This sketch shows the plan of the steps illustrated in the feature of Chapter 14, The Sheltered Garden. The plan was taken from John James's book *The Theory and Practice of Gardening* and was freely adapted by Edwin Lutyens and other Edwardian architects. It shows how to finish off one set of steps next to another flight.

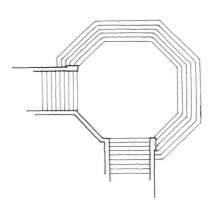

Setting Out a Parterre

Once the pattern has been drawn out on paper the setting-out lines should be added either to a copy or onto tracing paper overlaid on top of the design.

The lines must intersect the centre line at equal intervals. When they are transferred outside onto the terrace the lines should not be more than 6 ft or 2 m apart. If the pattern is complicated then the lines should be closer together. All measurements should be taken from the centre crossing lines. The lines should be pegged out exactly the same distance as scale on the plan. String can be stretched between the pegs and the distance between these lines and the design measured and marked out with different coloured pegs. These pegs should be joined up with string using a different colour to the setting-out lines and all the curves should be smooth out or set to a radius. The design can be marked on the ground by sprinkling a narrow line of sand or lime.

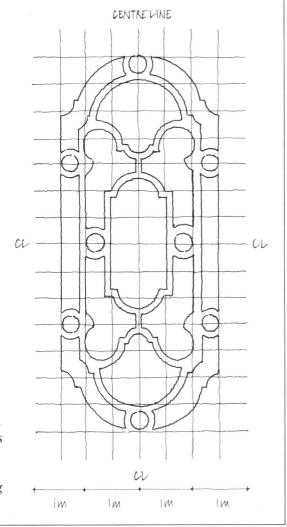

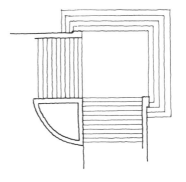

Planting Plan for a Sheltered Garden

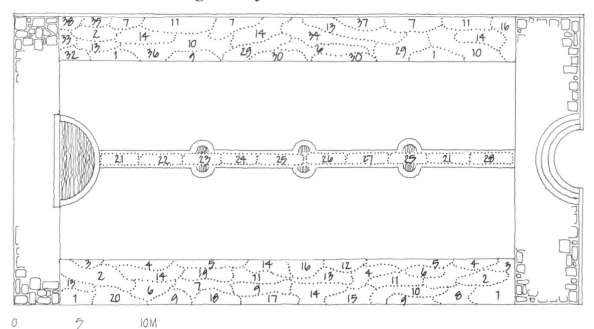

0   5   10M

1	Santolina chamaecyparissus	20	White VALERIAN
2	Pale blue DELPHINIUM	21	Sagittaria sagittifolia
3	Blue PANSY	22	Myosotis palustris
4	Blue IRIS	23	Sparghanium ramosum
5	Mignonette	24	Iris laevigata
6	PINK SNAPDRAGON	25	Butomus umbellatus
7	Echinops ritro	26	Iris pseudo-acorus
8	PINK VALERIAN	27	Menyanthes trifoliata
9	Pink HYBRID ROCK PINK	28	Alisma plantage
10	LAVENDER	29	Hydrangea serrata 'Rosealba'.
11	PINK HOLLYHOCK	30	White DIANTHUS
12	Lilac PANSY	31	Stachys lanata
13	White SNAPDRAGON	32	Yucca filamentosa
14	PINK CHINA ROSE	33	Yucca gloriosa
15	Dwarf LAVENDER	34	Purple GLADIOLUS
16	ROSEMARY	35	Clematis jackmanii
17	CATMINT	36	Chrysanthemum maximum
18	Veronica prostrata	37	Clematis flammula
19	Filipendula ulmaria flore pleno	38	Hamamelis mollis

Flower Stands and Tables

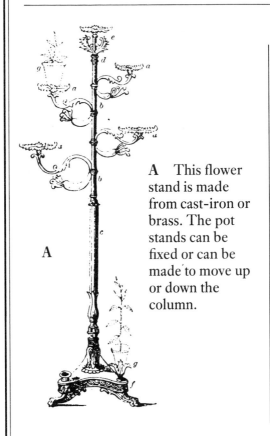

A This flower stand is made from cast-iron or brass. The pot stands can be fixed or can be made to move up or down the column.

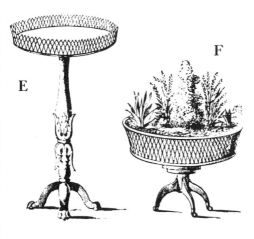

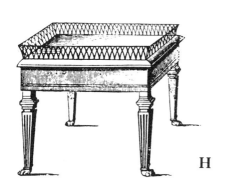

E F G and **H** are flower stands of wirework set on top of an elegant wooden table made from polished mahogany or oak. The baskets are lined with zinc. The plants are grown in pots and are arranged so that the tall plants are in the centre, with smaller and weeping plants around the outside. The pots are plunged into moist green moss. The table can be mounted on castors so it can be moved around the conservatory.

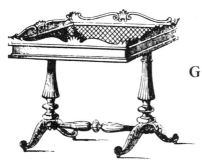

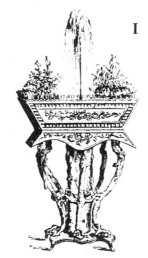

B C D are all samples of Wardian cases. **B** is about 4 ft 2 in (1.26 m) high, 3 ft (0.9 m) long and 2 ft (0.6 m) wide. The sides and legs are mahogany or oak and the glass top is set on brass rails. One side window is hinged and will lift up so that the plants can be handled. **C** and **D** are smaller and their glass cover lifts off completely. All the cases have small pipes with cork stoppers so that excess water can be drawn off.

I is very similar but is made from cast-iron or bronze. The stem of the table contains a small jet of water which sprinkles the plants.

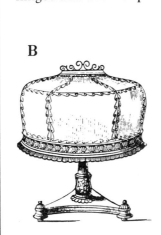

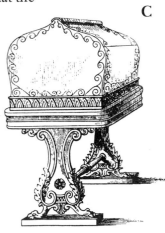

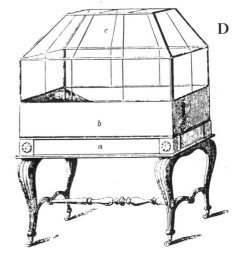

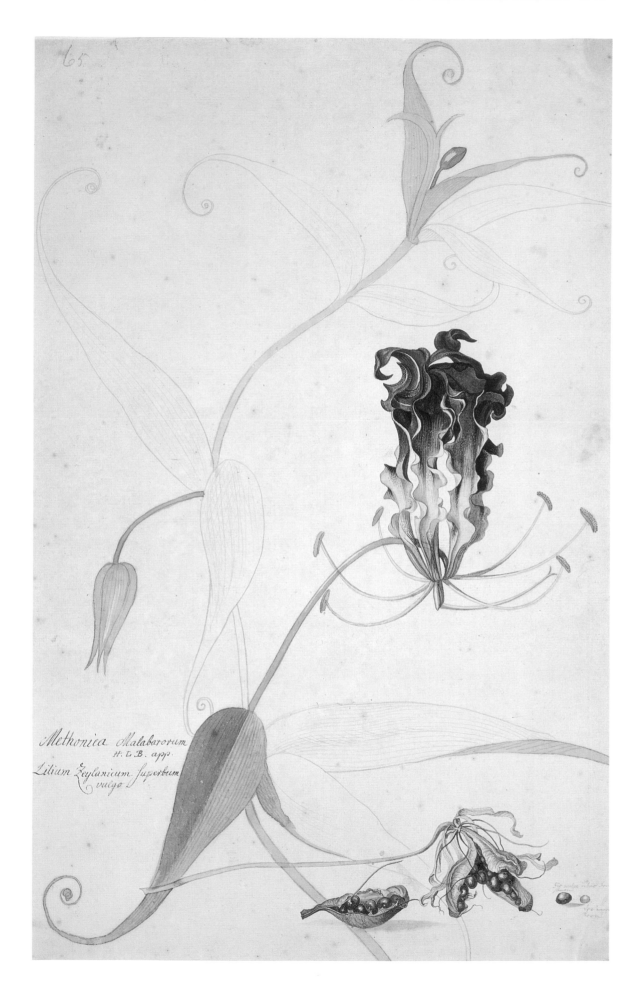

*Glory Lily (*Gloriosa superba*), a watercolour by Ehret.*

Methonica Malabarorum
H. L. B. app.
Lilium Zeylanicum superbum
vulgo

OPPOSITE
*Parrot tulip (*Tulipa gesneriana*), 1744, a painting on vellum by Ehret.*

206

GLOSSARY AND TERMS

Accoudoir balustrade or railing of a height to rest arms on.

Allée hedge-lined walk or ride.

Arbours, artificial made from trellis.

Arbours, natural made from trees.

Berçeau a vaulted arbour of trellis-work covered with foliage, or trees trained as an arbour without trellis.

Bosquet or **wilderness** an ornamental grove, thicket or shrubbery pierced by walks.

Boulingrin an ornamental sunken lawn 1–2 ft deep, or turf parterre; corruption of 'bowling green'.

Cabinets smaller versions of halls.

Cascades waterfalls where the water breaks regularly over stones.

Cloisters enclosed walk generally forming a square.

Fountain gerbe a fountain in the form of a powerful jet descending as spray all round.

Fountain piece d'eau a formal pond or basin usually of stone construction.

Fountain miroir d'eau a formal basin designed as a reflecting surface.

Gallery an arcade or covered walk overlooking a garden.

Gallery, green made from clipped trees.

Gallery, water trees clipped in an arch over a canal or water.

Goosefoot three rides joining at one place.

Glacis a slope at an angle less than 45 degrees from a retaining outside wall.

Halls open glades of a formal shape surrounded by woods.

Halls, covered halls covered with trellis or arbours.

Halls for comedy halls designed like a stage.

Labyrinth maze of walks, where the hedge is normally about 8–12 ft high.

Palisade a hedge of any height, the individual plants grown close together like a wooden upright fence and clipped to a smooth wall.

Parterre a flower garden laid out in an ornamental manner on the flat terrace adjoining the house.

Parterre broderie flowing plant-like designs of box against a background of coloured earth and bands of turf.

Parterre in the English manner or **Parterre a l'anglais** made of cut turf.

Parterre of cut work or **Parterre de pieces coupée** a design where the pattern is made of flower beds edged with box.

Plattes bandes narrow borders running around the outside of a parterre.

Plattes bandes isolées borders that lie free, around a parterre in the English Manner.

Quincunx trees planted in squares or fives like a five in playing cards.

Sentiers paths raked, not rolled.

St Andrew's cross parterre in the form of a diagonal cross.

Tazza a broad squat vase on a short base usually set on a plinth.

Urn a vase covered with a top.

Volute spiral walk up a mound.

Zic-zac chevrons zig-zag grass running through a surfaced path.

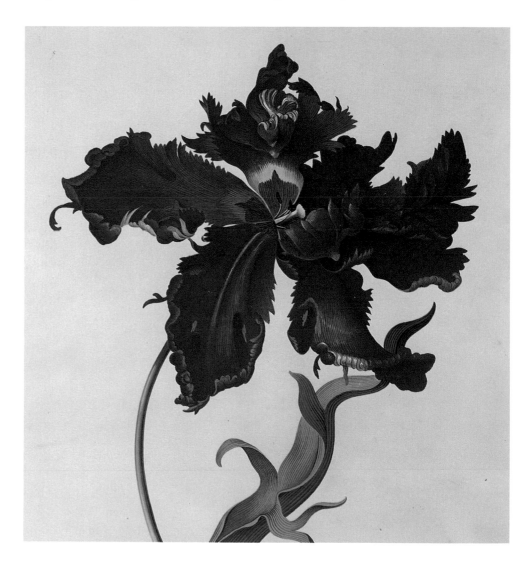

PLANT LIST

The plant list is a selection of the plants which gardeners may require when creating the period styles. Sadly, few of the varieties available in the seventeenth and eighteenth centuries have survived today. For example, at the end of the seventeenth century there were at least 150 varieties of tulip as well as many kinds of auriculas, primulas, carnations and pinks. There were also many different kinds of fruit trees. Thomas Rea's book, published at the end of the seventeenth century, gives over twenty kinds of pears, of which only three of those mentioned are grown today.

Plants that were most commonly used have been chosen. Native plants which were naturally available have not been listed unless they were of particular importance. Lists have been made for each period. Varieties noted under earlier periods may sometimes be appropriate for later styles as well although they have not always been repeated. There are obviously many plants available for the more recent styles and so only the ones most commonly used are given.

COMMON NAMES

Old Common Names	Name Today	Latin Name
Abele Tree	White Poplar	Populus alba
Alternus	Buckthorn	Rhamnus alternus
Apple of Jerusalem	Balsam Apple	Momordica balsamina
Arbor Judea	Judas Tree	Cercis siliquastrum
Balm of Gilead	Balsam Fir	Abies balsamea
Beane Trefoile	Golden Rain	Laburnum anagyroides
Blite	Love-lies-bleeding	Amaranthus caudatus
Checker Daffodil	Snake's Head	Fritillaria meleagris
Cornell Tree	Cornelian Cherry	Cornus mas
Crowfoot	Buttercup	Ranunculus acris
Dame's Violet	Sweet Rocket	Hesperis matronalis
Dens Canis/Dens Leonis	Dog's-Tooth Violet	Erythronium dens-canis
Dittaine	Burning Bush	Dictamnus albus
Dog's Bane	Silk-Weed	Asclepia syriaca
Flos Adonis	Pheasant's Eye	Adonis aestivalis
Flower Gentle/Prince's Feather	Amaranthus	Amaranthus hypochondriacus
Flower de Luce	Iris	Iris spp.
Gillyflower	Carnation/Pink/ Sweet William/Stock	Dianthus caryophyllus spp.
Hedgehog	Medicago	Medicago arborea
Holy Oak/Rose Tremiere	Hollyhock	Alcea rosea
Horehound	Betony	Stachys officinalis
Iacynth of Peru	Hyacinth of Peru	Scilla peruviana
Indian Pink	China Pink	Dianthus chinensis
Larkes-heele-Flowers	Larkspur	Consolida ambigua
Linden Tree	Lime	Tilia vulgaris
Mastic Tree	Turpentine Tree	Pistacia terebinthus
Minionet	Mignonette	Reseda odorata
Muske Grape Flower	Grape Hyacinth	Muscari racemosa
Nonsuch	Jerusalem Cross	Lychnis chalcedonica
Orientall Iacynth	Hyacinth	Hyacinthus orientalis
Park Leaves	Tutsan	Hypericum androsaemum
Passe Flower	Pasque Flower	Pulsatilla vulgaris
Persian Jessamine	Persian Lilac	Syringa x persica
Piony/Poeonia	Peony	Paeonia officinalis
Primrose Tree	Evening Primrose	Oenothera biennis
Quick Beam	Mountain Ash/Rowan	Sorbus aucuparia
Quick	Hawthorn	Crataegus monogyna
Sattin Flower	Honesty	Lunaria annua
Savin/Sabine	Savin	Juniperus sabina
Starry Iacynth	Squill/Scilla	Scilla bifolia
Tree St. John's Wort	Spirea	Spirea hypericifolia
Tree of Life	Arbor vitae	Thuja occidentalis
Trumpet Flower	Indian Bean Tree	Catalpa bignonioides
Trumpet Flower	Trumpet Vine	Campsis radicans
Venice Sumach	Smoke Tree	Cotinus coggygria
Vervain	Vervein	Verbena spp.
Wolfesbane	Monk's Hood	Aconitum spp.

Plants available before 1700

Latin Name	Common Name	Documented Use
Herbs		
Allium schoenoprasum	Chives	Parterre
Artemisia absinthium	Wormwood	Parterre
Artemisia abrotanum	Southernwood	Parterre
Carum carvi	Caraway	
Chamaemelum nobile	Camomile	Seat
Coriandum sativum	Coriander	
Crocus sativus	Saffron	
Cuminum cyminum	Cumin	
Foeniculum vulgare	Fennel	
Glycyrrhiza glabra	Liquorice	
Hyssopus officinalis	Hyssop	Parterre
Laurus nobilis	Bay	Parterre, Tub
Levisticum officinale	Lovage	
Melissa officinalis	Lemon Balm	
Mentha spp.	Mint	
Ocimum basilicum	Basil	
Origanum vulgare	Origano	
Origanum majorana	Marjoram	
Petroselinum crispum	Parsley	Parterre
Peucedanum graveolens	Dill	
Rosmarinus officinale	Rosemary	Parterre, Tub, Hedge
Rumex acetosa	Sorrel	
Ruta graveolens	Rue	Parterre
Salvia officinalis 'Icterina'	Variegated Golden Sage	Parterre
Salvia officinalis 'Purpurascens'	Purple Sage	Parterre
Santolina chamaecyparissus	Cotton lavender	Parterre, Hedge
Tanacetum balsamita	Costmary	
Thymus vulgaris spp.	Thyme	Parterre
Vegetables		
Allium cepa	Onion	
Allium sativum	Garlic	
Allium porrum	Leek	
Apium graveolens	Celery	
Asparagus officinalis	Asparagus	
Beta vulgaris	Beet	
Brassica rapa	Turnip	
Brassica oleracea	Cabbage	
Cichorium intybus	Chicory	
Cucumbus sativus	Cucumber	
Cynara scolymus	Globe Artichoke	
Daucus carota	Carrot	
Foeniculum vulgare	Fennel	
Helianthus tuberosus	Jerusalem Artichoke	(1617)
Lactuca sativa	Lettuce	
Peucedanum sativum	Parsnip	
Raphanus sativus	Radish	
Spinacia oleracea	Spinach	
Tropaeolum majus	Nasturtium	Frame (1686)
Vicia faba	Broad Bean	
Vigna spp.	Scarlet Runner Bean	Frame
Vigna spp.	Kidney Bean	
Fruit		
Cornus mas	Cornelian Cherry	
Cucumis melo	Melon	
Cydonia oblonga	Quince	
Ficus carica	Fig	Wall
Fragaria vesca	Strawberry	
Malus domestica	Apple	
Mespilus germanica	Medlar	
Morus alba	White Mulberry	
Morus rubra	Red Mulberry	(1629)
Morus nigra	Black Mulberry	
Prunus armeniaca	Apricot	
Prunus cerasus var.	Morello Cherry	Wall
Prunus domestica var.	Plum	
Prunus dulcis var.	Almond	
Prunus persica var.	Peach	Wall
Pyrus communis	Pear	
Ribes	Raspberry	
Ribes var.	Red Currant	
Ribes uva-crispa	Gooseberry	
Sambucus nigra	Elder	
Hedging		
Berberis vulgaris	Berberis	
Buxus sempervirens	Box	
Buxus sempervirens 'Suffructicosa'	Dwarf Box	
Corylus avellana	Hazel	
Crataegus monogyna	Hawthorn	Quickset
Ilex aquifolium	Holly	
Laurus nobilis	Bay	
Prunus spinosa	Blackthorn	
Salix purpurea	Purple Osier	Palisade
Salix viminalis	Osier Willow	Palisade
Taxus baccata	Yew	
Climbers		
Atropa bella-donna	Deadly Nightshade	
Bryonia dioica	White Bryony	
Calystegia sepium	Bindweed	
Clematis cirrhosa	Clematis	
Clematis flammula	Clematis	
Clematis vitalba	Old Man's Beard	
Clematis viticella	Clematis	
Hedera helix	Ivy	
Humulus lupulus	Hop	
Jasminum azoricum	Jasmine	Arbour (1690s)
Jasminum officinale	White Jasmine	
Lonicera caprifolium	Perfoliate Honeysuckle	

Lonicera periclymenum	Woodbine Honeysuckle	
Lonicera sempervirens	Trumpet Honeysuckle	(1656)
Passiflora caerulea	Passion Flower	(1699)
Pisum sativum	Pea	
Rosa rubiginosa	Sweetbriar	Arbour, Hedge
Rosa x alba	White Rose	
Rosa arvensis	Field Rose	
Rosa canina	Dog Rose	
Rosa Elegantine	Elegantine Rose	
Solanum nigrum	Black Nightshade	
Vitis vinifera	Grape	

Borders and Knots

Achillea ptarmica	Sneezewort	
Acanthus mollis	Acanthus	
Acanthus spinosa	Acanthus	
Allium schoenoprasum	Chive	
Allium sativum	Garlic	
Alcea rosea	Hollyhock	
Althaea officinalis	Marsh Mallow	
Amaranthus hypochondriacus	Amaranth	(1684)
Anemone pavonina	Double Anemone	
Anemone coronaria	Garden Anemone	
Anemone hepatica	Liverwort	
Antirrhinum majus	Snap-dragon	
Aquilegia canadensis	Canadian Columbine	
Aquilegia vulgaris	Columbine, Granny's Bonnet	
Aralia racemosa	Aralia	
Armeria maritima	Sea Thrift	
Bellis perennis	Daisy	
Calendula officinalis	Common Marigold	
Calendula officinalis flore pleno	Double Marigold	
Campanula latifolia	Bellflower	
Campanula persicifolia alba	White Bellflower	
Campanula persicifolia	Bellflower	
Campanula pyramidalis	Chimney Bellflower	
Campanula trachelium	Bellflower	
Cheiranthus cheiri	Wallflower	
Cistus albidus	Pink Rock Rose	
Cistus populifolius	Rock Rose	
Clematis recta	Border Clematis	
Clematis integrifolia	Border Clematis	
Convallaria majalis	Lily of the Valley	
Crocus sativus	Saffron	
Cyclamen europaeum	Autumn-flowering Cyclamen	
Cyclamen repandum	Spring-flowering Cyclamen	(1629)
Cytisus trifolium	Broom	
Delphinium consolida	Canterbury Bells	
Dianthus caryophyllus	Carnation	
Dianthus barbatus	Sweet William	
Dianthus deltoides	Maiden Pink	
Dianthus 'Old Crimson Clove'	Clove Carnation	

Dianthus superbus	Fringed Pink
Digitalis grandiflora	Foxglove
Eryngium alpinum	Sea Holly
Erythronium dens-canis	Dog's-Tooth Violet
Euphorbia myrsinites	Euphorbia

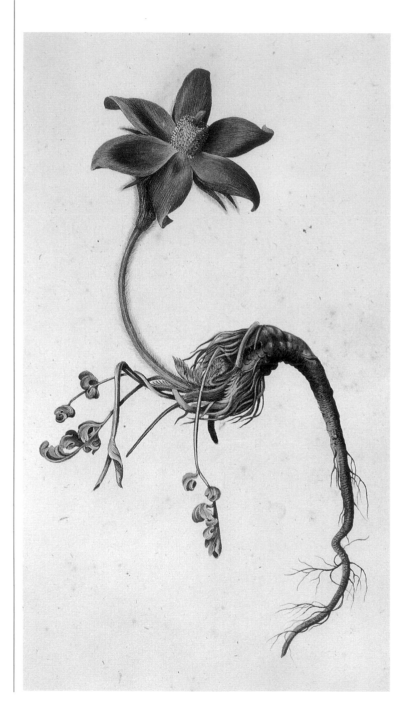

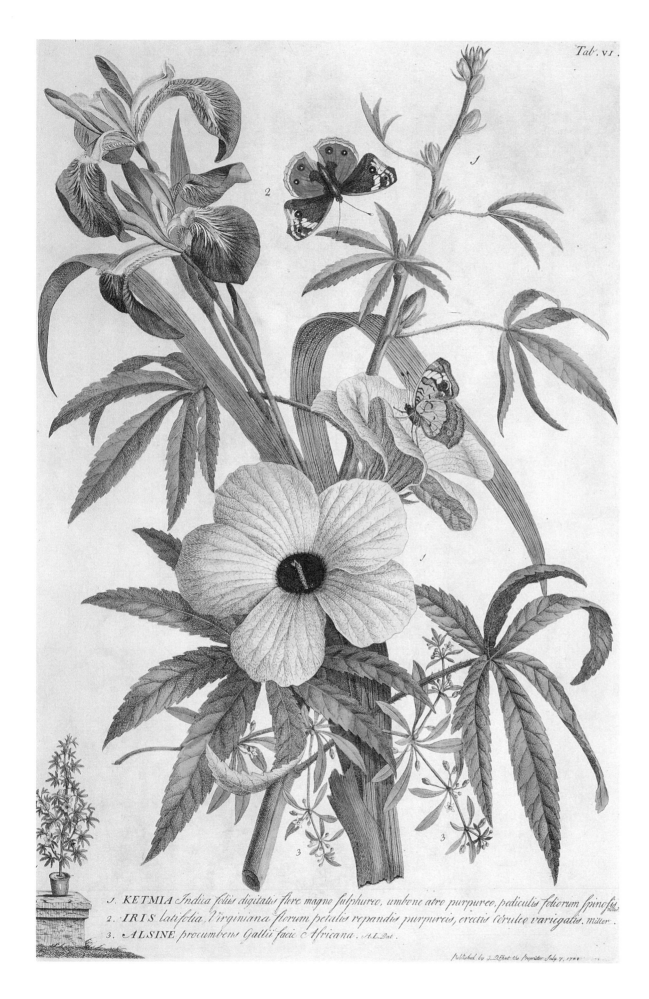

Tab. VI.

1. KETMIA *Indica foliis digitatis flore magno sulphureo, umbone atro purpureo, pediculis foliorum spinosis.*
2. IRIS *latifolia Virginiana florum petalis repandis purpureis, erectis cœruleo variegatis. Miller.*
3. ALSINE *procumbens Gallii facie Africana. A.L.Zut.*

Published by G. D. Ehret the Proprietor July 7, 1748.

Decan hemp (Hibiscus
cannabinus), with a
southern blue flag (Iris
virginica), on the left,
and carpet-weed
(Mollugo verticillata),
below, 1748, an engraving
by Georg Ehret.

OPPOSITE
Pasqueflower (Anemone
pulsatilla), 1732, a
watercolour by Georg
Ehret.

211

Euphorbia palustris	Euphorbia	
Fritillaria imperialis	Crown Imperial	
Galega officinalis	Goat's Rue	
Gentiana asclepiadea	Willow Gentian	
Geranium macrorrhizum	Pink Geranium	
Geranium pratense	Violet Geranium	
Geranium sylvaticum	Blue Geranium	
Gladiolus byzantinus	Gladiolus	
Galanthus nivalis	Snowdrop	
Gypsophila paniculata	Gypsophila	
Helleborus corsicus	Lenten Rose	
Helleborus foetidus	Lenten Rose	
Helleborus niger	Christmas Rose	
Helianthus annuus	Sunflower	
Hemerocallis fulva	Day Lily	
Hemerocallis minor	Day Lily	
Hepatica triloba	Hepatica	
Hesperis matronalis	Sweet Rocket	
Hyacinthus orientalis (vars)	Hyacinth	
Iberis spp.	Candytuft	
Iris persica	Persian Iris	(1629)
Iris germanica	Iris	
Iris florentina	White Iris	
Lathyrus latifolius	Everlasting Sweet Pea	
Lathyrus vernus	Sweet Pea	
Lavandula spica	Old English Lavender	Parterre
Lavandula stoechas	French Lavender	Parterre
Leucojum vernum	Snowflake	
Lilium candidum	Madonna Lily	
Lilium bulbiferum	Red Lily	
Lilium martagon	Martagon Lily	
Limonium vulgare	Sea Lavender	
Lupinus arboreus	Tree Lupin	
Lupinus albus	Lupin	
Lychnis chalcedonica	Jerusalem Cross	
Lychnis coronaria	Rose Champion	
Malva Moschata	Mallow	
Matthiola incana annua	Annual Stock	
Melianthus major	Melianthus	
Menthe pulegium	Pennyroyal	
Myrtus communis	Myrtle	Parterre, Tub
Narcissus jonquilla	Jonquil	
Narcissus jonquilla flore-pleno	Double Jonquil	
Narcissus minor	Dwarf Daffodil	(1629)
Narcissus odorus	Sweet Daffodil	(1629)
Narcissus poeticus	Daffodil	
Narcissus pseudonarcissus	Wild Daffodil	
Nepeta x faasenii	Catmint	Parterre
Nigella damascena	Love-in-a-Mist	
Oenothera biennis	Evening Primrose	
Oxalis acetosella	Wood Sorrel	
Paeonia officinalis	Peony	
Paeonia peregrina	Red Peony	
Papaver somniferum	Opium Poppy	
Phillyrea angustifolia variegata	Variegated Phillyrea	Tub
Polemonium caeruleum	Jacob's Ladder	
Polianthes tuberosa	Tuberose	(1629)

Potentilla recta	Yellow Potentilla	
Primula auricula spp.	Auricula	
Primula vulgaris	Primrose	
Pulsatilla vulgaris	Pasque Flower	
Pyracantha coccinea	Firethorn	Tub
Reseda odorata	Mignonette	
Rosa x centifolia	Cabbage Rose	
Rosa cinnamomea	Cinnamon Rose	
Rosa damascena 'Versicolor'	York & Lancaster Rose	
Rosa foetida 'Bicolor'	Austrian Copper Rose	
Rosa gallica 'Officinalis'	Apothecary's Rose	
Rosa gallica 'Versicolor'	Rosa Mundi	
Rosa hemisphaerica	Sulphur Rose	
Rosa moschata	Musk Rose	
Rosa mollis	Mollis Rose	
Rosa pimpinellifolia	Burnet Rose	
Rosa rubiginosa	Sweet Briar Rose	
Salvia argentea	Silver Clary	
Salvia sclarea	Clary	Parterre
Scilla peruviana	Hyacinth of Peru	(1607)
Syringa x persica	Persian Lilac	Parterre, Tub (1634)
Syringa vulgaris	Lilac	Parterre, Tub
Tagetes patula	French Marigold	
Tagetes erecta	African Marigold	
Teucrium chamaedrys	Germander	Parterre
Tulipa gesneriana	Tulip (Cvs)	
Valeriana officinalis	Valerian	
Veronica teucrium	Veronica	
Viburnum opulus	Guelder Rose	Parterre, Tub
Viburnum lanata	Common Viburnum	
Viola tricolor	Heartsease	
Viola odorata	Violet	
Viola spp.	Pansy	
Yucca filamentosa	Yucca	Tub (1656)
Yucca gloriosa	Yucca	Tub

CHAPTER 4: *The Geometrical Garden*

Plants available before 1740

Latin Name	*Common Name*	*Documented Use*
Small Trees and Shrubs for Groves and Bosquets		
Acer campestre	Field Maple	Coppice
Aralia spinosa	Aralia	
Arbutus andrachne	Strawberry Tree	
Arbutus unedo	Strawberry Tree	
Buxus sempervirens	Box	Hedge
Carpinus betulus	Hornbeam	Hedge, Palisade
Celtis australis	Nettle Tree	
Cercis siliquastrum	Judas Tree	
Colutea arborescens	Bladder Senna	
Cornus mas	Cornelian Cherry	
Cornus sanguinea	Dogwood	Coppice, Hedge
Corylus avellana	Hazel	Coppice, Hedge

Scientific Name	Common Name	Usage
Crataegus azarolus	Thorn	Coppice, Hedge
Crataegus monogyna	Hawthorn	Coppice, Hedge
Crataegus oxycantha	Hawthorn	Coppice, Hedge
Cupressus sempervirens	Italian Cypress	Allée, Evergreen Wood, Palisade
Cytisus scoparius	Broom	
Daphne mezereum alba	White Mezereon	
Diospyrus virginiana	Persimmon	
Diospyrus lotus	Date Plum	
Euonymus europaeus	Spindle Tree	Hedge
Ficus carica	Fig	
Hypericum calycinum	Rose of Sharon	
Ilex aquifolium	Holly	Hedge, Allée, Evergreen Wood
Ilex aquifolium 'Aureomarginata'	Variegated Holly	
Ilex aquifolium 'Ferox'	Hedgehog Holly	
Juniperus communis	Juniper	Hedge, Allée
Juniperus sabina	Juniper, Savin	Hedge, Allée
Laburnum alpinum	Scotch Laburnum	
Lonicera caprifolium	Perfoliate Honeysuckle	
Laurus nobilis	Bay Laurel	Hedge, Allée
Ligustrum vulgare	Privet	Hedge, Allée, Evergreen Wood
Mespilus germanica	Medlar	
Philadelphus coronarius	Mock Orange	
Phillyrea angustifolia	Alterna	Hedge, Evergreen Wood
Phillyrea latifolia	Alterna	Hedge, Evergreen Wood
Populus canescens	Dog Poplar	
Populus tremula	Aspen	Damp Ground
Prunus avium	Wild Cherry, Gean	Hedge, Allée
Prunus avium 'Plena'	Double Gean	Hedge
Prunus dulcis	Almond	
Prunus dulcis 'Roseo-plena'	Double Almond	
Prunus fruticosa	Ground Cherry	
Prunus laurocerasus	Cherry Laurel	
Prunus padus	Bird Cherry	
Prunus virginiana	Choke Cherry	
Pyracantha coccinea	Firethorn	Hedge
Rhamnus alaternus	Buckthorn	Hedge
Rhus typhina	Stag's-Horn Sumach	
Ribes uva-crispa	Gooseberry	Hedge
Robinia pseudoacacia	False Acacia	
Rosa damascena	Damask Rose	
Rosa gallica 'Versicolor'	Rosa Mundi	
Rosa moschata	Musk Rose	
Rosa rubiginosa	Sweet Briar	
Ruscus aculeatus	Butcher's Broom	Hedge
Salix caprea	Goat Willow	Coppice
Salix cinerea	Grey Sallow	Coppice, Hedge, Allée
Salix fragilis	Crack Willow	Coppice
Salix purpurea	Purple Osier	Coppice, Hedge, Allée, Basket
Salix viminalis	Osier Willow	Coppice, Hedge, Allée
Sambucus nigra 'Laciniata'	Cut-Leaf Elder	
Sorbus aucuparia	Mountain Ash	
Sorbus domestica	Service Tree	
Spartium junceum	Spanish Broom	
Syringa x persica	Persian Lilac	
Syringa vulgaris	Lilac	
Tamarix gallica	Tamarisk	
Taxus baccata	Yew	Hedge, Evergreen Wood, Palisade, Allée
Vaccinium myrtillus	Whortleberry	
Vaccinium vitis-idaea	Cowberry	
Viburnum opulus	Guelder Rose	
Viburnum tinus	Laurustinus	Hedge

Avenues and Woods

Scientific Name	Common Name	Usage
Abies alba	Silver Fir	Double Walk, Hedge (1696)
Abies balsamea	Balsam Fir	
Acer platanoides	Norway Maple	
Acer pseudoplatanus	Sycamore	
Aesculus hippocastanum	Horse Chestnut	Allée
Alnus glutinosa	Alder	
Betula pendula	Weeping Birch	
Betula pubescens	White Birch	
Carpinus betulus	Hornbeam	Colonnade, Arbour, Portico
Castanea sativa	Sweet Chestnut	
Cedrus libani	Cedar of Lebanon	
Fagus sylvatica	Beech	
Fraxinus excelsior	Ash	Bosquet
Fraxinus ornus	Manna Ash	
Juglans nigra	Black Walnut	
Picea abies	Norway Spruce	
Pinus sylvestris	Scots Pine	
Platanus x hispanica	London Plane	
Platanus orientalis	Oriental Plane	
Populus alba	White Poplar	
Populus tremula	Aspen	
Quercus ilex	Holm Oak	Hedge
Quercus robur	Oak	
Salix alba	White Willow	Damp Ground
Sorbus torminalis	Wild Service Tree	
Thuja occidentalis	Arbor-Vitae	
Tilia cordata	Small-Leaved Lime	Grove
Tilia x europaea (vulgaris)	Common Lime	Colonnade, Allée, Arbour, Portico, Grove
Tilia platyphyllos	Broad-Leaved Lime	Grove
Ulmus glabra	Wych Elm	
Ulmus procera	English Elm	Colonnade, Allée, Arbour, Portico

CHAPTER 5: *Theatrical Garden*

Amphitheatre Plants available before 1760

Pots

Citrus sinensis	Orange
Citrus 'Limonia'	Lemon
Myrtus communis	Myrtle

Flowers

Alcea rosea	Hollyhock
Amaryllis belladonna	Amaryllis
Aquilegia canadensis	Canadian Columbine
Aquilegia vulgaris	Columbine
Delphinium grandiflora	Delphinium
Eryngium bourgatii	Sea Holly
Fritillaria imperialis	Crown Imperial
Geranium maculatum	Geranium
Gypsophila paniculata	Gypsophila
Helenium autumnale	Sneezeweed
Hemerocallis fulva	Day Lily
Lilium candidum	Madonna Lily
Lobelia cardinalis	Cardinal Flower
Lychnis flos-jovis	Maltese Cross
Matthiola incana annua	Annual Stock

Canterbury bell (Campanula medium), 1757, a painting on vellum by Georg Ehret.

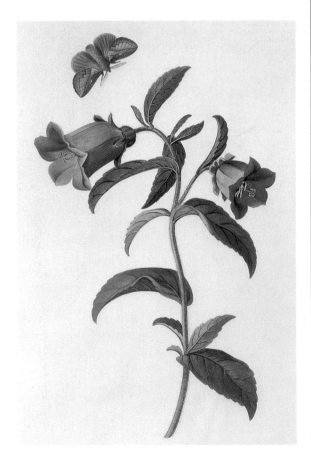

Narcissus jonquilla	Jonquil
Narcissus minor	Daffodil
Narcissus odorus	Daffodil
Narcissus poeticus	Pheasant's Eye.
Primula officinalis	Primrose
Veronica incana	Veronica
Vinca minor	Perrywinkle
Viola odorata	Sweet Violet
Viola odorata flore pleno	Double Violet

Deciduous

Low Shrubs

Rosa x centifolia	Cabbage Rose
Rosa damascena	Damask Rose
Rosa moschata	Musk Rose
Rosa rubiginosa	Sweet Briar
Spiraea hypericifolia	Spiraea

Shrubs, Medium and Large

Cistus laurifolius	Rock Rose
Cytisus scoparius	English Broom
Daphne mezereum	Mezereon
Laburnum alpinum	Scots Laburnum
Syringa vulgaris	Lilac
Viburnum opulus	Guelder Rose

Trees

Aesculus hippocastanum	Horse Chestnut
Alnus glutinosa	Alder
Carpinus betulus	Hornbeam
Castanea sativa	Sweet Chestnut
Corylus avellana	Hazel
Fagus sylvatica	Beech
Malus sylvestris	Crab Apple
Populus balsamifera	Balsam Poplar

Evergreen

Low Shrubs

Buxus sempervirens	Box
Euphorbia palustris	Spurge
Juniperus sabina	Juniper, Savin
Juniperus communis	Common Juniper
Viburnum tinus	Laurustinus

Shrubs, Medium and Large

Arbutus unedo	Strawberry Tree
Ilex aquifolium	Holly
Phillyrea angustifolia	Phillyrea
Prunus laurocerasus	Cherry Laurel
Rhamnus alaternus	Buckthorn
Taxus baccata	Yew

Trees

Abies alba	Silver Fir
Cupressus sempervirens	Italian Cypress
Picea abies	Norway Spruce
Pinus cembra	Arolla Pine
Pinus pinaster	Maritime Pine
Pinus sylvestris	Scots Pine

CHAPTER 6: *Landscape Garden*

Plants available before 1780

Trees

Acer pseudoplatanus	Sycamore
Acer saccharinum	Silver Maple
Acer rubrum	Red Maple
Acer platanoides	Norway Maple
Acer negundo	Box Elder Maple
Aesculus hippocastanum	Horse Chestnut
Ailanthus altissima	Tree of Heaven
Alnus glutinosa	Common Alder
Arbutus unedo	Strawberry Tree
Castanea sativa	Sweet Chestnut
Catalpa bignonioides	Indian Bean Tree
Cedrus libani	Cedar of Lebanon
Chamaecyparis thyoides	White Cypress
Fagus grandiflora	American Beech
Fagus sylvatica	Beech
Fraxinus americana	White Ash
Fraxinus excelsior	Ash
Fraxinus ornus	Manna Ash
Gleditsia triacanthos	Honey Locust
Halesia carolina	Snowdrop Tree
Juglans nigra	Black Walnut
Laburnum anagyroides	Laburnum
Larix decidua	Larch
Liquidambar styraciflua	Liquidamber
Liriodendron tulipifera	Tulip Tree
Magnolia grandiflora	Evergreen Magnolia
Magnolia tripetala	Umbrella Tree
Picea abies	Norway Spruce
Pinus strobus	White Pine
Pinus sylvestris	Scots Pine
Platanus x hispanica	London Plane
Platanus orientalis	Oriental Plane
Populus balsamifera	Balsam Poplar
Prunus avium 'Plena'	Double Gean
Prunus dulcis	Almond
Prunus padus	Bird Cherry
Quercus alba	White Oak
Quercus cerris	Turkey Oak
Quercus coccinea	Scarlet Oak
Quercus ilex	Holm Oak
Quercus robur	Oak
Quercus rubra	Red Oak
Rhus verniciflua	Varnish Tree
Robinia pseudoacacia	False Acacia
Salix babylonica	Weeping Willow
Sorbus aria	Whitebeam
Sorbus aucuparia	Mountain Ash
Tilia cordata	Small-Leaved Lime
Tilia x europaea (vulgaris)	Common Lime
Tilia platyphyllos	Broad-Leaved Lime

Shrubs in Pleasure Grounds

Amelanchier canadensis	Snowy Mespilus
Aralia spinosa	Devil's Walking Stick
Cistus ladanifer	Gum Cistus
Colutea orientalis	Bladder Senna
Cornus florida	Flowering Dogwood
Cytisus hirsutus	Hairy Broom
Cytisus scoparius	Broom
Daphne mezereum	Mezereon
Hippophae rhamnoides	Sea Buckthorn
Hypericum androsaemum	Tutsan
Hypericum calycinum	Rose of Sharon
Ilex glabra	Inkberry
Ilex opaca	American Holly
Juniperus sabina	Savin
Kalmia latifolia	Calico Bush
Ligustrum vulgare	Privet
Lonicera periclymenum	Woodbine
Lonicera sempervirens	Evergreen Honeysuckle
Mespilus germanica	Medlar
Phlomis fructicosa	Jerusalem Sage
Prunus laurocerasus	Cherry Laurel
Prunus lusitanica	Portugal Laurel
Rhododendron maximum	Rose Bay
Rhododendron ponticum	Rhododendron
Rhus typhina	Stag's-Horn Sumach
Rosa x alba	White Rose
Rosa x alba 'Maiden's Blush'	Maiden's Blush Rose
Rosa centifolia	Provence Rose
Rosa chinensis 'Old Blush'	Monthly Rose
Rosa x damascena bifera	Damask Rose
Rosa damascena 'Versicolor'	York & Lancaster Rose
Rosa gallica 'Versicolor'	Rosa Mundi
Rosa rubiginosa	Sweet Briar, Elegantine
Ruscus aculeatus	Butcher's Broom
Sambucus nigra	Elder
Sambucus nigra 'Laciniata'	Cut-Leaved Elder
Sambucus racemosa	Red-Berried Elder
Spartium junceum	Spanish Broom
Spiraea hypericifolia	Spiraea
Spiraea salicifolia	Bridewort
Syringa x persica	Persian Lilac
Syringa vulgaris	Common Lilac
Tamarix gallica	Tamarisk
Viburnum opulus	Guelder Rose

CHAPTER 7: *English Flower Garden*
CHAPTER 8: *Villa Garden*

Plants introduced before 1820

Latin Name	*Common Name*

Perennials, Annuals and Bulbs

Aconitum cammarum	Monk's Hood

Alcea rosea	Hollyhock	Iris pumila	Dwarf Iris
Anemone coronaria	Anemone	Iris susiana	Caledonian Iris
Anemone virginiana	Virginian Anemone	Iris xiphiodes	Bulbous-Rooted Iris
Antirrhinum majus	Snapdragon	Lilium martagon	Martagon Lily
Aquilegia vulgaris	Columbine	Lobelia cardinalis	Cardinal Flower
Armeria maritima	Thrift	Lunaria annua	Honesty
Bellis perennis	Daisy	Lupinus perennis cvs	Lupin
Caltha palustris plena	Double Marsh Marigold	Lychnis chalcedonica	Maltese Cross
Campanula bononiensis	Bellflower	Lychnis coronaria plena	Double Rose Campion
Campanula carpatica	Bellflower	Matthiola incana annua	Stock
Campanula latiloba	Bellflower	Narcissus jonquilla vars	Jonquil
Campanula persicifolia	Peach-Leaved Bellflower	Narcissus poeticus	Pheasant's Eye
Campanula punctata	Bellflower	Narcissus pseudonarcissus	
Campanula pyramidalis	Chimney Bellflower	vars	Daffodil
Campanula versicolor	Bellflower	Narcissus tazetta	Polyanthus Narcissus
Cheiranthus cheiri	Wallflower	Nigella damascena	Love-in-a-Mist
Consolida ambigua	Larkspur	Paeonia mascula	Peony
Convallaria majalis	Lily of the Valley	Paeonia officinalis vars	Peony
Crocus x sativus	Saffron	Phlox drummondii	Phlox
Crocus vernus	Crocus	Phlox maculata	Phlox
Cyclamen europaeum	Autumn-flowering	Phlox paniculata	Phlox
	Cyclamen	Polianthes tuberosa	Tuberose
Cyclamen repandum	Spring-flowering	Primula auricula	Auricula
	Cyclamen	Primula vulgaris vars	Primrose
Delphinium elatum	Delphinium	Pulsatilla vulgaris	Pasque Flower
Dianthus alpinus	Alpine Pink	Ranunculus aconitifolius	White Bachelors' Buttons
Dianthus barbatus	Sweet William	Reseda odorata	Mignonette
Dianthus caryophyllus	Carnation	Saxifraga urbium	London Pride
Dianthus superbus	Fringed Pink	Scilla peruviana	Blue Hyacinth of Peru
Digitalis ferruginea	Iron-Coloured Foxglove	Scilla peruviana alba	White Hyacinth of Peru
Digitalis grandiflora	Great Yellow Foxglove	Silene armeria	Catchfly
Digitalis purpurea	Purple Foxglove	Silene vulgaris	Campion
Erythronium dens-canis	Dog's-Tooth Violet	Tagetes erecta	African Marigold
Euphorbia polychroma	Spurge	Tagetes patula	French Marigold
Euphorbia rigida	Spurge	Tradescantia virginiana	Spiderwort
Fragaria vesca	Wild Strawberry	Trillium erectum	Lambsquarters
Fritillaria imperialis	Crown Imperial	Tropaeolum majus	Nasturtium
Fritillaria meleagris	Snakeshead Fritillary	Tulipa gesneriana	Double Early Tulip
Galanthus nivalis	Snowdrop	Tulipa sylvestris	Wild Yellow Tulip
Gentiana acaulis	Gentian	Valeriana officinalis	Valerian
Geranium endressii	Pink Geranium	Veronica exaltata	Veronica
Geranium ibericum	Cranesbill	Veronica gentianoides	Veronica
Geranium pratense	Meadow Cranesbill	Veronica incana	Hoary-Leaved Speedwell
Geranium wallichianum	Blue Geranium	Veronica officinalis	Speedwell
Gladiolus communis	Corn-flag	Vinca major	Greater Periwinkle
Helianthus annuus	Sunflower	Vinca minor	Lesser Periwinkle
Helleborus niger	Christmas Rose	Viola odorata	Sweet Violet
Hemerocallis fulva	Day Lily	Viola tricolor	Heartsease
Hepatica triloba	Hepatica		
Hepatica triloba caerulea	Blue Hepatica	**Climbers**	
Hesperis matronalis	Sweet Rocket	Clematis alpina	Clematis
Hosta lancifolia	Plantain Lily	Clematis cirrhosa	Clematis
Hosta plantaginea	Plantain Lily	Clematis flammula	Clematis
Hyacinthus orientalis	Hyacinth	Clematis orientalis	Clematis
Iberis sempervirens	Candytuft	Clematis vitalba	Old Man's Beard
Iris florentina	White Florentine Iris	Clematis viticellá	Clematis
Iris germanica	German Iris	Jasminum officinale	White Jasmine
Iris persica	Persian Iris	Lonicera x americana	American Honeysuckle
Iris pseudacorus	Yellow Water Iris	Lonicera caprifolium	Perfoliate Honeysuckle

Lonicera etrusca	Honeysuckle		
Lonicera implexa	Honeysuckle		
Lonicera periclymenum	Woodbine		
Lonicera sempervirens	Trumpet Honeysuckle		
Passiflora caerulea	Blue Passion Flower		
Wisteria sinensis	Wisteria		

Trees and Shrubs

Arbutus unedo	Strawberry Tree
Daphne mezereum	Daphne
Ginkgo biloba	Maidenhair Tree
Hydrangea arborescens	Hydrangea
Jasminum humile	Jasmine
Juniperus virginiana	Pencil Cedar
Kalmia latifolia	Calico Bush
Larix decidua	Larch
Larix x pendula	Weeping Larch
Liriodendron tulipifera	Tulip Tree
Lonicera caerulea	Honeysuckle
Magnolia grandiflora	Magnolia
Nerium oleander	Oleander
Philadelphus coronarius	Mock Orange
Pinus strobus	Weymouth Pine
Rhododendron arboreum	Tree Rhododendron
Rhododendron canescens	White Azalea
Rhododendron hirsutum	Rhododendron
Rhododendron luteum	Yellow Azalea
Rhododendron maximum	Rose Bay
Rhododendron nudiflorum	Pink Azalea
Rhododendron ponticum	Rhododendron
Rhododendron roseum	Rose Azalea
Rhodendron viscosum	Swamp Azalea
Rosa chinensis var.	Old China Rose varieties
Rosa moschata	Musk Rose
Salix babylonica	Weeping Willow
Tsuga heterophylla	Western Hemlock

CHAPTER 9: *Walled Garden*

Plants available before 1830

Apples

'Adams Pearmain'	'Tom Putt'
'Ashmead Kernel'	'Warner's King'
'Autumn Pearmain'	'White Transparent'
'Bess Pool'	'Wyken Pippin'
'Brownlees' Russet'	
'Cornish Gillyflower'	**Apricots**
'Court Pendu Plat'	'Early Moor Park'
'Cox's Pomona'	'Moor Park'
'D'Arcy Spice'	
'Gravenstien'	**Blackberry**
'Hambledon Deux Ans'	'Parsley-Leafed'
'Harvey'	Rubus fruticosus
'Keswick Codling'	Rubus laciniatus
'Orleans Reinette'	
'Pitmaston Pineapple'	**Cherry**
'Reinette Rouge Etoile'	'Bigarreau Gaucher'
'Ribston Pippin'	'Morello'
	'Napoleon Bigarreau'

Fig
'Brown Turkey'
'White Marseilles'

Grape
'Black Hamburg'
Vitis Brandt

Medlar
Mespilus germanica

Mulberry
Morus alba
Morus nigra

Nectarine
'Lord Napier'
'Rivers Prolific'

Peach
'Duke of York'
'Peregrine'

Nuts

Corylus avellana	Hazelnut
Juglans nigra	Black Walnut
Juglans regia	Common Walnut
'Kent Cob'	Lambert's Filbert
Prunus dulcis	Almond

Pear
'Autumn Bergamotte'
'Black Worcester'
'English Windsor'
'Monsieur John'
'Spring Bergamotte'
'Williams' Bon Chrétien'

Plum
'Count Althuann's Gage'
'Kirkes Blue'
'Mirabelle de Nancy'
'White Magnum Bonum'
'Yellow Egg'

Quince
Cydonia oblonga

CHAPTER 10: *Ornamental Garden*

Plants available before 1850

Perennials

Alstroemeria aurantiaca	Peruvian Lily
Aquilegia vulgaris	Columbine
Aster alpinus	Aster
Aster amellus	Aster
Campanula alliarifolia	Bellflower
Campanula bononiensis	Bellflower
Campanula carpatica	Bellflower
Campanula garganica	Bellflower
Campanula lactiflora	Bellflower
Campanula latiloba	Bellflower
Campanula persicifolia	Peach-Leaved Bellflower
Campnula punctata	Bellflower
Campanula pyramidalis	Chimney Bellflower
Campanula rotundifolia	Harebell
Campanula sarmatica	Bellflower
Campanula versicolor	Bellflower
Dianthus gratianopolitanus	Cheddar Gorge Pink
Dianthus superbus	Fringed Pink
Dicentra spectabilis	Bleeding Heart
Dictamnus albus	Dittany
Galtonia candicans	Summer Hyacinth
Gentiana acaulis	Gentian
Gentiana asclepiadea	Willow Gentian
Gentiana lutea	Bitterwort Gentian
Geranium ibericum	Cranesbill

Geranium pratense	Meadow Cranesbill
Geranium sanguineum	Bloody Cranesbill
Hesperis matronalis	Sweet Rocket
Iris germanica	Iris
Lathyrus latifolius	Perennial Pea
Lathyrus tuberosus	Pea
Lilium auratum	Golden-Rayed Lily
Lilium tigrinum	Tiger Lily
Lobelia cardinalis	Cardinal Flower
Lobelia fulgens	Lobelia
Lychnis chalcedonica	Maltese Cross
Lychnis viscaria	Catchfly
Lysimachia nummularia	Creeping Jenny
Malva moschata	Musk Mallow
Mimulus moschatus	Mimulus
Oenothera acaulis	Evening Primrose
Oenothera missouriensis	Evening Primrose
Paeonia mascula	Peony
Paeonia officinalis	Peony
Pelargonium peltatum	Ivy-Leaved Geranium
Pelargonium zonale vars	Geranium
Potentilla atrosanguinea	Red Daisy Potentilla
Potentilla recta	Yellow Daisy Potentilla
Romneya coulteri	Tree Poppy
Salvia fulgens	Cardinal Red Sage
Salvia involucrata	Sage
Salvia patens	Sage
Tigridia pavonia	Peacock-Tiger Flower
Trollius europaeus	Globe Flower
Verbascum phoeniceum	Purple Mullein
Verbena peruviana	Verbena
Verbena rigida	Verbena
Veronica officinalis	Speedwell
Viola tricolor	Heartsease

Annuals and Biennials

Alcea rosea	Hollyhock
Althaea officinalis	Marsh Mallow
Anagallis Tenella	Anagallis
Antirrhinum majus	Snapdragon
Clarkia elegans	Clarkia
Clarkia pulchella	Clarkia
Eschscholzia californica	Californian Poppy
Lathyrus odoratus	Sweet Pea
Lupinus littoralis	Lupin
Lupinus luteus	Lupin
Mattiola incana annua	Annual Stock
Myosotis caespitosa	Forget-Me-Not
Reseda odorata	Mignonette
Tropaeolum majus	Nasturtium

Shrubs

Calceolaria integrifolia	Slipperwort
Cotinus coggyria	Venetian Sumach, Smoke Tree
Fuchsia magellanica	Fuchsia
Fuchsia magellanica 'Gracilis'	Fuchsia
Hypericum calycinum	Rose of Sharon

Lupinus arboreus	Tree Lupin
Rosa 'Celestial'	pink
Rosa 'Bourbon Queen'	pink
Rosa 'Blanchefleur'	white
Rosa 'Hermosa'	pink
Rosa 'Old Blush'	pink
Rosa 'Mme Hardy'	white
Rosa 'Ispahan'	pink
Rosa 'Charles de Mills'	purple
Rosa 'Gloire de France'	pink
Rosa 'Desprez à Fleur Jaune'	yellow

CHAPTER II: *Rosarie*

Roses available before 1880

R. 'Burnet Double Marbled Pink'	marble pink
R. 'Burnet Double Pink'	pink
R. 'Burnet Double White'	white
R. ecae	yellow
R. foetida	Austrian Briar
R. foetida bicolor	Copper Austrian Briar
R. pimpinellifolia	Scotch Rose, Burnet Rose
R. sericea	white
R. gallica	French Rose
R. gallica officinalis	Apothecary's Rose, Red Rose of Lancaster
R. gallica versicolor	Rosa Mundi

Hybrids

'Alain Blanchard'	crimson
'Belle de Crécy'	pink, fragrant
'Belle Isis'	double, pink
'Boule de Nanteuil'	double, pink
'Camaieux'	double, pink striped
'Cardinal de Richelieu'	purple, fragrant
'Charles de Mills'	purple
'Complicata'	bright pink
'Conditorum'	red, fragrant
'D'Aguesseau'	crimson
'Duc de Guiche'	violet crimson
'Duchess d'Angoulême'	double pink
'Duchesse de Buccleugh'	magenta
'Duchesse de Montebello'	double, pink
'Empress Josephine'	deep pink, slightly fragrant
'Georges Vibert'	striped, carmine
'Hippolyte'	magenta
'Ipsilanté'	lilac-pink
'Président de Sèze'	magenta-lilac
'Rose du Maître d'Ecole'	double, pink

'Tricolor de Flandres'	striped, purple-pink
'Tuscany Superb'	velvet red
R. x centifolia	Cabbage Rose
R. x centifolia alba	White Provence
Hybrids	
'Blanchefleur'	pink, fragrant
'Fantin Latour'	pink
'Juno'	pale pink, fragrant
'La Noblesse'	double, silver pink, fragrant
'Petite Lisette'	deep pink
'Pompon de Bourgogne'	rosy claret
'Reines des Centfeuilles'	double, pink, fragrant
'Robert le Diable'	crimson
'Rose de Meaux'	double, pink, fragrant
'White Provence'	Unique Blanche, white
R. x centifolia muscosa	Moss Rose
Hybrids	
'Alfred de Dalmas'	semi-double, creamy pink, fragrant
'Baron de Wassenaer'	double, red
'Blanche Moreau'	double, white, fragrant
'Capitaine John Ingram'	double, crimson, fragrant
'Célina'	semi-double, pink
'Chapeau de Napoléon'	double, deep pink, fragrant
'Common Moss'	Old Pink Moss, fragrant
'Eugenie Guinoisseau'	violet purple, fragrant
'Felicité Bohain'	pink
'Général Kléber'	pink
'Gloire des Mousseux'	double, soft pink, fragrant
'Henri Martin'	crimson, fragrant
'James Mitchell'	double, pink
'James Veitch'	purple
'Jeanne de Montfort'	pink, fragrant
'Lanei'	Lane's Moss, crimson
'Little Gem'	crimson
'Louis Gimard'	double, pink
'Maréchal Davoust'	purple, pink
'Marie de Blois'	pink, fragrant
'Mme de la Roche-Lambert'	purple
'Mme Louis Levêque'	soft pink
'Mrs William Paul'	red
'Mousseux du Japon'	semi-double, lilac pink
'Nuits de Young'	dark maroon
'Pélisson'	double, red
'Reine Blanche'	double, white
'René d'Anjou'	pink, fragrant
'Salet'	double, rose
'Shailer's White Moss'	white, fragrant
'Striped Moss'	pink-red stripes
'William Lobb'	semi-double, purple, fragrant
'Zenobia'	pink
'Zoe'	double, pink
R. x damascena	
R. x damascena versicolor	York and Lancaster

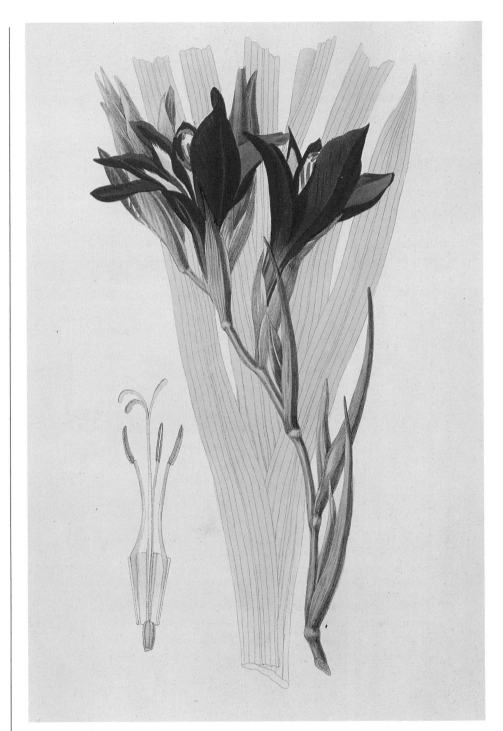

Gladiolus cardinalis, 1825, a watercolour by William Clark.

Hybrids

'Blush Damask'	double, deep pink
'Botzaris'	double, creamy
'Celsiana'	pink, fragrant
'Ispahan'	semi-double, pink, fragrant

'Kazanlik'	pink
'La Ville de Bruxelles'	pink
'Leda'	pink, fragrant
'Mme Hardy'	white, fragrant
'Quatre Saisons'	pink, fragrant

R. portlandica	Portland Rose
Hybrids	
'Comte de Chambord'	pink, fragrant
'Jacques Cartier'	deep pink, fragrant
'Pergolese'	lilac
'Rose du Roi'	mottled red

R. x alba	White Rose of York
Hybrids	
'Celestial'	pink, fragrant
'Félicité Parmentier'	pink
'Königin von Dänemark'	Queen of Denmark, pink
'Maiden's Blush Great'	blush pink, slightly fragrant
'Maxima'	Jacobite Rose, white
'Mme Legras de St Germain'	cream
'Mme Plantier'	white, near climber

R. rubiginosa	Sweet Briar
Hybrids	
'Manning's Blush'	pink
R. villosa	Apple Rose
R. carolina	pink
R. nitida	pink
R. palustris	Swamp Rose
R. virginiana	Virginian Rose

R. x l'héritierana	Boursault Rose, pink
Hybrids	
'Blush Boursault'	pink
R. banksiae lutea	Yellow Banksia
R. moschata	Musk Rose
R. rugosa	pink
R. rugosa alba	white

R. sempervirens	Evergreen Rose
Hybrids	
'Adélaide d'Orléans'	semi-double, pinkish
'Felicité et Perpétue'	small clusters, pink
'Princess Louise'	lilac-pink

R. chinensis	China Rose
Hybrids	
'Cramoisi Supérieur'	semi-double, red
'Hermosa'	pink
'Louis XIV'	red
'Minima'	Fairy Rose, light pink
'Old Blush'	Monthly Rose, China pink
'Papa Hémeray'	pink
'Slater's Crimson China'	pink
'Viridiflora'	The Green Rose

R. x bourboniana	now extinct
Hybrids	
'Boule de Neige'	white, fragrant
'Bourbon Queen'	pink
'Princesse de Lamballe'	rose, slightly fragrant
'Commandant Beaurepaire'	pink, purple, marbled white
'Coupe d'Hérbé'	pink
'Gros Choux d'Hollande'	soft pink
'La Reine Victoria'	lilac-pink
'Louise Odier'	rose-pink
'Mme Lauriol de Barny'	silver-pink
'Mme Pierre Oger'	silver-pink
'Souvenir de la Malmaison'	Queen of Beauty, pale pink
'Variegata de Bologna'	striped
'Zephirine Drouhin'	pink, thornless

Noisette Hybrids

'Aimée Vibert'	double, white, fragrant
'Blush Noisette'	semi-double, pale pink
'Céline Forestier'	climber yellow
'Desprez à Fleur Jaune'	yellow and buff
'Gloire de Dijon'	pale yellow
'Maréchal Niel'	yellow, fragrant
'Mme Alfred Carrière'	climber, white
'Rêve d'Or'	yellow
'William Allen Richardson'	apricot

Hybrid Perpetuals

'Alfred Colomb'	brick red
'Archduchesse Elisabeth d'Autriche'	rose
'Ardoisée de Lyon'	rich red
'Baron Girod de l'Ain'	crimson
'Baroness Rothschild'	rose, fragrant
'Baronne Prévost'	rose
'Charles Lefèbvre'	crimson-maroon
'Comtesse Cécile de Chabrillant'	pink
'Dupuy Jamain'	cerise-red
'Empereur du Maroc'	crimson-maroon
'Ferdinand Pichard'	red striped white
'Frau Karl Drushki'	white
'Général Jacqueminot'	General Jack, red
'Gloire de Ducher'	pink red, fragrant
'La Reine'	rose pink
'Le Havre'	double, red, fragrant
'Mme Gabriel Luizet'	double, pink
'Paul Neyron'	pink, fragrant
'Prince Camille de Rohan'	deep red
'Reine des Violettes'	violet, fragrant
'Souvenir du Docteur Jamain'	double ruby red
'Victor Verdier'	double, rose, fragrant
'Yolande d'Aragon'	pink, fragrant

Hybrid Teas

'Captain Christy'	climber, soft pink
'La France'	silver-pink
'Reine Marie Henriette'	climber, red

CHAPTER 12: *Rock and Quarry*

Plants introduced before 1900

Alpine and Rock Plants

Alchemilla alpina	Alchemilla
Androsace helvetica	Androsace
Androsace sarmentosa	Androsace
Androsace villosa	Androsace
Antirrhinum majus var.	Snapdragon
Arabis caucasia	Snow-in-Summer
Armeria maritima	Sea Thrift
Armeria montana	Alpine Thrift
Artemisia absinthium	Wormwood
Aubretia deltoidea vars.	Aubretia
Aurinia saxatilis	Alyssum
Campanula carpatica	Bellflower
Campanula garganica	Bellflower
Cheiranthus cheiri	Wallflower
Dianthus deltoides	Maiden Pink
Dianthus fragrans	Pink
Gentiana acaulis	Gentian
Gentiana alpina	Gentian
Gentiana verna	Gentian
Geranium cinereum	Geranium
Gypsophila repens	Gypsophila
Iberis saxatilis	Candytuft
Iris cristata	Eransia Iris
Iris pumila	Dwarf Bearded Iris
Lychnis alpina	Lychnis
Mimulus cupreus	Mimulus
Mimulus luteus	Monkey Musk
Papaver burseri	Alpine Poppy
Phlox bifida	Phlox
Phlox nana	Phlox
Phlox procumbens	Phlox
Phlox subulata	Phlox
Polygonum affine	Polygonum
Potentilla alchemilloides	Potentilla
Primula allionii	Primula
Primula auricula	Auricula
Primula forestii	Primula
Primula x pubescens	Primula
Primula rosea	Pink Candelabra Primula
Primula sieboldii	White Lacecap Primula
Primula vulgaris	Primrose
Saponaria ocymoides	Soapwort
Saxifraga burseriana	Saxifrage
Saxifraga fortunei	Saxifrage
Saxifraga longifolia	Saxifrage
Sedum acre	Stonecrop
Sedum spurium	Stonecrop
Sempervivum arachnoideum	Houseleek
Sempervivum montanum	Houseleek
Silene alpestris	Silene
Stachys lanata	Lamb's Tongue
Thymus serphyllum	Thyme

Bulbs, Corms and Tubers

Anemone x fulgens	Anemone
Anemone nemorosa	Wood Anemone
Anemone pavonina	Great Peacock Anemone
Crocus corsica	Crocus
Crocus chrysanthus	Early Crocus
Crocus imperati	Crocus
Crocus susianus	Crocus
Crocus vernus	Crocus
Cyclamen cilicium	Autumn-flowering Cyclamen
Cyclamen coum	Spring-flowering Cyclamen
Cyclamen purpurascens	Summer-flowering Cyclamen
Fritillaria acmopetala	Fritillary
Fritillaria imperialis	Crown Imperial
Fritillaria pyrenaica	Fritillary
Fritillaria persica	Fritillary
Iris reticulata	Iris
Lilium auratum	Golden-Rayed Lily
Lilium candidum	Madonna Lily
Lilium henryi	Lily
Lilium martagon	Martagon Lily
Lilium regale	Regal Lily
Lilium speciosum	Lily
Narcissus asturiensis	Daffodil
Narcissus assoanus	Daffodil
Narcissus nanus	Daffodil
Scilla bifolia	Blue-Flowered Scilla
Scilla siberica	Siberian Squill

Hardy Ferns

Adiantum pedatum	Maidenhair Fern
Adiantum venustum	Maidenhair Fern
Asplenium adiantum-nigrum	Black Spleenwort
Asplenium trichomanes	Maidenhair Spleenwort
Athyrium filix-femina	Lady Fern
Blechnum penna-marina	Blechnum Fern
Blechnum spicant	Blechnum Fern
Cheilanthes lanosa	Cheilanthes Fern
Cystopteris bulbifera	Bladder Fern
Cystopteris fragilis	Bladder Fern
Dryopteris spinulosa	Buckler Fern
Gymnocarpium dryopteris	Gymnocarpium
Gymnocarpium robertianum	Gymnocarpium
Phyllitis scolopendrium	Hart's-tongue
Polypodium vulgare	Adder's Fern

Shrubs

Calluna spp.	Heather
Cytisus spp.	Broom
Daphne petraea	Daphne
Daphne jasminea	Daphne
Erica spp.	Heath
Genista lydia	Genista Broom

Helianthemum
  nummularium — Rock Rose
Hypericum rhodopeum — St. John's Wort
Lavendula spica — Lavender
Rhododendron
  ferrugineum — Alpine Rose
Rhododendron hirsutum — Rhododendron
Rhododendron myrtilloides — Rhododendron
Rosmarinus officinalis — Rosemary
Santolina
  chamaecyparissus
  corsica — Santolina

CHAPTER 13: *The Wild and Woodland Garden*

Bulbs, Corms and Tubers

Anagallis tenella — Anagallis
Anemone blanda — Anemone
Anemone nemorosa — Wood Anemone
Crocus angustifolius — Crocus
Crocus biflora — Crocus
Crocus etruscus — Crocus
Crocus speciosus — Crocus
Cyclamen coum — Spring-flowering Cyclamen
Cyclamen repandum — Spring-flowering Cyclamen
Erythronium dens-canis — Dog's-Tooth Violet
Erythronium revolutum — Erythronium
Eschscholzia californica — Californian Poppy
Galanthus gracilis — Snowdrop
Galanthus nivalis — Snowdrop
Galanthus plicatus — Snowdrop
Hyacinthoides non-
  scriptus — Bluebell
Leucojum aestivum — Summer Snowflake
Narcissus bulbocodium — Daffodil
Narcissus minor — Daffodil
Narcissus poeticus — Pheasant's Eye
Narcissus pseudonarcissus — Wild Daffodil
Scilla bifolia — Bluebell
Scilla siberica — Siberian Squill

Perennials

Artemisia stelleriana — Dusty Miller
Aster novi-belgii — Michaelmas Daisy
Caltha palustris — Marsh Marigold
Hemerocallis fulva — Day Lily
Hemerocallis minor — Day Lily
Iris foetidissima — Stinking Iris
Primula denticulata — Candelabra Primula
Primula elatior — Oxlip
Primula vulgaris — Primrose
Smilacina racemosa — False Spikenard
Vinca major — Greater Periwinkle
Vinca minor — Lesser Periwinkle

Climbers

Clematis cirrhosa — Clematis
Clematis flammula — Clematis
Clematis montana — Clematis
Hydrangea petiolaris — Climbing Hydrangea
Tropaeolum speciosum — Flame Flower

Shrubs

Amelanchier canadensis — Snowy Mespilus
Forsythia x intermedia — Forsythia
Philadelphus 'Beauclerk' — Mock Orange
Viburnum plicatum — Japanese snowball
Viburnum rhytidophyllum — Viburnum

Rhodendrons

Azuma-kagami — Kurume Azalea
Byron — Rustica Hybrid Azalea
Coccinea speciosa — Ghent Hybrid
Cornielle — Ghent Hybrid
Hinode-giri — Kurume Azalea
Hinomayo — Kurume Azalea
Hollandia — Mollis Hybrid
Palestrina — Vuyk Hybrid
Rh. arboreum — Tree Rhododendron
Rh. augustinii — Specie Rhododendrons
Rh. barbatum
Rh. 'Beauty of Littleworth'
Rh. 'Betty Wormald'
Rh. 'Britannia'
Rh. 'Cremorne'
Rh. decorum
Rh. 'Erebus'
Rh. eriogynum
Rh. falconeri
Rh. griersonianum
Rh. 'Idealist'
Rh. kaempferi
Rh. 'Lady Chamberlain'
Rh. 'Loderi'
Rh. luteum — Yellow Azalea
Rh. macabeanum
Rh. 'May Day'
Rh. neriiflorum
Rh. 'Praecox'
Rh. sutchuenense
Rh. williamsianum
Rh. yakushimanum

Trees

Abies magnifica — Californian Red Cedar
Acer davidii — Snakebark Maple
Acer griseum — Grey-Leaved Maple
Acer grosseri — Snakebark Maple
Acer saccharinum — Silver Maple
Betula papyrifera — Paper Birch
Betula pubescens — Common Birch
Cedrela sinensis — Cedrela
Cedrus atlantica — Atlas Cedar
Davidia involucrata — Pocket Handkerchief Tree
Drimys winteri — Winter Bark
Magnolia campbellii — Pink Tulip Tree
Magnolia kobus — Japanese Magnolia

Magnolia liliiflora — Purple Magnolia
Magnolia sieboldii — Magnolia
Magnolia x soulangeana — Magnolia
Magnolia stellata — Magnolia
Magnolia wilsonii — Magnolia
Paulownia tomentosa — Paulownia
Prunus padus — Bird Cherry
Quercus coccinea — Scarlet Oak
Quercus rubra — Red Oak
Quercus palustris — Pin Oak
Sequoia sempervirens — Californian Redwood
Sequoiadendron
  giganteum — Wellingtonia
Tsuga heterophylla — Western Hemlock
Zelkova carpinifolia — Zelkova

Meadow Grass Mixes

Meadow	Percentage Mix	
Agrostis capillaris	Browntop	10%
Cynosurus cristatus	Crested Dog's Tail	20%
Festuca ovina	Sheep's Fescue	40%
Festuca rubra spp. pruinosa	Slender Creeping Red Fescue	20%
Poa pratensis	Smooth-Stalked Meadow Grass	10%

Shaded Meadow		
Agrostis capillaris	Browntop	9%
Cynosurus cristatus	Crested Dog's Tail	18%
Deschampsia caespitosa	Tufted Hairgrass	3%
Festuca ovina	Sheep's Fescue	36%
Festuca rubra spp. pruinosa	Slender Creeping Red Fescue	18%
Poa nemoralis	Wood Meadow Grass	7%
Poa pratensis	Smooth-Stalked Meadow Grass	9%

CHAPTER 14: *The Sheltered Garden*

Annuals and Biennials

Ageratum houstoniana vars — Ageratum
Alcea rosea — Hollyhock
Antirrhinum majus — Snapdragon
Dianthus barbatus vars — Sweet William
Myosotis caespitosa — Forget-Me-Not
Reseda odorata — Mignonette
Tagetes erecta — African Marigold
Tagetes patula — French Marigold
Tropaeolum majus vars — Nasturtium

Perennials

Acanthus mollis — Bear's Breeches
Acanthus spinosus — Bear's Breeches
Achillea filipendulina — Achillea
Agapanthus campanulatus — Blue African Lily
Agapanthus inapertus var. — Blue African Lily

Alchemilla mollis — Alchemilla
Allium campanulatum — Allium
Alstroemeria aurantiaca var. — Peruvian Lily
Alstroemeria ligtu – hybrids — Peruvian Lily
Anemone x hybrida — Japanese Anemone
Aquilegia vulgaris var. — Granny's Bonnet
Artemisia lactiflora — White Mugwort
Artemisia ludoviciana — White Wormwood
Artemisia stelleriana — Dusty Miller
Aster novae-angliae vars — Michaelmas Daisy
Aster novi-belgii vars — Michaelmas Daisy
Aster sedifolius vars — Blue Michaelmas Daisy
Bergenia cordifolia vars — Megasea
Brunnera macrophylla — Anchusa
Campanula lactiflora vars — Bellflower
Campanula persicifolia — Bellflower
Chrysanthemum coccineum – hybrids — Pyrethum Daisy
Chrysanthemum x superbum — Shasta Daisy
Clematis x durandii — Border Clematis
Crambe maritima — Sea Kale
Crocosmia – hybrids — Montbretia
Dahlia coccinea vars — Dahlia
Delphinium elatum – hybrids — Delphinium
Dianthus 'Dad's Favourite' — Garden Pink
Dianthus 'Brympton Rcd' — Gardcn Pink
Dianthus 'Fragrans Plenus' — Garden Pink
Dianthus 'White Ladies' — Garden Pink
Dianthus 'Mrs Sinkins' — Garden Pink
Dianthus 'C. T. Musgrave' — Garden Pink
Dicentra formosa vars — Bleeding Heart
Digitalis grandiflora — Foxglove
Eryngium bourgatii – hybrids — Sea Holly
Euphorbia characias — Spurge
Euphorbia myrsinites — Euphorbia
Euphorbia palustris — Milkweed
Euphorbia polychroma — Euphorbia
Galega officinalis vars — Goat's Rue
Geranium pratense vars — Blue Geranium
Geranium psilostemon — Purple Geranium
Geranium 'Russell Pritchard' — Pink Geranium
Gladiolus x colvillei – hybrids — Gladiolus
Gunnera manicata — Gunnera
Gypsophila paniculata vars — Gypsophila
Helenium autumnale — Sneezeweed
Helianthus decapetalus – hybrids — Sunflower
Helleborus atrorubens — Red-Flowered Christmas Rose
Helleborus corsicus — Lenten Rose
Helleborus foetidus — Lenten Rose
Helleborus niger — Christmas Rose

Helleborus orientalis vars	Christmas Rose
Hemerocallis flava	Day Lily
Hemerocallis flava – hybrids	
Hosta albomarginata	Day Lily
Hosta crispula	Funkia, Plantain Lily
Hosta fortunei vars	Lilac-Flowered Hosta
Hosta plantaginea	Hosta
Hosta sieboldiana	Hosta
Iberis sempervirens vars	Large-Leaved Hosta
Iris germanica – hybrids	Candytuft
Iris pallida	Bearded Iris
Kniphofia – hybrids	Dalmatian Iris
Lathyrus grandiflorus	Red Hot Poker
Lilium regale alba	Everlasting Sweet Pea
Lilium vars	White Regal Lily
Lobelia cardinalis – hybrids	Lily
Lupinus polyphyllus – hybrids	Cardinal Flower
Lychnis coronaria vars	Lupin
Meconopsis betonicifolia	Maltese Cross
Meconopsis paniculata	Himalayan Blue Poppy
Nepeta x faassenii	Himalayan Yellow Poppy
Oenothera tetragona	Catmint
Paeonia – hybrids	Evening Primrose
Papaver orientale – hybrids	Peony
Phlomis russeliana	Oriental Poppy
Phlox paniculata – hybrids	Yellow Phlomis
Polygonatum x hybridum	Phlox
Rheum palmatum vars	Solomon's Seal
Rodgersia pinnata	Ornamental Rhubarb
Rudbeckia fulgida	Cut-Leaved Rodgersia
Salvia fulgens	Black-eyed Susan
Salvia nemorosa	Cardinal Sage
Schizostylis coccinea var.	Sage
Senecio x hybridus	Kaffir Lily
Stachys olympica	Cineraria
Verbascum phoeniceum	Lamb's Ears
Verbascum chaixii	Purple Mullein
Veronica exaltata	Mullein
	Blue Veronica

Shrubs for Borders

Arbutus andrachne	Strawberry Tree
Choisya ternata	Mexican Orange Blossom
Cistus x cyprius	Rock Rose
Cortaderia selloana	Pampas Grass
Danae racemosa	Alexandrian Laurel
Fuchsia magellanica	Fuchsia
Hydrangea macrophylla	Lacecap Hydrangea
Ilex altaclerensis – hybrids	Highclere Holly
Ilex aquifolium – hybrids	Holly
Kerria japonica	Kerria
Olearia phlogopappa	Daisy Bush
Phlomis fructicosa	Phlomis
Sambucus racemosa 'Plumosa Aurea'	Golden-Leaved Elder
Skimmia japonica	Skimmia
Syringa vulgaris – hybrids	Lilac
Yucca gloriosa	Spanish Dagger

Plants Flowering by Season

Winter

Acacia dealbata	Mimosa
Azalea var.	Azalea
Begonia var.	Begonia
Camellia var.	Camellia
Chrysanthemum – hybrids	Chrysanthemum
Citrinum var.	Orange and Lemon
Coronilla valentina	Yellow Coronilla
Crocus var.	Crocus
Cyclamen – hybrids	Cyclamen
Euphorbia – hybrids	Poinsettia
Helleborus niger	Christmas Rose
Hyacinth – hybrids	Hyacinth
Jasminum azoricum	Jasmine
Jasminum mesnyi	Primrose Jasmine
Jasminum polyanthum	Fragrant White Jasmine
Narcissus var.	Daffodil
Orchidaceae	Orchid
Rhododendron var.	Rhododendron
Salvia splendens	Salvia
Senecio – hybrids	Cineraria
Tulip var.	Tulip
Viola var.	Violetl

Summer

Araujia sericofera	Cruel Plant
Billardiera longiflora	Billardiera
Bougainvillea spectabilis var.	Bougainvillea
Calceolaria var.	Calceolaria
Cissus antarctica	Kangaroo Vine
Convallaria major	Lily of the Valley
Fuchsia – hybrids	Fuchsia
Gloxinia – hybrids	Gloxinia
Jasminum dispermum	White Jasmine
Lapageria rosea	Chilean Bell Flower
Lilium – var.	Lily
Nerine var.	Nerine
Nerium oleander	Oleander
Orchidaceae	Orchid
Passiflora caerulea	Passion Flower
Passiflora exoniensis	Pink Passion Flower
Passiflora racemosa	Red Passion Flower
Pelargonium	Geranium
Plumbago auriculata	Blue Plumbago
Rosa var.	Rose

Ferns

Adiantum pedatum	Maidenhair Fern
Cyrtomium falcatum	Japanese Holly Fern
Dicksonia antarctica	Tree Fern
Woodwardia radicans	Chain Fern

LIST OF GARDENS

The following list is a selection of gardens which contain good examples of period styles. Most are open to the public but dates and times should be checked before visiting. **Chapter names** are used to indicate period style.

KEY:

Ownership:

NT – National Trust
NTS – National Trust for Scotland
EH – English Heritage
T – Trust – Private Trusts

Pr – Private
Pub – Public – Local Authority, or Government

Opening Times:

All year	– every day except Bank Holidays
Summer daily	– from Easter to the end of September/October
Summer days	- certain days from Easter to the end of September/October
Winter days	– certain days from November to April

ADMIRAL HOUSE, Chatham Docks, Kent. T; **Villa**. By appointment.
ALTON TOWERS, Alton, Staffordshire. 0538 702200. T; **Ornamental, Rock & Quarry, Wild & Woodland, Conservatory**. All year.
ASHDOWN HOUSE, Nr. Lambourn, Oxfordshire. NT; **Knot, Geometric**. Summer days.
AUDLEY END, Saffron Walden, Suffolk. 0799 22399. EH; **Landscape, Ornamental, Rosarie**. All year.
BARRINGTON COURT, Ilminster, Somerset. 0460 40601. NT; **Walled Sheltered**. Summer daily.

BATEMANS, Burwash, East Sussex. 0435 882302. NT; **Rosarie, Topiary, Wild & Woodland**. Summer daily.
BATTERSEA PARK, London SW 10, Pub; **Rock & Quarry**. All year.
BELSAY HALL CASTLE AND GARDENS, Belsay, Northumberland. 066 181 636. EH; **Landscape, Ornamental, Rock & Quarry, Wild & Woodland**. All year.
BELTON HOUSE, Nr. Grantham, Lincolnshire. 0476 66116. NT; **Landscape, Ornamental, Conservatory**. Summer daily.
BIDDULPH GRANGE, Biddulph, Stoke-on-Trent, Staffordshire. NT; **Ornamental, Rock & Quarry, Wild & Woodland**. Summer daily.
BLAISE HAMLET, Henbury, Avon, Somerset. Pr; **Villa**. By appointment.
BLENHEIM PALACE, Woodstock, Oxfordshire. 0993 811325. Pr; **Landscape, Ornamental**. Summer daily.
BLICKLING HALL, Aylsham, Norfolk. 0263 733084. NT; **Knot, Landscape, Ornamental, Topiary**. Summer days.
BOWHILL, Nr. Selkirk, Scotland. 0750 20732. Pr; **Landscape, Ornamental**. Summer days.
BOWOOD, Calne, Wiltshire. 0249 812102. Pr; **Landscape, Ornamental, Rock & Quarry, Wild & Woodland, Conservatory**. Summer daily.
BRAMHAM PARK, Wetherby, West Yorkshire. 0937 844265. Pr; **Knot, Geometric, Landscape**. Summer daily.
BRIGHTON PAVILION, Brighton, East Sussex. 0273 603005. Pub; **Villa, Ornamental**. All year.
BROADLANDS, Romsey, Hampshire. 0794 516878. Pr; **Landscape**. Summer daily.
BURGHLEY HOUSE, Stamford, Lincolnshire. 0780 52451. Pr; **Landscape**. Summer daily.
BUSCOT PARK, Nr. Faringdon, Oxfordshire. 0367 20786. NT; **Walled**. Summer days.

CALKE ABBEY, Nr. Derby, Derbyshire. NT; **Landscape, Ornamental**. Summer daily.
CASTLE HOWARD, York, North Yorkshire. 065 384 333. Pr; **Geometric, Landscape, Ornamental, Rosarie, Wild & Woodland**. Summer daily.

The cascade at Mellerstain, designed so that the water splashes down the waterfall noisily.

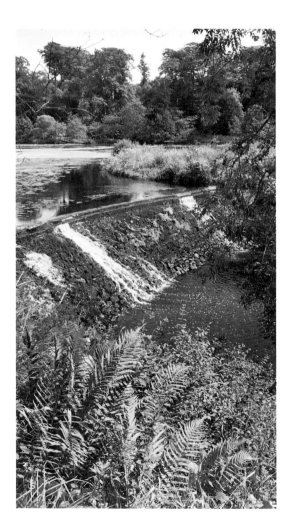

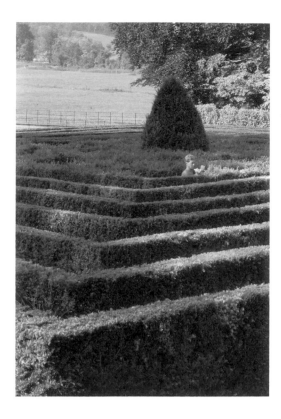

The gardener clipping the maze at Chevening, first planted in 1812.

CHATSWORTH, Bakewell, Derbyshire. 024 688 2204. Pr; **Geometric** (remnants). **Landscape, Ornamental, Rock & Quarry, Conservatory**. Summer daily.

CHEVENING, Sevenoaks, Kent. 0732 454091. T; **Geometric,Landscape, Ornamental**. By appointment only.

CHISWICK HOUSE, Chiswick, London, W10. EH/Pub; **Geometric,Theatrical, Ornamental, Conservatory**. All year.

CLAREMONT LANDSCAPE GARDEN, Esher, Surrey. NT; **Theatrical**. Summer daily.

CLIVEDEN, Maidenhead, Buckinghamshire. 062 86 5069. NT; **Ornamental, Rosarie**. Summer daily.

CRAGSIDE HOUSE, Rothbury, Northumberland. 0669 20333. NT; **Rock & Quarry, Wild & Woodland**. Summer daily. Winter days.

CRANBORNE MANOR, Cranborne, Dorset. 072 54 248. Pr; **Knot,Landscape, Topiary, Rosarie, Sheltered**. Summer daily.

CULZEAN CASTLE, Maybole, By Ayr, Strathclyde, Scotland. 065 56 269. NTS; **Landscape, Walled, Ornamental, Conservatory**. All year.

DARTINGTON HALL, Totnes, Devon. T; **Sheltered** (B. J. Ferrand). Summer days.

DRUMLANRIG CASTLE, Nr. Thornhill, Dumfries, Scotland. 084830248. Pr; **Geometric, Landscape, Ornamental**. Summer days.

DRUMMOND CASTLE, Muthill, Tayside. Pr; **Landscape, Ornamental**. Summer days.

DUBLIN, BOTANIC GARDENS, Glasnevin, 9 Dublin. 010 353 1 377596. **Conservatory**. All year.

DUNHAM MASSEY, Altrincham, Cheshire. 061 941 1025. NT; **Geometric**. Summer daily.

EDZELL CASTLE, Edzell, Tayside. NTS; **Knot**. Summer daily.

GLASGOW, BOTANIC GARDENS, Great Western Road, Glasgow 12. 041 334 2422. **Conservatory**. All year.

GREAT DIXTER, Northiam, East Sussex. 07974 3160. Pr; **Sheltered**. Summer daily.

GREENWICH PARK, London. Pub; **Geometric** (remnants).

HAGLEY HALL, Nr. Stourbridge, Warwickshire. 0562 882408. Pr; **Theatrical**. Summer days.

HAMPTON COURT PALACE, Hampton Court, East Molesey, Surrey. 081977 8441. Pub; **Pleasaunce, Knot, Geometric, Ornamental, Conservatory**. All year.

HATFIELD HOUSE, Hatfield, Hertfordshire. 0992 763849. Pr;**Knot, Geometric, Landscape**. Summer daily.

HAWKESTONE PARK, Nr. Shrewsbury,

OPPOSITE

Planting at the edge of a woodland at Heale House. The enormous leaves of the gunnera overshadow grass, ferns, and skunk cabbage. In the middle distance is the attractive feature of a Japanese lantern.

At Hestercombe Gertrude Jekyll used Virginia creeper to draw attention to the form of the circular niche designed by Edwin Lutyens.

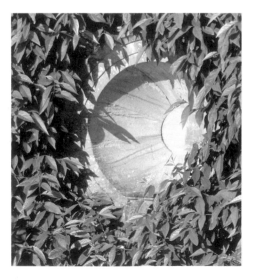

Shropshire. Pr; **Theatrical, Rock & Quarry**. By appointment.

HEALE HOUSE, Woodford, Salisbury. 072 273 504. Pr; **Walled, Wild & Woodland, Sheltered** (Peto). Summer daily.

HERGEST CROFT GARDENS, Kington, Herefordshire. 0544 230160.Pr; **Walled, Wild & Woodland, Conservatory**. Summer daily.

HESTERCOMBE HOUSE, Cheddon Fitzpaine, Taunton. 0823 87222. Pr; **Sheltered**. Days all year.

HEVER CASTLE, Nr. Edenbridge, Kent. 0732 865224. Pr; **Ornamental, Topiary, Rosarie**. Summer daily.

HIDCOTE, Hidcote Bartrim, Nr. Chipping Campden,Gloucestershire. 0386 333. NT; **Sheltered** (L. Johnston). Summer daily.

HIGH BEECHES, Handcross, West Sussex. Pr; **Wild & Woodland**. Summer daily.

HIGHCLERE CASTLE, Nr. Newbury, Berkshire. 0635 253210. Pr; **Walled, Ornamental, Wild & Woodland**. Summer days.

IFORD MANOR, Bradford-on-Avon, Wiltshire. 02216 3146. Pr;**Sheltered** (Peto). Summer days.

INVEREWE, Poolewe, Wester Ross, Scotland. NTS; **Wild & Woodland**. Summer daily.

KEATS HOUSE, Hampstead, London NW3. 081 435 2062. T; **Villa**. All year.

KENTWELL HALL, Long Melford, Suffolk. Pr; **Pleasaunce,Conservatory**. All year.

KENWOOD, Hampstead, London NW3. 081 348 1286. EH; **Ornamental, Conservatory**. All year.

KEW ROYAL BOTANICAL GARDENS, Richmond, Surrey. 081 977 8441.Pub; **Examples of all Styles except Geometric, especially plants and Conservatory**. All year.

LAMPORT HALL, Lamport, Northampton. T; **Rock & Quarry**. Summer days.

LANHYDROCK, Nr. Bodmin, Cornwall. 0208 73320. NT; **Landscape, Ornamental, Wild & Woodland**.

LEONARDSLEE, Horsham, West Sussex. Pr; **Wild & Woodland**. Summer daily.

LEVENS HALL, Kendal, Cumbria. 053 95 60321. Pr; **Geometric,Ornamental, Topiary**. Summer daily.

LUTON HOO, Luton, Bedfordshire. 0582 22955. Pr; **Landscape, Ornamental**. Summer daily.

MANDERSTON, Duns, Scotland. 0361 83450. Pr; **Sheltered**. By appointment.

MAPPERTON, Beaminster, Dorset. 0308 862645. Pr; **Ornamental, Topiary**. By appointment.

MARSH COURT, Stockbridge, Hampshire. 0264 810503. Pr; **Sheltered**. By appointment.

MEGGINCH CASTLE, Errol, Perth. Pr; **Walled, Ornamental, Topiary**. By appointment.

MELBOURNE HALL, Derby. Pr; **Geometric**. By appointment.

MELLERSTAIN HOUSE, Gordon, Berwickshire. 057 381 225. Pr; **Geometric, Landscape, Ornamental**. Summer daily.

MOTTISFONT, Mottisfont, Hampshire. 0794 40757. NT; **Rosarie**. Summer daily.

MOUNT EDGCUMBE, Nr. Plymouth, Cornwall. 0752 822236. Pub; **Theatrical** (remnants), **Landscape, English Flower, Rosarie, Conservatory**. All year.

NYMANS, Handcross, West Sussex. 0444 400321. **Wild & Woodland**. Summer. NT

OXFORD BOTANIC GARDENS, Oxford. Pub; **Geometric, Plants, Conservatory**. All year.

OXBURGH HALL, Swaffham, Norfolk. 036 621 258. NT; **Knot, Ornamental, Sheltered**. Summer daily.

PAINSHILL PARK, Cobham, Surrey. 0932 68113. T; **Theatrical**. By appointment.

PECKOVER HOUSE, Wisbech, Cambridgeshire. 0945 583463. NT; **Ornamental, Rosarie, Conservatory**. Summer daily.

PENCARROW HOUSE, Bodmin, Cornwall. 020 884 369. Pr; **Ornamental, Rock & Quarry**. Summer daily.

PETWORTH PARK, Petworth, West Sussex. 0798 42207. NT; **Landscape**. All year.

PITMEDDEN, Udny, Scotland. 065 13 2445. NTS; **Knot**. Summer daily.

POLESDEN LACY, Nr. Dorking, Surrey. 0372 58203. NT; **Landscape, Ornamental, Rosarie**. Summer daily.

POWERSCOURT, Enniskerry, Co. Wicklow, Ireland. 010 353 867676. Pr; **Ornamental, Wild & Woodland**. Summer daily.

POWIS CASTLE, Welshpool, Gwynedd, Wales. 0938 4336. NT; **Geometric, Ornamental, Rosarie**. Summer daily.

QUEEN MARY'S ROSE GARDEN, Regents Park, London W1. **Rosarie**. All year.

QUEEN ELEANOR'S GARDEN, Winchester, Hampshire. T; **Pleasaunce**. All year.

RED LODGE MUSEUM, Bristol. 0272 503573. T; **Pleasaunce**. All year.

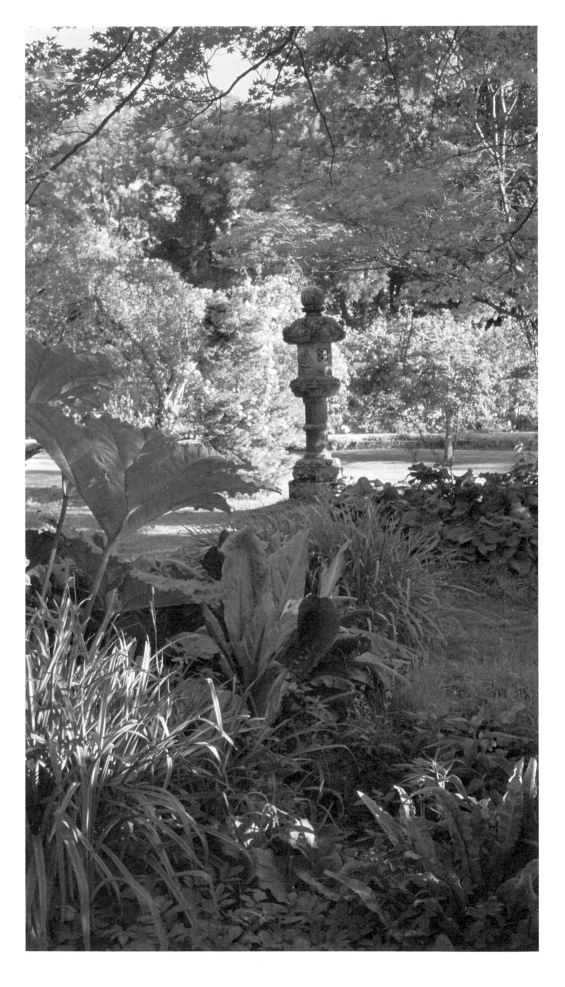

ROCKINGHAM CASTLE, Nr. Corby, Northamptonshire. 0536 770240. Pr; **Geometric** (remnants), **Landscape, Ornamental, Rosarie**. Summer daily.

ROSEMOOR, Great Torrington, Devon. 0805 2256. T; **Rosarie, Wild & Woodland**. All year.

ROUSHAM, Steeple Aston, Oxfordshire. 0869 47110. Pr; **Theatrical, Walled, Landscape, Conservatory**. Summer daily.

SALTRAM HOUSE, Plymouth, Devon. 0752 336546. NT; **Landscape, Wild & Woodland, Sheltered, Conservatory**. Summer daily.

SCOTNEY CASTLE, Lamberhurst, Kent. 0892 890651. NT; **Rock & Quarry, Wild & Woodland**. Summer daily.

SEZINCOTE, Moreton-in-Marsh, Gloucestershire. Pr; **Landscape, Conservatory, Rock & Quarry**. Summer daily.

SHRUBLAND HALL, Coddenham, Suffolk. 0473 830404. Pr; **Ornamental**. By appointment.

SHUGBOROUGH, Stafford. 0889 881388. NT; **Landscape, Ornamental, Rosarie, Wild & Woodland**. All year.

SISSINGHURST, Sissinghurst, Kent. 0580

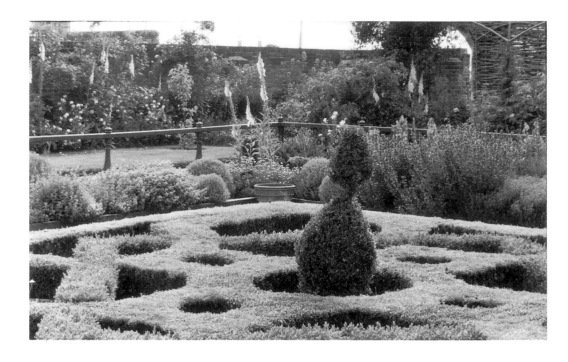

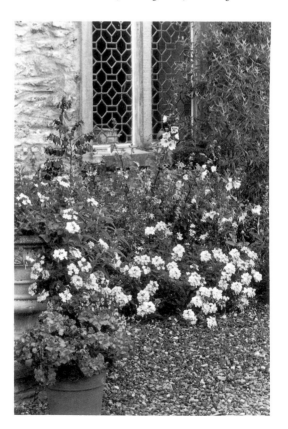

BELOW
At Levens Hall phlox and mallows form a cottage-garden effect in a large formal garden.

712850. NT; **Sheltered**. Summer daily.

SIZERGH CASTLE, Kendal, Cumbria. 05295 60070. NT; **Rock & Quarry**. Summer daily.

STONEFIELD CASTLE HOTEL, Tarbet, Argyll. 0880 820836. **Wild & Woodland**. Summer daily.

STOURHEAD, Stourton, Nr. Mere, Wiltshire. 0747 840348. NT; **Theatrical**. Summer daily.

STOWE, Buckingham. NT; **Theatrical, Landscape**. Summer days.

SYON HOUSE, Brentford, London. 01 560 0881. Pr; **Geometric, Ornamental, Conservatory**. All year.

TATTON PARK, Knutsford, Cheshire. 0565 54822. NT; **Landscape, Ornamental, Rosarie, Conservatory**. All year.

TINTINHULL, Nr. Yeovil, Somerset. NT; **Sheltered** (M. Fish). Summer daily.

TRENTHAM PARK, Nottingham. Pub; **Ornamental, Conservatory**. All year.

TRESCO ABBEY, Isles of Scilly. Pr; **Wild & Woodland**. Summer daily.

TUDOR HOUSE MUSEUM, Southampton. 0703 226248. T; **Pleasaunce**. All year.

WADDESDON MANOR, Nr. Aylesbury, Buckinghamshire. 0296 651211. NT; Ornamental, **Rosarie**. Summer daily.

The little knot garden at Tudor House shows how the square pattern interweaves through the rest of the hedge.

WEALD & DOWNLAND MUSEUM, Singleton, Nr. Chichester, West Sussex. 024 363 348. T; **Pleasaunce**. All year.

WEST DEAN GARDENS, Nr. Chichester, West Sussex. 0243 63205. T; **Landscape, Rock & Quarry, Wild & Woodland, Sheltered**. Summer daily.

WESTBURY COURT GARDEN, Westbury-on-Severn, Gloucestershire. 045 276 461. NT; **Pleasaunce, Knot**. Summer daily.

WESTON PARK, Nr. Shifnal, Shropshire. 095 276 207. T; **Ornamental, Landscape**. Summer daily.

WILTON HOUSE, Salisbury, Wiltshire. Pr; **Fantasy, Landscape**. Summer daily.

WIMPOLE HALL, Wimpole, Nr. Cambridge. 0223 207257. NT; **Landscape**. Summer daily.

WISLEY GARDENS, Royal Horticultural Society's Garden, Wisley, Surrey. 0483 224234. T; **Rock & Quarry, Wild & Woodland, Conservatory, Sheltered**. All year.

WOBURN ABBEY, Woburn, Bedfordshire. 0525 290666. Pr; **Theatrical, Landscape, Ornamental, Conservatory**. Summer daily.

WREST PARK, Silsoe, Bedfordshire. 0525 60718. Pr; **Geometric, Ornamental, Conservatory**. All year.

DIRECTORY

SELECTION OF SUPPLIERS

Architectural Ornaments, Antiques

Ainleys Industrial Estate, Elland, West Yorkshire HX5 9JP. 0422 375595. Antique ornaments, statues.

Architectural Heritage, Taddington Manor, Taddington, Nr. Cutsdean, Cheltenham, Gloucestershire GL54 5RY. 038 673 414. Second-hand ornaments and architectural details.

Christie's, 85 Old Brompton Road, London SW7 3LD. 071 581 7611. Auctioneers, specialist sales.

Clifton Little Venice, 3 Warwick Place, London W9. 071 289 7894. Second-hand ornaments.

Crowther of Syon Lodge, Syon Lodge, Busch Corner, London Road, Isleworth, Middlesex TW7 5BH. 081 560 7978/7985. Antique ornaments.

H. Crowther, 5 High Road, Chiswick, London W4 2ND. 081 994 2326. Antique ornaments.

T. Crowther, 282 North End Road, Fulham, London SW6 1NH. 071 385 1375. Antique ornaments.

Phillips, 101 New Bond Street, London W1Y 0AS. 071 629 6602. Auctioneers, specialist sales.

Sotheby's, Summers Place, Billingshurst, Sussex. RH14 9AD. 0403 783933. Auctioneers, specialist sales.

Sussex Garden Statuary, Burwash, East Sussex TN19 7HX. 0435 882496. Antique garden statuary, ornaments and furniture.

Bridges

CTS, Concrete and Timber Services Ltd., Colne Valley Workshops, Manchester Road, Linthwaite, Huddersfield, Yorkshire HD7 5QG. 0484 846487. Timber foot bridges and parapets.

Stuart Garden Architecture, Barrington Court, Barrington, Ilminster, Somerset TA19 0NQ. 0460 42003. Trellis, arbours, seats, furniture, bridges, gazebos, pavilions and pergolas.

Woodscape, Upfield, Pike Lowe, Brinscall, Nr. Chorley, Lancashire PR6 8SP. 0254 830886. Timber bridges.

Conservatories

Elegant Structures Ltd., Elegant House, 2a Alexandra Grove, Finchley, London N12 8NU. 081 446 2512. Conservatories.

Frolics of Winchester (see Furniture)

Halls Traditional Conservatories, 1-3 Revenge Road, Lords Wood, Chatham, Kent ME5 8UD. 0634 687155. Conservatories.

Machin Designs Limited, 4 Avenue Studios, Sydney Close, London SW3 6HW. 071 589 0773. Conservatories.

Marston & Langinger Ltd., 20 Bristol Gardens, Little Venice, London W9 2JQ. 071 286 7643. Conservatories.

Mitre Conservatories, P.O. Box 55, Tonbridge, Kent TN12 8BY. 0892 83 5166. Conservatories.

Ollerton Gazebos, Samlesbury Bottoms, Preston, Lancashire PR5 0RN. 025 485 2127. Conservatories and pavilions.

Town and Country Conservatories, 53 Ellington Street, London N7 8PN. 071 609 9919. Conservatories.

Fencing and Gates

British Gates and Timber Ltd., Biddenden, Nr. Ashford, Kent, TN27 8DD. 0580 291555. Fencing, gates and gate furniture.

Dorothea Ltd. (see Ironwork)

The English Basket Centre, Curload, Stoke St. Gregory, Nr. Taunton, Somerset TA3 6JD. 0823 69 418. Wattle fencing, rustic hurdles and arches.

Jacksons Fencing, Stowting Common, Nr. Ashford, Kent TN25 6BN. 023 375 393. Fencing, gates, tree supports, arches, plant climbers and wickerwork.

Renzland Ltd. (see Ironwork)

Victorian Lace (see Ironwork)

Wessex Hurdles, 6 Haggetts, Witchampton, Wimborne, Dorset BH21 5BS. 0258 840694.

Fountains and Water Features

Stapley Water Gardens Ltd., Stapley, Nantwich, Cheshire CW5 7LH. 0270 628111. Pumps, liners, fittings and illumination.

Water Techniques, Unit D3, Sandown Industrial Park, Mill Road, Esher, Surrey KT10 8BL. 0372 66408. Water display specialists.

Watermation Ltd., Monument Way East, Woking, Surrey GU21 5LY. 0483 770303. Water display specialists.

Wildwoods Water Gardens Ltd., Theobalds Park Road, Crews Hill, Enfield, Middlesex EN2 9BP. 01 366 0243. Water display specialists.

Wright Rain, Crow Arch Lane, Ringwood, Hampshire BH24 1PA. 0425 472251. Irrigation specialists.

Furniture

Andrew Crace Designs, Bourne Lane, Much Hadham, Hertfordshire SG10 6ER. 027984 2685. Garden furniture, gazebos and structures, old fashioned garden labels.

Barnsley House Garden & Decorative Furnishings, Barnsley, Cirencester,

Gloucestershire. 028 574 561. Garden and decorative furnishings.

Bath Metal, 61 Walcot Street, Bath BA1 5BN. 0225 446107. Reproduction metal furniture.

Chatsworth Carpenters, Estate Office, Edensor, Bakewell, Derbyshire DE4 1PH. 024 688 2242. Garden furniture.

Dorothea Ltd. (*see* Ironwork)

Frolics of Winchester, 82 Canon Street, Winchester SO23 9JQ. 0962 56384. Furniture and conservatories.

Hickson Landscape Structures (*see* Pergolas and Trellis)

Lloyd Christie (*see* Pergolas and Trellis)

Robin Eden, Pickwick End, Corsham, Wiltshire SN13 0JB. 0249 713335. Garden furniture.

Shedlow Ltd., Badingham Road, Framlingham, Woodbridge, Suffolk IP13 9HS. 0728 723041. Garden furniture.

Shedlow, Harrisons Joinery Ltd. (*see* Ironwork)

The Landscape Ornament Co. Ltd. (*see* Stonework)

Stuart Garden Architecture (*see* Pergola and Trellis)

Sussex Garden Statuary (*see* Statuary)

Ironwork

County Forge Ltd., The Welshmill, Park Hill Drive, Frome, Somerset BA11 2LE. 0373 72440. Wrought ironwork and garden lighting.

D. G. Masters, Oakhill Forge Ltd., 39 St. Cuthbert Street, Wells, Somerset BA5 2AW. 0749 72984. Ornamental ironwork, containers.

Dorothea Ltd., Pearl House, Hardwick Street, Buxton, Derbyshire SK17 6DH. 0298 79121. Architectural ironwork and furniture.

Renzland Ltd., London Road. Copford, Colchester, Essex CO6 1LG. 0206 210212. Decorative wrought ironwork. Gates, brackets and architectural details.

Shedlow, Harrisons Joinery Ltd., Stratford St. Andrew, Saxmundham, Suffolk IP17 1LF. 0728 4264. Cast iron garden furniture, wirework, gazebos and arches.

Victorian Lace, Unit 5, Woodside Park, Catteshall Lane, Godalming, Surrey GU7 1LG. 04868 20366. Decorative iron ornaments and fencing.

Lead

Christopher Pote & Russell G. Sheen, 6 Chapel Road, Reach, Cambridgeshire CB5 0JJ. 0638 742011. Statuary, fountains and planters.

Stonework, Balustrading, Walls, Ornaments and Vases

Arundel Stone, 62 Adwick Road, Bognor Regis, Sussex PO21 2PE. 0243 829151. Balustrades.

Chilstone Garden Ornaments, Sprivers Estate, Horsmonden, Kent TN12 8DR. 089 272 3553. Ornaments, balustrades and architectural details, vases and statuary.

Haddonstone Ltd., The Forge House, East Haddon, Northamptonshire NN6 8DB. 060 125 365. Ornaments, balustrades, architectural details, vases, plinths and statuary.

Kingfisher Ornamental Stone, 46 North Road, Wells, Somerset BA5 2TL. 0749 73601. Ornaments, balustrades.

Malta Stone, Clerks House, Shoreditch Church, London E1 6JM. 071 739 1848. Stonework containers, fountains and architectural details.

Minsterstone Ltd., Wharf Lane, Ilminster, Somerset TA19 9AS. 046 05 2277. Ornament, statuary, vases and details, balustrades.

Peachstone, 1 Somers Way, Bushey, Herts WD2 3HR. 081 950 9488. Balustrades.

Sedgemoor Stone Products, Pen Hill, Station Road, Yeovil, Somerset BA5 2TL. 0935 29797. Balustrades.

Senlac Stone, Marley Lane, Battle, East Sussex TN33 0RD. 04246 2244. Balustrades.

The Landscape Ornament Co. Ltd., Voysey House, Barley Mow Passage, Chiswick, London W4 4PN. 081 995 9739. Ornament and furniture.

Statuary

Architectural Heritage Ltd., Taddington Manor, Taddington, Cutsdean, Cheltenham, Gloucestershire GL54 5RY. 038 673 414. Antique garden statuary.

Chilstone Garden Ornaments (*see* Stonework)

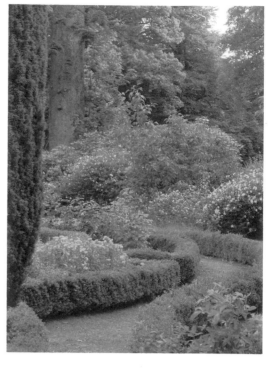

The serpentine box hedges bordering the paths at Belsay give design to the garden.

Christopher Pote & Russell G. Sheen (*see* Lead)

Drummonds of Bramley, Birtley Farm, Horsham Road, Bramley, Guildford, Surrey GU5 0LA. 0483 898766. Reclaimed building materials, period garden statuary and architectural antiques.

Haddonstone Ltd. (*see* Stonework)

Minsterstone Ltd. (*see* Stonework)

Pergolas and Trellis

Hickson Landscape Structures, Wheldon Road, Castleford, West Yorkshire WF10 2JT. 0977 556565. Pergolas, screens, furniture and timber structures.

Lloyd Christie, 10 Acorn Production Centre, 105 Blundell Street, London N7 9EN. 081 609 3667. Trellis panels, arbours and archways.

Shedlow, Harrisons Joinery Ltd. (*see* Ironwork)

Stuart Garden Architecture, Barrington Court, Barrington, Ilminster, Somerset TA19 0NQ. 0460 42003. Trellis, arbours, seats, furniture, bridges, gazebos, pavilions and pergolas.

The English Basket Centre (*see* Fencing)

Trellisworks, West Mead Nursery, Clay Lane, Chichester, West Sussex, PO19 3JG. 0243 774238. Trellis and screens.

Paving, Natural Stone and Path Surfaces

B. & S. Natural Stone, Eastern Avenue, Shoreham-by-Sea, West Sussex BN4 6PD. 0273 46 4804. Natural stone.

Building & Landscape Supply Co., Unit 4, Devonshire Drive, Chinley, Stockport, Cheshire SK12 6AS. 0663 50911. Natural stone.

Civil Engineering Developments, 728 London Road, West Thurrock, Grays, Essex RM16 ILU. 0708 867237. Natural stone, aggregates, flint, granite, quartzite, sandstone, etc.

Drummonds of Bramley (*see* Statuary)

Silverlands Stone, The Genet Group, Holloway Hill, Chertsey, Surrey KT16 OAE. 0932 569277. Natural stone.

Vases, Orange Cases and Planters

Adrian J. Black, 36 Freeman Street, Grimsby, South Humberside DN32 7AG. 0472 55668. 'Versailles Tubs'.

D. G. Masters (*see* Ironwork)

Barrie Quinn Antiques, 34 Broxholme House,

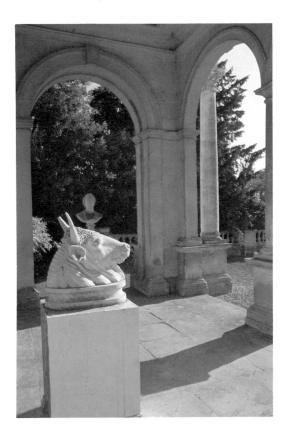

At Shrublands a marble bull surveys the ornamental garden.

New Kings Road, London SW6. 01 736 4747. Garden *jardinières*.

Chilstone Garden Ornaments (*see* Stonework)

Christopher Pote & Russell G. Sheen (*see* Lead)

Courtyard Pottery, The Welshmill, Groundwell Farm, Cricklade Road, Swindon, Wiltshire. 0793 727884. Terracotta and terranigra pots.

Crowther of Syon Lodge, Busch Corner, London Road, Isleworth, Middlesex TW7 5BH. 081 560 7978. Antique garden ornaments.

Dibco Ltd., 49 Dartford Road, Sevenoaks, Kent TN13 3TE. 0732 460022. Classical and decorative terracotta pots, tubs and planters.

Haddonstone Ltd. (*see* Stonework)

Malta Stone (*see* Stonework)

Minsterstone Ltd. (*see* Stonework)

The Olive Tree Trading Co. Ltd., Lep Building, Corney Road, London W4 2SN. 071 995 5281. Terracotta pots.

Ware Planters, Sedgegate Nursery, Sedge Green, Nazing, Essex EN9 2PA. 0992 462378. Planters in oak and mild steel.

Whichford Pottery, Shipston-on-Stour, Warwickshire CV36 5PG. 060884 416. Terracotta pots.

SELECTION OF SPECIALIST NURSERIES

Bulbs and Alpines

Jacques Amand, Clamp Hill, Stanmore, Middlesex HA7 3JS. 081 954 8138.

Avon Bulbs, Burnt House Farm, Lambrook, South Petherton, Somerset TA13 5HE. 0460 42177

Rupert Bowlby (Bulbs), Gatton, Reigate, Surrey RH2 OTA. 07374 2221.

Broadleigh Gardens (Bulbs), Barr House, Bishops Hull, Taunton, Somerset TA4 IAE. 0823 286231.

Paul Christian Rare Plants, Box 468, Wrexham, Clwyd, LL13 9XR. 0978 366399.

Jack Drake Nurseries, Inshriach, Aviemore PH22 IQS. 05 404 287.

Edrom Nurseries, Coldingham, Eyemouth,

Borders TD14 5TZ. 08907 71386.

Hartside Nurseries, Low Gill House, Alston, Cumbria CA9 3BL. 0498 81372.

Holden Clough, Holden, Bolton by Bowland, Clitheroe, Lancashire BB7 4PF. 05242 61626.

W. E. Th. Ingwersen Ltd., Birch Farm Nursery, Gravetye, East Grinstead, Sussex RH19 4LE. 0342 810236.

Conservatory Plants

Long Man Gardens, Lewes Road, Wilmington, Polegate, East Sussex BN26 5RS. 0323 870816.

Newington Nurseries, Old School, Newington, Oxford OX9 8AH. 0865 891401.

Reads Nursery, Hales Road, Loddon, Norfolk NR14 6QW. 0508 46395.

The Palm Centre, 563 Upper Richmond Road West, London SW14 7ED. 081 876 3223.

The Palm Farm, Thornton Hall Gardens, Thornton Curtis, Nr. Ulcebury, North Humberside DN39 6XF. 0469 31232.

Fruit Trees

Deacons Nurseries (RHS), Godshill, Isle of Wight PO38 3HW. 0983 40750.

Keepers Nursery, 446 Wateringbury Road, East Malling, Maidstone, Kent ME19 6JJ. 0622 813008.

Olivers Orchard Ltd., Olivers Lane, Colchester, Essex CO2 OHH. 0206 330208.

J. Tweedie Fruit Trees, Fruit Trees Nursery, 504 Denby Dale Road West, Calder Grove, Wakefield WF4 3DB. 0924 274630.

Herbs and Wild Flowers

Candlesby Herbs, Cross Keys Cottage, Dandelsby, Spilsby, Lincolnshire PE23 5SF. 075484 211.

John Chambers, 15 Westleigh Road, Barton Seagrave, Kettering, Northants NN15 5AJ. 0933 681632.

Fold Garden, 26 Fold Lane, Biddulph, Staffordshire ST8 7SG. 0782 513028.

Hollington Nurseries Ltd., Woolton Hill, Newbury, Berkshire. RG15 9XT. 0635 253908.

Iden Croft Herbs, Herb Centre of Kent, Frittenden Road, Staplehurst, Kent TN12 0DH. 0580 891432.

Oak Cottage Herb Garden, Nesscliffe, Nr. Shrewsbury, Shropshire SY4 IDB. 074381 262.

The Herb Farm, Peppard Road, Sonning Common, Reading RG4 9NJ. 0734 724220.

The Herb Garden, Capel Ulo, Pentre Berw, Gaerwen, Anglesey, Gwynedd, North Wales.

Herbaceous Plants, Nurseries specializing in Old Varieties

Beth Chatto Gardens, Elmstead Market, Colchester, Essex CO7 7DB. 020 622 2007.

Bressingham Gardens, Bressingham, Diss, Norfolk IP22 2AB. 0379 88 469.

Carlisle's Hardy Plants, Carlisle's Corner, Twyford, Reading, Berkshire RG10 9PU. 0734 340031.

Cotton Manor Garden, Northampton NN6 8RQ. 0604 740219.

Cranborne Garden Centre, Cranborne, Wimbourne, Dorset BH21 5PP. 07254 248.

Fortescue Garden Trust, The Garden House, Buckland Monachorum, Yelverton, Devon PL20 7LQ. 0822 854769.

Herterton House Nursery, Hartington, Cambo, Morpeth, Northumberland NE61 4BN. 067074 278.

Langthorns Plantery, Little Canfield, Dunmow, Essex CM6 ITD. 0371 872611.

Lye End Nurseries, Lye End Link, St. Johns, Woking, Surrey GU21 ISW. 04862 69327.

Margery Fish Nursery, East Lambroke Manor, South Petherton, Somerset TA13 5HL. 0460 40328.

Perryhill Nurseries, Hartfield, East Sussex TN7 4JP. 089277 3778.

Plants From The Past, The Old House, 1 North Street, Bellhaven, Dunbar, Lothian Region EH42 INU. 0368 63223.

Roses

David Austen Roses, Bowling Green Lane, Albrighton, Wolverhampton WV7 3HB. 0907 22 3931.

Peter Beales Roses, London Road, Attleborough, Norfolk NR17 IAY. 0953 454707.

E. B. LeGrice (Roses) Ltd., North Walsham, Norfolk NR28 0DR.

John Mattock Ltd., The Rose Nurseries, Nuneham Courtenay, Oxfordshire OX9 9PY. 086738 265.

Roses du Temps Passé, Woodlands House, Strepton, Nr. Stafford ST19 9LG. 0785 840217.

Seeds

Chiltern Seeds, Bortree Stile, Ulverston, Cumbria LA12 7PB. 0229 581137.

Sandeman Tree and Shrub Seeds, The Croft, Sutton, Pulborough, West Sussex RH20 IPL. 07987 315.

Samuel Dobie and Son Ltd., Broomhill Way, Torquay, Devon TQ2 7QW. 0803 616281.

Seeds By Size, 70 Varney Road, Warners End, Hemel Hempstead, Hertfordshire HP1 2LR.

Stewarts (Nottm) Ltd., 3 George Street, Nottingham NG1 3BH. 0602 476338.

Suttons Seeds, Hele Road, Torquay, Devon TQ7 7JQ. 0803 612011.

Thompson and Morgan (Ipswich) Ltd., Poplar Lane, Ipswich, Suffolk IP2 0BA. 0473 690743.

Garden Centres

Bridgemere Nurseries Ltd., Bridgemere, Nantwich, Cheshire CW5 7QB. 09365 375.

Hillier Garden Centre, Sunningdale Nurseries, London Road, Windlesham, Surrey GU20 6LQ. 0344 23166.

Hillier Garden Centre, Ampfield House, Ampfield, Romsey, Hampshire SO51 9PA. 0794 68733.

Notcutts Nurseries Ltd., Woodbridge, Suffolk IP12 4AF. 03943 3344.

Wyevale Garden Centre, King's Acre Road, Hereford HR4 0SE. 0432 266261.

Trees and Shrubs

Burncose South Down Nurseries, Gwennap, Redruth, Cornwall R16 6BJ. 0209 861112.

Glendoick Gardens Ltd., Glencarse, Perth, Tayside, Scotland PH2 7NS. 073 886 205.

Hergest Croft Gardens, Kington, Herefordshire HR5 3EG. 0544 230218.

Hydon Nurseries, Clock Barn Lane, Hydon Heath, Godalming, Surrey GU8 4AZ. 048 632 252.

Helpful Societies and Organizations

Agricultural Development and Advisory Service, Ministry of Agriculture, Fisheries and Food, Nobel House, 17 Smith Square, London, SW1P 3HX. 071 238 3000.

Building Centre Group Ltd., 26 Store Street, London WC1E 7BT. 071 637 1022.

Centre for the Conservation of Historic Parks and Gardens, Institute of Advanced Architectural Studies, University of York, The King's Manor, York YO1 2EP. 0904 433966/63.

Countryside Commission, John Dower House, Crescent Place, Cheltenham, Gloucestershire GL50 3RA. 0242 521381.

Countryside Commission for Scotland, Battleby, Redgorton, Perth PH1 3EW. 0738 27921.

English Heritage, 23 Savile Row, London W1X 2BT. 071 973 3000.

Fountain Society, 16 Gayfere Street, Smith Square, London SW1. 071 222 6037/2917.

Garden History Society, 5 The Knoll, Hereford HR1 IRU. 0432 354479.

Georgian Group, 37 Spital Square, London E1 6DY. 071 377 1722.

Historic Houses Association, 2 Chester Street, London SW1X 7BB. 071 259 5688.

Horticultural Trades Association, 19 High Street, Theale, Reading RG7 5AH. 0734 303132.

Landscape Institute, 6/7 Barnard Mews, London SW11 IQU. 071 738 9166.

National Council for the Conservation of Plants and Gardens, The Pines, The Royal Horticultural Garden, Wisley, Woking, Surrey GU23 6QB. 0483 224234.

National Gardens Scheme, 57 Lower Belgrave Street, London SW1W 0LR. 071 730 0350.

The National Trust, 36 Queen Anne's Gate, London SW1H 9AS. 071 222 9251.

The National Trust for Northern Ireland, Rowallane House, Saintfield, Ballynahinch, County Down BT24 7LH. 0238 510721.

The National Trust for Scotland, 5 Charlotte Square, Edinburgh EH2 4DU. 031 226 5922.

The Royal Horticultural Society, Vincent Square, London SW1P 2PE. 071 834 4333.

The Royal Institute of British Architects, 66 Portland Place, London W1N 4AD. 071 580 5533.

The Thirties Society, 18 Comeragh Road, London W14 9HP. 071 381 9797.

The Victorian Society, 1 Priory Gardens, Bedford Park, London W4 ITT. 081 944 1019.

BIBLIOGRAPHY

General

CECIL, Hon. Mrs Evelyn (Alicia Amherst) *A History of Gardening in England*. London, 1896. Includes a bibliography of early gardening books.

CLARKE, H. F. *The English Landscape Garden*. London, 1948.

CLIFFORD, Derek *A History of Garden Design*. London, 1962, Faber.

COLVIN, Howard *A Biographical Dictionary of British Architects 1600–1840*. 2nd edition, London, 1978, John Murray.

COLVIN, Howard (ed.) *The King's Works*. 6 vols., London, 1963–80.

COLVIN, Howard and HARRIS, J. (eds.) *The Country Seat*. London, 1970.

DESMOND, Ray *Bibliography of British Gardens*. Winchester, 1984, St. Paul's Bibliography.

DUTTON, Ralph *The English Garden*. London, 1937, Batsford.

The Glory of the Garden. Sotheby's & Royal Horticultural Society catalogue, January 1987.

HADFIELD, Miles *A History of British Gardening*. London, 1979, Murray.

HADFIELD, Miles, HARLING, Robert and HIGHTON, Leonie *British Gardeners: A Biographical Dictionary*. London, 1980, Zwemmer.

HARRIS, John *The Artist and the Country House: A History of Country House and Garden View Painting 1540–1870*. London, 1979, Sotheby Parke Bernet.

HARRIS, John *A Country House Index*. London, 1979, Pinhorns.

HARRIS, John (ed.) *The Garden*. Victoria and Albert Museum exhibition catalogue, 1970.

HENREY, Blanche *British Botanical and Horticultural Literature Before 1800 . . . A History and Bibliography, etc.* 3 vols., London, 1975, Oxford University Press.

HUNT, Peter (ed.) *The Book of Garden Ornament*. London, 1974, Dent. Reprint of G. Jekyll.

HUXLEY, Anthony *An Illustrated History of Gardening*. London, 1978, Paddington Benn.

JELLICOE, Geoffrey *The Landscape of Man*. London, 1979, Thames & Hudson.

JONES, Barbara *Follies and Grottoes*. London, 1974, Constable.

LANCASTER, M. and GOODE, P. *Oxford Companion to Gardens*. Oxford, 1986, Oxford University Press.

MALINS, Edward and the KNIGHT OF GLIN *Lost Demesnes, Irish Landscape Gardening 1660–1845*. London, 1976.

PRINCE, Hugh *Parks in England*. Isle of Wight, 1967, Pinhorns.

STUART THOMAS, Graham (ed.) *Re-creating the Period Garden*. London, 1984, Swallow Publishing.

TUNNARD, C. *Gardens in the Modern Landscape*. London, 1938; and New York, 1948.

WEAVER, L. and RANDAL Philips R. *Small Country Houses of Today*. 3 vols, 1910–25.

WATKINS, David *The English Vision*. London, 1982, John Murray.

SECTION I
Gardens of Embroidery

ADAMS, W. H. *The French Garden, 1500–1800*. London, 1979, Scolar Press.

BRADLEY, Richard *The Gentleman's and Gardener's Kalendar*. London, 1728, W. Mears.

CAMPBELL, Colen *Vitruvius Britannicus*. 3 vols., 1717–25; continued by T. Badeslade and J. Rocque. 1 vol., 1739; J. Wolfe and J. Gandon. 2 vols., 1767–71.

COOK, Moses *The Manner of Raising, Ordering and Improving Forest-Trees, etc.* London, 1676, Peter Parker.

CRISP, Sir Frank *Mediaeval Gardener*. 2 vols., London, 1924, Bodley Head.

CULPEPER, Nicholas *The English Physitian or an Astrologophysical discourse on the Vulgar Herbs of this Nation, etc.* London, 1652, Peter Cole.

DEFOE, Daniel *Tour Thro' the Whole Island of Great Britain*. (1724). Various editions.

EVELYN, John *Kalendarium Hortense*. London, 1666, J. Martyn, J. Allestry.

EVELYN, John *Sylva or Discourse of Forest Trees*. London, 1664, J. Martyn.

FOX, Helen M. *André Le Nôtre*. London.

GERARD, John *Herball*. London, 1597, John Norton.

HARVEY, John *Early Gardening Catalogues*. Chichester, 1972. With complete reprints of lists and accounts of the 16th– 19th centuries.

HARVEY, John *Early Nurserymen*. Chichester, 1975, Phillimore.

HARVEY, John *Medieval Gardens*. London, 1981, Batsford.

HILL, Thomas *The Gardener's Labyrinth* (1577). Reproduced Oxford, 1987, Oxford University Press.

JACQUES, David *The Gardens of William and Mary*. London, 1988, Christopher Helm.

JAMES, John *The Theory and Practice of Gardening*. 1712 (2nd edition 1728).

KIP, J. and KNYFF, L. *Britannia Illustrata*. 1707 etc.

KNYFF, Leonard *Nouveau Théâtre de Grand Bretagne*. 1724.

LAWRENCE, John *The Clergy-Man's Recreation*. London, 1729, Lintot.

LANGLEY, Batty *New Principles of Gardening*. London, 1727.

LEITH-ROSS, Prudence *The John Tradescants - Gardeners to the Rose and Lily Queen*. London, 1984, Peter Owen.

MASCALL, Leonard *The Country-Man's Recreation*. London, 1654, Mabb. Translated from Dary Brossard.

MEAGER, Leonard *The English Gardener*. London, 1670, P. Parker.

McLEAN, Theresa *Medieval English Gardens*. London, 1981.

MILLER, Philip *The Gardener's Dictionary*. 1731 (6th edition 1771). London.

MILLER, Philip *The Gardener's Kalendar.* 1732 (16th edition 1775).

MORRIS, C. *The Journeys of Celia Fiennes.* 1682-1712, London, 1947, Cresset Press.

PARKINSON, John *Paradisi in Sole Paradisus Terrestris* (Herbal), London, 1629, Humfrey Lownes and Robert Young.

STRONG, Roy *The Renaissance Garden in England.* London, 1979, Thames & Hudson.

SWITZER, Stephen *Ichnographia Rustica* or *The Nobleman, Gentleman, and Gardener's Recreation.* 3 vols., London, 1718.

VAN DE PASS, Crispin *Hortus Floridus.* 1615.

WILLIS, P. *Charles Bridgeman and the English Landscape Garden.* London, 1977, Zwemmer.

WOODBRIDGE, Kenneth *Princely Gardens.* London, 1986, Thames & Hudson.

WOOLRIDGE, John *Systema Horticulturae, or The Art of Gardening.* London, 4th edn 1700, W. Freeman.

SECTION II
Gardens of Paradise

ABERCROMBIE, John *The Gardener's Pocket Dictionary.* 3 vols., London, 1786.

BOUTCHER, William *A Treatise on Forest Trees.* 2nd edition, Edinburgh, 1778, John Murray.

CARTER, George, GOODE, Patrick and LAURIE, Kedrun *Humphry Repton, Landscape Gardener 1752–1818.* Exhibition catalogue for an exhibition at Sainsbury Centre for Visual Arts, University of East Anglia and at the Victoria and Albert Museum. London, 1982, John Murray.

CHAMBERS, W. *Designs of Chinese Buildings.* 1757.

CHAMBERS, W. *A Dissertation on Oriental Gardening.* London, 1772.

DIXON-HUNT, John *William Kent, Landscape Garden Designer.* London, 1987, Zwemmer.

DIXON-HUNT, John and WILLIS, Peter J. (eds.) *The Genius of the Place: the English Landscape Garden 1620–1820.* London, 1975, Paul Elek.

GILPIN, W. S. *Practical Hints upon Landscape Gardening: with some remarks on Domestic Architecture as connected with Scenery.* 1832, 2nd edition 1835.

HARRIS, E. *Thomas Wright Arbours and Grottos, a fascimile . . . with a catalogue of Wright's work in architecture and garden design.* 1979, Scolar Press.

HASSELL, J. *Views of Noblemen and Gentlemen's Seats.* 1804-5.

HUSSEY, Christopher *English Gardens and Landscapes 1700-1750.* London, 1967, Country Life.

HYAMS, E. *Capability Brown and Humphry Repton.* 1971.

JACQUES, David *Georgian Gardens: Reign of Nature.* London, 1982, Batsford.

JONES *Views of the Seats, Mansions, Castles, etc. of Noblemen and Gentlemen in England, Wales, Scotland and Ireland.* 3 vols., 1829.

LOUDON, J. C. *The Landscape Gardening and Landscape Architecture of the late Humphry Repton, Esq. Being his entire works on these subjects.* 1840, Longman.

LOUDON, J. C. *Hints on the Formation of Gardens and Pleasure Grounds.* London, 1812, John Harding.

LOUDON, J. C. *Observations on the Formation and Management of Useful and Ornamental Plantations.* Edinburgh, 1804, Archibold Constable.

LOUDON, J. C. *Encyclopedia of Gardening.* London, 1823, Longman, Hurst, Rees, Orme, Brown and Green (many editions).

LOUDON, J. C. *Encyclopedia of Cottage, Farm and Villa Architecture and Furniture.* London, 1833.

LOUDON, J. C. *The Suburban Gardener and Villa Companion.* London, 1838.

LOUDON, J. C. *A Treatise on Farming, Improving and Managing Country Residences.* 2 vols., London, 1802.

MARSHALL, W. *Planting and Ornamental Gardening.* London, 1775, J. Dodsley.

MASON, W. *The English Garden.* London, 1772–9.

MEADER, James *The Modern Gardener or Universal Kalendar.* London, 1771.

MEADER, James *The Planter's Guide.* London, 1770.

PAPWORTH, John Buonarotti *Hints on Ornamental Gardening.* London, 1823, R. Ackermann.

PAPWORTH, John Buonarotti *Rural Residences . . . with Observations on Landscape Gardening.* London, 1818.

POCOCKE, R. *Travels through England during 1750, 1751 and later years.* 2 vols., London, 1888–9.

PRICE, Sir Uvedale *An Essay on the Picturesque.* 1794-8. (expanded in the final edition, 1810, 3 vols., under the title *Three Essays on the Picturesque*).

REPTON, H. *Observations on the Theory and Practice of Landscape Gardening.* London, 1803.

REPTON, H. *Sketches and Hints on Landscape Gardening.* London, 1794.

REPTON, H. *Fragments on the Theory and Practice of Landscape Gardens.* London, 1816.

STEWART, Sir Henry *The Planter's Guide.* 2nd edition. Edinburgh, 1828, John Murray.

STROUD, D. *Capability Brown.* London, 1950.

STROUD, D. *Humphry Repton.* London, 1962.

TAIT, A. A. *The Landscape Garden in Scotland 1735–1835.* Edinburgh, 1980.

WALPOLE, Horace *The History of the Modern Taste in Gardening.* 1780.

WALTER, Nicol *Villa Garden Directory.* 1809. London.

WATKINS, David *The English Vision: The Picturesque in Architecture, Landscapes and Garden Design.* London, 1982, John Murray.

WATTS, W. *Seats of the Nobility and Gentry.* London, 1779.

WHATELY, T. *Observations on Modern Gardening.* Dublin, 1770.

WILSON, Michael *William Kent, Architect, Designer, Gardener, 1685–1748.* London, 1984, Routledge & Kegan Paul.

YOUNG, A. *A Six Weeks' Tour through the Southern Counties of England and Wales.* 1768.

YOUNG, A. *A Six Months' Tour through the North of England.* 4 vols., 1770.

Perennial plants in a parterre at Wrest Park give year-round colour.

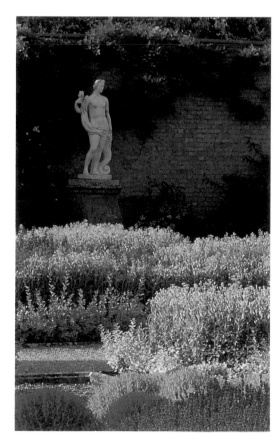

SECTION III
Gardens of Romance

AGAR, Madeline *Garden Design in Theory and Practice.* 2nd edition, London, 1913, Sidgwick & Jackson.

BEETON, Mrs *The Beeton Book of Garden Management.* London, 1890; Hertfordshire, 1985, Omega.

BLOMFIELD, Reginald *The Formal Garden in England.* London, 1901, Macmillan.

BROWN, Jane *Gardens of a Golden Afternoon.* London, 1985, Penguin.

CANE, Percy *Modern Gardens.* London, 1926–7, The Studio.

CHADWICK, George F. *The Park and the Town: Public Landscapes in the 19th and 20th Centuries.* London, 1966, Architectural Press.

CONDER, Josiah *Landscape Gardening in Japan.* Tokyo, 1893.

COOKE, T. (ed.) *The Century Book of Gardening.* London, n.d., Country Life.

DILLISTONE, George *The Planning and Planting of Little Gardens.* London, 1920, Country Life.

ELLIOT, B. *The First Table Decoration Competition. The Garden,* 1988, Home & Law Pub.

ELLIOT, B. *Victorian Gardens.* London, 1986, Batsford.

GODWIN, E. W. and ADAMS, M. B. *Artistic Conservatories.* 1860.

HAIG THOMAS, Rose *Stone Gardens.* London, 1905.

HOLME, Charles (ed.) *The Gardens of England.* 4 vols., London, 1908-27.

JEKYLL, Gertrude *Garden Ornament.* 1918;

reprint 1982, Antique Collector's Club.

JEKYLL, Gertrude *A Gardener's Testament.* London, n.d., Batsford.

JEKYLL, Gertrude *Wood and Garden.* 1899, Longmans Green.

JEKYLL, Gertrude *Lilies for English Gardens.* 1901, Newnes/Country Life.

JEKYLL, Gertrude *Wall and Water Gardens.* 1901, Newnes/Country Life.

JEKYLL, Gertrude *Roses for English Gardens.* 1902, Newnes/ Country Life.

JEKYLL, Gertrude *Colour in the Flower Garden.* 1908, Newnes/ Country Life.

JEKYLL, Gertrude and WEAVER, Lawrence *Gardens for Small Country Houses.* 1912, Newnes/Country Life.

KEMP, Edward *How to lay out a Garden.* London, 1858, Bradbury & Evans.

LE LIEVRE, A. *Gardens Among the Chimney Pots.* London, 1988, Country Life.

At Biddulph Grange the fantasy of a rock garden merges into the woodland garden.

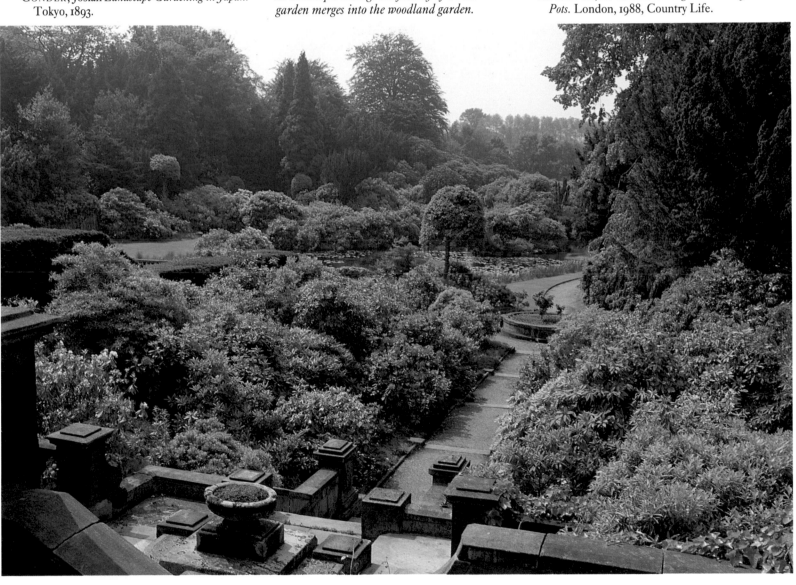

LOUDON, J. C. *A Treatise on Farming, Improving, and Managing Country Residences.* 2 vols., London, 1806, Longmans.

MASSINGHAM, Betty *Miss Jekyll: Portrait of a Great Gardener.* London, 1966, Country Life.

MAWE, Thomas and ABERCROMBIE, John *Everyman His Own Gardener.* 16th edition 1800.

MAWSON, Thomas *The Art and Craft of Garden Making.* London, 1908.

MAWSON, T. H. *The Life and Work of an English Landscape Architect. An Autobiography.* 1927.

MCINTOSH, Charles *The Book of the Garden.* Vol. 2, Edinburgh, 1853, William Blackwood & Sons.

MEREDITH, Lewis B. *Rock Gardens, How to Make and Maintain Them.* London, 1910, Williams & Norgate.

MILNER, H. E. *The Art and Practice of Landscape Gardening.* London, 1890.

OTTEWILL, David *The Edwardian Garden.* New Haven and London, 1989, Yale University Press.

PANKHURST, A. *A Corridor of Camellias. The Garden,* London, 1988, Home and Law Pub.

PAUL, William *The Rose Garden.* 2nd edition, London, 1863, Kent & Co.

PEMBERTON, Joseph H. *Roses, Their History, Development and Cultivation.* London, 1908, Longman.

ROBINSON, William *Garden Design and Architects' Gardens.* London, 1892, John Murray.

ROBINSON, William *The English Flower Garden.* London, 1883, John Murray. Many editions.

ROBINSON, William *The Wild Garden.* London, 1870, John Murray.

ROGERS, W. S. *Garden Planning.* London, 1910, T. Fisher Unwin.

SCOTT-JAMES, Anne *Sissinghurst, The Making of a Garden.* London, 1975, Michael Joseph.

TAYLOR, G. *Some Nineteenth-Century Gardeners.* London, 1951.

TAYLOR, G. *The Victorian Flower Garden.* London, 1952.

TIPPING, H. Avray *English Gardens.* London, 1925, Country Life.

TIPPING, H. Avray *Gardens Old and New.* London, n.d., Country Life.

TRESIDDER, J. and STAFFORD, C. *Living Under Glass.* London, 1986, Thames & Hudson.

VARDEN, Philip *The Encyclopedia of Villa Architecture.*

Plants

BEAN, W. J. *Trees and Shrubs Hardy in the British Isles.* 4 vols., 8th edition, London, John Murray.

BEALES, Peter *Classical Roses.* London, 1985, Collins Harvill.

BRICKELL, Christopher *Gardeners' Encyclopaedia of Plants and Flowers.* London, Royal Horticultural Society.

BRICKELL, Christopher and SHARMAN, Fay *The Vanishing Garden.* London, 1986, John Murray.

CHATTO, Beth *The Dry Garden.* London, 1980, Dent.

COMPTON, James *Success with Unusual Plants.* London, 1987, Collins.

COX, Peter *The Larger Species of Rhododendron.* London, 1979, Batsford.

GRIEVE, Mrs M. *The Modern Herbal.* London, 1931, reprinted 1975, Jonathan Cape.

HAY, Roy (ed.) *Reader's Digest Encyclopaedia of Garden Plants and Flowers.* London, 1971, Reader's Digest.

HAY, Roy and SYNGE, Patrick M. *The Dictionary of Garden Plants.* London, 1969, Ebury Press and Michael Joseph.

HILLIERS, Manual of Trees and Shrubs. Devon, 1973, David & Charles.

INGWERSEN, Will *Manual of Alpine Plants.* England, 1978, Dunnsprint.

KRUSSMANN, G. *Manual of Cultivated Broad-Leaved Trees and Shrubs.* 3 vols., London, 1984, Batsford.

KRUSSMANN, G. *Manual of Cultivated Conifers.* London, 1985, Batsford.

MATHEW, Brian *The Smaller Bulbs.* London, 1987, Batsford.

MILLAR GAULT, S. *The Dictionary of Shrubs.* London, 1976, Peerage Books.

PHILLIPS, Roger *Trees in Britain, Europe and North America.* London, 1978, Pan.

RIX, Martyn and PHILLIPS, Roger *The Bulb Book.* London, 1981, Ward Lock.

ROYAL HORTICULTURAL SOCIETY *Dictionary of Gardening.* 5 vols., Oxford, 1951, Clarendon Press (shortly to be revised).

STUART THOMAS, Graham *Climbing Roses Old and New.* London, 1965, Phoenix House.

STUART THOMAS, Graham *Gardens of the National Trust.* Great Britain, 1979, National Trust/Weidenfeld and Nicolson.

STUART THOMAS, Graham *Perennial Garden Plants or The Modern Florilegium.* 2nd edition, London, 1982, Dent.

STUART THOMAS, Graham *Plants for Ground-Cover.* London, 1971, Dent.

STUART THOMAS, Graham *The Old Shrub Roses.* London, 1963, Phoenix House.

VAN GELDEREN, D. M. and VAN HOEY SMITH, J. R. P. *Conifers.* London, 1986, Bradford.

Construction

LITTLEWOOD, Michael *Landscape Detailing.* 2nd edition, London, 1986, Architectural Press.

LITTLEWOOD, Michael *Tree Detailing.* London, 1989, Architectural Press.

COUNTRYSIDE COMMISSION FOR SCOTLAND Perth. Information sheets outside detailing and planting information.

Journals

Garden History, The Journal of the Garden History Society. 1972–.

Journals of Garden History. 1981–.

Victoria History of the Counties of England. 1904–.

Country Life Cumulative Index. Vol. I–CLXX, London, 1982, IPC Magazines.

Directory Publications

The Plant Finder. Published by Headmain for Hardy Plant Society. c/o Lakeside, Gaines Road, Whitbourne, Worcestershire WR6 5RD.

Historic Houses, Castles and Gardens open to the Public. Leisure Publications, Windsor Court, East Grinstead House, East Grinstead, West Sussex RH19 1XA.

Graham Rose and Peter King *The Good Gardens Guide 1990.* London, 1990, Century Hutchinson.

Martyn Rix and Alison Rix *Gardens Open Today.* London, 1987, Viking.

The National Gardens Scheme, Gardens of England and Wales. Annual Publication.

Landscape 90. The Environmental Review. Landscape Design Trust, 5a West Street, Reigate, Surrey RH2 9BL.

Landscape Institute Yearbook and Directory. Landscape Design Trust, 5a West Street, Reigate, Surrey RH2 9BL.

Environmental Directory. Civic Trust, 17 Carlton House Terrace, London SW1Y 5AW.

INDEX

The most significant debt
is to Lawrence, Richard and Edward Banks,
to whom this book is dedicated.

The publisher and author acknowledge the help and generosity of the following: Mr W.L. and Mr R.A. Banks, Major David and Lady Anne Rasch, the Trustees of the Tudor House Museum, the Somerset Fire Brigade, the National Trust, the National Institute of Agricultural Engineering, Mr Ian Pollard, Mr and Mrs John Montagu, the Trustees of Chevening Estate, the Royal Horticultural Society, Painshill Park Trust, Mr C. Cotterell-Dormer, English Heritage, the Earl of Haddington, the Grimsthorpe and Drummond Castle Trust Limited, Mr H. Bagot, Lord Saumarez, Shrubland Hall Health Clinic, Suffolk, the London Borough of Camden, Mrs C. MacCarthy and Mr D. MacCarthy, Sir David Barran, Pearsons Plc, Brent Elliott (Librarian RHS Lindley Library), Mr Anthony Huxley, Mrs Mavis Batey, Lord and Lady Dickinson and the Hon. Mrs Gascoigne.

The publisher wishes to make the following reproduction and copyright acknowledgements: Reproduced by Gracious Permission of Her Majesty the Queen: 23. Phaidon Press: 8, 210, 211, 214, 219. Bibliothèque Nationale, Paris (service photographique): 34. Yale Center for British Art, Yale: 38-9. Devonshire Collection, Chatsworth. Reproduced by permission of the Chatsworth Settlement Trustees and Courtauld Institute of Art, University of London (print): 44. Buckinghamshire County Museum: 62-3. RIBA, the British Architectural Library, London: 70, 90, 110 (above), 139. The Hon. Mrs Gascoigne: 92, 93, 100. Bodleian Library, Oxford: 100. Camden Council: 109. Norfolk County Library (Colman Collection) and George Carter: 110 (below). Geremy Butler: 70, 90, 110 (above), 139. Royal Horticultural Society, Lindley Library, and Weidenfeld & Nicolson Archives: 135. Tania Midgley: 166. Bridgeman Art Library: 170. Lord and Lady Dickinson: 98. Derek Balmer: 98. British Library: 52. British Museum (Natural History): 206. Victoria and Albert Museum: 207. H. Inigo Triggs, *The Formal Gardens in England and Scotland*, London (Batsford), 1902: 15, 125, 128, 148. Sir Frank Crisp, *Mediaeval Gardener*: 149. John James, *The Theory and Practice of Gardening*: 56. J. C. Loudon, *A Treatise on Farming . . .*: 72. McIntosh, *The Book of the Garden*: 124, 128, 158.

Phaidon Press Limited
Summertown Pavilion
Middle Way
Oxford OX2 7LG

First published 1991

© 1991 Phaidon Press Limited
Text © 1991 Elizabeth Banks
Drawings © 1991 Lucy Cuddon
Photographs © Jerry Harpur

Designed by Simon Bell

A CIP catalogue record for this book is available from the British Library

ISBN 07148 2622 7

All rights reserved. No part of this publication may be reproduced, stored in a retrieval system or transmitted, in photocopying, recording or otherwise, without the prior permission of Phaidon Press.

Printed and bound in Great Britain by
Butler & Tanner Ltd, Frome and London

Endpapers: Detail from 'A plan of the Buildings and Gardents at [W]rest . . .', *Vitruvius Britannicus*, 1737

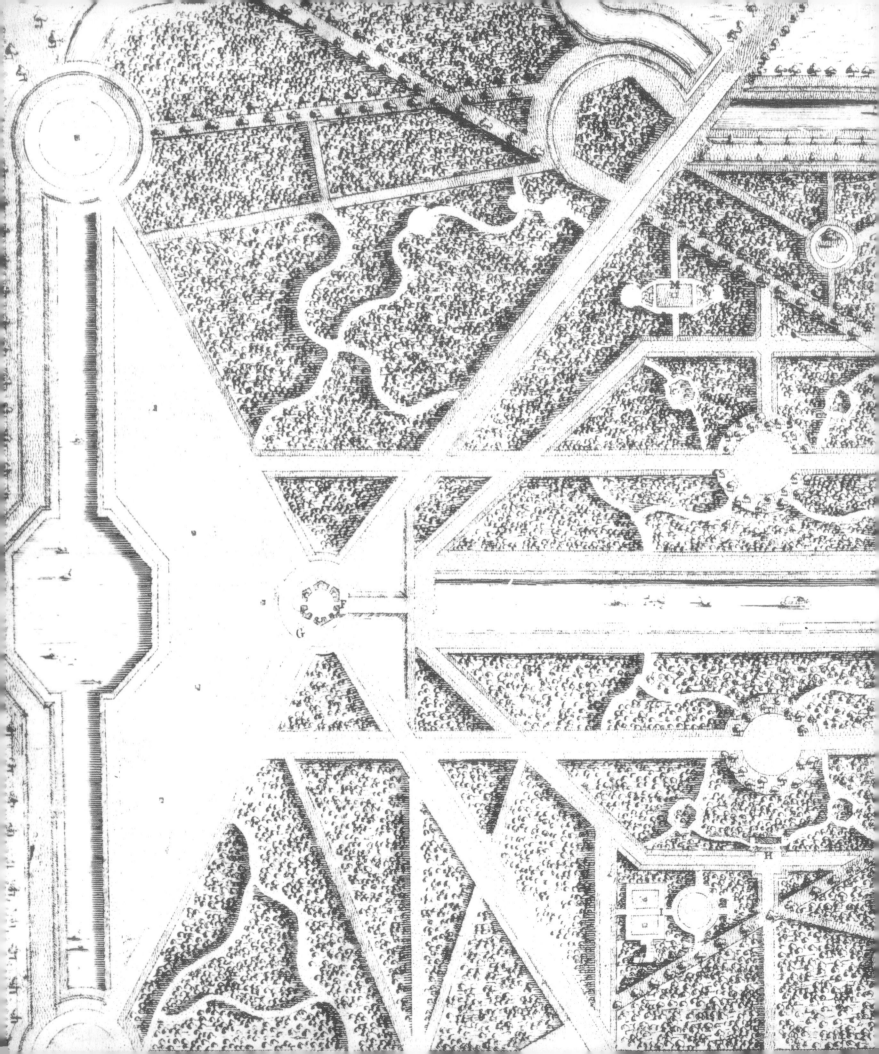